City of Women

City of Women,

SEX AND CLASS IN NEW YORK, 1789–1860

Christine Stansell

Alfred A. Knopf New York 1986

Library of Congress Cataloging-in-Publication Data
Stansell, Christine.
City of women.
Bibliography: p.
Includes index.
1. Women—Employment—New York (N.Y.)—History—
19th century. 2. Women—New York (N.Y.)—History—
19th century. 3. New York (N.Y.)—Economic conditions.
4. New York (N.Y.)—Social conditions. I. Title.
HD6096.N6S8 1986 305.4'2'097471 86-45283
ISBN 0-394-51534-X

To
Herbert Gutman
in loving memory

and to
R. S. W.

Contents

Part Three
Wage Work
103

Part Four
The Politics of the Streets, 1850–1860
169

Acknowledgments

Many friends and colleagues have helped me, intellectually and spiritually, to write this book. I am grateful to all those who read and criticized various drafts: my adviser, David Brion Davis, Nancy Cott, David Montgomery, Jessica Benjamin, Mari Jo Buhle, Eric Foner, Linda Kerber, Elizabeth Lunbeck and especially Mary Ryan and my editor Alice Quinn. The extraordinarily generous aid and copious knowledge that fellow historians of New York lent me was testimony to the enriching possibilities of shared scholarly endeavors. I thank Elizabeth Blackmar, Peter Buckley, Paul Gilje and above all William R. Taylor. I have benefited greatly from Helen Wright's skilled and impeccable typing and Johanna Wilson's meticulous research assistance, and from the research skills of Marybeth Hamilton and Gerry Pearlberg. I am grateful to the American Council of Learned Societies and the Mrs. Giles Whiting Foundation for financial support in crucial stages of the research and writing.

Some debts stretch far back into the past. From Ann Douglas I learned as an undergraduate to love nineteenth-century America. I remain indebted to her inspiration and her confidence in me. Peter H. Wood's vision of a democratic kind of history writing helped me to see scholarship as an enterprise that might transcend the academic. The study of social and historical theory I shared with John Faragher long ago has given me incalculable benefits over the years. Finally, I owe much to my mother and father, Mary Dressler Stansell and the late John W. Stansell, whose deep curiosity about early America and whose love of the work of the hands gave me an abiding interest in the lives of laboring people.

Four friendships have been particularly rich sources of sustenance. For many years Ellen Ross and Judith Walkowitz have shared with me their thoughts and research. Working with two such fine historians has been a constant pleasure. Ann Snitow and Sharon Thompson, with their brilliant turns of mind, have many times helped me to see things fresh. I am grateful to all of them for their devotion.

Without the patience of the New York archivists, I could never have done this research: John Lovari and Barbara Schickler, former staff members of the New-York Historical Society, and the obliging staff members of the New York Municipal Archives, who uncomplainingly hauled out dozens of dusty boxes for me. All historians of New York are indebted to Idilio Gracia-Peña, director of the Municipal Archives, who over the past twenty years has saved countless records from destruction and has established, against all odds, a center for their preservation and use.

Fifteen years ago I first read the work of Herbert Gutman, and it gave me confidence in setting out on my own intellectual project. For the last five years I was lucky enough to be his friend, and to encounter firsthand the irreverence, wisdom and acuity that made him so beloved. His early death was a grievous loss. The first part of the dedication is a token of how much I, like so many others of my generation, owe to his capacious spirit.

Of the many gifts that life in New York City bestowed on me, certainly the greatest was meeting Sean Wilentz. His intellectual passion and emotional support have contributed immeasurably to my ambitions and desires. Looking back on the years I have known him, a time contiguous with the writing of this book, a line of Louise Bogan's comes to my mind: "Now that I have your heart by heart, I see."

Introduction

Between the founding of the republic and the Civil War, a new conception of womanhood took shape in America, preeminently in Northeastern towns and cities. Within the propertied classes, women constituted themselves the moral guardians of their families and their nation, offsetting some of the inherited liabilities of their sex. Laboring women were less fortunate: The domestic ideals from which their prosperous sisters profited did little to lighten the oppressions of sex and class they suffered. They were also more troublesome, since their actions—indeed, their very existence as impoverished female workers—violated some of the dearest held genteel precepts of "woman's nature" and "woman's place."

This book is about the misfortunes that laboring women suffered and the problems they caused. It examines how and why a community of women workers came into existence in America's first great city; it analyzes the social conflicts in which laboring women were involved and the social pressures they brought to bear on others. It explores a city of women with its own economic relations and cultural forms, a female city concealed within the larger metropolis of New York.

New York stood at the center of the momentous processes that recast American society in the nineteenth century. Once a modest seaport, the city early took the lead in developing new forms of commerce and mass production; by 1860 it was both the nation's premier port and its largest manufacturing city. The appearance of new social classes was both cause and result of industrial development and commercial expansion. Wealth from investments in trade and manufacturing ventures supported the emergence of an urban bourgeoisie; the expansion of capitalist labor arrangements brought into being a class of largely impoverished wageworkers. The resulting divisions fostered, on each side, new and antagonistic political ideas and social practices.

We know most about the male participants in these conflicts, working-men and employers. Politically, bourgeois men upheld their right to protect, improve upon and increase the private property on which rested, they believed, their country's welfare. In return, many workingmen affirmed a belief in the superior abilities of those who worked with their hands—as opposed to the idle, acquisitive, parasitical owners of property—to direct American society in accordance with republican values of social equality, civic virtue and yeomanry that they inherited from the Revolution. Class conflict ebbed and flowed, pulling in different groups at different times and casting up different objects of contention: economic (strikes, labor disputes), political (elections, party platforms, municipal regulations) and a wide range of social issues (temperance, Sabbath observance, common schools, abolitionism).[1]

Class formation was related to, but not synonymous with, the thoroughgoing transformation of the gender system in the first half of the nineteenth century: that is, the changes in all those arrangements of work, sexuality, parental responsibilities, psychological life, assigned social traits and internalized emotions through which the sexes defined themselves respectively as men and women. Women of the emerging bourgeoisie articulated new ideas about many of these aspects of their lives. Designating themselves moral guardians of their husbands and children, women became the standard-bearers of piety, decorum and virtue in Northern society. They claimed the home as the sphere of society where they could most effectively exercise their power. In their consignment to the household as the sole domain of proper female activity, women suffered a constriction of their social engagements; at the same time, they gained power within their families that also vested them with greater moral authority in their communities.[2]

While the cult of domesticity spoke to female interests and emerged from altered relations between men and women, it also contained within it conflicts of class. As urban ladies increased their contacts with the working poor through Protestant missions and charity work, they developed domestic ideology as part of a vision of a reformed city, purged of the supposed perfidies of working-class life. Domesticity quickly became an element of bourgeois self-consciousness. In confronting the working poor, reformers created and refined their own sense of themselves as social and spiritual superiors capable of remolding the city in their own image. From the ideas and practices of domesticity they drew many of the materials for their ideal of a society that had put to rest the disturbing conflicts of class.

Female class relations, then, were central to the tremendous efflorescence and self-confidence of bourgeois life in the first half of the nineteenth century. It was the ladies who expanded on its possibilities and the workingwomen who bore the brunt of its oppressions. Female needleworkers and domestic servants fashioned the clothes, stitched the fancywork and tended the homes that together formed the physical basis of gentility; the burgeoning female occupations provided much of the discretionary money and leisure that allowed reform-minded men and women to undertake their energetic forays out into the city to investigate and admonish. Women, as self-appointed exemplars of virtue, were especially fitted to make that trek, since it was often members of their own sex who seemed most in need of moral correction—all the varieties of working-class women whose sexual and social demeanor subverted strict notions of female domesticity and propriety.

Glancing at the history books, it is difficult at first to discern those problematic poor women. When laboring women do appear in scholarship about the nineteenth century, it is usually as timid and downtrodden souls, too miserable and oppressed to take much of a part in making history. Mired in terrible working conditions, they toil long hours for starvation wages, seemingly powerless in the face of employers' abuse. At moments, inexplicably, they fight back by organizing short-lived, generally ineffectual trade unions. In general, however, they seem to succumb to the timeless fatalism of the poor—archetypal victims caught in a history of bondage and determinism. In this context of silence and passivity, it is easy to imagine these women simply as pale reflections of more articulate and active historical participants, as either feminine versions of working-class men or working-class versions of middle-class women.

On closer inspection, however, more varied and lively characters materialize: shrewd little girls, truculent housewives, feckless domestic servants, astute trade unionists. All these women played a part in the thoroughgoing changes in work, family and politics in nineteenth-century New York, initiating and responding to change in ways that were often different from both men of their class and their sisters in the middle class. This book is an attempt to illuminate their complicated milieu, thus far largely submerged in the histories of others. I hope to deepen our understanding of just what—and how much—was at stake in the wider urban world, the dense and conflict-ridden antebellum city.

A word about organization. The structure is loosely chronological. The first chapter begins in 1789, the year that saw the creation of the republic, and ends in 1820, which more or less marked the closing of the early national period and inaugurated the decade when New York's population and economy began to expand to the scale of a major city. The last two chapters focus on the decade 1850–60, which witnessed a full-scale crisis of urban life, the culmination of social problems that had been in the making for forty years. Chapters in between treat the intermediate decades, roughly 1820–50, from varying perspectives. In all the chapters there are chronological over-laps. The account proceeds from an analysis of those tensions between men and women that remained confined to the gender system ("The Politics of Sociability") to the developments in wage work that directly reshaped the place of women in urban political economy ("Wage Work") to those sexual conflicts which spilled over into the formal politics of the municipality ("The Politics of the Streets").

New York was *sui generis,* a place set off from the rest of the country in many ways. In its cosmopolitanism, its extremes of wealth and poverty, its breadth of human enterprise, it resembled London and Paris, those other great cities of the nineteenth-century Western world, as well as Boston and Philadelphia, its more modest American counterparts. But if unique, New York was far from irrelevant to the rest of America: It was a historical stage writ large for encounters that reverberated across the rest of the nation. It was the home of a radical working class and the site of intense class conflicts before the Civil War; it was also at the forefront of middle-class commercial and domestic culture. The opportunities and the difficulties it posed for women anticipated changes that would occur nationally throughout the century. Already by the 1840s an arbiter of gender fashions and expecta-tions, New York was a testing ground for much that was new between the sexes. For poor women in this city, a new configuration of suffering and possibility was just beginning to move into place.

Part One

Precarious Dependencies: Women in the Republican City, 1789–1820

Chapter 1 Female Work and Poverty

To imagine New York City in 1789 is to conjure up the figures of the eighteenth-century picaresque: tattered beggars, silk-stockinged rich men, pompadoured ladies and their liveried footmen, leather-aproned mechanics and shabby apprentice-boys, sleek coach horses, pigs. It was a volatile, contentious, politicized place, where the riotous world of the laboring poor surrounded a small, self-enclosed enclave of the wealthy and urbane. New York was still only an outpost of international commerce, but its inhabitants already displayed some of the traits of the metropolitans they would become in the next half century: stylishness, high self-esteem and an awareness of social tensions barely held in check.

The economic and social changes that swept the city after the Revolution and transformed it into the leading port and, then, manufacturing center of America greatly altered the lives of its laboring people. Poverty increasingly defined the experience of many of those living in the dark, dirty, overcrowded little plebeian neighborhoods along the East River. Poverty was closely connected to economic development. The successes of New York's early manufacturers were in no small part due to the ready availability of the cheap labor of the working poor. Earlier in the eighteenth century, poverty had usually been associated with the *inability* to work—with the crippled, the aged and the very young. By the early nineteenth century, poverty was becoming connected to the changing structure of work itself —to the difficulties laboring people had in supporting themselves in manufacturing employments that paid insufficient wages and gave insufficient work.

These rearrangements also involved changes between men and women. Within the swelling ranks of the laboring poor, urban migration and the beginnings of urban manufacturing spelled the disintegration of the customary household economies that had formerly absorbed the energies and loyalties of women. The growing uncertainty of employment for many men eroded the older, familiar configuration of male provider and female household manager, an actuality for many laboring families up to the Revolution and a reasonable expectation for many more. The disruption of household economies fostered new forms of insecurity: for women, uncertainties about men's support and commitment; for men, the loss of accustomed kinds of authority within their households and workplaces.

The City

By 1820, New York had become a center of capitalist development, a staging ground for the great transformations of the industrial wage system.[1] The 1790s saw the first stage of this phenomenal expansion, as American neutrality gave the city's merchants the opportunity to corner the Atlantic shipping trade between European belligerents. New York shipping flourished throughout the series of events that eventually drew all Europe into war. With profits from their newly won preeminence on the Atlantic routes, New York shippers turned a modest provincial harbor into a hub of international commerce.[2] The population more than doubled between 1800 and 1820, from 60,000 to more than 123,000 people.

Merchant capitalism shaped the social geography of the city. Lining Broadway, the street of fashion, were the fine town houses of wealthy shippers and financiers, which extended from the lovely park at the southern tip of the island north to the park around City Hall. Four-storied brick and Georgian in style, they reminded British travelers of the residences of London's aristocratic West End, down to their brass and silver doorplates. Scattered up and down Broadway were artisan shops that catered to the luxury trade, turning out goods that could rival the finest in London: silver, linen, silk hose, beaver hats, powdered wigs and elegant coaches. Many trans-Atlantic visitors remarked on the pampered tastes so evident on Broadway, decidedly at odds with the Europeans' preconceptions of republican simplicity. Dressed to the hilt in the latest British styles, trailed about by servants, the New York rich showed a flair for fashion that led travelers to compare the Broadway throng to that of London's Bond Street. "English luxury displays its follies," a disappointed French visitor complained in 1788.[3]

Although the merchants were ambitious, their search for profits did not extend to the new factories with which their New England counterparts were experimenting. The beginnings of the city's manufacturing sector, already evident by 1820, lay rather with men of more modest means, master artisans who, beginning in the 1790s, produced goods for the merchant capitalists' distant markets. Proximity to the seaport gave these entrepreneurs connections to the lucrative export trade; the necessity of furnishing goods in bulk encouraged them to abandon traditional methods of handicraft and to implement rudimentary methods of mass production. In their workshops, they began to use their journeymen as hired wage laborers rather than as craftsmen due an accustomed price for their work. In changing around their workshop arrangements, the masters laid the groundwork for urban industrialization.[4]

This flourishing economy pulled into it people from all across the Western world; international turmoil cast up poor people as well as riches on Manhattan's shores.[5] Because the city was the main point of debarkation for immigrant ships, it became a way station of Atlantic misery, an asylum for all kinds of survivors looking for another chance. "Vagrants multiply on our hands to an amazing degree," lamented Richard Varick, soon to be mayor, in 1788.[6] The term "vagrants" dates back to the Elizabethan poor law; with its connotations of an undifferentiated class, it can mislead us. These people were not a homogeneous group but rather the motliest of crews, bound together by the one common circumstance of having arrived in New York with little or no position in life. Some were born wanderers, children or grandchildren of the rootless proletarians who drifted about the English empire: soldiers and sailors, prostitutes and peddlers, beggars, thieves and rogues.[7] The fictional vagaries of Moll Flanders were not far removed from the tale of the three thousand women a British agent shipped from the Liverpool slums to serve as prostitutes to British troops stationed in New York during the occupation. Patriotic citizens drove out a thousand of the women after the British evacuation, but many remained as part of the "idle and profligate Banditti" who troubled respectable citizens in the 1790s. Likewise, many of the "strolling poor" of the American Northeast gravitated to New York, drawn by the hope of employment and the city's liberal relief policies.[8]

Other poor people had once been settled folk. English and Irish farmers, squeezed by enclosures and a run of bad harvests, came by the thousands searching for ways to turn their luck. Land shortages in the nearby countryside and in lower New England sent young men and women to the city

searching for some means to establish themselves in life. Politics had motivated others to set sail from home: wealthy planters and their mulatto
supporters who sought refuge from the Santo Domingo Revolution in 1801,
Irish patriots who had fled the repercussions of the failed rebellion of 1798,
English radicals in flight from Pitt's repression.[9] Other British working
people migrated for the rumored high wages of the New World. All
contributed to "the prodigious influx of indigent foreigners" which the
Almshouse superintendent lamented in 1796.[10]

The immigrant poor were castaways set adrift by the storms of distant
places; other "vagrants" were insiders, laboring people from New York
with their own troubles to bear. Beginning in the early eighteenth century,
long-term factors of economic distress pushed increasing numbers of urban
artisans out of taxable status—one index of a decent livelihood—into the
ranks of the propertyless. The growth of the colonial seaport cities did little
or nothing to benefit the great majority of their residents; urban prosperity
between 1700 and the eve of the Revolution took the form of a redistribution
of wealth toward the wealthiest residents.[11] A cycle of wartime boom and
postwar recession, with attendant price increases, accompanied the conflicts with the French and Indians which occurred at least once a generation
up to the Revolution. By 1776, as many as a third of the residents of
America's large towns lived in poverty.[12]

The trend continued after the Revolution. Although wage rates rose for
journeymen and unskilled laborers between 1790 and 1830, seasonal and
intermittent unemployment undercut these gains.[13] High prices made periods of unemployment all the more difficult, especially since saving was
nearly impossible. In those trades where the shift to entrepreneurial, profit-
accumulating methods of production was pronounced, journeymen suffered increased competition for work, irregularity of employment and a
lowering premium on skill (which resulted in the breakdown of apprenticeship and the hiring of semiskilled and unskilled workers). In other words,
they experienced what Marxist economists call the casualization of labor.
Some master craftsmen successfully adapted to the exigencies and opportunities of the booming seaport economy (the renowned cabinetmaker
Duncan Phyfe, who made his fine furniture into a trademark of American
elegance, is a good example). But most small masters, squeezed by mer-
chant-controlled credit and committed to, or caught in, an order far
removed from capitalist ambitions, shared the lives of the working poor.[14]

As in other eighteenth-century cities, the situation in New York does not
bear out the oft-repeated assumption that laboring people profited by some
fabled scarcity of labor in America. Seasonal unemployment kept sailors,
unskilled laborers, many small masters and most journeymen at the margins
of poverty and liable to periods of indigence. During the winter, cold

weather and harbor ice brought shipping nearly to a standstill and threw dock laborers, artisans in the maritime trades and sailors out of work. With good luck and a moderate winter, these men worked about two-thirds of the year. Severe winters, however, disrupted the delicate balance of employment and idleness and created serious hardship. In the hard winter of 1817–18, for instance, when the adventurous could walk on solid ice from Manhattan to New Jersey, poor relief soared.[15] Seasonality also affected the building trades, which depended on the weather, and the consumer finishing trades, especially shoemaking and tailoring, which as mass production proceeded apace, followed yearly cycles of demand. The journeymen masons in 1819, appealing for public support during a strike, calculated they worked about 213 days a year and estimated their surplus income (what was left over for clothes, recreation, illness and emergency) at $27; the journeymen carpenters, in a similar statement in 1809, estimated their wages allowed them to maintain only the smallest margin above subsistence. In the slow seasons, unemployed men made do by using any small savings they had accumulated or, more typically, by turning to odd jobs and migration to pull themselves and their families through. Journeymen sometimes went tramping for work; laborers set off for the docks of Charleston, Savannah and New Orleans. Thomas, a journeyman printer (who affords us a rare glimpse into an individual life because of his part in a murder trial in 1811), occupied himself when unemployed by killing stray dogs for a fee from the city. A rise in the price of necessities could mean widespread distress for those whose livelihoods were so shaky. Some 600 journeymen in the winter of 1797, for instance, requested assistance from the Common Council because of high prices: "By reason of large families," they claimed, they could not buy enough wood for their fires.[16]

The result was a spartan standard of living. Accident and disease spelled disaster, and both were rife in late eighteenth-century cities. Poor sanitation and crowding made disease endemic; dock work and streets teeming with horses and wagons posed considerable hazards to life and limb. The relatively primitive state of medical care meant that simple injuries—a broken leg, for example, or a laceration—could be permanently crippling. The situation of Abraham Fincher, a house carpenter who asked the city for aid in 1786, was dreaded but not rare: He had fallen at work, injured his thigh and could no longer work at his trade. When a breadwinner was thus incapacitated, he and his family faced pauperism. The Almshouse was in part populated by men of working age who suffered from running sores and broken limbs. Likewise, the common respiratory diseases and persistent infections brought on by cold weather could also reduce the able-bodied to dependence on charity.[17]

The problems of poverty were becoming a continuing crisis. From 1790 to 1800, the population of New York nearly doubled; in the next twenty years it doubled again. The pressures strained the old municipal relief system nearly to the point of collapse. New York had had its troubles with the poor throughout the eighteenth century, since its inefficiency in enforcing provincial and, later, state settlement laws—which mandated the expulsion of paupers to their last place of settled residence—made it something of a sanctuary for the indigent. Still, settlement laws had helped to hold down the numbers of public charges. By the 1790s, however, it was impossible to limit the numbers of the impoverished. The settlement laws, suspended during the Revolution, were virtually ineffectual. Indeed, their enforcement elsewhere worked to New York's disadvantage, since upstate towns learned to rid themselves of foreign-born paupers by shipping them back to the port of entry, which was, technically, their place of settlement. The numbers of people living on "indoor relief" in the Almshouse increased gradually through the 1790s and then, with the construction of a new facility, climbed sharply.[18]

The hostilities with Britain precipitated a full-scale social crisis and ushered in a sustained visitation of economic ill fortune. The disastrous embargo of 1807–09 on Atlantic trade badly damaged an economy geared to maritime commerce and caused widespread suffering among the unemployed. The War of 1812, which again paralyzed merchant shipping, pushed the numbers of those who sojourned in the Almshouse in 1813 and 1814 up to 1,430 people. In the winter of 1813, as many as 1,000 people a day sought municipal relief. The end of the war brought little respite, since once trans-Atlantic shipping resumed, immigrants poured into the city. In 1817, a conjuncture of circumstances—an unusually severe winter, an economic slump and the arrival of over 7,000 immigrants—created what amounted to a state of emergency. An estimated one-seventh of the population—15,000 people—depended on relief that winter. Over the next few years the crisis continued, sustained by more heavy immigration, another bad winter in 1820–21 and an outbreak of yellow fever in 1822. For the vulnerable, the weather, an economic downturn and sickness could be calamities that destroyed the carefully collected resources of a lifetime and pushed a family of respectable means into indigence.[19]

The character of the poverty-stricken population was changing. Certainly the traditional poor of the colonial period still figured among New York's dependents: orphans, cripples, the blind and deaf, widows, disabled soldiers, the aged, the sick, and aging slaves freed by their masters because they were infirm. There had always been an admixture of able-bodied men and women among the strolling poor: landless younger sons, sailors, failed farmers, women outcast for illegitimate pregnancies. But after the turn of the century, the proportion of the able-bodied among those dependent on relief seems to have climbed. The numbers of the "outdoor poor"—those who were able to or insisted upon maintaining themselves outside the Almshouse—were, by 1809, "already incalculable and rapidly increasing," the Almshouse superintendent noted. Between 1813 and 1815, the numbers of persons granted outdoor relief doubled, from 8,253 people to 16,417. These indigent people, dependent on relief but able to work—indeed, often working—were too closely identified with the laboring classes for officials to dismiss them as vagabonds. The problems the working poor posed were becoming, by 1820, critical issues of political economy, public welfare and public health.[20]

Those problems were most evident in the living conditions of the laboring classes, which deteriorated visibly in this period. Although visitors to New York always lauded the New World splendor of airy Broadway, most of the city was cramped, gloomy and noisome, not much different from the humble quarters of an English provincial port like Liverpool or Bristol. For blocks and blocks northward up the island and between Broadway and the East River docks, "the streets are small and crooked; the foot-paths, where there are any, narrow, and interrupted by the stairs from the houses, which makes the walking on them extremely inconvenient . . . the houses are mean, small, and low."[21] There were still a few fine mansions scattered throughout the east side and plenty of well-preserved old Dutch houses, gable-ended brick, which prosperous shopkeepers and master craftsmen pridefully kept up: The sharp class segregation that would mark residential patterns in the nineteenth century was only beginning. But as newcomers crowded into these already congested districts, the east side came to be more identified with the poor, while the wealthy began to withdraw from the streets where they had once lived to move uptown to country houses or to more homogeneous elite districts. Boardinghouses for sailors, day laborers, journeymen and their families became wedges for the movement of masses of the poor into the east side streets. In response to rising rents, laboring people doubled and tripled up in what had once been single-family dwellings and packed into town houses abandoned by their wealthy owners and subdivided into tenements and boardinghouses. In 1819 at one address in Corlears Hook, 103 people lived in one building. In the outer wards at the city's edge, too, journeymen and laborers crowded, two and three families together, into little cottages strewn along the dirt roads and open tracts of ground. But it was the area between Broadway and the eastern waterfront that comprised the main quarter of the working poor, those without "even a stool to sit on, nor a bed to lie upon" and the journeymen and laborers one step removed from their lot.[22]

Overcrowding aggravated already serious sanitation problems. Methods that had served the modest Dutch town collapsed. Garbage and waste collected in open sewers that ran down the middle of the streets and congealed into a fetid mire around the street pumps and docks where servants, slaves and the municipal scavengers dumped refuse and slops every night. Horses, dogs, cattle and pigs compounded the problem of street sewage. Water was in short supply. To some degree, the stench and filth oppressed all classes of citizens, but the laboring classes, predictably, suffered the most. In the households of the prosperous, servants provided some of the amenities of cleanliness, and the affluent could retreat to the country during epidemics and the especially foul summer months. Moreover, their houses stood on the airiest and most salubrious spots on the island, while the tenements of the working poor lay close to unhealthy and low-lying land. The notorious Five Points slum, for instance, a few blocks east of City Hall, had grown up on a marsh shunned by those who could afford to avoid its pestilential properties. The new journeymen's neighborhoods at the undeveloped north side of the city, even if they benefited from comparatively open air, grew up in proximity to the "noxious" trades that made their homes there: tanneries, distilleries and slaughterhouses, whose stench and piles of waste were a breeding ground for vermin and disease.[23]

Yellow fever was the most ominous consequence of overcrowding and bad sanitation. The first cases appeared in the summer of 1791 in a poor neighborhood near the waterfront, "a part of the city thickly inhabited, its houses generally small, and badly ventilated." By the fall, the "malignant fever" had subsided, only to appear again for the next three summers. In 1795 it broke out into an epidemic that, by its end, had killed some 750 people. The poor, unable to flee, were its chief victims. It swept through again in 1798 and then in 1803, 1805 and 1822. Its etiology was a mystery to the baffled city fathers. They knew that it came from ships in the West Indies trade, but how and why it took root in their once healthful port was a mystery. Theories abounded, but those who mulled over the question agreed there was some relationship between the epidemics and the influx of poor people.[24]

Eighteenth-century people were no strangers to squalor. The affluent and the poor alike were accustomed to bodily discomfort and uncleanliness. What was new by 1820 was not dirt and disease but their heavy concentration in some districts. The yellow fever epidemics were the most startling images of this process, as the quarters of the laboring poor became literal threats to public health. In subsequent decades, the New York bourgeoisie would conflate the problems of poverty with those of disease. For the moment, it is enough to note that by 1820, few New Yorkers could fail to perceive either the increasing bounty or the deepening misery of their city.

Women's Work

The growth of merchant capitalism, the spread of wage relations in manufactories and artisan workshops and the decline of living standards all
altered the ways in which laboring women worked for a living. The disappearance of productive households, in both the city and the rural areas from
which many newcomers came, pushed women into new employments. As
the livelihoods of many men became less dependable, families increasingly
needed women's cash earnings to get by.

To analyze the disintegration of productive household economies is a
complicated enterprise. This extremely uneven process spanned at least a
century, perhaps 150 years. It occurred in different parts of America at
different times. In the seaboard cities, household economies could be characterized as mixed—partly depending on men's cash earnings and commer-
cially purchased goods, partly depending on women's produce—as early as
1750. Except for the rural hinterlands, there were no "pure" household
economies—where women themselves crafted all domestic necessities—by
the time of the Revolution. In many families, domestic production was only
makeshift (a bit of spinning here, a little soap making there), as family
resources in land and household declined. Finally, women of the strolling
poor were entirely uprooted from household production.[25]

Still, domestic production in one form or another would have been an
experience that remained within the living memory of most laboring people
in turn-of-the-century New York. Many of them did come directly from
family farms in the American countryside and from tenancies, freeholds
and peasant plots in the British Isles. In such rural societies, household
production prevailed. Even women who had grown up in the city would
probably have worked as servants or daughters in households where mistresses tended gardens and kept chickens, pigs and cows. By 1820, this
household regimen was possible only for those women whose husbands and
fathers earned a steady income. These descendants of colonial goodwives
still kept pigs and chickens in their little backyards (the pigs also trotted
about the streets, to the perennial amusement of European visitors); they
tended gardens and crafted many of their domestic goods themselves;
women in master craftsmen's families probably helped out in the shops or
workshops that adjoined their domestic quarters.[26]

The working poor, however, lacked such domestic resources. Some poor
journeymen's wives who lived on the outskirts of town might still keep
gardens and poultry. But the well-stocked larder of the respectable artisan's

wife was unattainable for the wives of poor artisans and casual laborers crowded into the tenements and for the many destitute female immigrants who had once kept their own pigs and spun their own yard in Irish and English villages.

The causes of female poverty were both economic and familial. Some women, of course, were born paupers: destitute daughters of indigent mothers, driven from one country village to another until, in the Revolution and its aftermath, they drifted into the comparatively secure harbor of the city. Others came on hard times with the declining fortunes of the men in their families. For others, poverty ensued from a sudden loss of male support. Widowhood was virtually synonymous with impoverishment. So was the sudden disappearance of a man, for one reason or another. Sailors' women, for instance, suffered great hardship while their husbands and lovers were at sea. The exodus of men to the Revolution and, later, to the War of 1812 precipitated a crisis of female poverty from which many of those who were subsequently widowed by the wars—or deserted by roving men—never recovered. Ann Hallam was probably such a case: In 1815 she petitioned the Common Council for aid for herself and three small children, since "her husband has been long absent and she does not know if ever he will return." Male absence and desertion may also have generally increased. The difficulties men experienced in supporting their families made it more likely they would leave them, either permanently or temporarily, in the perennial search for work that took migrating laborers and tramping artisans up and down the East Coast. Women, one New York charity noted in 1818, were generally more vulnerable to impoverishment than men, being "more exposed to a sudden reverse of circumstances."[27]

As much as they could, these women tried to hold together disintegrating family economies. Some kept pigs or bits of gardens. Others gave up altogether any lingering ambitions toward the role of household mistress and dedicated their energies instead to the makeshift housekeeping of the city, the catch-as-catch-can routine of the destitute. Whatever their relationship to older forms of domestic production, cash became crucial to many women, either to support themselves or to supplement men's wages.

Domestic service was probably the most common waged employment. "Helps" (a more common term than "servant" in the early nineteenth century) worked alongside mistresses in the demanding routines of household crafts and the labor-intensive tasks of housekeeping in an age before utilities like running water and gaslight were available. Service was generally a more casual affair than it was to become in the Victorian era, certainly as toilsome but less bound up in rituals of class deference. Mistresses, if prosperous enough to employ help, nonetheless often came from the same community of laboring people as their servants. Except among the very rich, the elaborate distinctions between employer and employed, mistress and servant had not yet developed. Margaret Banks, for example, the common-law wife of a peddler, could be found in 1804 drinking ale in the victualing house where she worked, near her cellar lodgings; her mistress was privy to Margaret's quarrels with her husband and spoke of her as a friend. White women often worked in such neighborhood arrangements; black women were more likely to work for the wealthy, since slave owning at the turn of the century was still sufficiently widespread to make the black skin of a servant, either freedperson or slave, a sign of the employers' (or owners') affluence.[28]

Other kinds of paid employment were extensions of household work. Providing lodgings was one way for women to bring in money. There was always a demand for lodgings in a seaport, since so many transients passed through, but the need grew greater as immigration increased after the War of 1812 and as growing numbers of employers eschewed the old practice of lodging their employees in their own houses. Taking lodgers could be as simple a matter as letting someone sleep on your floor for a few pence a week; it could also be a more formal operation, as it probably was for the seventy-nine women who identified themselves in the 1805 city directory as boardinghouse keepers. Laundressing work was available year round. Washing clothes was an onerous task that required strength and submitting to extremes of hot and cold. Black women often took on this lowly labor, one of the few paid employments they could obtain. In the late summer and fall, women could also venture out into the country—to rural New Jersey, Connecticut, Long Island, Westchester County and the Hudson Valley—where farm families took them on to help with the harvesting, canning and preserving.[29]

The provisioning trades also offered women some foothold. In a growing city where householders might live some distance from the markets and stores, where growing numbers of workplaces were separate from households, and where some transient people had no households at all, women could make a living by hawking and vending foods and domestic supplies. Street peddling was work for black women, the very poor and women too frail to work at service. It required only the strength to carry a basket about and a shilling or two to invest in a day's wares. The numbers of street peddlers increased after 1800 along with the numbers of poor people who bought from them. Female hucksters sold fruits and vegetables, candies and cakes door-to-door, on busy corners and around the docks and countinghouses. Their cries gave a special flavor to city life. The black women who sold hot corn, Manhattan's special delicacy, were renowned for their cry, a strange, melancholy tune:

Hot corn, hot corn, here's your lily white hot corn
Hot corn all hot, just come out of the boiling pot.[30]

But although peddling was often the only way very poor women could support themselves, it earned scarcely a subsistence. The Reverend Ezra Stiles Ely was a Presbyterian minister to the Almshouse whose stern views on salvation commingled with a genuine empathy for his flock. His appreciation of the difficulties the poor faced makes his observations unusually free of the biases that shaped the remarks of his contemporaries. Ely remarked ruefully on the prospects of an old woman peddler he had encountered on his rounds, who was laid up in the Almshouse hospital with a broken leg: "She will recover, to suffer more pain, and hawk pincushions to procure some of the conveniences of life, which cannot be distributed in the public almshouses. O! it is astonishing that the heirs of heaven should be found in such circumstances."[31]

More fortunate women had some chance to establish a small proprietorship. A bit of money could go toward building a little stand on some frequented spot in the business and workshop districts or on the docks, where the women owners then sold refreshments to passersby and workingmen. Some women rented stalls in the public markets where they vended fresh produce and dairy products. A few owned small food shops of their own. In the census of New York occupations in the 1805 city directory, 18 women were counted among the city's 793 grocers, 5 among 27 fruit sellers, 2 cookshop owners out of a total of 7, a confectioner ("Grovers widow") and 7 tavern or coffee-house keepers out of 113 in the city. Prosperous enough for the city directory to notice them, these were probably widows—like Mrs. Grover the confectioner—who had inherited already established businesses. Widowhood was a common road to female proprietorship.[32]

On a more modest scale, the easy movement of people between households and streets allowed women to set up accommodations for eating and drinking in their own rooms, where they sold fruits, candies, cakes and liquor. Thus the Society for the Relief of Poor Widows (SRPW), the earliest female charity in the city, agreed to loan five dollars to a Mrs. McLeod "to assist her in setting up a little shop." In 1804, however, with an eye sharpened toward improving as well as relieving the poor, the society's ladies resolved to withhold their help from any widow who was found vending liquor. They wished to discourage their charges from running "disorderly houses," as they were known to the authorities. Called "bawdy houses" by the public, these little places sold cheap liquor to patrons of the "lowest" sort: free blacks, journeymen, apprentices, sailors and women on the loose—courting girls, prostitutes and runaway wives.

The bawdy houses catered to sexual license, male rowdiness and *bonhomie* and to working people's love of drinking and dancing. High times went on there, "dancing, kissing, cursing and swearing" until all hours of the night, to the great disturbance of neighbors, who periodically took their grievances to court. Raucous patrons collected about their doors, catcalling at passersby and brawling among themselves. At one end of the spectrum, bawdy houses shaded into groceries, retreats where people stopped to relax and gossip; at the other, into brothel-like establishments that rented rooms for illicit sex. Here, too, black women could earn money, since bawdy houses often catered to an interracial clientele.[33]

The realm of commodity production generally excluded women, except insofar as its employments overlapped with those of families. The only women counted among the city's artisans in 1805—a female hatter and the Widow Harris, a shoemaker—had probably learned their trades as helpers to their husbands.[34] The exceptions were those sewing trades that were traditionally female. In dressmaking and millinery, women followed the regular artisan sequence of training and mastery, as apprentices, journeywomen and mistresses. Only in these trades were women a substantial presence. There were 31 seamstresses in New York in 1805; 51 of 59 mantuamakers (dressmakers) were women and 22 tailoresses were listed as compared to 166 tailors. (See Table 1, p. 225.) Status as a craftswoman was a privilege, one of the few tickets for women in the early national years— besides shopkeeping, midwifery and perhaps nursing—to a decent and steady livelihood.

In most craftwork, women received no formal training, and their position was marginal. Their employments were either an extension of tasks they performed as helpers to men—shoe binding, for instance—or continuations of domestic crafts they learned in family households. The "putting-out" or "giving-out" system, which encompassed most of the women who did work in commodity production, drew on both artisanal and domestic arrangements. In the years after the Revolution, city merchants and village storekeepers along the Northeastern seaboard began distributing raw materials to women to work up at home into ready-made goods, which the entrepreneurs then sold: flax and wool to spin into yarn, yarn to weave into cloth and stockings, stockings to seam, straw to braid into the makings for hats, shoes to bind, cloth to sew into gloves and shirts. Although putting out flourished mostly in rural New England, some given-out work was also available in New York. Master cordwainers began to put out shoes to bind early in the nineteenth century, and spinning and given-out work were the few remunerative employments the SRPW could encourage among its beneficiaries in the same years.[35]

Spinning was, in fact, something of a panacea for the plight of poor

women. Beginning in 1734, when the first municipal poorhouse was established, and continuing through the War of 1812, charitable benefactors
distributed spinning wheels to needy females as the one conceivable remedy
for their difficulties. Patriotic and, later, profit-oriented motives mingled
with concern for the female poor. In 1764, a Society for the Promotion of
Arts, Agriculture and Economy set up a linen manufactory in the city
where women and children spun flax as part of the movement to stop the
importation of British goods; again in 1789, the New York Manufacturing
Society established a cloth manufactory with an eye both to employing the
poor and promoting American industry. Both enterprises languished: the
first with the decline of the homespun movement, the second for lack of
water power, which fueled identical endeavors in New England.[36] For a
short time during the War of 1812, several hundred war widows and enlisted
men's wives took given-out work from the House of Industry, a female-run
charity founded to alleviate destitution among the "honest" female poor.
The House gave out flax and wool to spin, stockings to knit, gloves and
a few fine linen shirts to sew. Although the charity's managers created a
protomanufactory by centralizing some of the work on their premises, the
ties of wage work to domestic work were still strong. One mother brought
her youngest children with her to work, a young widow spun with her
baby on her lap and old women knit stockings, much as they all would have
done in households where they lived as dependent sisters, wives, grand-
mothers, great-aunts and spinsters.[37]

Despite its earlier popularity with charities, however, put-out work of
this sort was dwindling in importance. By 1820, textile mills had mostly
usurped hand spinning and weaving; the House of Industry itself folded
under the pressure of the cheap manufactured goods British industry
"dumped" on New York after the war. Moreover, put-out work was insufficient for women like the Widow Morris ("she having seven children under
the age of 10 years") to whose "peculiarly distressing situation" the SRPW
alluded. Burdened with small children, she could not go out to service, and
wages for put-out work were too low and employment too intermittent to
support her family.[38] Ezra Stiles Ely acknowledged this reality in writing
of a widow in his spiritual charge: "This woman, I positively know, has
been industrious," he avowed, wrestling with the equation his contemporaries made between idleness and poverty. "Poverty in her case is not her
fault; unless it be a crime to find needles and silk, to close and bind Morocco
shoes at the rate of 4 s. for twelve pair, when every cord of wood costs her
more money than she can accumulate in a month." The ladies of the
SRPW, more sympathetic than most of their philanthropist peers to the
actualities of their beneficiaries' lives, recognized in 1815 that their employment schemes of the past few years, which had mostly depended on putting

out, were inadequate to the needs of the widows. "We trusted better times were at hand. When opportunities, for the exertion of their own industry might be afforded them. . . . But even should work abound—We appeal to those who are Mothers—how much time, can a widow with infant children sometimes 4, and 5 in number, never less than 2, how much time can she have to gather sufficient to provide bread and clothing, for herself, and them: and pay the rent of her dwelling?" Those women who did work solely at given-out tasks were probably from artisan families where men were steadily employed; self-supporting women and those attached to casually employed men needed other sources of income.[39]

Most commonly, poor women worked at different employments throughout the year. Two women charged by authorities in 1820 with keeping a disorderly house, for example, also did washing and sewing on the side. A street seller might turn to laundressing in cold weather; a laundress might supplement her earnings with put-out work. When all else failed, laboring women turned to poor relief, either "outdoor"—cash, wood or food—or institutional "indoor" relief in the Almshouse or Almshouse hospital.[40] For old women, the shift to relief was often permanent. Many Almshouse inhabitants would live out their days there, although hardly happily. When the eighty-eight-year-old widow Elizabeth Burns lost her street stall, she had a literate friend or a professional letter writer tell the Common Council in plain language what was demeaning to her about the poorhouse: "She is in trouble not knowing what to do or where to seek an Asylum and being far advanced in years the Multiplicity of people in the Almshouse would be rather irksome." "It is easy to teach the duty of contentment to the affluent," the Reverend Ely mused of one in his congregation, an old woman heartsick at ending her days an Almshouse charge: "But to the poor—'who wants to die in the Hospital?'"[41]

Younger women seemed to have used the Almshouse as a temporary resort during the winter, when expenses were highest, or when men were absent, out of work, or ill. With good fortune, a woman could leave when circumstances eased; with a run of bad luck, she might be in and out for some time, forced to piece together ragged employments with indoor relief. The troubles of an Irish woman who emigrated in 1811 illustrate just what bad luck could mean. She entered the Almshouse with her four children in the winter after her husband had abandoned them all for the pleasures of tavern life; Ezra Stiles Ely met her there, ill with a fever, in a ward crowded with women in the same predicament. He next saw her on the Battery, her children clustered about her; she was seeking to meet with her husband who had signed on to a ship in the harbor. If she could get half his pay, she explained, she and the children could leave the Almshouse; if they could again live in "fresh air" she believed they could recover from

the fever which had overtaken all of them. Unsuccessful, she returned to
the Almshouse for an extended sojourn which resulted in one child's death.
She finally left in the spring, but soon fell ill again in the raw May rains
and, when Ely next met her, was on her way back. Although her travails
were especially dire, they were by no means rare, as the figures on female
admissions to the Almshouse attest. Periods of precarious dependency on
a man alternated with hand-to-mouth self-sufficiency; both were coupled
with the ongoing struggle to fend off disasters like a child's death.[42]

The disruptions of the early national period made women's subsistence
from male-headed households shaky, but New York's economy as yet
provided them almost no other ways to make a living. When Edward
Livingston, mayor in 1803, proposed a municipal workshop to employ the
indigent, he was able to specify some tasks for men, but could propose
nothing more for women than vague "labours suited to their strength."
Even the stern gentlemen of the Society for the Prevention of Pauperism,
ever vigilant against the idle propensities of the poor, acknowledged that
it was difficult for women to make a living: "throughout the country, it may
be said, there is often a defect of profitable employment for women and
children of indigent families" . . . "women have fewer resources than men;
they are less able to seek for employment."[43] Paid work was sparse and
unstable. Laboring women were confined within a patriarchal economy
predicated on direct dependence on men, although that system was severely
strained. The hardest-pressed of the working poor, they formed a vast
reserve of labor that enterprising employers had only to tap.

Chapter 2 The Problem of Dependency: Men and Women, Rich and Poor

As poverty in New York intensified, the civic-minded elite began to scrutinize the comportment and manners of the laboring poor. Before 1800, there had been no systematic discussion of the sources of poverty. The ruling merchant/professional class saw the poor as an unremarkable presence, their dependency to be tolerated with a mixture of distaste and lofty benignity. Charity, accordingly, had been an unquestioned if sometimes irksome obligation of urban life. By 1820, however, philanthropists were coming to view the dependencies of the poor as an imposition on the good will of the prosperous. Once seen by the charitable as a condition bequeathed by divine providence, poverty was becoming a distasteful situation for which the poor themselves were responsible.

Poor women, the humblest members of a generally obscure group, did not at first figure prominently in the new discourse. The early organized charities spoke of an abstract, homogeneous mass, "the poor," differentiated by virtue or vice, not by sex, age or ethnicity. Before 1820, popular ideas about women's character and capacities tended to subsume all women, rich, middling and poor, under the common and disdainful rubric of "the sex." In a republican culture which placed the independence of the male citizen at its zenith, the dependent status of all women put them in the same lowly category as servants, children, apprentices, slaves and the poor—all inferiors whose lack of reason and virtue necessitated for the common good that they live under the care and supervision of wise citizens. By 1820, women of prosperous families had managed to free themselves from some of the

most unflattering views of "the sex" by casting themselves as civic-minded
mothers educating their children in the new nation's service. Laboring
women, however, remained right at the crossroads where views of the
contemptible, dependent poor intersected with views of contemptible, dependent women. There, they were left to shoulder the burden of persistent
misogynist ideas.

Eve's Daughters
in the Republican City

While many laboring women found it difficult in the changing social and
economic circumstances of New York to sustain their actual dependencies
on male-headed households, the *ideology* of female dependency still informed popular notions. Indeed, the republican beliefs of the Revolution,
broadly disseminated among New York laboring men, amplified and
strengthened assumptions of female subservience and male authority that
were already widely current in eighteenth-century Anglo-American society. Elite women in the decades after the war had held onto some ideological and cultural resources that protected and even improved their perceived
position. Laboring women, however, had barely examined the possibilities
the Revolution held out for their sex; moreover, their class position made
them more vulnerable to sexual antagonisms which grew worse in the next
twenty years.

It was not that patriarchal views of women were anything new, or that
there was a direct causal relation between republican politics and contemptuous attitudes toward women. Rather, the ideological climate of the post-
Revolutionary decades seems to have reinvigorated, rather than undercut,
an already established, popularly based misogyny. Women had never rated
high in the canons of eighteenth-century thought. Seventeenth-century
dissenting Protestantism had done something to elevate female status by
breaking with a centuries-old European tradition that viewed women as
daughters of Eve, mankind's ill fortune, prey to vanity, folly and concupis-
cence. Yet the old suspicions of women cropped up on all levels of seventeenth-century American religious society, from ministers' sermons to
judgments against village shrews to witchcraft accusations.[1] In the eighteenth century, the image of the traducing Eve faded with the general
attenuation of Calvinist orthodoxy, but Eve's vices lingered on, to be translated into the quintessentially feminine follies that advice and etiquette

books admonished women to curb and men to beware of. Although the ideas in these writings were not necessarily those of their readers (not to speak of all those who did not read books), they nonetheless reveal what literate men and women thought in all possibility they could expect of themselves and each other.

From this perspective, the belief in women's potential for deviousness is striking. Women's dependent status supposedly fostered in them all the vices and stratagems of the weak: They were foolish, easily corrupted by flattery, immodest and frivolous, artful and vain. And *because* they were so prone to these vices, they were rightfully and properly dependent on men for direction and moral authority. Thus Lord Chesterfield, whose letters (collected and published as an advice manual) were popular on both sides of the Atlantic, made one of his typically low assessments of the female character: "They have but two passions, vanity and love," he remarked.[2] Chesterfield was a confirmed misogynist, and his ideas define the outer limits of articulated antagonisms toward women, but he was by no means alone. More liberal-minded writers implicitly sided with him, if not in the tactics he advocated, then at least with his low estimation of female character. Throughout the century, a variety of reform-minded Anglo-American writers, from Mary Wollstonecraft to Benjamin Franklin, held up an alternative ideal of female piety, modesty and prudence; although they proposed that the sources of women's defects lay not in their nature but in their upbringing, they, too, implied that the female character was morally deficient.[3]

Even in a society that talked about liberty as much as did post-Revolutionary America, such weak and willful people could not be left to their own devices. To exercise virtue and ensure the capacity to maintain the republic, a citizen had to be *independent:* that is, he had to be at liberty to act according to his own reasoned judgments about what served the public good. He could not be dependent upon another for his well-being, lest he be influenced or coerced. That was the problem in England, American patriots believed, where an oligarchy had ensnared the freeborn in a corrupt political and economic system in which men of modest means depended for their livelihoods upon the favors of the great. No one who depended on another could fully exercise republican virtue, and thus no dependent—woman, servant, child or slave—possessed the moral status necessary for citizenship.[4] Thus the ideological legacy of the Revolution shaped men's—including laboring men's—sense of their place in the gender system as well as in the entirety of American society. The political importance of the male-headed household was confirmed; republican patriarchalism was synonymous with citizenship; independence demanded the subordination of morally suspect dependents. Linda Kerber has noted that insofar as republican writers thought of women at all (which was seldom), they thought of qualities to avoid. Femininity was associated with self-indulgence, luxury and ignorance. "If Americans lived in a world of the political imagination in which virtue was ever threatened by corruption, it must be added that the overtones of virtue were male, and those of corruption, female."[5] Women, then, were rightfully subjected within their households to the authority of those male heads who could properly watch out for their interests and protect the liberties of all.

The implications of republican ideology for women were not all negative. Popular republicanism, with its stress on the reasonable abilities of all human beings, provided women themselves some ways to attack the belief in the innate folly of their character. During the Revolution and the early national period, women, especially the wives and daughters of patriot leaders, raised tentative questions about women's rights (recall Abigail Adams's admonition to her husband at the beginning of the Revolution to "remember the ladies").[6] They also improved the social estimation of their sex by creating a republican imagery of motherhood. If virtue was necessary to citizenship, they proclaimed, then women could play a part in the new republic as mothers who educated their sons in republican values. Gone were the follies of the lady; reason and prudence, not vanity and frivolity, would characterize the republican mother. For privileged women, this perspective on woman's social role was to foster, in turn, the nineteenth-century cult of domesticity: Not only were women *as* virtuous as men, the proponents of domesticity would declare, they were *more* virtuous. By 1820, changes in family relations and the first excitements of evangelical religion (which put a premium on respect toward women) had marked out among the propertied classes a sphere in which women could be assured, at least in theory, of social respect.[7]

There were, then, competing republican images, one group invented and promoted primarily by women, the other inherited from the past and articulated chiefly by men. On balance, it was the latter that prevailed, especially (we will see) in regard to laboring women. As in any revolution, only a self-conscious women's movement could have made real for women the emancipatory potential of the patriots' ideas of liberty. Not only did the American Revolution do little to improve the female condition; in many ways it strengthened negative opinions of women. Indeed, by the 1790s, the campaign for recognition of women's full dignity had *lost* ground, especially in New York, where British influence remained strong among the elite. There, republican motherhood (whatever its appeal to high-minded patriots) ran against the grain of a culture that took its cues from Regency London. "The sink of British manners and politics," Benjamin Rush acerbically termed fashionable New York.[8] However ardently New York women may have worked to enhance the dignity of their sex, their efforts occurred in a city where self-styled libertines swaggered about the streets, the blood sports beloved by Regency rakes persisted as popular pastimes and the double standard of sexual behavior remained a source of unabashed masculine pride.[9]

If anything, male license for sexual aggressiveness increased in the two decades after the Revolution, especially toward women in public. Feminist agitation during the French Revolution and the publication of Wollstonecraft's *Vindication of the Rights of Women* combined to create a specter of female heterodoxy on both sides of the Atlantic between 1793 and the War of 1812. In England, anti-Jacobinism and anti-feminism (entwined in Edmund Burke's splenetic characterization of French feminists as "the revolutionary harpies of France, sprung from night and hell") fueled the fire of the evangelical reaction. In the United States, Wollstonecraft was "held in general abhorrence," one woman reported in 1803; female advocates of a widened women's sphere were ridiculed as pretentious bluestockings; the association of women's rights with social anarchy and sexual license grew stronger.[10]

These antagonisms toward women were never fully elaborated into explicit ideas that men considered and debated. Mostly, assumptions about women were expressed within a structure of feeling rather than a body of explicit ideas. What shaped the gender relations of ordinary people were unconscious or half-conscious beliefs, intuitions, reactions—the culturally conditioned sense of what was obvious and proper, a matter of common sense. Republican ideas of government, authority and power supported already familiar justifications of sexual hierarchies.[11] To understand the roots and implications of these darker perceptions of women, we must piece together fragments.

A series of events in 1793 provides an especially valuable source of information about how men could act out and explain to themselves their hostilities toward women, and how those hostilities connected with popular politics. Harry Bedlow, a gentleman, was charged with raping seventeen-year-old Lanah Sawyer, a seamstress and daughter of a seaman. Sawyer had met Bedlow one evening when she was out walking; he introduced himself as "Lawyer Smith" and asked to see her again. When the pair walked out together, Bedlow at first treated his companion to chaste and genteel entertainments, ice cream and a tour around the Battery. On the way back, however, well after midnight, he demanded payment for his favors and either forced the girl (according to her) or invited her (according to him) into a bawdy house, where they spent the night and had sexual "connection."[12]

Bedlow's defense in the ensuing trial constitutes a digest of misogynist thought girded by class contempt. Rather than defending Bedlow's intentions or actions, his phalanx of distinguished attorneys shrewdly shifted the focus of the trial from the duplicity of the seducer to the weak-mindedness of the seduced. The girl, they argued, should have been better attuned to the etiquette of debauchery. When a poor girl meets a rich man on the street, what else should she assume but that he intends to make use of her sexually? "Considering the difference of their situations, to what motive could she attribute his assiduities? Could she imagine that a man of his situation would pay her any attention . . . unless with a view of promoting illicit commerce? Was it probable that Lawyer Smith had any honorable designs in his connection with a sewing girl?" This was not rape but seduction by an accomplished practitioner of the art, the counsel proudly affirmed.[13]

This argument drew on very old beliefs about men's rights to women's bodies. But the identification of heterosexual relations with treachery and cold-blooded exploitation was particularly characteristic of eighteenth-century Anglo-American culture. In the lawyers' argument that Bedlow's intentions were perfectly clear—what else could a gentleman want with a poor girl?—courting appears as a barely concealed contest of duplicity between men and women. The prescriptive literature of the times viewed frank sexual hostility as a fact of polite society. "The greater part of either sex study to prey upon one another," avowed the fashionable London preacher Dr. Fordyce, author of a popular advice manual published in an American edition in 1787; thank goodness, he added parenthetically, men had the edge. "The world," he lamented, "in too many instances, is a theatre of war between women and men. Every stratagem is tried, and every advantage taken, on the side of both." Courtship was a war of wits, each sex jockeying to turn the other to its own exploitative uses. Marriage was a prolonged siege of female guile against male authority: *Female Policy Detected: or the Arts of a Designing Woman Laid Open* ran the title of one popular satire.[14] In this context, writers exhorted men to use dissimulation as a weapon. Reasonable men, Lord Chesterfield wrote, only trifled with women and always kept in mind that "they" could turn vicious: "It is necessary to manage, please, and flatter them, and never to discover the least marks of contempt, which is what they never forgive"—all the more difficult, since contempt was just what Chesterfield assumed would be uppermost in men's minds.[15] Although Chesterfield's views of women were especially derisive, the popular reception of the *Letters* shows the extent to which polite society tolerated extreme sexual antagonisms and saw sexual aggression—even brutal aggression—as one way for gentlemen to get on in the world.

While men's power in the struggle derived from their superior authority, reason and intelligence (their "strength and daring," as Fordyce put it),[16] women's flowed from "passion." If chastity was the cardinal virtue of womanhood, passion was its chief vice. Passion was women's legendary carnality, the curse of Eve, capacious receptacle for all the foolishness, wantonness and greed of the sex. It knew no limits of age. Any female could be a passionate creature, as the defendants in trials for child rape sometimes contended. The attorney for a weaver charged with raping a thirteen-year-old girl in 1800, for example, based the argument for the defense on the claim that carnality comprised the essence of even a female child's character: "The passions may be as warm in a girl of her age as in one of more advanced years."[17] As for the traduced Lanah Sawyer, it was her "desire of gratifying her passions," the defense attorneys argued, which led her to entertain the man's acquaintance in the first place. Passion was not simply lasciviousness, but sexual greed fused with other kinds of acquisitiveness in a peculiarly female mode of exploitation. By these lights Sawyer was not the victim she appeared; only trickery, "art," preserved the appearance of innocence—a "fair outside, while all was foul within."[18]

After fifteen minutes of deliberation in the Bedlow/Sawyer rape trial, the jury returned a verdict of not guilty. The acquittal touched off a riot, in which a crowd of six hundred (men, it seems) converged on the bawdy house where the accused, Bedlow, had taken the girl. The mob ransacked it, and proceeded on to several other brothels and the houses of Bedlow's attorneys before mounted militia turned them back.[19]

Against the backdrop of the bloody events in France in 1793, political passions—pro- and antirevolutionary—ran high in the new republic.[20] In the Bedlow affair, popular dissatisfaction with the privileged crystallized into an image of aristocratic sexual license. Sympathy for the girl herself does not seem to have been particularly important in the affair. Her own father vowed "if his daughter was wrong he would turn her out of doors" and loyalty not to the girl but to the father, a man "well known amongst the seafaring People," seems to have motivated the "Boys, Apprentices, Negroes and Sailors" who made up the crowd. The spectacle of gentlemanly license protected by a court was what touched off a wave of "popular indignation,"[21] turning a drama of female sexual vulnerability into a conflict between men.

Into this fray entered "Justitia," probably a woman of some learning, certainly a highly literate one (her real identity remains hidden). Angered by Bedlow's acquittal, Justitia wrote a letter to the newspaper denouncing Bedlow as "a *wretch* . . . whose character is too vile to be portrayed" and took the occasion to air some of her own sexual grievances. The attack on the bawdy houses had been, no doubt, "a matter of great grief for many of our *male* citizens," she observed with unladylike sarcasm, "considering

what comfortable hours they have passed in these peaceful abodes far from
the complaints of a neglected wife." She went on to suggest—archly—that
the bawdy houses might be policed far more effectively if it weren't for the
fact that the magistrates themselves patronized them.

Justitia's intrepid foray into print set off a flurry of abuse. No respectable
woman could even know of such things, her respondents maintained sar-
donically. They dropped hints about her identity and to top it off belittled
the "weakness of her misunderstanding and the indelicacy of her pen." The
exchange quickly shifted ground from the political matter of the bawdy
houses to the question of Justitia's own honor. In the end she was reduced
to recruiting a gentleman who, she informed her adversaries in her final
letter, would call on the writer who had most directly sullied her name
through his imputations.[22] These were not women's matters, Justitia had
learned, even if rape and prostitution directly concerned them. Men
guarded the public discourse of sexuality.

In the Bedlow case and the Justitia exchange, the implicit sexual connotations of the weak-mindedness of women became explicit. Popular views
of female folly converged with the notion of passion. Both were defects that
warped women's ability to act reasonably. Dominated by emotional imperatives, women could not comport themselves with the fairness and independence required of the citizen. In the trial, Bedlow's attorneys, drawing on
such assumptions, had suggested that unleashing women in a court of law
in itself threatened the civil process. The life of a citizen (rape was a capital
crime until 1796) was in jeopardy because of a woman's testimony, and such
testimony was inherently suspect. "Putting the life of a citizen in the hands
of a woman to be disposed of almost at her will and pleasure," the defense
grimly characterized the proceedings, and went on to denounce the legitimacy of all female testimony in the trial as fundamentally compromised by
the supposedly loose sexual proclivities of the women in question. The
female neighbors had testified that Lanah Sawyer was a girl of good character, unlikely to go to bed willingly with Bedlow. In response, the prosecu-
tion argued that the neighbor women's testimony was worthless, since by
virtue of their sex and their humble position, they knew nothing of good
character themselves: "Their being of the same condition of life with the
Prosecutrix gives us a right to doubt what they mean." The sexual practices
of such women—"accustomed . . . to allowing male friends liberties"—
partook of the same vices which deformed Sawyer's character.[23]

The intersection of class and gender, then, signified a sexual wantonness
that weakened women's credibility. More broadly, assumptions about female passion discredited women's authority over their own persons. Men
could with some justification make women, especially laboring women,
their sexual prey, since a foul nature exempted the latter from the cus-

tomary protections of virtuous womanhood. Justitia had stepped out of place, thereby abnegating those protections, by venturing into the public discourse of sexual politics. Other women did so simply by walking unescorted on the streets. Harassing women in public was a favorite entertainment of the "bloods," rakes whose chief pastime was lounging about the streets. Progenitors of the midcentury dandies, the bloods affected (perhaps parodied) the languorous, bored and disdainful manner associated with patrician men. Fancy dress was their insignia; contempt for women, their emblem of high style. A phalanx of young men hung about the streets, ready to jeer and jolt a victim. "If she essays to proceed by the wall, they instantly veer that way, and defeat her intention. In this manner she is often obliged to pass and repass several times in front of the line, each one making his impertinent remarks on her as she tried to get forward—'An Angel, by H——s!' 'Dam'd fine girl, by g——d!' 'Where do you lodge, my dear?' " "Language the most obscene, and actions the most gross" accompanied the hooting and catcalling. Laboring women, more likely than ladies to be out on the streets alone, must have been frequent targets. Certainly the effect of the insults (which included "the drawing up of the upper, or pouting out of the nether lip, accompanied with a sort of hissing") was to stigmatize women as rightful prey on the streets.[24]

The celebration of women as fair game was also at work in another gentleman's scandal of the era, the trial of the merchants William Wilson and Alexander Buchanan in 1820 for kidnapping Nancy Martin, a washerwoman's daughter.[25] The story had all the elements of a Richardson novel (or, closer to home, one of Susanna Rowson's plots): a villainous rake, an innocent girl, abduction and forcible assault (although the heroine's resistance fell decidedly short of novelistic standards). Buchanan had met Nancy Martin somewhere in the city and had determined to have her for his own; he decided on abduction—or elopement, as he presented it to her —to accomplish his ends. Encouraged by her suitor's promises of liveried servants, a two-story brick house and other accoutrements of fashion— "everything she wanted to make her happy"—Martin slipped away from home and took up residence in lodgings Buchanan had taken for her. There the two consummated their relationship. The arrangement remained consensual—that of a kept mistress and her lover—for ten days, Buchanan stringing her along with more promises until remorse and disillusion overtook her. Meanwhile, her mother pleaded in vain for her return with Buchanan's friend Wilson, whom Nancy's sister had pointed out in City Hall Park.

Along with her virtue, Nancy had apparently, in the eyes of her lover, given up the rights over her person. Wilson flatly refused to share any information about the girl's whereabouts with the distraught mother. To her insistence that Buchanan had no right to hide the girl, the friend countered, "*You don't know but that he has,*" since "she was a poor, ordinary insignificant thing—that had lost her virtue and been intimate with other *men.*" The girl was safe, contended Wilson, and if she suffered any anguish in the episode, then her abductor would "make it up" with a little money. The lines of self-justification here are important. Wilson was rationalizing an obviously illegal act with a deeper, half-conscious sense of how men could lawfully treat women. If men acted as unabashed predators, even captors, as they did in this case, it was in response to women who, from the male perspective, had set themselves up both as prey and as avaricious aggressors in their own right.

But contempt for women was not the attitude exclusively of wealthy gentlemen. Indeed, it was probably a bond that men shared across class lines in a "plebeian" culture where sporting gentlemen might consort with workingmen at bawdy houses and cockfighting rings and in political affrays. Images of women as bawds and tricksters were a staple in the conversations of laboring people, and the lusty moll of sailors' ballads and journeymen's jokes was close kin to the greedy whore of gentlemen's lore. The figure of the affable wench, an integral part of the bawdy popular culture of the early eighteenth century, was still alive in the first two decades of the nineteenth. Sometimes amiable, sometimes scheming, she was one way or the other out to get her way with men. For "The Orange Woman," a Dublin girl in a sailors' broadside, this meant simply satisfying her carnal appetites. "I always fancy pretty Men,/Wherever I can find 'em," the "hearty buxom Girl" declares unabashedly.

> I'll never marry, no indeed,
> 　For Marriage causes trouble;
> And after all the priest has said,
> 　'Tis merely hubble bubble.
> The rakes will still be counted rakes,
> 　Not hymen's chains can bind 'em. . . .

"And so," she happily concludes

> Preventing all mistakes
> I'll kiss where'er I find 'em.[26]

The Orange Woman was a sailor's dream come true, the proverbial whore with a heart of gold who took pleasure in men and asked for little in return. Similarly, the obliging Mrs. Huggins, in this bit of allusive doggerel from her husband's advertisement for his hairdressing establishment in 1808, seems content with an evening with "a good jolly cock":

> At eve, by the fire, like a good jolly cock,
>   When my day's work is done and all over;
> I tipple, I smoke, and I wind up the clock,
>   With sweet Mrs. Huggins in clover.[27]

Real women, of course, demanded a return on their favors, and other renditions of the bawd from before the Revolution also indicate laboring men's view that sexuality was a female weapon, the instrument by which women duped men and then took them for all they were worth. "A father said to his son, what is your wife quick already?" ran a joke from an almanac aimed at a readership of skilled workers. "Yes, said he, a pox on her, she is too quick, for we have been married but a month, and she is ready to lie in." The source of humor in such jokes was a shared view of women as inseparable from the babies they bore and of both babies and women as parasites on men's lives. "A man complained to his wife she brought him nothing. You lie like a rogue, says she, for I bring you boys and girls without your help."[28]

If women were parasitical dependents, then they lived in men's households on sufferance. When that sufferance was too sorely tried, men could feel themselves justified in withdrawing what they had bestowed. In anger, men sometimes acted out a drama of patriarchal proprietorship of the household and all that it contained. Not even the birth of his child stopped the woodworker Laurence Bracken from showing his wife and the neighbors that he rationed out the resources of his household as he saw fit; indeed, the baby may have set him off, as a bevy of women took over the house for his wife's lying-in. Six hours after she gave birth he marched into her chamber and "observed that the bed on which . . . [she] was then lying was his Bed and that [she] should not lie upon it," whereupon he seized her by the hair and dragged her naked to the floor.[29] George Hart's hostility toward his common-law wife, who had taken four shillings from his pockets, was similarly uncompromising; he beat her to death and then explained to the neighbors this was only her just deserts: "I will serve any d———d w———e so, who robs me of my money." John Banks, a sailor, used similar language to brag about the bloody murder of his common-law wife, with whom he had quarreled over the marketing (he beat her with a shovel and slit her throat with a razor): "I would kill a dozen like her, for she was a dam'd bitch."[30]

These last two statements are the words of criminals, and admittedly, we could discount them as evidence of *common* male attitudes on those grounds alone. But others who spoke in a similar vein were not murderers but simply aggrieved husbands. Certainly, not all men detested their wives. At the turn of the eighteenth century, just as years before and years later, there were harmonious and affectionate relations between men and women. The point is rather that, in this period, men did not expect tender feelings to develop as a matter of course in their marriages; on the contrary, they saw hostilities between the sexes as normal and even natural.

Within such a comprehension of gender relations, there were few territories where men and women could meet on dependably peaceful terms. The double standard, by these lights, was a legitimate male weapon in sexual warfare rather than a regrettable consequence of male lust—the construction the Victorians would later give it. So was sexual antagonism and even, sometimes, sexual violence. True, there were powerful ideological traditions, including republicanism, that celebrated the family as an entity of heterosexual harmony and mutuality. This cooperative image, however, stood in tension with another view of the family as a place for disciplining women, a means of cloistering them and protecting society at large from their depredations.

It was not these assumptions alone, of course, that consigned women to the family and men to the public world. Centuries of tradition dictated that women be responsible for household labor and that they be excluded from many kinds of public life. But the assumptions about women's nature did legitimate this familiar division, constraining women from walking the streets, engaging in a trade or seeking amusement for themselves. Meanwhile, the structures of household life that supported beliefs in masculine authority and female moral weakness eroded under economic and social pressures. The consequent rearrangements in women's work, part and parcel of the experience of proletarian life, were in many cases to aggravate sexual hostilities. The working-class city of the nineteenth century, however, would also create openings for more amiable negotiations between the sexes.

Charity and Class Relations

At the turn of the century, caring for the poor was primarily an obligation of the city's elite. The ministration of charity was one of many patrician duties that had devolved on wealthy merchants and professionals by virtue of their social position and their perceived right to rule their city. After the

Revolution, prominent New Yorkers had begun to express their sense of social responsibility in a network of organizations modeled on English humanitarian societies: secular societies for helping poor widows, the sick poor and distressed slaves, church-sponsored societies to aid the indigent and charity schools for poor children. The idea of benevolence, philosophically elaborated by a variety of eighteenth-century thinkers, made humanitarian charity part of a broad-minded, cosmopolitan Anglo-American sensibility. Benevolence was the practice of disinterested goodness, an innate moral sense that existed independent of the threat of damnation. Within the framework of Enlightenment ideas of progress, benevolence happily united the self-interest of the giver with altruism.[31] "Providence has wisely allied the interest of the individual with the interest of the human race," the New York Humane Society cheerfully asserted.[32] In the churches, likewise—the Quaker meetings and the wealthy Episcopalian, Presbyterian and Dutch Reformed congregations—Christ's reminder that "ye have the poor always with you" (Matthew 26:11) strengthened the belief in charity as an eternal duty of those whom God had materially blessed.[33] Those of his people on whom God "bestows the comforts of this life," John Rodgers, popular Presbyterian minister and philanthropist in his own right, reminded his listeners, "are hereby constituted his *Almoners* to dole out his charity to their poorer brothers and sisters . . . one great design of Heaven in giving them such Plenty is that they may be hereby enabled to supply the wants of the necessitous."[34]

Providence thus wisely utilized class differences to ensure a benevolent interdependency, one basis for social intercourse between superiors and inferiors in a hierarchical world. Charity elicited generosity from the former and patience and submission from the latter. "We are speaking to the hearts of all," testified the founders of the New York Dispensary in 1800, "by showing that a common interest still unites the different classes of the community, and bridges over the immense gulf which, at first sight, seemed to separate them."[35] In a city where class distinctions were dramatic, ritualized benevolence supposedly bridged the gap and bound the wealthy into a commonalty with the poor.

From these ideas and beliefs, the New York elite constructed a fairly confident relationship with "their" poor, one in which civic-mindedness and patrician self-interest met in a felicitous union of benign urbanity.[36] Understanding poverty as a natural and ordained feature of society, the charities saw their work as practical and ameliorative. The city's first philanthropists wanted to mitigate the worst distresses of the poor; they did not even consider the possibility of eradicating poverty itself. They sought to help the poor with firewood, groceries and handed-down clothes, not to change their habits or attitudes. Poverty was not a moral failing, but a condition bequeathed by providence. "Riches or poverty happen at the wise disposal of God," John Romeyn, one of the city's first revival ministers, asserted in 1810.[37]

To be sure, this was no golden age of humanitarianism. Tolerance coexisted with sterner, punitive attitudes derived from Calvinist doctrine and from the old tenets of the English poor law, which stressed the importance of vigilance against the "vicious," unworthy and idle poor and gave rise to severe and punitive practices.[38] Even so, while the old idle/honest distinction played an important role in judging the suitability of applicants for charity, philanthropists seldom employed it in analyzing poverty as a social question. When the societies spoke of the "peculiar claims" of the poor, they referred to needs that might be overwhelming, insistent and vexing, but that nonetheless seemed to them to be legitimate.[39]

Patrician confidence in urban benevolence faltered before the pressing demands of the poor during and after the War of 1812. By 1817, it had all but collapsed. Pessimism, ironically, fostered higher ambitions. Philanthropists began for the first time to speak of doing away with poverty altogether, if only out of their own fatigue with coping with the crisis of need that began during the embargo. The wealthy insurance broker Thomas Eddy spoke for many of his colleagues when he admitted he was "tired" of helping the unfortunate: "It appears to me more wise," he wrote to the former mayor and philanthropist Dewitt Clinton in 1817, "to fix on every profitable plan to prevent their poverty and misery."[40] In municipal government, too, authorities came to reject benevolence as inadequate to the problems before them. As late as 1813, a calm acceptance of obligation still framed the comptroller's reminder to the Common Council that adequate poor relief must be a priority in the budget: "Care should be taken to husband all our resources . . . the demands of support of the poor the ensuing season will far exceed all antecedent periods." But this kind of pragmatism was waning before a growing anxiety. From 1798 to 1816, expenditures for the Almshouse more than doubled; during the disastrous season of 1818–19 they soared to over $100,000. The city's liberal poor relief system had become a heavy burden to taxpayers.[41]

Even in the 1790s, critics of benevolence as public policy had argued that municipal relief, in alleviating the worst distress, simply encouraged the poor to rest easy in their situations. During the war, this point of view prompted a discussion among philanthropists themselves about the adverse effects of "indiscriminate" giving: charity that was given too freely and uncritically and thus unwittingly promoted vice and idleness.[42] New York philanthropic luminaries, especially the Quakers, were closely connected to English humanitarians. Their discouragement over the situation in New York made them especially receptive to ideas their English friends and colleagues were promoting in the poor-law debate in Britain, especially to the Malthusian theory that benevolence bred (literally!) poverty.[43]

Philanthropic exasperation and disaffection with benevolence were also reactions to the growing importunity of the poor after the Revolution. It was one thing for God to direct His stewards to share their wealth; it was another for poor people themselves to ask for their share, as seamen and laborers had done during the embargo when they pressured the Common Council for relief. The petition was couched in the customary language of deference to social betters, but throughout the protestations of humility the men hinted at more threatening actions (the possibilities of thieving, or breaking the embargo to sign up on foreign vessels).[44] While the embargo demonstrations were only a fleeting outburst, there were also other signs that poor people had come to see relief as their prerogative. Increasingly, both the local and the migratory poor incorporated relief into their survival patterns; poor relief was, for many, not simply a recourse in a catastrophe but a structural element of subsistence. As a consequence, the character of the Almshouse changed, from a last resort for those permanently disabled from working (cripples, the elderly, the sick, mothers with small children) to a seasonal or episodic way station for the theoretically able-bodied. Ezra Stiles Ely thus found that the poor made their own uses of the Almshouse. The entire residency of one ward he visited turned over in three weeks, and he noticed that in cold weather, the population swelled with the admission of those who "could not endure the frosts of winter" (ten years later the Common Council would denounce the unworthy poor who expected to spend "the Summer Season in idleness and the winter in the Almshouse").[45] The greatest change in the relief system, however, was the great expansion of outdoor relief, always a problematic category in Anglo-American charity since it lacked the punitive and controlling elements inherent in institutionalization. Recipients of outdoor relief could continue to live as they were inclined, which meant, as the Common Council put it in 1817, that taxpayers supported a "class of persons whose sole object appears to be a life of idleness and dissipation."[46] New York's largesse seemed in some cases only to stimulate the poor's impudence rather than to strengthen their gratitude: During the yellow fever epidemic of 1805, the Almshouse superintendent complained, all too many applied for charity not because they were truly needy but because "as they generally termed it, they would have their share of it."[47]

During 1817 dissatisfaction with existing practices, disgust with the "unworthiness" of charity recipients and esteem for English innovations all led to the formation of the Society for the Prevention of Pauperism (SPP).[48] Organized by leaders of the mercantile, religious and professional communities—including Thomas Eddy—the SPP signaled a shift of philanthropic effort from meliorism to active reform. While the gentlemen who organized it had no hopes of eradicating poverty, they did (as the name indicates) intend to abolish pauperism, poverty's most extreme and pernicious form: "That condition in society, which implies *want, misery*, distress, and approaching ruin."[49]

In the refocusing of charitable attention, the habits of the poor took on great importance. Historians have noted the moralism which entered the views of urban charities after 1815, and this is true of the SPP.[50] The SPP's analysis of the causes of poverty, freighted with British-inspired statistics and taxonomic classifications, consisted entirely of what the gentlemen perceived to be the vices of the urban poor: "imprudent and hasty marriages," ignorance, idleness, intemperance, thriftlessness, gambling, and promiscuous sex[51] ("Want of employment" was entirely omitted in the first three annual reports). These were social as well as moral categories: The "evils" were the SPP's own renditions of familiar aspects of life in poor neighborhoods. Indeed, these were such familiar aspects of poor people's lives that eighteenth-century humanitarians scarcely mentioned them: common-law marriage, illiteracy, habitual drinking, gambling and carousing, looseness with money—all the "idle" ways, in short, of a laboring poor with little use for emerging bourgeois values of industry, sobriety, thrift and sexual restraint.

Here were the makings of a bourgeois understanding of the problem of poverty. Gone was the acceptance of things as they were, to be replaced by a prescription of hard work as a panacea for misery, a view of charitable giving as the means to endorse hard work, and a rudimentary apparatus of intervention and discipline to implement "charity": stricter licensing laws for taverns, savings banks for the prudent, treadmills for the lazy. Gone also was the tolerance for the diversity of city life that had colored a variety of interactions between the wealthy and the laboring poor, from the charity visits of humanitarians to the sexual slumming of rakes. In contrast, the new agenda promoted cultural homogeneity: the ever-calculating, self-interested *homo economicus,* image of bourgeois man, would serve as a model for the downtrodden. Although emulating the prosperous would never lead the poor to social equality (poverty was desirable, since if it weren't for the poor, who would enrich the wealthy?),[52] it would remove the worst excesses of indigence. In refashioning the poor man's self-expectations, philanthropists believed they could renovate him to compete successfully in the market, the equilibrator of all social relations.

What were the consequences of the redirection of philanthropic interest? The SPP would not directly have touched the lives of many of the laboring poor. Only a handful would have endured the drudgery of the treadmill, which the SPP succeeded in installing in the penitentiary in 1823, or ploughed their way through the dry moralisms of the society's tracts on thrift, prudence and industry. Many more, however, would have felt the tightening of constraints on public relief that the SPP effected. The society's Benthamite utilitarianism and its belief in the destructive effects of benevolence became the guiding notions of philanthropic innovation between 1817 and 1830. In 1817 the Common Council cut back on its grants to private charities and considered curbing promiscuous almsgiving by suspending all municipal donations in the future.[53] Four years later, it discontinued the assize on bread, an old municipal tradition that limited the price of bread in order to ensure the poor an adequate supply of food (political economy judged the bread assize, like indiscriminate charity, to interfere with the equilibrating mechanism of the market).[54] A repudiation of obligation began to replace the language of stewardship in the Council's deliberations on the condition of the poor. "It is confidently believed," the aldermen asserted in 1821 in language borrowed from the SPP, "that a great portion of the pauperism in this country arises from a reluctance to labor and dependence on the public bounty." SPP recommendations for punitive work requirements for the indigent strongly influenced the Yates Report to the state legislature in 1823, which codified a new and harsh poor law for the state.[55]

Not everyone agreed. Cadwallader Colden, mayor in 1819, challenged the proposition that benevolence bred indigence, and a committee under his auspices, investigating the increase in indoor relief, found no one in the Almshouse who was an "unfit" object of charity and sensibly reminded the public that as the city grew, the numbers of the poor were bound to increase also.[56] Older notions of charity persisted, especially (we will see) among charitable ladies, who incorporated the eighteenth-century ideal of benevolence into a belief in their own obligation to help the unfortunate of their sex.

Nonetheless, it was the SPP gentlemen whose interpretations prevailed in public policy and in the popular understanding of poverty. Where charity had once been seen as an expression of organic social bonds, beneficent for giver and receiver alike, it came to be construed as an activity fraught with irritation for the former and moral peril for the latter. Through the antebellum period, the evangelical movement in New York was to disseminate ideas first developed by the SPP to a constituency of religious activists and readers of the revivalist press. In the discourse that ensued, the social context of laboring people's lives—the supposed breeding ground of poverty—took on compelling interest.

The early charities developed a set of assumptions about the depraved character of the laboring poor that were to influence class relations for the entire antebellum period. Their views did not simply represent, as histori-

ans of American cities have sometimes implied, a neutral or objective response to an escalating urban crisis. Rather, as the privileged classes formulated the problem of poverty, these charities also exercised power within
a field of intensifying class conflicts.

Later, women were to play an important role in refining and implement-
ing the reformist approach as they made their own determinations about
how social change could occur. As bourgeois wives and mothers strengthened their sense of their own redemptive powers, they elaborated a sentimental imagery of poverty and a set of prescriptions for a renewed family
life within the working classes. Charitable ladies directed the attention of
their male colleagues, already fastened on the milieu of the laboring poor,
into a more specific focus on the domestic arrangements of the tenements.
As the poor moved into the foreground of nineteenth-century views of the
city, constructions of the meaning of manhood and womanhood, motherhood and childhood fused with the already established categories of virtue
and vice.

For laboring women, the thirty years after the Revolution were especially
difficult. Marginalized by the republican political movements that were the
most hopeful developments in the lives of the popular classes, they endured
the full force of the economic and social distress of the period. They stood
at the center of the emerging problem of poverty. Deprived of many of the
protections of customary household economies, as yet women had little
ability to eke out a living from the wage-labor system.

The Revolution did little to change the situation of American women.
This was especially true for poor women, whose low social position barred
them from the few concrete benefits the war bestowed on their sex—
reforms in education and the law. As propertied women began their ascent
to republican motherhood, laboring women became the receptacle for all
the unsavory traits traditionally assigned their sex. Laboring men had taken
from the Revolution the materials for a transposed identity as citizens,
freemen, and republican fathers. In ensuing years, the growth of metropolitan industry was to undermine these men's sense of their own political,
social and patriarchal importance; at the same time, it was to create the
conditions for expanding and strengthening a masculine community of
labor devoted to defending their prerogatives in the workplace, at the ballot
box and in the family. As laboring men tried to salvage and then vindicate
their citizenship and paternal prerogatives, they often looked balefully on
the women who, in a city where slavery was in decline, struggled on at the
very bottom of the social hierarchy, figures of a supposed dependency
which, for the would-be patriarchs, was at once desirable and irksome. The

new republic gave poor women only fragments of an ideological language with which to press their own claims, and their social and working lives provided few materials to invent a new set of ideas for understanding their situation.

Except for the occasional scandal about a poor girl and a gentleman, the lives of laboring women excited little public interest. The impoverished woman, a crucial figure to the early Victorian comprehension of poverty and class, had yet to materialize in the minds of the socially concerned. It was, indeed, the entrance of bourgeois women en masse into the philanthropic movement that introduced this figure, and the considerations of gender she embodied, to elite discussions. In charitable and reform work, these genteel women were finding their own voice and articulating their sense of their own importance. There was little in their language, however, that could help laboring women, whose identities were rooted outside the sphere of religion and the home. Even in this early period, when feminine class identities were somewhat fluid, laboring women increasingly diverged from their more prosperous sisters' sense of propriety. In the coming years, the task of domesticating the women of the streets, bawdy houses and tenements would prove one of the most challenging tasks that urban reformers, male and female, set themselves.

Part Two

The Politics of Sociability,
1820–1850

Chapter 3 Women in the Neighborhoods

By the 1820s, men and women of the urban bourgeoisie were coming to see households as more than just lodgings. The "home," their own term for the domestic setting, had become for them a pillar of civilization, an incubator of morals and family affections, a critical alternative to the harsh and competitive world of trade and politics. The home was based on a particular configuration of family members: woman at home, man at work, children under maternal supervision or at school. In its psychological form, it embodied the emotional self-sufficiency of the conjugal family and the suitability of women to private life; as a material setting, it elaborated the physical elements of the household into an embellished inner space cut off from the public world.[1]

In this sense, the home was absent from the lives of urban laboring women, who observed no sharp distinctions between public and private. Rather, their domestic lives spread out to the hallways of their tenements, to adjoining apartments and to the streets below. Household work involved them constantly with the milieu outside their own four walls; lodgers, neighbors, peddlers and shopkeepers figured as prominently in their domestic routines and dramas as did husbands and children. It was in the urban neighborhoods, not the home, that the identity of working-class wives and mothers was rooted.

At the turn of the century New York's residential pattern had been a patchwork of class; by the 1830s, the enclaves of laboring people were coming to constitute separate territories, so extensive and distinct that they

seemed to genteel observers something like a foreign domain. Ned Buntline's fictional hero Peter Precise found one way of expressing this as he
stood in 1848 looking down a street in the especially wild and especially
poor Five Points: "Oh God! Can this be a Christian city?"[2] Certainly the
standards of genteel propriety, synonymous with Christianity to Buntline's
respectable readership, were almost entirely lacking in the Five Points, as
well as in the vast precincts of Corlears Hook, the little black ghetto of
Bancker Street, the North (Hudson) River waterfront district off Green-
wich Street, Kleindeutschland to the north and east, the shantytown Dutch
Hill to the north and the eastern side of the island from Fourteenth to
Twenty-third streets.[3] There, what struck visitors most forcibly was the
unabashedly raucous and contentious public life: the drinking, the fighting,
the carousing and quarreling and lovemaking. Notions of domestic privacy
seemed entirely absent, as people circulated continually between the streets
and their own and each others' lodgings.

Much of this was familiar. Drunkenness and contentiousness were such
well-known aspects of life in Western cities as to seem endemic among the
poor. As for domestic privacy, what was new was the value attached to it
by the bourgeoisie, not its absence among laboring people. The concept of
familial intimacy was quite new and ran counter to the patterns of everyday
life that had shaped the experience of most Europeans and Americans, not
just the poor, up to 1800.

Nonetheless, the particular kind of urban neighborhood which so disturbed civic-minded bourgeois New Yorkers was different from earlier
forms. One new element was the extensive community of women that
developed within the transient and disruptive circumstances of urban migration. Of course, the most visible inhabitants of the neighborhoods were
men. They were the preponderance of drunken brawlers and street loungers and the most noticeable workers, as they trudged to and from the docks
or labored at the open doors of the craft shops that dotted the streets.
Another, less noticeable round of female activity, however, went on around
this masculine sphere, a cycle of pinching and saving, of cleaning and
borrowing and lending, of taking—and of being taken. With unremitting
labor, wives, mothers and female neighbors kept the "tenement classes"
going from day to day—whether stitching shirts for the clothing shops or
bargaining down street peddlers. Out of the precarious situations into
which immigration, poverty and (for many) the erosion of male support
thrust them, women formed particular attachments to each other and to
their children that made the neighborhoods important resources in the
negotiations and battles of daily urban life.

Industrialization and
Working-Class Formation

The residents of these gregarious neighborhoods helped to transform New York into what was, by 1860, the largest manufacturing city in America and the capital of the country's finance and commerce.[4] Its small workshops, stacked floor by floor in the new cast-iron warehouses that lined the narrow, crowded streets, were as important to America's Industrial Revolution as the better-known mills of New England. Between 1820 and 1860, the population quadrupled to over 800,000; the city's border moved a mile and a half north from City Hall to Forty-second Street. "How this city marches northward!" marveled diarist George Templeton Strong after a walk in 1850. "Wealth is rushing in upon us like a freshet."[5]

New York's spectacular rise began in the 1820s. The disruption of shipping in the war had seriously damaged the port, but recovery was steady, and by 1820 the maritime economy was sturdy and thriving. In the next few years, in a series of remarkable leaps, its merchants gained control of the American import/export economy. In 1825, the completion of the Erie Canal, the final step to preeminence, linked the city to the Great Lakes and secured its position as an entrepôt for the enormous hinterland the canal penetrated.[6] "Not a tree will be felled which does not necessarily operate to increase the trade and riches of New York," a contemporary observed in 1819.[7]

These commercial developments stimulated a phenomenal growth of the small manufacturing sector that had appeared in the 1790s. The opening of the Erie Canal, with its profitable possibilities for new inland markets, alerted many more craftsmen to the advantages of mass production and the entrepreneurial-minded began to expand their operations. The steady flow of people into the city allowed ambitious master craftsmen to restructure and enlarge their work forces and to cut labor costs by hiring unskilled and semiskilled immigrants and women as wage laborers rather than journeymen who had served regular apprenticeships. When skilled workers faced this competition they, too, accepted lowered wages and intermittent work.

The genius of the city's entrepreneurs, its favored situation in trade and, above all, its cheap labor brought about New York's Industrial Revolution. In contrast to the pattern usually associated with industrial development— the mechanization of work in factories—New York employers generally did not adopt new machines but rather incorporated handicraft workers into wage-labor arrangements. With the exception of a few trades where journeymen continued to craft custom goods for a luxury market, wage labor and its attendant insecurities came to affect most New York laboring people in the years after 1820. Metropolitan industrialization greatly reduced the chances that journeymen might own their own shops, and greatly enlarged the scale of proletarian dependency: the state in which workers own no means of a livelihood other than their own ability to labor. The distinction between skilled and unskilled, artisan and laborer had been meaningful in the eighteenth century when chances were good that a journeyman might in due time become a proprietor of his own shop. It became far less so in the nineteenth century, as craftsmen and laborers alike were pulled into the working class, and as proprietorship itself became a shaky business. Shoemaking, for instance, was already in decline by 1820, prey to competition from New England towns; by the 1840s, the pressures of credit and an expanding national market had impoverished both journeymen and small masters in the trade. The great majority of tailors suffered a similar fate between 1820 and 1860, although a privileged majority fared well. (Those tailors lucky enough to serve as head cutters in the large clothing shops were probably the best paid workers in New York by the 1840s, earning an income large enough to give their wives an entrée to gentility.)[8] Thus industrialization heightened differences *among* skilled workers as well as blurred their differences from the unskilled.

Between 1820 and 1860, the working class became largely immigrant: English, German and (most of all) Irish. The foreign-born population soared from 18,000 in 1830 to more than 125,000 in 1845, a proportional increase from 9 percent of the city's residents to 35 percent; by 1855, the Irish accounted for 28 percent of New York's populace, the Germans for 16 percent.[9] Before 1846, the newcomers tended to be poor but not necessarily penniless: The Irish, for instance, were often Protestant farmers and skilled craftsmen from the North, although canal and railroad construction projects also drew thousands of Catholic peasants and cottiers who ended up as day laborers in the States. After the first crop failures of the potato famine in Ireland in 1845, however, distress became desperation, and Irish refugees began to arrive bereft of all but the clothes on their backs. Depression in the grain-exporting regions of northern Germany also sent a small, steady flow of poor German peasants into the tide of pauperized Irish. In 1855, an estimated three-quarters of the work force were immigrants.[10] To be Irish in antebellum New York was almost certainly to belong to the working poor: a day laborer, a sweatshop worker, or an ill-paid manufactory hand. The situation of the Germans was a bit more varied. Those German farmers who had been able to sell off their land before migrating put their small capital into often successful shopkeeping—as bakers, tobacconists, tavern keepers and grocers. Most Germans, however, joined the working class—as cabinetmakers, tailors and shoemakers in low-paid and insecure situations.

A small black population also figured in the ranks of the working poor. Strictly speaking, slavery did not altogether end in New York until 1827. It had long been declining in the city, however, and beginning with the Revolution (when the British occupying the city had announced a general emancipation), the black community consisted primarily of freed men and women. As in other Northern cities, racial segregation was marked. Although blacks lived in pockets scattered throughout the whole city (a pattern of dispersal among whites that accounts for the frequency of inter-racial domestic feuds in the court records), they were often denied the use of public conveyances and almost always barred from working in the crafts. Black men worked as seamen, day laborers, waiters, barbers and whitewashers, generally in menial, ill-paid and casualized situations.[11]

The political economy of the city of women was distinct, although not unrelated to that of race, ethnicity and occupation. Family situations propelled women into the working class, and the relations of gender gave a distinct shape to the female experience of proletarianization. A woman's age, marital status, the number and age of her children and, above all, the presence or absence of male support determined her position in working-class life. Any woman, whether the wife of a prosperous artisan or a day laborer's daughter, was vulnerable to extreme poverty if, for some reason, she lost the support of a man. With the expansion of manufacturing employment after 1830, young single women might earn some kind of a living for themselves, but married women with children experienced the loss of men's wages, either through death or desertion, as devastating. The seasonal moves that men made to find work enhanced their women's vulnerability. Tramping artisans and migrant laborers could die on the road or take advantage of the moment to abandon their families, and even loyal husbands could find it hard to get news and money back to children and wives in New York. The frequency of occupationally related accidents and disease in men's employments contributed to a high rate of male mortality, which also left many women as the breadwinners for their families.[12] Men, too, suffered when their wives died or left them. The loss of women's housekeeping services, along with whatever income they contributed, created hardships for widowers and deserted husbands. Nonetheless, a woman's absence alone was not sufficient to imperil a husband's livelihood, while a wife cast on her own faced the specter of the Almshouse.

Domestic Labor in the Tenements

For all laboring women, native-born and immigrant, black and white, wives of skilled men and daughters of the unskilled, working-class life meant, first and foremost, the experience of living in the tenements. The tenements were remote from the middle-class home, and they were also different from the households of the urban laboring classes in the late eighteenth century. The difference was not in standards of living, although there has been great historical debate over whether the material conditions of the laboring classes improved or declined with industrial capitalism. Certainly, eighteenth-century New York, as compared to the nineteenth century, was no golden age of prosperity for working people. What did distinguish the industrial metropolis from the eighteenth-century port was not the existence of poverty but rather its context and scale, as the uncertainties of wage work spread out from the lowest ranks of laborers to artisans accustomed to some measure of domestic security, and encompassed multitudes of immigrants who arrived each decade.

Women experienced this partly as a change in the nature of housekeeping. We have seen that after the Revolution urban domestic production had become the privilege of a minority of prosperous artisans' wives; after 1820 it virtually disappeared along with its symbols, the peripatetic pigs and cows who trotted about the streets. Even those women still prosperous enough to carry on household production, the wives of successful artisan entrepreneurs, largely abandoned it for commercial goods. Poorer women lacked the steady income, the space or the facilities to engage in household crafts. Another pattern took hold in the tenements, the catch-as-catch-can struggle to make ends meet. A ceaseless round of scraping, scrimping, borrowing and scavenging came in some measure to dominate the housekeeping of all working-class women.

Tenement life overrode distinctions between ethnic and occupational groups and played an important role in the creation of a metropolitan working-class culture. Tenements were one response to the acute housing shortage that began in New York with the surge in immigration in the 1820s and lasted unabated through the mid-1850s. Tenements differed from earlier housing for the poor in that they were constructed or refurbished specifically for multiple occupancy. Before 1850, landlords had generally subdivided existing buildings, usually single-family houses, into "reconstructed" tenements to accommodate more people and generate more rents[13]— "dilapidated, crazy old houses," one urban reformer called them.[14] Landlords rented out hives of subdivided space, packing people into attics, outlying stables and sheds, and damp basements. In 1842, a public health survey found that more than 7,000 people lived in cellars, and by midcentury, the number had grown to 29,000.[15] The old wooden tenements stood for decades. The infamous Old Brewery, a five-story tenement in the heart of the Five Points, supposedly housed more than 1,000 people in its labyrinth of rooms, cellars, subcellars and hidden passageways.[16] Several families might occupy a large room; it was common for one family to crowd into a single room. In 1839, for instance, an evangelical tract distributor in lower Manhattan visited six families living in a garret. A sick woman lay on a few rags on the floor. "The place where she lay was so low that the shingles of the roof could be reached by the hand," he related.[17] In another tenement in 1845, a reporter for a *Tribune* series on labor found a shoemaker living with his family in a room in which a man could not fully stand. The furnishings were his workbench, a cradle made from a dry-goods box, one pan and a few broken chairs.[18]

In the early 1830s, a few speculators erected buildings specifically for occupancy by the poor. In the next decade, builders began to construct working-class tenements divided into standard units of space. Recalling the English model of workers' block housing, regimented lines of the bare brick buildings appeared in the upper reaches of the east side in the newly settled wards above Fourteenth Street. The typical apartment in a new tenement had a front room, which served as kitchen and parlor, and one or two sleeping cubicles, often windowless.[19] Even so, the new construction did not meet the demand: Lodgers and whole families doubled up in the back rooms, "space filtered from within working class neighborhoods," as Elizabeth Blackmar has put it.[20] Lodgings in the standardized tenements could be even worse than the odd-size crannies of the reconstructed tenements, since builders often erected tenements in the centers of blocks, nearly flush with the back walls of those that fronted the streets, thus blocking off light and air. The rear buildings themselves lacked direct light and cross-ventilation. Often adjoining the privies, the rear tenements were the recourse of the very poor and became the scenes of some of the worst horrors of metropolitan housing.[21]

In the worst tenements, there was little that went on that visitors from charitable organizations could recognize as housekeeping. The households of the poorest people—the day laborers, free blacks, underpaid craftworkers and single mothers who crowded into the back rooms of their neighbors and into basements and attics—were packed with people but bare of domestic effects. There was no furniture to speak of, few clothes to wash, little food to prepare. The reports of social investigators at midcentury described an overwhelming domestic inertness in the tenements. The poor "crowded beneath mouldering, water-rotted roofs, or burrowed among rats in clammy cellars," observed one; another exclaimed that tenement dwellers "exist almost comfortably in conditions which others of refinement would find intolerable."[22] The Irish seemed especially bad housekeepers: "accustomed in their own country to live like pigs, they can stow themselves away into all sorts of holes and corners, and live on refuse,"[23] noted a sardonic journalist. What such observers could not see was that despite the odds against them, most women, no matter how poor, took pride in neat and clean lodgings. Even the Irish, commented an English workingman with all the prejudices of his countrymen, were proud of their domestic amenities, their " 'bits of carpits on their flures.' "[24] A well-swept hearth and scoured floor were symbols of self-esteem still within the reach of even the very poor: The *mise en scène* of many a charity visitor's account is a bare room where a woman or child is scrubbing the floor.

Slightly more prosperous working people were likely to win bourgeois encomiums as the "respectable" poor, especially if they approximated the family patterns of the prosperous: father at work, mother at home, children in some apprenticed position or at school. "Their habitations, though generally small and crowded, and in very unpleasant situations, nevertheless present the appearance of neatness and order, which widely distinguishes their occupants from the more wretched portion of society," a tract-distributing minister reported in 1834. "Their children are many of them decently clad and sent to school, and when they arrive at a suitable age, are generally apprenticed to some mechanical art."[25] Respectable families could maintain furnished interiors which also garnered the charity visitors' approval: chairs, bedsteads and icons of decency like clocks and prints on the wall.[26] These were people who, for the moment, benefited from a fairly steady male income—most notably, those attached to journeymen or small masters who had gained some secure foothold in their trades or those who worked in trades comparatively untouched by industrialization. But the line which the minister confidently drew between them and the "wretched" was a thin one. The family economies of "respectable" artisans were delicate, savings usually impossible, so that "when overtaken by sickness, or when business is unusually depressed, they are at once deprived of their means of subsistence." A journeyman printer, in a letter to a labor newspaper, stated that a single man might lay by some of his wages, "but if a workingman be married and have a family of young children, his wages cannot do more than command the mere necessities of life—it is impossible for him to lay by anything against the periods of sickness or old age."[27] A case from a lying-in charity shows how fragile the security of some artisanal families had become by the 1820s. Rebecca Williamson's husband, a rigger, was a "worthy man," she said, but in the fall of 1828 he could not get work and the couple was wholly without means to provide for the imminent birth of their child. The lying-in charity summed up such situations as "the various accidental causes and visitations, as afflicting as unforseen . . . to which working people are peculiarly liable."[28] "Respectable" women afflicted by such "visitations" easily slid into the ranks of the destitute, the garret and cellar dwellers, where they earned the contempt of charity visitors for their broken furniture and ragged clothes.

What the charity visitors were unable to see was that keeping house in the tenements in any circumstances was hard work. Dirt and trouble abounded.[29] "Even the better houses of the poor are discouraging to women," observed the writer Catharine Sedgwick, a resident New Yorker. "They get wearied out with their necessary work, and no strength and time left to clean a house that always wants cleaning."[30] Washing and cleaning were difficult, since all water had to be carried up the stairs. People tracked in dirt from the muddy streets; plaster crumbled; chimneys clogged and stoves smoked. The winter wind blew through broken windows and scattered ashes about. Children knocked over slop pails; rains flooded basement rooms. Eighteenth-century women, to be sure, had battled the same enemies. " 'New York, I perceive'—said a gentleman the other day, scraping the mud from his boots, [in 1837] 'still holds her own. She had, as far back as I can remember, the reputation of being the dirtiest city in the Union; and she maintains it still!' "[31] For the most part, housekeepers before 1860 did not yet have to contend with the industrial dirt—coal smoke and smog —that plagued women in Manchester and the Midlands. "The clearness of the atmosphere, and the absence of coal smoke, are particularly pleasing to those who are accustomed to the dingy and coloured walls of the houses in Liverpool," attested an Englishwoman who visited in 1848.[32] Still, overcrowding and an urban accumulation of dirt took their toll. If the dirt was the same as in earlier times, there was more of it, with few compensations in improved sanitation and none in improved housing.

For all the lack of substantial household effects, domestic labor in these tiny rooms absorbed the energies of women morning to night. The poorer the family, the heavier was woman's work. Cleaning was only a small part of complicated and arduous family economies. The major effort went into acquiring necessities—food, fuel and water—a task that took up hours of the day and entailed scores of errands out of the house. This work was by nature public, knitting together the household with the world of the streets. It generated its own intricate network of exchange among neighbors and between parents and children and created the material basis for a dense neighborhood life.

Women and children spent a great deal of time on work that, in the twentieth century, utilities would perform. Although by the 1840s the

privileged classes were beginning to enjoy the first fruits of domestic technology—running water, piped gas and water closets—the tenements had
no utilities.[33] Privies were in the back courts; light came from candles and
kerosene lamps; water, from rain barrels, street-corner pumps and, for a
fortunate few, sinks in downstairs hallways. New York completed its
much-touted Croton water system in 1842, and gas was introduced in the
early 1830s, but tenement landlords seldom went to the expense of piping
either into their buildings; the few who purchased water only ran it to the
first floor. The burden of "the almost entire absence of household conveniences" usually fell on young children not otherwise employed; like their
peers in rural America and Ireland, they toted water up the stairs and
hauled slops back down (less fastidious mothers tossed their slops right out
the window). Children also ran the many errands required when there was
never enough money in hand for the needs of the moment. Mothers sent
them out to fetch a stick of wood for the fire, thread for their sewing,
potatoes for dinner. Purchases were necessarily piecemeal, "by the small,"
and often on credit: one candle, an ounce of tea, three cents' worth of
Godfrey's Cordial for a colicky baby.[34]

Children's street scavenging also produced objects for domestic use.
Scavenging seems to have been a widespread practice among the laboring
classes in the eighteenth century, but after 1820, those who could afford to
probably began to desist from sending children out to the streets, since child
scavengers were liable to be arrested for vagrancy, and the habit of mixing
scavenging with petty theft and prostitution had become common. The
poor, however, had no choice. For them, scavenging was an essential way
to make ends meet, even if the chore might lead their children into thieving
or illicit sex. "Of the children brought before me for pilfering," wrote a
police magistrate in 1830, "nine out of ten are those whose fathers are dead,
and who live with their mothers, and are employed in this way. The petty
plunder . . . finds a ready market at some old junk shop, and the avails are
in part carried home as the earnings of honest labor."[35]

Scavenging was the chore of those too young to earn income through
wage work or street selling. Six- or seven-year-olds were not too small to
set out with friends and siblings to gather fuel for their mothers. Small
platoons of children scoured the docks for food—tea, coffee, sugar and flour
spilled from sacks, barrels and wagons. Streets, shipyards and lumberyards,
building lots, demolished houses and the precincts of artisan shops and
factories held chips, ashes, wood and coal to take home or peddle to neighbors.[36] As children grew more skilled, they learned how to pillage other odd
corners of the city. "These gatherers of things lost on earth," a journalist
called them in 1831. "These makers of something out of nothing."[37]

Street scavenging has probably been a practice of the urban poor for centuries, but this was a specifically nineteenth-century form, which depended on a demand for raw materials from an urban manufacturing system where commercial lines of supply were not fully in place. Besides taking trash home or peddling it to neighbors, children sold it to junk dealers, who in turn vended it to manufacturers and artisans to use in industrial processes. On the waterfront, children foraged for loose cotton, which had shredded off bales on the wharves where the Southern packet ships docked, as well as for shreds of canvas and rags; junk dealers bought the leavings and sold them to manufacturers of paper and shoddy (shoddy, the cheapest kind of cloth, made its way back to the poor in the form of "shoddy" ready-made clothing). Broken bits of hardware—nails, cogs and screws—went to iron and brass founders and coppersmiths to be melted down; bottles and bits of broken glass to glassmakers. Old rope was shredded and sold as oakum, a fiber used to caulk ships. The medium for these exchanges was a network of secondhand shops along the waterfront. In 1850, public authorities made some efforts to close down the junk trade, but police harassment seems to have had little effect. "On going down South Street I met a gang of small Dock Thieves . . . had a bag full of short pieces of old rope and iron," William Bell, police inspector of secondhand shops, reported on a typical day on the beat. The malefactors were headed for a shop like the one into which Bell, ever-earnest about his job, slipped incognito just in time to witness an illicit transaction between the proprietor and a six-year-old boy, who sold him a glass bottle for a penny.[38]

Pawning was also a feature of domestic work. Through pawning, women made use of less-needed goods in the service of procuring necessities. The traffic was especially heavy toward the end of the week, since rent was usually due on Saturday morning. "Sunday clothes are put in pawn during the week, and redeemed again on Saturday night" when wages were paid.[39] Clothes were the most common pledge—winter clothes in summer, extra clothes in winter, Sunday clothes any time. A substantial wardrobe was one edge against adversity. The pawning cycle functioned fairly smoothly as long as income was steady enough for a woman to redeem the possessions when she needed them—shoes, for instance, when the cold weather came. In hard times, however, women gave up absolute necessities, a sign a family was in trouble: pots, pans, bedding and treasures of respectability like watches, clocks and books.

"Everything that can be imagined is offered in pledge," observed a metropolitan journalist in 1854. "All is fish that come to the pawn-broker's net."[40] One of his fellows, fascinated like other Victorian writers with the profusion of commodities in city life, took pains in 1849 to catalogue the curious species piled up in the dark little shops. Under masses of old clothes hanging from the ceiling was a veritable menagerie of objects, among them many women's tools and women's treasures: irons, calicoes, crimping irons, cradles, dustpans, dictionaries, fiddles, frying pans, inkstands, jew's harps, lamps, lavender water, mattresses, necklaces, pie pans, pincushions, quack medicines, rings, rattraps, umbrellas, wicker baskets.[41] Suspenders, shawls and scrub brushes went, too, but when worse came to worst, women gave up their furnishings—chairs, tables and featherbeds. The bare rooms where charity visitors saw people sleeping on straw pallets and chairs spoke of a series of transactions with the pawnbroker.

In the tenements, even laundry was a feature of public life, strung up high above the streets and alleys. The solitary housewife would not emerge within the urban working class until the late 1920s, when cheap utilities first became available in the tenements. In the first half of the nineteenth century, the boundaries between private and public life were fluid and permeable. Laboring women made their lives as wives and mothers on the streets as much as by their hearthsides.

Children and the Family Wage Economy

Domestic labor in the tenements and economic survival in the city demanded help from all family members. Traditions of family cooperation ran deep among the laboring poor. In those European and American rural societies from which so many New Yorkers had emigrated, earning a living from the land demanded that children and parents work together. Among urban artisans, the moral values of mutual aid and the economic ties of cooperation were also strong. Craft shops, which provided work for sons, daughters and wives (along with apprentices and journeymen), had long been an index of the well-being of the master craftsman. Proprietorship was the surest footing for patriarchal authority, since family workshops gave men a direct claim on the labor of household members. As immigration brought farm people to the city and as industrial capitalism pushed more and more artisans into permanent wage earning, the working poor adapted these patterns of cooperation to the exigencies of proletarian life. Children no longer necessarily worked alongside their parents, but they just the same learned their duty to contribute to the common family good.

The family wage economy, in which parents and children pooled their individual earnings toward a common subsistence, was the basis of urban working-class life. Parents set their children to work in many different combinations of wage earning, domestic labor and paid work. An older child might look after the younger ones, thus freeing up more hours for a mother to do wage work; one son might help a craftworker father with simple tasks, another might be sent out to the streets to scavenge or peddle. Daughters could be kept home to do the cooking and washing for boarders, or they might be sent out to earn money at domestic service. Whatever the case, parents expected their children to "earn their keep"—to contribute either their unpaid labor or their cash earnings toward the family's needs.

Family loyalties, however, did not always win out over the temptations New York held out to the young: the allure of things to buy, places to go, pleasures of one's own. Families were not simply mutualistic groups, whose members were bound together by reciprocal ties of obligation and devotion. They were also little hierarchies in which men dominated women, and parents commanded the labor and deference of children. When children worked under the direct supervision of their parents on farms or in workshops, they had little chance to evade their parents' discipline. But when they worked on their own, the duties their parents exacted from them could begin to chafe. Then spending money on an evening at a dance hall could seem far preferable to handing it over to your mother; leaving home altogether to run about the streets with friends, picking up a living this way and that, could be far more alluring than staying on with a father who whipped you or with a mother who was constantly scolding. The tensions between the meager independence of wage work and the pull of family loyalties defined one dimension of working-class life.

This tension helps to explain the problem of juvenile crime in New York between 1820 and 1860. Juvenile crime was very much bound up with issues of family authority and family labor. The infractions of those children who ended up in the House of Refuge, the city's asylum for the "correction" of youths, were as often against their families as against public order. The malefactors included children who ran away from home or from wage-earning positions, others who used their earnings to strike out on their own in the city and still others who refused to earn their keep. William Codman ended up in the asylum in 1835 because his mother asked the city watchmen to take him there, "because he would not work, and she could not support him." George Cadwell's parents committed him because he would not remain at the employments they found for him but ran away to live "in the company of City Boys." George "did not like to live at home as his Father scolded." Mary Ann Corbitt had done something at home but she did not know what, when the evidently dissatisfied aunt with whom she lived sent her to the House in 1825.[42]

Many children landed in the House of Refuge because official definitions of crime collided with working-class uses of the streets (scavenging
is a case in point). But the extent to which working-class parents themselves committed their children shows that the movement against juvenile
crime was a means of family as well as class control. The House of Refuge began as an institution sponsored by the SPP to discipline the unruly
progeny of the poor, but it quickly became a resource that parents of the
laboring classes used to strengthen their own authority. In 1825, two years
after the institution had opened, municipal authorities initiated all but
a fraction of the commitments; in 1835, parents themselves initiated 47
percent.[43]

While the family wage economy developed out of working-class
solidarities, there were also contradictions inherent in this pattern of subsistence. Working-class poverty increased the importance of cooperation,
but city life could make it seem onerous and avoidable to the young.
Parental control was also patriarchal control, allowing fathers to make
crucial decisions about others' futures. On farms, men controlled the disposition of land; in craft shops, they allocated the work and the earnings;
in both city and country, they largely determined their children's futures
through the disposition of dowries and marriage portions. "It will be for
you to judge," wrote a still-dutiful immigrant daughter back to her father
in County Cork. When he arrived in New York, it was up to him
whether the family would cast their lot in the city or travel further
west.[44] In Ireland, the growing impoverishment of smallholders in the
pre-Famine years undercut this power in some ways; when there was so
little to pass on to sons, fathers lost important leverage. Yet at the same
time, declining fortunes could *strengthen* patriarchal determination: Irish
smallholders increasingly made their children accountable to severe sexual
prohibitions to prevent effectively any but eldest sons and daughters from
marrying, in order to apportion intact small bits of family property. As
the economic basis of patriarchal and familial control diminished, parents
lost the ability to limit their children's social adventures—where they
went, what they did with their money, how they earned a living and who
they courted. Rebellious boys were bad enough, but defiant daughters
were worse, raising as they did fears of female passion on the loose and
burdensome out-of-wedlock pregnancies. In a culture in which people of
all classes viewed with consternation the tremendous changes wrought in
New York life, working-class children by the 1850s were to become a
powerful symbol of urban disorder. In particular, unruly daughters
would create reverberations within a propertied class preoccupied with
the maintenance of female chastity and within a working class concerned
with the decline of masculine authority.

The Moral Economy of the Tenements

Neighborhoods both mitigated and aggravated conflicts within families. Neighbors helped parents—especially mothers—extend their authority over their offspring when the children were out working on their own, and they also entered briskly and forcefully into domestic frays between husbands and wives. The neighborhoods collected and concentrated married women's resources.

While trade unions were a predominantly male manifestation of the new kinds of communities the city made possible, the tenement neighborhoods were a female form of association and mutual aid, a crucial buffer against the shocks of uprootedness and poverty. In some senses there was nothing new about this; since the seventeenth century, London's East End and the *faubourgs* of the Parisian poor had been centers of enormous migration from the countryside.[45] But conditions for the creation of urban communities had greatly changed. The scale of urbanization was much greater in the nineteenth century, transiency far more widespread. Because the erosion of artisanal work had undermined the stability of so many of its residents, New York lacked a settled laboring population of any significance proportional to the numbers of newcomers who poured in. As a result, tens of thousands of strangers between 1820 and 1860, and especially after 1845, faced the difficulties of settling in and assimilating themselves amidst the most daunting circumstances of underemployment and penury, with little to call on except the help of other strangers.

A number of American historians, in arguing against an older view that immigrant cultures succumbed to demoralization, vice and crime under the strains of urban poverty, have correctly stressed that immigration was not as anomic and uprooting as one might think. Many immigrants entered the city as welcomed arrivals, greeted by friends and family members who had migrated before them.[46] Like the country people who migrated to European cities in the seventeenth and eighteenth centuries, the Irish and Germans clustered in enclaves of kin and fellow villagers in New York.[47] Still, these forms of association did not encompass all newcomers. In New York, people shifted about, moving once, twice, several times a year. "A tenement population is a migratory one," observed a physician at a city dispensary for the poor.[48] If demographic patterns in other Northeastern cities are any indication, poor people also moved in and out of New York as well as within it: Studies of geographic mobility in the Northeast between 1830 and 1860 have found that between 44 and 70 percent of adult men moved away

in any decade.[49] Kin networks and provincial groupings, once reconstituted, could also break down. The strands of family, regional and village
loyalties ran through working-class neighborhoods, but they were only part
of the web.[50]

To some degree, the working poor, especially immigrant women, were
able to create urban communities in the context of massive transiency. In
doing so, they drew on traditions of cooperation and mutual aid reminiscent of life in poor neighborhoods in early modern London or even Paris.
In the volatile circumstances of this nineteenth-century city, however,
these traditions became more elastic and adaptable. Laboring women in the
antebellum years helped to lay the basis for the intimate and engaged
neighborhood life that flourished among Eastern European Jews and Ital-
ians in the late nineteenth and early twentieth centuries.

The interchange between households and the streets, a common feature
of poor neighborhoods, allowed women to involve themselves, often
deeply, in the lives of passing acquaintances. Women moved easily in and
out of different households. People spent a great deal of time outside, and
doors were seldom locked, even at night. "In the warm summer evenings
all were out of doors or at the windows," recalled an English workingman
who had lived in New York. "Numbers of females would be sitting on the
'stoops,' their chins in their hands, their elbows on their knees, convers-
ing."[51] It was not exceptional for passersby or loungers from the streets,
especially drunks, to wander into someone's lodgings on the ground level
of a tenement with requests for help.[52] Catherine Gallagher, on an early
morning trip to the privy in 1854, found a drunken woman on her stoop.
Gallagher gave her water and watched her stumble into another ground
floor room where she again requested water. The female occupant there
complied, then asked the drunk to go about her business. "She said she
would in a few minutes," lay down and promptly died.[53] Although the
outcome of this incident was dramatic, neither Gallagher nor her neighbor
seemed to have regarded the encounter itself as extraordinary. It was not
only drunks who presumed on strangers' hospitality. Bridget Clarke had
met the seamstress Mary Galloway one morning in 1858 when the latter
stopped by her grog shop. Clarke knew only that Mary was out of work
and hanging "around the neighborhood." That evening Mary Galloway
returned to spend the night and to borrow some of Bridget's fancy clothes.
"Mary was an entire stranger to me," Bridget Clarke claimed, "I never saw
her two hours before that night. My doors were unlocked, because the lock
is broke."[54] The city's records of foundling children tell similar stories of
strangers asking for help. In 1839, a female shopkeeper on the Bowery
agreed to watch an infant while its mother, a customer, went to get a friend
to look at a hat in the store. Like the other women making these depositions,

the shopkeeper ended up with an abandoned child—a tale that also illumi-
nates the underside of mutual aid, the ways in which women could use
expectations of domestic cooperation, especially within the anonymity of
a city, to exploit, trick and prey upon others.[55]

The value of these stories does not necessarily lie in their veracity. Judges
and poor-law officials took down this evidence from the poor people involved, and deference, fear and wiliness may have fashioned the facts to suit
the listeners. For the Irish, feigned ingenuousness before the law was second nature, a reflex acquired over several centuries spent under the thumb
of English officialdom. Bridget Clarke, whom we met above, may have been
trying to distance herself from the legal trouble in which Mary Galloway
was embroiled by claiming she had never met Galloway. In the cases of
abandoned children, there were clear reasons why a complainant might
disclaim acquaintance with the mother. If the former held onto the child,
the city would pay her a nurse's fee; knowing this, some mothers (or so the
poor-law commissioners claimed) colluded with friends who, representing
themselves as unwitting strangers left with abandoned children, secured the
weekly fees which, presumably, they then shared with the mothers.[56] But
even dissimulation is likely to hide itself behind a cloak of plausibility. If
the deponents in these cases were lying, the explanations are still similar
enough from case to case to add up to a recognizable pattern, and the
evidence can tell us something about what kind of help people saw as lying
within the bounds of the credible.

Involvement with neighbors was less circumstantial than was aid proffered to strangers, not so much a matter of generosity on the spur
of the moment as of structured expectations of reciprocal help. In a calamity, neighbors' help made the difference between survival and destitution.
After a fire on the working-class outskirts of town in 1845, the aldermen
reported, over two hundred families were homeless, having saved little else
but their clothes. Those friendly with neighbors had moved in with them,
while those "not so fortunate as to have any friends" were living in the
basements of the burned houses "in a very destitute condition."[57] But
neighborliness was also a matter of day-to-day routines. Emotionally gregarious and materially needy, neighbor women moved about the tenements
constantly, visiting round from one household to the next to gossip and
drink, nurse the sick or mind a baby, upbraid an abusive husband or a
negligent wife, borrow and lend. Neighbors saved women tiring trips to
the street pump by sharing their rainwater or (for the lucky few) their sinks;
they lent each other cutlery, bedding for the sick, cooking pots. When a
very poor woman lacked wood, she might warm herself by a neighbor's fire.
The attentiveness of neighbor women to others' affairs could be a round-
the-clock affair: Depositions in domestic murder trials record the observa-

tions of wakeful women who, through the thin tenement walls, noted entrances and exits, conversations and cries, sounds of discord and crying babies through the entire night.

But cooperation did not automatically engender harmony, and demands for help and services gave rise to hostility as well as cooperation. Although women often responded to others' needs with kindness, they also met presumptions with blows and curses. The mutuality of domestic work pulled neighbors through difficult times, but it also bred innumerable quarrels. Fights flared up over whose turn it was to put her water barrel under the rainspout or, after the advent of Croton water, who might use the first-floor sink. The practice of borrowing scarce domestic goods also sparked contention. "Quarrels occur between women about the most trifling things," wrote Mike Walsh, newspaper editor, labor politico and a resident of the very poor Sixth Ward who knew the tenements firsthand. "A broom is left on the stairs, the back door is left open, or the front door is shut and locked when one of the husbands is out late at night. A row and a fight begins in consequence." One recourse was to sabotage an antagonist's housekeeping arrangements, hexing her with dirt and disarray: "The clothes lines are cut; the water in the cistern is used up, or ashes are left on the back stoop and trod into the hall carpet."[58]

These neighbors' quarrels are testimony not to the antisocial "pathologies" which all too many analysts attribute to the urban poor, but rather to the existence of durable networks of cooperation. The parties in the court proceedings from which this evidence comes were precisely those neighbors who could not contain their conflicts within the ordinary daily round of courtesies, slights and rebuffs. Although female neighbors tolerated, supported and even encouraged neighborhood brawls, they also stepped in to mediate antagonisms. Tenement quarrels were seldom, if ever, private matters. The participants habitually took their accusations and grievances to others to adjudicate and reconcile.

One way to do so was to take the fight to the streets. In venting their anger there, women publicized their side in the quarrel to the assemblage of the neighborhood. The wilder fights involved curses and name-calling. Hannah Corwin finally took Mary Flinn to court for such insults in 1824. Flinn, who lived opposite Corwin on Cherry Street in Corlears Hook, was in the habit of calling Corwin and her sister whores and shouting other obscene epithets.[59] Cursing of course attracted a crowd, which in turn provided an audience for the attacker's slurs on her antagonist's reputation. This kind of maligning could go on for months. The Clements women, who lived in 1830 in a waterfront neighborhood on the North (Hudson) River, had quarreled with their neighbor, the respectable lodging house keeper Rhoda Horton, over their apparently irregular sexual doings. After yelling insults at Horton for a time, the Clementses escalated the fight by cutting out letters from bills and signs and pasting them together on Horton's front fence into "vulgar and indecent words." Attackers could devote considerable time and energy to a feud. The Clements women watched Horton's comings and goings like hawks; she could not go outside to hang out her wash, she complained, without incurring a stream of abuse.[60]

Once a woman had succeeded in bringing a feud to the attention of the neighborhood, more raucous involvement from the community could ensue. When Mrs. Young shouted out her insults at James Wilson's family over the course of two years in the late 1820s, she was in the process of "raising a mob," as the legal language described it, marshaling her forces: a group of friends, acquaintances and hangers-on who could coalesce into a solid bloc of moral support.[61] Cursing could function as a sort of carny barking, an invitation to the coming show if verbal abuse should spill over into fisticuffs. Then, women lit into each other, usually with their bare hands—scratching, pummeling and tearing each other's clothes—sometimes with domestic objects—sticks of wood, wet rags, shovels, brooms and chamber pots. "Mobs" gathered to take sides, cheer on favorites and, if the fight became too violent, to call the watch. Extravagant and histrionic, these demonstrations of passionate grievances were directed not simply at beating up the antagonist but at securing sympathy and solidarity from the audience. For the Irish, such staged contentions were familiar from the old country. The ferocious "faction fights" of the Irish countryside, fierce collective rows in which women cheered on the opponents and supplied the combatants with weapons, were a marvel of public pugnacity to nineteenth-century travelers, all the more so since, at the end, the opponents parted apparently amicably.[62] Cities, of course, provided men with a greatly enlarged arena for violent conflict: Men fought as members of rival gangs and political parties, as Irish against native-born, Protestant against Catholic, white against black and trade unionist against strikebreaker, as well as from drunkenness mingled with a myriad of personal motives. But cities also fostered modes of public female belligerence.[63] This was a woman's theater of discord, replete with the rhetorical flourish of insult and revenge.

Obviously, not *every* woman took to her neighbor with a broom. Like the stories of people's involvement with strangers, we know about these incidents from court depositions—in this case, trials for assault. By nature, the encounters are out of the ordinary, since they ended up in a magistrate's court. But if the parties in assault cases were more belligerent or litigious than others, there is no indication they were deviants or outlaws. Their "crimes" were exceptional not in their violent character but in the degree of violence. Whatever their personal predilections, laboring women were sufficiently exposed to physical aggression to see it as one possible outcome

of any antagonism between women or, as we shall see later, between
women and men.

People also acted out larger sorts of conflicts on the streets. In eighteenth-century New York, as in London and revolutionary Paris as well as
Boston and Philadelphia, street mobbing had been a powerful political tool
of the *menu peuple*. Politically explicit crowd actions waned after the Revolution, as party politics (with its own theater of parades, election brawls and
gang warfare) subsumed many of the energies of the mob. Mobbing itself
persisted; its targets changed to local, often domestic issues rather than
government policies. Abolitionists, black cartmen, unpopular English actors, strikebreakers and police all sparked crowd violence.[64]

Although women were only on the fringes (if that) of the large, politically directed crowds, they were active in smaller mob actions which enforced a domestically based neighborhood justice. Two, three or half a
dozen people might set upon and rough up some offender of neighborhood
mores. Usually women joined a male assault, egging on the men and
helping from the sidelines: When John Roach and three other men broke
into William Donahue's store in 1828 and smashed up his property, Roach's
wife Elizabeth fought to hold the door open so the men could beat their
retreat.[65] But women occasionally took on malefactors on their own. Ellen
Doyle, Mary Haley and Mary Geary, all neighbors on Bayard and Mott
Streets in 1820, "by force and violence took possession of a room" of
William McElvain's on Bayard Street "& turned him out."[66] Ann Mullins
took three women to court in 1831 for attacking her: They had followed her
through the streets, "using towards her low and abusive language & pelted
her with stones."[67]

It is difficult to tell much about the grievances of neighborhood mobs
from the formulaic testimony of court depositions, but there are some
outlines to these shady conflicts. Disputes over tenancy were one cause of
mob fights. In New York's intricate system of letting and subletting, landlords often lived in close proximity to tenants (in the case of lodgers, they
often lived in the very same room) so that domestic irritations inflamed
disputes over rent. Noise was, not surprisingly, a source of contention: In
1821, for instance, Betsy Hyland had taken her landlords John Hogan and
his wife to court for assaulting her; the next day, Hyland and three men
attacked the landlord when he called the watch to stop their noisy carousing.[68] Evictions could also prompt mob actions, as when a crowd threatened the life of a landlord who began proceedings against his tenants in
1827.[69] Landlords, however, were themselves often part of the neighborhood
and could raise mobs in their own interests, as when a quarrel over a
subtenancy arrangement in 1826 led the woman who was the "lessor" to
raise a mob which tried to break down the door of her tenants.[70]

Fragments of evidence hint at other causes. Depositions identify the object of attack: a grocer (a collector of debts like the landlord), a bawdy house proprietor (the noise, drunkenness and loose morals of bawdy houses aggrieved respectable neighbors). Bawdy houses that attracted an interracial clientele frequently offended whites in the environs. In a city where the black community was small, but where racial tensions often ran high, animosity between black women and white women sometimes led to fights. Racial hostilities, when women were involved, seem often to have touched on issues of sexuality, as when one black woman accused another late on a spring night in 1820 of consorting with a white man, and a mob gathered to egg on the brawl.[71] Questions of heterosexual propriety seem to have often been the province of the crowd. In 1847 in Brooklyn, a large Irish mob gathered for a classic European charivari. The object was a notorious minister, charged with various acts of seduction and adultery, who was marrying the young stepdaughter of a judge. The mob surrounded the house at which the wedding was taking place and serenaded the couple with "groans, yells, and hootings" and a clamor of "cow horns, marrow bones and cleavers, tomb-stone fiddles, tin kettles and thunder mugs" and continued for hours, undaunted by the appearance of the mayor himself who arrived to read the Riot Act.[72] Political party machinations probably underlay such a large, well-organized ruckus; more commonly, sexual policing, chastisement and revenge took place on a small scale. The evidence only allows us to guess, but behind cases of women who forcibly evicted a man from his room, there may have been some breach of the rules of neighborliness or of a sexual or marital code; at issue in an attack on a woman taunted by her assailants "with low and abusive language" were probably violations of domestic etiquette or sexual propriety.[73] The woman attacked by another woman who lived with her former husband might, in turn, raise an *ad hoc* regiment in retaliation. Elizabeth Sayre was the object of a mob of about one hundred people that gathered one winter day in 1831, led by one John Furrell; she might have been a sexual malefactor—an adultress or bawdy house keeper —or a landlady or storekeeper who had somehow angered Furrell.[74]

Amiability and anger, reciprocity and resentment lent the working-class neighborhoods the volatile, contentious, emotionally fierce character that so disturbed polite observers. Laboring women's kindnesses were generally invisible to the prosperous, but their pugnacity at moments cropped up in New York's public culture, an element of urban "color." Lydia Maria Child, feminist and abolitionist, recorded one such episode, which occurred when a gentleman in a downtown crowd ordered an old Irish woman to move out of his way. " 'And indade I won't get out of your way; I'll get right *in* your way,' said she. . . . She placed her feet apart, set her elbows akimbo, and stood as firmly as a provoked donkey."[75] There was something appealing and cathartic about this incident, a flash of defiance in the urban crowd. Neighborhood quarrels were different: smouldering embers rather than sparks. Monotonous, ritualistic, obsessive, they revealed themselves in the oft-repeated phrases of court depositions: "she had beat him . . . and would beat him again"; she would "knock her brains out"; she had "repeatedly threatened her with violence to wit with beating her brains out, and killing her"; she "would tear his . . . guts out."

These shifting communities of cooperation and contention had none of the counterbalancing elements of the female domestic sphere of calm and affection that bourgeois men and women prized. Poor women created their communities out of a sometimes boundless emotional energy, a voracity for involvement in the lives of others. For their social betters, who were beginning to pride themselves on the ability of women to create a private space in a city they perceived as corrupt and alienating, the domestic turbulence of the working-class neighborhood posed a serious threat.

Chapter 4 Places of Vice:
Views of the Neighborhoods

"The city has been made the grand lurking-place of vice," a speaker at an evangelical meeting announced in 1835.[1] Since the days of Jefferson, Americans had voiced similar denunciations of urban corruption. This man's point, though, was not a general lament about the inherent baseness of city life but a specifically framed indictment: He was protesting what he saw to be the infestation of one particular city, New York, by the forces of sin. Others echoed his condemnation. A map of the city limned bright and dark according to the moral state of the district, another evangelical subsequently speculated, would present an alarming picture. Tucked away off the avenues, down the side streets and alleys, were lodged appalling concentrations of viciousness, multitudes which "probably outnumbered the whole Christian portion of the city . . . ignorant, careless, deprived, perishing."[2] By the 1830s, New York was daunting in its complexity; religious activists were well aware how easily sin—"inebriation, squalid wretchedness, Sabbath profanation and vices"[3]—could conceal itself in such a city from the vigilance of the devout.

These places of vice were the incarnation of bourgeois perceptions of the working-class neighborhoods. The evangelicals were devout Protestants who, spurred by a series of revivals that began after the War of 1812, invaded the poor neighborhoods in search of souls lost to grace. Their numbers swelled in the years 1829–35, when the great evangelical minister Charles Finney preached his New York revivals; by 1835, the evangelical movement encompassed a score of moral reform organizations. The pious view of the iniquity of working-class life had developed from attitudes toward the "unworthy" poor which had been germinating in the city's elite since 1812. But there were also new elements in the evangelicals' metaphors of danger, sin and secrets, which embodied the class prejudices and perceptions they formed as they saw firsthand the realities of the working poor. The imagery of concentrated vice was one response to the movement of laboring people into recognizably working-class neighborhoods.

Ideals of family life and womanhood also played into the images of depravity. On their errands of mercy into the tenements, evangelical men and women encountered patterns of womanly behavior and child rearing that clashed with their deepest-held beliefs. As genteel writers and ministers after 1820 articulated more clearly their expectations of women in the home, the evangelicals sharpened their own ideas about domesticity in the context of their disapproving encounters with the laboring poor. Antebellum domesticity—at least in its urban form—emerged within a field of class antagonisms and in turn incited and intensified those antagonisms. Through the efforts of the evangelicals to transform working-class neighborhoods, issues of gender and family entered into class conflicts.[4]

Evangelical Reform and the Home Visit

In 1829, the New York City Tract Society, the city's leading evangelical organization, reorganized its work with the unregenerate. Volunteers were assigned a group of families on whom they would regularly call with inspirational tracts, Bibles, and the message of salvation. These home visits, the evangelicals hoped, would penetrate the entire city: Christ's legions would leave no resident untouched.[5]

The emphasis on mass conversions came from the evangelicals' view of the role of human will in securing salvation. While orthodox Calvinists had believed that God saved whom He chose, the evangelicals gave much more credit to human agency. God would help with His divine grace those who helped themselves. By 1829, the evangelicals had taken their faith in human ability one step further: If people could help to save themselves, then they could also expedite the salvation of others. Divine grace, moreover, had a social as well as a spiritual purpose. From its beginnings, the evangelical movement had concerned itself with urban poverty. Fortified by a faith in the limitless powers of the redeemed to transcend earthly circumstance, the evangelicals saw salvation (rather than the prudent pursuit of self-interest the SPP advocated) as the solution to the problem of poverty in the city.[6]

Twenty years earlier, the home visit was unknown. The first generation of New York philanthropists minimized their direct contact with the ungodly poor; the first evangelical groups which appeared after the War of 1812 often used salaried agents or poorer volunteers who were not themselves church members in the city missions and Sunday schools they established.[7] The zeal of the NYCTS, however, and the cultural imperatives around which it took shape, dictated a departure from customary benevolent practices. The conception of the home visit grew out of the great moral importance attributed to the home by just such men and women as adhered to the evangelicals.[8]

The ideology of domesticity thus provided the initial impetus for what would become a class intervention, the movement of reformers into the working-class neighborhoods and the households of the poor between 1830 and 1860. Home visiting quickly became standard practice. Later charitable and moral reform associations were to implement home visits as a matter of course. Although the Tract Society had not initially limited its calls to the poor (the Finneyite activists believed that damnation hid everywhere, in high places and low), its members soon came to focus primarily upon the laboring population, who were *collectively* identified with unregeneracy. By the mid-1830s it was clear that the great masses of laboring people in their own city of New York, "Satan's empire,"[9] demanded special attention. Religious duty lay not just in responding to need—or vice—when it presented itself, but in actively ferreting out opportunities to minister to or struggle with the benighted souls hiding away in those dark urban places. Before 1820, home visiting was random and spontaneous, an act of personal patronage. The standardized, organizationally based home visit put what had been an act of special concern on an efficient and programmed basis. It allowed the beneficent to become acquainted systematically with their recipients by entering their households and scrutinizing not only "their wants but . . . their habits and dispositions."[10] It streamlined the technology of reform.

Home visiting took genteel men and women out of the safe environs of religious institutions and into the poor neighborhoods. Their contact with "the growing moral desolations of the city"[11] increased accordingly. On their rounds, pillars of New York commerce like the wealthy Arthur Tappan stalked small boys headed out for a game of Sunday ball, adjuring them to Sabbath observance. Devout ladies urged tracts on swearing cartmen. Visitors pressed Bibles on reluctant tenement dwellers, probed into the state of their souls and tried to engage them in prayer.[12]

As the devout fanned out "from house to house, through . . . streets and lanes,"[13] their experience of tenement life grew accordingly. The resultant discussion of the poor, however, was not simply a thoughtful response to the conditions they encountered. Rather, through the medium of their own peculiar perceptions, they translated these experiences into certain conventions of the imagination—so much so that home visitors' accounts, with their formulaic situations, cast of stock characters and ritualized conversations, came to constitute a fictional genre in themselves. Stories of last-ditch repentances (on death beds of rags) and hard-won temperance pledges (sworn in squalid garrets) were staples of the visitors' notes, the descriptions of actual encounters with the poor that were the real meat of the Tract Society's annual reports. The visitors took the poignant, appealing qualities attributed to the already well-known virtuous poor and fashioned from them other pleasingly pious figures: the temperate if downtrodden workingman, the reformed and reinspired Catholic, the repentant sailor. The origins of urban sentimentalist novels of the 1840s and 1850s, those popular tales of virtue and vice, rags and riches in the big city, lie partly with the charity visitors' accounts, where fantasies about class turned newly illuminated details of tenement life to their own uses. Indeed, the connections between experiential accounts and fiction were so close that some novelists structured their tales around a charitable lady's or gentleman's encounters with the virtuous poor. By the 1850s, social reformers made their own ventures into fiction in the form of "sketches," cloaked as social reportage, of generic figures they supposedly encountered in their work— the fallen woman, the starving seamstress, the ragged match girl.[14]

Home visiting furthered the shift of philanthropic attention, evident a decade earlier in the activities of the SPP, toward the conditions of urban society. As the fictional narrative took shape, it was as much about class— rich meets poor, the respectable help the ragged—as it was about religion. The language of virtue and vice, traditionally laden with social connotations, became for the evangelicals a code of class, which described their own mission of social domination in the language of ethical mandate. "Sin here exists in its most concentrated form," lamented a Baptist minister in 1841,[15] nowhere more apparent than in the crowded working-class neighborhoods; concentration bred a moral contagion which threatened the entire Christian community. New York was a place where, as one minister pointed out, a Christian walking out on a Sunday might well ask, "Is it possible that these streets be within the dominion of the God of heaven?"[16]

The evangelicals directed their efforts at a generally irreligious poor. There is little evidence that, even with all the "excitements" of the revivals, middle-class evangelicalism ever made significant inroads into the urban working class. Among literate, self-educated journeymen, a tradition of freethinking, both atheistic and deistic, ran strong in the antebellum period, drawing its legitimacy from the republican authorities Jefferson and Tom Paine. Other native-born journeymen and laborers, however, were simply indifferent. Certainly, some working people were caught up in lower-class sects like the Baptists and, in the 1840s, the chiliastic Millerites. These groups were distinct, however, in both doctrine and organization, from the genteel Finneyites. In general, no denomination had the success in making working-class converts that the Methodists did in England. Before 1845, Christian invocations and exhortations leave little trace in the formal language of trade union deliberations and proclamations—either men's or women's—let alone the court depositions which record something of the language of daily life. Partly, of course, hostility to the evangelicals came from the obstinately Catholic Irish. In the eyes of the revivalists, a Catholic was not a Christian but a superstitious heathen, and no accommodation with this priest-ridden lot—short of conversion—was possible. But working-class dislike of the evangelicals was also more general, stemming from class antagonism to prudish Magdalene reformers, temperance zealots and sour Sabbatharians. Overall, then, the home visitors knocked on the doors of people who tended to view them as "meddlesome folks, always prying into other people's business."[17]

Religious zeal, however, was not simply a cloak for class domination. Rather, evangelical men and women understood class in religious terms. The joys of the spirit could not have been negligible in work that involved pressing oneself, often as an unwanted guest, on one family after another. But genuine spiritual ardor does not rule out the exercise of power, if one sees power over others as necessary for their redemption. The men who led the New York City Tract Society and similar groups were members of a rising commercial and industrial bourgeoisie, distinct from the old merchant elite: The Tappan brothers were country boys who had made good in the silk trade, the temperance zealot Joseph Brewster was a successful master hatter, and Anson G. Phelps was an iron manufacturer.[18] Through their home visiting, they sought to teach the poor virtues of thrift, sobriety, hard work and deference to employers which they also fought hard to inculcate in their workers—traits that ultimately would contribute to their own profits. The campaign for temperance they carried on is the clearest-cut example of their "benevolent entrepreneurialism." Evangelical employers attempted to abolish among their workmen the long-established custom of drinking at work, a reform which, if accomplished, would lend to both the good order and productivity of the workplace and the virtue and spiritual decorum of the men.[19]

Beyond self-interest, however, evangelical moral reform served as a nexus of social identity, "an impulse toward self-definition, a need to avow publicly one's own class aspirations" which led people to seek each other out across a range of incomes and occupations, differentiating themselves from the classes above and below them. Evangelicalism made sense of and gave coherence to the position of an as yet ill-defined group in the city. The revivals gathered middling and newly wealthy people from varying backgrounds in a common endeavor. Evangelicalism bred in its leading adherents the sense of membership in a newly empowered bourgeoisie more fit to direct the city than its old patricians. For the ill-paid clerks and accountants who made up a large part of the movement's rank and file, religious associations opened up social connections outside the shabby boardinghouses where they resided, a life in which they could exercise impulses of piety and civic responsibility that found few outlets in the countinghouses where they worked (Melville's Bartleby might have avoided his sad end had he taken up home visiting). For all these people, evangelical associations provided a wider network of friends and acquaintances.[20] Home visiting, in particular, gave them a way to explore a city well on its way to acquiring a baffling heterogeneity.

Evangelicalism and
Female Class Relations

The public life of the evangelical revivals was especially valuable to women. Nationwide, they poured into the fold in great numbers, "the workers, the fund raisers, the emotionally committed supporters of tract and Bible societies, of Sunday schools and of charity sewing societies."[21] They took spiritual command of their own families, assigning themselves traditionally patriarchal duties like leading family prayers. In the excitements of the revivals, women put the finishing touches on the new imagery of womanhood they had been promoting since the late eighteenth century. Evangelical women and the ministers who encouraged them turned the republican mother into a moral leader. This figure, the "true" woman, powerfully repudiated misogynist assumptions about the weaker character of the sex and studiously ignored the well-worn tales of Eve's transgressions in favor of more flattering Biblical texts about industrious, faithful and pious females. Banished to the upper and lower reaches of society (to the frivolous rich and the depraved poor) was the image of the vain, foolish, sexually duplicitous woman. The dignified Christian woman demanded respect and esteem for her sex.[22]

In New York, the elevation of women's ideological status must have been one factor that gave female evangelicals the courage to breach the boundaries that barred them from certain parts of the city. Early nineteenth-century Protestantism, Nancy Cott has observed, enabled women "to rely on an authority beyond the world of men and provided a crucial support to those who stepped beyond accepted bounds."[23] Late eighteenth-century custom had largely excluded ladies from public life, and sexual delineations of urban geography persisted into the antebellum years. In old Knickerbocker families, which as late as the 1830s still observed the decorum of the Federalist era, ladies unattended by men did not enter even the most genteel restaurants; the text to a book of pictures of New York published in 1832 explained about an illustration of Pearl Street that women seldom, if ever, ventured into the crowded business district in that area.[24]

Clear boundaries delimited respectable, propertied womanhood: To violate them was to find oneself in the shady realm of the demimonde. Home visiting, however, allowed respectable women to cross with impunity some of the same class boundaries that gentlemen-about-town habitually transgressed. The Society for the Relief of Poor Widows (SRPW) was founded in 1797 as New York's first female charity; after 1820 it was closely allied with the evangelicals. This women's association, one of the city's largest and most powerful, confronted the geographical circumscriptions of gender, beginning in the early 1820s, with a string of resolutions that limited home visits to certain sections of the city. Off-limits were streets "the managers cannot visit with propriety" like those around Five Points, a veritable sink of iniquitous pleasures in the eyes of the genteel. The ladies continually expanded the limits of propriety, however, as the laboring poor moved uptown.[25] Others were bolder. The zealous members of the Female Moral Reform Society, founded in 1834 to abolish prostitution, traveled to the "low" brothels of Corlears Hook and Five Points, the most powerfully tabooed spots for women in the entire city, to stand outside and read Scripture, to pray and to urge repentance on all who entered and exited.[26] Admittedly, the Moral Reform ladies were extreme in their ardor and their actions. Nonetheless, evangelicalism gave women the spiritual armor—the self-protection that Justitia had sorely lacked—to defend their reputations from the slurs women incurred when they ventured onto men's sexual terrain.

Through religiously motivated exploration, then, bourgeois women made some progress in making the city their own.[27] What their advances meant for their laboring sisters is a more complicated question. Deeply invested in a particular construction of gender as the basis of respect for their sex, the religious women encountered in the neighborhoods of the working poor an alien mode of womanhood and family life. To some extent they responded sympathetically, in ways that differed from moralistic male charities and reform associations. While empathy for their sex tinged evangelical women's perceptions of the poor, however, those perceptions still drew upon and reinforced bourgeois biases.

For charitable women, a strong commitment to proving the "worthiness" of applicants reconciled stringent exclusionary policies with a genuine solicitude for some who sought aid. Women's charities required verifiable character references and marriage certificates from applicants, a practice which ruled out the great majority of those in the most desperate straits, the immigrants. Although travelers' guides advised emigrating Irish to take along such papers, many did not (or could not, if theirs were common-law marriages), and those who did often found the letters from Ireland useless, since they could not be verified in New York. Practical concerns, of course, also entered into this policy. The ladies needed principles of selection all the more because they were inundated with requests for help. Moral criteria helped the ladies justify to themselves and to their applicants why they could help some and not others, and at times soothed their own distress at their inability to give aid.[28]

The logic of reconciliation between gender-based sympathies and class-based moralism is especially striking among the ladies who ran the Asylum for Lying-In Women, where the appeal to the common afflictions of womanhood was especially strong. The asylum was a refuge for pregnant women bereft of the resources for giving birth. For a small fee the patients obtained room and board, a midwife's services and postpartum care. "It is our own sex appealing to us," the ladies stressed to members and supporters. Poverty, they believed, only increased the burdens that all women endured in pregnancy and childbirth. "Daughters of affliction, how hard is your lot!" the recording secretary exclaimed in 1830, in sympathy with a woman in an especially sad situation.[29]

But it was virtue, not affliction, the ladies were willing to succor. However "interesting" or miserable a woman's circumstances, she could not enter without references. The ladies found Mrs. Donnally's case, for instance, especially touching. Pregnant and with four small children, she had followed her husband to New York; the day she arrived he took sick and died. This unfortunate woman's letters of character were good, but "the testimonials of marriage were wanting" (even if her husband was dead, the ladies needed to be sure the pregnancy was legitimate) and the board regretfully turned her away, noting that "her widow'd heart seem'd ready to burst as she spoke of her helpless children." Mrs. Byrnes, already handicapped by her residence in the disreputable Five Points, was damned by the very urgency of her need: "From her abject appearance she appeared not a fit association for patients." But the most chilling instance of the limits of sisterly charity was that of Maria Burley in 1827. Her case was "pitiable and urgent," the admissions committee noted. Her husband had left her and their child to go tramping for work. She had spent the money he left her on caring for her sick mother, who had then died. Destitute, she went to live with a friend, but she had no bed of her own: Nine months pregnant, "she was shivering with cold without comfortable apparel." Yet Mrs. Burley lacked the requisite letters and the ladies sent her back out into the bitter cold of a New York January until they could ascertain her character from reliable sources. Consequently, the woman almost died.

> It is painful to relate that after a walk of two miles in this extreme cold she was obliged to seek refuge for the night in an open garret with only one quilt for covering and before morning and alone she was delivered of a female infant, which when she was found by two men was frozen to her clothing and with great difficulty restored to life.

By the next day the ladies had made their inquiries, and the half-frozen Mrs. Burley could be admitted. But even these terrible travails were not enough to convince the ladies they had given charity to a "proper object." The following summer, the admissions committee noted sorrowfully that they had learned that "Mrs. Burley who was confined here last winter does not appear to sustain as good a character as was hoped." Such were the contradictions embedded in sisterly charity or, as the ladies of the asylum described it, "the difficulties of meeting at the same time the demands of justice and charity."[30]

At the same time, an appreciation of the specific dilemmas of women did mitigate the judgments charitable ladies made. Women's charities tended more than men's to favor "charity" over "justice." In part, this more sympathetic cast of mind led the ladies to bring some of the particular debilities of poor women to the light of charitable discourse: The first mentions in New York of women's low wages, for example, occurred in the reports of the SRPW.[31] In part, it meant that the women's policies seldom took on the punitive tone common to the men's associations. In 1826, for example, the SRPW alluded in none too veiled terms to its differences with the SPP. The ladies' work had taught them something about the limitations of exhortations to industry and thrift, at least when directed at women: "It has been alledged," the managers noted sharply, "that if people are honest and industrious they may always make some decent living in this happy Land; there may be some truth in this assertion as it respects the other Sex, for they are well paid for their labour: but what can a bereaved widow do, with 5, or 6 little children, destitute of every means of support but what her own hands can furnish (which in a general way does not amount to more than

25 cents a day). . . . Oh! such as say she cannot need assistance have no heart."[32]

The language of the heart was evangelical, counterposed to the arid directives to hard work which came from secular, utilitarian minds. The ladies could see that labor and thrift were not cure-alls for the plight of their widows. Neither could the pursuit of rational self-interest have seemed to them to be a help: Mothers themselves, they must have sensed how irrelevant utilitarian virtue was to women struggling to support their children. If the heart alone was not enough to discern the objects of charity, neither were the familiar categories of worthy and unworthy adequate to what the ladies saw were sometimes sufferings peculiar to women.

The figure of the solitary poor woman that emerged within the female charities between 1820 and 1830 implicitly addressed this dilemma. Generally, the evangelically inspired women's charities did not actively contribute to the evolving discussion of social depravity, but rather embroidered a sentimentalist image of the female victim, a gentle and wounded spirit who partook of the piety and deference of the traditional worthy poor. The virtues of the image were elaborated within the emerging ideal of true womanhood. Such a proper object of women's sympathy was "poor yet industrious, modest quick neat," frail, vulnerable, timid and self-sacrificing:

> Warm'd by labor all day long. . . .
> Ill clad, and fed but sparsely. . . .
> The frugal Housewife trembles when she lights
> Her scanty stock of brush Wood, blazing clear. . . .
> And while her infant race with outspread hands
> And crowded knees, still cow'ring o'er the sparks—
> Retires, content to quake, so they be warm.[33]

Above all, the worthy poor woman was alone (except for her children). She abnegated the "bad associations" which surrounded her; she was, accordingly, a "lonely" and "desolate" woman who tearfully "look'd round in vain for friend or succour," the metaphorical (if hardly actual) inhabitant of a "solitary dwelling." Her moral independence from the milieu in which she lived—or, from another perspective, her social isolation—made her dependent on womanly charity not just for material help but for emotional support. "The thought that there is someone who cares for her . . . is like a balm to her wounded spirit, and causes hope to spring up where before, nothing but withering despondency was felt."[34] In practice, then, sentimentalism did little to promote understanding across class lines; rather, it reinforced the categories of worthy/unworthy and fleshed them out with a specifically female content.

Female worthiness, in the eyes of the women's charities, stemmed partly from the same virtues required of male applicants—a deferential manner, for instance. But it also depended on matters particular to women. Children were especially important, their activities a litmus test of their mothers' virtue. The SRPW made their placement at paid work a condition of assistance (a troublesome policy, since the widows often balked at putting their younger children out to work); most charitable aid to women after 1820 hinged to some degree on the manner in which they raised their children.[35] As the ladies discovered more about their dependents' households through home visiting, housekeeping itself became an issue. In 1824, the ladies of the SRPW voted to deny aid to "every Widow . . . of habits which are inimical to their own comfort, and thereby rendering the Visits of the Managers to their Houses disagreeable, and useless." Women's paid work, too, came under scrutiny: Waged sewing, other put-out work and domestic service were acceptable, but the other employments by which married women earned a living in their own neighborhoods—taking in boarders, street selling, keeping a shop or a bawdy house—rendered them ineligible. Similarly, women too closely connected to certain neighborhoods—those who lived in "disreputable streets" or who lived near people of "bad reputation" were ruled out. The "true" woman of the poor was an isolated woman.[36]

The figure of the solitary woman quaking in her garret allowed the members of female charities to acknowledge the specific injustices to which their sex was subject and at the same time to maintain their contempt for the milieu in which poor women lived. It was an image fashioned from both sex and class loyalties, the progenitor of all the shivering seamstresses and disinherited match girls, weepy but valiant, who frequented the pages of charity reports and urban fiction in the Victorian period.[37] Insofar as the ladies of religious charities could associate the women they helped with this image, they extended to them the emotional bonds of womanhood. In effect, however, such a community of sex could only incorporate a tiny minority of laboring women. By the very unsolitariness of their lives, most of the female laboring poor excluded themselves.

The sentimentalist imagery of female poverty became a convention of nineteenth-century urban social thought. For all its remoteness from the actualities of experience, it nonetheless embodied a new empathy for women; as such, it could only have developed within a reform movement in which women were active. In practice, however, such figures of the imagination did little to help female benevolent associations cope with the realities of poor women's lives in those dense neighborhoods laced through with the intimacies of loyalty, anger and affection. Sentimentalism did, however, serve to reconcile, however unevenly, the competing claims of class and sex.

The urban geography of vice charted by the ministers and tract visitors was neither an accurate rendition of plebeian reality nor a figment of an anxious bourgeois imagination. Rather, it represented the charities' hostile perceptions of certain kinds of working-class assumptions and associations. Prepared to aid the silent and solitary sufferers, charitable visitors were repelled by the gregarious clamor of the tenements. Nathaniel Willis, although not himself a reformer, voiced what must have been the surprise many experienced when he discovered the distance between what he had imagined the poor to be like and what he saw firsthand: "At the Five Points," he observed on a tour of the city's exotica of poverty, "nobody goes in doors except to eat and sleep. The streets swarm with men, women, and children. . . . They are all out in the sun, idling, jesting, quarrelling, everything but weeping, or sighing, or complaining. . . . A viler place than Five Points by any light you could not find," he concluded. "Yet to a superficial eye, it is the merriest quarter of New York."[38]

But neither will Willis's sketch of the jolly carefree poor suffice. Laboring women certainly had troubles which did not dissipate "out in the sun." The ceaseless duties of female housekeeping—the scraping, scavenging, pawning and borrowing—were a response to the decimations wreaked by worsening conditions in waged employment. The notorious independence of laboring children was economically useful to their families, but it also caused mothers many problems, as children learned to edge their way around parental discipline. Women's feuds and mobs represented mechanisms of a neighborhood-based arbitration and justice, but they also embodied the strains of forced intimacy.

A developing history of family instability framed the passions and dramas of the tenements. Men's relationships to their families shifted, as old patterns of involvement and authority disintegrated. The same circumstances that loosened men's ties bound their wives in all the more tightly. Situated at the heart of the household economy, mothers almost always stayed on, no matter how dire the situation. Consequently, it was they who often felt most keenly the hardships of wages insufficient to feed their children, and the fatigue of enforced dependency on others who themselves had little to share. The exigencies of working-class life, on the one hand, increasingly assigned women major responsibilities for their children's survival and, on the other, denied them the means to support their families.

It was, in part, the consolidation of these domestic networks that contributed to the evangelicals' perceptions of the "concentration" of wickedness in the city. As they came to identify working-class mores as inherently vice-ridden, the neighborhood took on the appearance of the breeding ground of sin. The ways laboring women helped one another, raised their children and played out their pleasures and grievances on the streets only seemed to the pious to manifest a belligerent iniquity. Home visiting provided all the more opportunity to witness the supposed coalescence of depravity in the tenements and on the streets. Journalists and writers, in translating the experiences of the home visitors into narratives, popularized the geography of vice as a metaphor through which genteel New Yorkers could see themselves as both brave explorers of a dangerous city and elect guardians of civilized culture.

By constituting themselves in evangelical work as *especially* moral, women could also set off to investigate the geography of vice. Through the cult of domesticity, they thus gained some freedom of movement and a wider sphere of influence and activity. These improvements in bourgeois women's lives, however, generated few benefits for the women they sought to help. Their sympathy for the collectivity of women, real indeed in some cases, took the form of an imagined womanhood which had little to do with the actual difficulties of laboring women and their working-class neighborhoods.

Chapter 5 Women and Men

Like other female relationships, women's involvement with men depended on practical matters of daily life and survival as well as on emotional connections. Imagination and need, passion and practicality flowed together into courtship and marriage; the need to get a living, as well as love and desire, brought lovers and spouses together. The exchange, of course, was far from equal: In a city where it was difficult for any woman to support herself and where no mother could earn a living wage, women needed men more than men needed women. The fact of female economic dependency continued to breed hostility on both sides.

As in other areas of domestic life, however, the working-class neighborhoods gave women leverage in their dealings with men. Neighbor women often challenged, if not misogynistic ideology, then at least the ways in which men turned sexual hostilities into physical abuse. Similarly, outside the tenement neighborhoods, groups of young women helped to create a working-class youth culture which, by the 1840s, offered single women some latitude of movement and play. The self-conscious feminine solidarities of the propertied classes, the "bonds of womanhood," held little meaning for tenement mothers and factory girls. Nonetheless, new female presences in the city's streets, workshops, dance halls, and even (fitfully) in the labor movement helped to shift somewhat the balance of power between the sexes. In these overlapping domains, small and cramped as they were, women found some freedom from customary modes of masculine control.

Marriage

Like other family relationships, the marriages of laboring men and women harbored little explicit, articulated tenderness. Courting was a time for private strolls and seductions, but its end was a practical household arrangement based on reciprocal obligations. In marriage, men provided their wages in exchange for women's help and domestic services. In this, working-class conjugality did not differ structurally from genteel marriage, although the celebration of romantic love distinguished bourgeois marriages ideologically.[1] In the vexed social and economic circumstances of antebellum working-class life, this traditional bargain between the sexes also presented problems that, as in other areas of private life, became the stuff of neighborhood intrigues and dramas.

There was much in working-class relationships that recalled the belligerent plebeian heterosexuality of the eighteenth century, but the context in which men and women experienced their difficulties had greatly changed. As industrial capitalism modified gender relations, working people often felt the shocks of the wage system most keenly in family ways. As the family wage economy undermined parental authority, so it threw into question relationships of male authority and female subservience long taken for granted, based on the power husbands and fathers derived from supervising work under their own roofs or on their own farms. In the American countryside, women might act as mistresses of their own preserves—the dairy, the kitchen, the henhouse or the garden—but men had the final word in land transactions and wills.[2] In Ireland, at least among smallholders and cottiers, women seem to have lacked much independence in their work: Domestic drudgery, a variety of household serfdom, defined their position. On peasant plots, they worked alongside the men in the fields, where, a traveler reported in 1812, they were "subjected to all the drudgery generally performed by men," but were viewed as subordinates, not partners. Domestic industry—spinning and stocking knitting—afforded women an economic sphere of their own, but the decline of Irish domestic industry in the early nineteenth century pushed even craftswomen into field cultivation.[3]

As people moved to the city and into wage earning, men found it difficult to reconstitute their economic authority. The role of family breadwinner that antebellum society proffered to journeymen and laborers was unreliable: All too often, the episodic character of men's employment meant that wives and children, not fathers, supported families with their earnings. Although all but the most impoverished men could support themselves, a wage sufficient to support a family was an elusive ideal for most.[4] Working-men responded in a variety of ways. Trade unions, we will see, articulated their own version of the cult of domesticity. They called for wages high enough to support wives and daughters at home and voiced a newfound respect for the domestic dignity of working-class wives. There was some distance, however, between trade union rhetoric and household realities. Within the day-to-day experience of tenement life, the mutuality of domes-ticity shaped married people's relationships, but so did sexual antagonism. Men's violence toward their wives was not only a displacement of the anger generated by unemployment or the loss of status in the work force—one explanation that comes easily to mind—but was also an attempt to recapture and enforce older kinds of masculine authority.

The same passions of anger and loyalty, love and hate that roused the neighborhoods also kindled the lives of married couples. Devotion, jeal-ousy, ardor and resentment trailed back over a common road traveled for years. The tale of the cabinetmaker Russ and his wife is a poignant illustra-tion that love, in all its circumlocutions, was not antithetical to violence. Russ was arrested in 1846, having beaten his wife to death in a drunken rage. The neighbors had known him for some time. He had a reputation for abusing his wife, a quiet and seemingly well-liked woman. Out of work in New York, Russ returned alone to Albany, where the two had lived previ-ously. There he found employment in his trade and set about making plans to bring her to join him. His letters to her, rare scraps of intimate testimony from a workingman, reveal an adoring but deeply troubled husband, aware of the couple's painful history and his own destructive part in it. Come to Albany, he implored. Here was prosperity, peace and happiness, "no fighting no cursing no bussle or confusion." In contrast to New York, he wrote, "when I look around me every thing I se reminds me of the happy moments we have passed hear in each others company." But he also wor-ried: "When I know that you are in New York without any protection and liable at any moment to be led astray a shuder passes over me." As the weeks passed and his wife, ill and unable to travel, failed to appear, his anxieties turned into suspicion and jealousy. Finally, he returned to New York to fetch her. On his first night home he drank himself into a rage and killed her.[5]

This case is unusual in the annals of New York homicide because of the explicitness of the assailant's psychological motives. In the records of most domestic quarrels, conflicts over practical household arrangements un-leashed men's rage. The passion is evident in the fury of the fights; the practicality, in the causes—money and domestic services, the currency of the marriage relation. Issues of money engendered literally murderous feelings. Mr. Twomey in 1853, for instance, was unsatisfied with his wife's account of money he had given her for groceries. Irritated at her vagueness, he "asked her did she think he picked this money up in the street. . . . He said if she did not give him a full account of what she got out of this money he would kill her or something like it." Later, the neighbors found him kneeling over her dead body, "calling her name and asked if she didn't love him and he her."[6]

Such a response suggests that husbands saw domestic violence in something of the same way parents viewed child discipline, as a corrective measure congruent with family loyalties. A moral reformer encountered this view of wife beating when she reproached a workingman at the Five Points Mission for his treatment of his spouse. " 'Oh, Mr. H.!' said the lady, 'a man should never strike a woman.' 'It is because she was drinking, Ma'am,' he replied, 'I never would strike her if she were sober.' " [7] This particular man posed to the city missionary as something of a reformer himself; in general, however, men tended to punish women not for violations of decorum, but for lapses that interfered with their own comfort. Insofar as husbands acted as disciplinarians, they judged women by a domestic code that was also a moral code. A bad wife was a bad woman, and it was the husband's duty to set her straight.

As it was a husband's right to know where his money went, so it was his prerogative to receive certain domestic services. Women's failure to satisfy men on this score precipitated many fights. A black man in 1822, for instance, beat his wife over some laundry or mending: "All I want Betsey is my Shirt," he explained, "and you may go as soon as you please." Mrs. Twomey, mentioned above, met her death over a turkey. Incensed about the way she had prepared the fowl as well as about the money she had spent on it, her husband set about beating her, interspersing his blows with sarcastic reproaches: " 'You made great preparations didn't you.' " Patrick Carroll was also unhappy with what awaited him when he arrived home for dinner in 1845. "He had two salt shad with him," his wife Bridget recounted, "and half a pound of candles which were pretty much all broke." She, in turn, was irritated with the meager provisions, and over supper the two went at each other with mutual recriminations. "He asked for his supper & what I had, I gave it too him on the table—he was not well pleased at the kind of supper I had for him but I had no better—that raised words betwixt us & then he catched me by the throat and knocked me down & tramped on me & kicked me all over."[8]

Such stories suggest that the marriage bargain was not symmetrical. So do the statistics, which indicate that six to ten times more women than men reported violent assaults from the opposite sex to the police.[9] Although men

certainly incurred reproaches from women for their behavior and failures
to provide, women's reprisals were not likely to take the form of physical
attack.[10] When women, however, failed to keep their households to men's
liking, they might risk violent reprisals.

The asymmetry of marriage is especially apparent in conflicts over
drunkenness. Drunkenness was not only a male problem. Both sexes drank
throughout the day: men at work, when they could (although after 1830
evangelical employers and reformed employees mostly abolished the practice) and at grog shops in the evenings; women at local groceries and in each
other's rooms; men and women together in their rooms, on the streets, and
at local bawdy houses and grog shops. Drunkenness carried different consequences, however, for men and women. Drunken men were familiar figures
to their wives, annoying, often frightening in their belligerence, but an
accustomed burden to bear. Indeed, in the 1840s one path for women to
working-class religious activism was temperance work for the Martha
Washingtonians.[11] A drunken woman, however, was a likely subject for
corrective beating, as the Five Points workingman had explained to the
female missionary. Thus an Irish laborer in 1831 claimed he had no intention
of beating his wife to death: He had only hit her to admonish her "because
she was drunk & no signs of dinner."[12] Another woman provoked her
spouse when he had bought food and given her the parcels to carry home,
and "she had fallen in the street drunk & thrown them about."[13] Drunken
women were often bad housekeepers who disregarded men's domestic
needs; these lapses made female insobriety not a common foible that women
shared with men but a cardinal sin. Such offenses did more than violate
expectations of domestic cooperation. They were breaches of the customary deference due to men: in some cases, as providers who distributed their
earnings as they saw fit; in others, as husbands and fathers who could
command the labor of others. Drunkenness was maddening because it
dramatized, however perversely, a woman's determination to serve herself
at the expense of others.

Turn-of-the-century beliefs still largely set the terms in which these
nineteenth-century workingmen expressed their hostilities toward women.
The defenses of the wife beaters and murderers before the Court of General
Sessions echo the contention of George Hart, whom we encountered earlier, that when a woman stole money from a man's pocket, she deserved the
worst. Women were whores, liars and thieves; the rage at female drunkenness, with its implicit accusations of idleness, evokes eighteenth-century
images of women as parasites.

But there are also elements which make this a very particular drama of
the early nineteenth-century metropolis. Taken together, these hundreds
and thousands of often bitter quarrels constitute not a skirmish in an eternal

battle of the sexes, but rather a great renegotiation of what, exactly, men and women owed each other. In a period when the productive household economy was disappearing and the family wage economy had yet fully to take shape, there could be considerable disagreement on just this issue. Hard times and the irregularity of employment made many husbands poor providers and weakened their control of their families. At the same time, female wage work, however lowly, provided many women some means of support apart from men.

The mutual aid of the neighborhoods provided women sources of strength on which to draw for their part in this struggle. Neighbors intervened in family fights and, on occasion, made their own judgments about the justice of men's demands on women. They pleaded with angry men, sought to temper their violence and often called the watch or the police when their efforts failed.[14] Custom dictated the timing of intervention, which took the form of a patterned series of moves and countermoves, even in the midst of a fight seemingly out of control. Crying "murder" was the signal for help; unless the victim shouted this word, neighbors only listened through the walls. When one woman came downstairs to complain about a beating from her husband, for instance, her friend inquired "why she did not halloe when William struck her" so that others could step in. Conversely, if the victim was too ready with her pleas, neighbors might cease to respond. Female troublemakers were known for their propensity to cry murder when there was no cause. When a husband beat his wife to death within earshot of a neighbor woman in 1831, the latter defended her inaction on the grounds that she "was so accustomed to hear the same cry day & night that she did not think it worth while to get up." A neighbor reproached Mary Molloy for calling for help when the situation did not, in the neighbor's mind, merit it: "Well what harm if he has," the neighbor snapped when Molloy complained her husband was beating her. "Don't make such a noise about it."[15]

If a woman behaved by the rules, then, neighbors might protect her, even if she were a stranger or a casual acquaintance. Neighbor women nursed the victims of beatings and sheltered those who had been threatened; they sometimes took conjugal quarrels, as they did other conflicts, to the streets. Their gestures of solidarity could be extravagant, as in 1822, when three women were arrested for beating a man to death who had just beaten his wife. More commonly, women publicized male transgressions in the theater of the streets and tenements, where they verbally attacked abusive husbands with energy and rhetorical force. A neighbor of the candlemaker William Carroll, hearing him beating his wife late one night in 1840, woke up the occupants of at least two other households with her cries: "I called out to him and said you dirty William you are killing your wife by inches."

"You murdering villain you have murdered your wife," cried out a chorus of neighbor women to a man; he, in turn, dazedly responded, "There is not much harm." He had stabbed his wife before, testimony subsequently revealed, and may have justified this new attack as simply another episode of well-merited chastisement.[16] When men invoked their absolute authority in their own households, when they minimized ill treatment of women on the grounds of their conjugal prerogatives, neighbor women could loudly voice their contrary opinions.

Women certainly depended on each other's help in navigating the perils of daily life. But they could also turn their hostilities on each other. Neighbors were busybodies as well as helpers; more precisely, the two identities were inseparable. The neighborly involvement which could literally save a woman's life from a beating could also turn against her if she violated some moral code. Poor Mrs. McGreen, who gave birth to an illegitimate child in 1855, experienced the full force of the punitive powers of the neighbor women. She had been married four months to her husband, a tailor, and had apparently concealed her pregnancy by another man. Although the husband seems to have been entirely ignorant of any trouble, Mrs. McGreen had already aroused the suspicions of her neighbors so that, on the morning when they heard furtive moaning through the walls, they snapped into action. A phalanx of female inquisitors paraded through her room to ferret out her secret. Mrs. McGreen continued to insist she was only ill. The neighbors were implacable. "I came in several times afterwards and searched about the rooms and closets," stated Bridget Gallagher, "but could not find it [the baby]. She told me and others who came in that she did not want me to interfere." Undeterred by the woman's request to be left alone, the women did not stop until they finally discovered the dead baby—either stillborn or a victim of infanticide—in the back alley, whereupon they marched triumphantly inside to announce their discovery to the husband.[17] Throughout the early nineteenth century, women seem to have tried to prevent infanticide, and publicized the act when it did occur, but this particular vendetta, with its pursuit of the husband's interests, seems motivated by the intention to punish adultery as much as by an ethos which deplored infanticide.[18]

No doubt women friends had helped each other with abusive husbands in eighteenth-century cities—and in the Irish and German villages from which so many laboring women migrated—but female aid in these large nineteenth-century urban communities coalesced into almost institutional forms, patterned and dependable, which were flexible enough to draw in vast numbers of women. These particular bonds of womanhood did not translate, as did female networks among the bourgeoisie, into an articulated ideology of womanhood. But neighborly relations between women could modify men's abusiveness. A neighbor woman in 1841 had known an abused wife only a short time when she risked the husband's reprisals by threatening to call the watch on him. When the newcomers were evicted, she gave them lodgings in her rooms, but told the husband if he beat his wife again she would evict him: "I would not have such a man in my place." A German storekeeper, known to beat his wife, pointed to her, as she lay on the bed passed out in a drunken stupor, and complained to a neighbor woman, "You see some of the neighbors will say I am always in the wrong." In publicizing his wife's transgressions he was defending himself against the adverse judgments of just this community.[19] The neighborhood was an alternative court, judge and jury, that, although predisposed to look favorably on women, did not always render verdicts in their favor. In the pursuit of justice it could be cruel and vengeful. Nonetheless, the collective power that women found there, for all its terrors, counterposed itself to men's privileges.

Single Women

The life of the tenements circumscribed much of young women's lives, but the milieu of the city also released them, if only episodically, offering great numbers the ability to live somewhat removed from the constraints of patriarchal families. Trans-Atlantic immigration separated many daughters from their parents and sent them off on their own. The expansion of female wage work into other employments besides domestic service meant that, for the first time, daughters could earn their livings outside household settings. Patriarchal controls over young women's leisure, time, earnings and sexuality weakened accordingly. In this new social space, single women helped to create a youth culture of sexual and commercial pleasures, purchased with wages and time freed up from domestic obligations and family discipline.

New York was full of single young women. A slight surplus of women in the population as a whole became a dramatic imbalance among people twenty to thirty years old. Until 1830, the sex ratio was even, but by 1840 there were over a quarter again more young women than men in the city. The Irish Famine migration temporarily mitigated the imbalance, since whole families were more likely to migrate in the crisis years. By 1860, however, there were again 125 women of marrying age for every 100 men.[20]

The sexual imbalance cannot be explained on the basis of immigration. In the trans-Atlantic migration, comprised mostly of young people, men

predominated over the entire period 1820–60, although women became
more numerous over time (by 1855–60, they counted for 43 percent of the
arrivals). Rather, the imbalance had to do with the conditions of the urban
labor market. Young men traveled widely in search of work *outside* the city
and thus their demographic presence in New York was diminished; young
women, however, were confined to local employment opportunities.[21]
While more men emigrated to New York, many also moved around in or
out of the city; in contrast, the prospects for single women beyond New
York remained slight.

But whatever restrictions awaited young immigrant women on arrival,
America still held special promise for them. There was the anticipation of
living away from the confines of the village and the drudgery of the cottier's
plot; there was also the hope of marrying better than one could ever hope
to in Ireland. One young woman rejoiced over her exemption from an Irish
marriage in a letter to her father, still in County Cork, in 1850: "Oh how
happy I feel . . . as The Lord had not it destined for me to get married to
some Loammun or another at home that after a few months he and I may
be an incumberance upon you or perhaps in the poor house."[22] The hope
of marriage itself became a lure, as the prospects for marrying in Ireland
dimmed.[23]

These girls and young women were departing from a centuries-
old pattern whereby a girl growing up moved as a dependent from one
household to another—from her father's house to her employer's to her
husband's. Traditionally, girls were more tightly bound into the web of
domestic industry and thus less mobile than boys.[24] Although in
eighteenth-century America the numbers of single women among the
strolling poor drifting into the cities increased greatly, those women seem
to have either moved into servants' positions or ended up in almshouses.
In Philadelphia in 1775, for example, the self-supporting woman living on
her own or with other women was virtually unknown.[25]

In antebellum New York, new patterns of female residence developed.
Of course, families in the New World, insofar as they could, did stretch to
incorporate solitary young immigrants. Girls who left Ireland alone often
moved in with uncles, aunts or married siblings once in New York. Other
young women on arrival went immediately into domestic service, where
the supervision of their employers' households limited whatever independence they might have gained in migrating. Still others, however, lived
outside family networks, as lodgers on their own. My survey of the residences of 600 workingwomen in New York in 1855 shows that, in fact, 224
of 400 single workingwomen were living independently of uncles, aunts,
grandparents and parents.[26] Working girls might double up with sisters or
workmates, "sleeping anyhow and anywhere"[27] in households headed by

workmates' parents or fellow villagers; they supported themselves through manufacturing employment, alternating factory or outside work with spells in domestic service. By the 1850s, the community of single women also reached beyond family households. Working girls crammed together into shared rooms in previously all-male boardinghouses and in tenements. "Many of these shop girls sleep half a dozen to a garret," Virginia Penny, a self-styled New York version of the London social investigator Henry Mayhew, reported in 1863. Factory workers only slept there, but outworkers—sewing workers who labored at home—also could turn shared rooms into all-female cooperative workshops.[28]

Admittedly, few girls lived altogether free of family authority, which diffused itself through other modes of community control. The neighborhood, we have seen, had its own intricate networks of surveillance; young women could find themselves subject to neighborhood interdictions which stretched back across the Atlantic to the sorts of criticism and supervision they might have experienced from their families in Ireland. When a seamstress took six men to court for a gang rape in 1858, she ran up against the judgmental powers of the neighborhood. During the trial, the witnesses— a cousin, the cousin's friend and their respective wives—had contradictory things to say about the victim's character. The disagreement hinged on what those still in Ireland had to say about her. One witness had heard others "speak badly of her in consequence of accounts they heard from the old country" while another claimed there was nothing against the girl in the letters from home.[29] Even so, such neighborhood criticisms did not lead to the direct and immediate discipline to which young girls were subject in their parents' households, the kind of interference about which a sister in the New World gently chided her father in a letter back home. "So my Dear Father according as I had stated to you I hope that whilst you are at home I hope that you will give my Sister Mary that privilage of Injoying herself Innocently on an accation that she pleases so far as I have said innocently."[30] Most important, women on their own were free of the obligations of domestic labor, perhaps the most powerful set of controls to which daughters were subject. Lodgers did not live with fathers and siblings to whom they owed the services of cooking, washing, hauling water and carrying wood. Although lodgers might even reside in working groups —for instance, in the households of men who employed them as assistants in garment making—the deference they owed in terms of domestic services and personal obedience would have been less than that daughters owed their parents. Even within the degrading and impoverished situation of female wage laborers, the break with deeply rooted conventions of family residence opened up new possibilities for single women in the city.

Young women and girls on their own played an important role in the development of an urban culture of young single people, male and female. Although much of the terrain of popular culture continued to be men's up through the Civil War, sociable resorts and practices began to open up for the mingling of the sexes as early as the 1790s. When Harry Bedlow, the rake we met in Chapter 1, enticed Lanah Sawyer out for an evening, it was to this milieu. He took her to an ice cream parlor and then for a promenade around the Battery with another couple. As girls reached puberty and beyond, street chores and outdoor games led into a landscape of sexual desire, where heterosexual machinations opened up new vistas. Sexuality was often the ticket of admission—the key to social pleasure, the coin of heterosexual exchange.

Antebellum working-class youth culture encompassed the bawdy houses and some of the traditional rowdy pastimes of what was still a rough maritime town, but as early as 1820 it also occupied new corners of the city. Holiday excursions to the country, for example, were special treats in which women included themselves. Parties of young men and women or groups of women set out on Sundays on ferry rides to Long Island, boat trips on the East River and carriage rides to the rural retreats of northern Manhattan. Rose Butler, a servant-girl on trial for arson in 1819, in detailing her descent into crime, chronicled some of these amusements. She had first used money pinched from her mistress to take some friends carriage riding; later, on the Fourth of July, she "went with some girls, on board the steam-boat, on a party of pleasure, and paid the charges," and spent the rest at a bawdy house "on a frolic." "It was in this manner," she concluded, "I squandered away the money I had stolen—in frolicking and rioting in the dance-houses and other places" at Corlears Hook, where poor girls mingled with workingmen and sailors.[31]

"Walking out" was another way young men and women met. Walking out was a prelude to courting, a means of flirting and pairing off. Young girls fell into walking out as they hung about the streets in groups in the course of doing their daily chores. Walking out was a patterned promenade on the avenues and in public places like City Hall Park; there, on Broadway and the Bowery, the crowds and the jumble of people and classes shielded the young from the scrutiny of their neighborhoods.[32] If walking out gave young women greater independence from adult supervision, however, the custom also provided, as in Lanah Sawyer's case, the latitude for some disastrous mistakes. As single women ventured outside the restrictions of their neighborhoods, they left behind the protections that kin and neighbors provided in enforcing men's sexual propriety. Although flirtations on the avenues were freer, they were also more dangerous, especially in a city where seduction, even debauchery, remained sources of male self-esteem into the antebellum years.

For a small number of Protestant women, church membership was a more decorous path to sociability. Although working-class revivalism was only a minor strain within a bourgeois movement, some of the free evangelical churches did have limited success in attracting working-class worshipers. Women figured disproportionately in the working-class revivals, as they did in the regular evangelical churches. In the Brainerd Presbyterian, a church established in 1833 to minister to the uptown working-class Eleventh Ward, over three-quarters of the congregation were women or girls. Of these, nearly half were single and unrelated directly to any other church members: They were young women on their own, many of them probably from the nearby countryside. While their pleasure-seeking sisters were off on Sunday excursions, these devout seamstresses and domestic servants found friendship and self-affirmation in the shared experience of God's word.[33]

Certainly young women must have benefited from the companionship. Being on one's own was, in general, a very risky business. The trials suffered by Caroline, whom Ezra Stiles Ely met in 1811 in his ministry to the Almshouse, show how seriously a girl could injure herself in cutting herself loose from her family. Caroline had been engaged to a young man in her hometown in Vermont; with her mother's blessing, the pair went off to visit his parents in another town, where the suitor promised they would marry. They eloped instead to New York, where he took a room for them in a waterfront boardinghouse. Shortly thereafter he abandoned Caroline, leaving her penniless and infected with gonorrhea. Without friends or kin in the city, she went to the Almshouse for treatment, where her country looks and repentant ways brought her to the minister's attention. But despite her professions of repentance to Reverend Ely, Caroline had seen enough of New York in her short stay to perceive that "keeping company" with men could be a way of supporting herself alone in the city. So when she left the Almshouse cured, she made her way back "on the town," to the same boardinghouse where she had lived with her young man, to support herself through prostitution.[34]

Caroline's story shows both the pleasures and the dangers involved when a girl set off on her own. Courtship was one part of a system of barter between the sexes, in which a woman traded sexual favors for a man's promise to marry. Premarital intercourse then became a token of betrothal. This was, however, a problematic exchange for the woman, since she delivered on her part of the bargain—and risked pregnancy—before the man came through with his. In the settled European and rural communities in which this practice was rooted, a young woman could count on family, neighbors and (in Ireland) local magistrates to hold the man to his vows should she become pregnant while courting.[35] Even in the more volatile circumstances of cities, neighbors and kin did what they could to supervise courtships. One of Lanah Sawyer's neighbors, for instance, had warned her that the "smart beau" who walked her home one night was not "lawyer smith" at all but "Harry Bedlow, a very great rake. . . ."[36] The already developed *genteel* code of female chastity had little bearing here. It was not "walking out" for which the neighbor admonished Lanah Sawyer, but the reputation of the one with whom she walked. Other young couples consummated their courtships practically under the eyes and with the tacit knowledge of the girls' families. In 1800, for instance, a respectable Quaker family watched calmly while a cousin, Alma Sands, disappeared into various bedrooms with the boarder Levi Weeks. The warmth of the courtship was occasion for remarks, but not the form the courtship was taking; the family assumed that the sexual activity was in itself proof (in general) of the pair's commitment and (in particular) of Levi Weeks's seriousness. "I always thought Levi a man of honor," attested the aunt, "And that he did not intend to promise further than he could perform."[37]

When people moved around, however, from city to city, from the Old World to the New, and from country to city (as in Caroline's case), these methods of ensuring male responsibility weakened. A young woman on her own in New York could enjoy the pleasures of promenading the avenues in fine dresses purchased with her own wages, but those "frolics," as the servant-girl Rose Butler called them, could also leave her bereft, stranded, and pregnant. Even single girls like Lanah Sawyer and Alma Sands, surrounded by people with an eye to their well-being, could run into trouble with men in the mobile and anonymous circumstances of the city. The neighbor's warnings failed to dissuade Lanah Sawyer from a disastrous liaison; Alma Sands was murdered the night she was to marry Levi Weeks, and suspicions that Weeks had tried to evade his obligations by killing the girl led to his indictment for the crime. The slow breakdown of betrothal practices was perhaps one reason that the Sawyer rape case became a *cause célèbre*. Like the trial of Harry Bedlow, the Sands murder also became a magnet for popular fantasies and fears. Hundreds of people came to view the girl's body; rumors swirled about the murderer's identity and the details of the killing; peddlers hawked handbills which conjured up "ghouls and goblins . . . dancing devils . . . accounts of witchcraft . . . strange and wonderful prophecies."[38] These were early and especially lurid acts in a narrative of seduction and betrayal that had probably already touched many urban families, and that in ensuing decades was to become a staple of nineteenth-century popular melodrama.

Early in the century, then, single women claimed their part in a youthful milieu where they could conduct—to a greater or lesser degree—their own pleasures and affairs. But sexual territory was also dangerous ground where the same mobility that gave women some degree of freedom—the continual movement of people in and around each others' lives—also rendered them more vulnerable to male entrapment and abandonment.

The mentality of early national life also enhanced that vulnerability. As long as rakes like Harry Bedlow remained exemplars of fashion, and as long as laboring men looked on women as antagonists to be outfoxed and out-maneuvered, severe sorts of exploitativeness toward young women—especially young women of spirit—would seem legitimate and unremarkable. And as long as the heterosexual marketplace of leisure remained closely connected to the older, male-dominated milieu of the bawdy houses, different conceptions of relations between men and women had little chance to emerge. The development of new possibilities awaited a more distinct working-class culture, where men's consciousness of how much they held in common with other wage earners—in other words, a working-class consciousness—would lead them to look more kindly on their female peers. This was a culture where the self-conscious community of class experience would to some degree encompass women, and where the slumming gentle-man would prove an unwelcome guest.

The Bowery

That milieu began to materialize in the 1830s on the Bowery, the broad avenue running up and down the east side of the island. Lined with work-shops, manufactories and workers' and small masters' dwellings, the Bow-ery was the plebeian counterpart of elegant Broadway to the west. In the two decades before the Civil War, it became a byword for working-class culture. As an 1863 guidebook informed newcomers to the city, "To deni-zens of New York, society is usually known under the generic divisions of Broadway and the Bowery."[39] All sorts of working people frequented its environs. The Bowery was the main thoroughfare for cheap goods, the heart of the butcher district, and a staging ground for public amusements —parades, horse races, and fights between the juvenile gangs for which the street became notorious.[40] Evenings on the Bowery were the special prov-ince of young people. At the end of the working day and on Saturday night, the dance halls, oyster houses and the famed Bowery Theater, built in 1827, came alive with workingwomen, journeymen and laborers looking for marital prospects, sexual encounters and general good times. In many ways, this culture resembled that of the bawdy houses. Men set the tone, and abusiveness toward women, if no longer explicitly celebrated in jokes and songs, still entered into the proceedings. Still, Bowery culture involved changes in the relations of single, young men and women; it marginalized older forms of misogyny and celebrated instead the possibilities of gregariousness between the sexes. While the reality often fell short, the ideal still represented an opening in gender relations. In the late eighteenth century, laboring men had tended to see themselves as a fraternity united against parasitical, corrupt females as well as the parasitical, corrupt rich. On the Bowery, a new imagery of community crystallized, in which class became a heterosexual association, one that granted women the ability to claim something of the republican pride that had been the workingmen's heritage for some fifty years.

Through the 1830s, the peculiar features of Bowery life—vociferous crowds at the theaters, riotous volunteer fire companies and truculent street gangs—became sufficiently well known to cohere into a cultural identity recognizable to outsiders; in the early 1840s, the Bowery produced its first metropolitan "type," the Bowery Boy.[41] Valorous, generous and unabashedly rough-hewn in manners and speech, the Boy descended from the Bowery "fire laddie" of the famed workingmen's volunteer fire companies in the 1830s; unlike the latter, however, the Bowery Boy aspired to fashion and style. An ordinary journeyman or apprentice, "he was but little seen during the day, being engaged at his employment," but at night, he appeared as a very different person. "These 'B'hoys' had fashions of their own . . . they were the most consummate dandies of the day," Abram Dayton, born into the prestigious old Knickerbocker elite, amusedly recalled. The Bowery Boy made up his costume according to a precise code of dress.

> The hair . . . was one of his chief cares. . . . At the back of the head it was cropped as close as scissors could cut, while the front locks permitted to grow to considerable length were matted by a lavish application of *bears grease,* the ends tucked under so as to form a roll, and brushed until they shone like glass bottles . . . a black, straight, broad-brimmed hat, polished as highly as a hot iron could effect, was worn with a pitch forward . . . a large shirt collar turned down and loosely fastened, school boy fashion, so as to expose the full proportions of a thick, brawny neck; a black frock coat with skirts extending below the knee; a flashy satin or velvet vest . . . pantaloons tight to the knee. . . . A profusion of jewelry as varied and costly as the b'hoy could procure. His rolling swaggering gait on the promenade on the Bowery; his position, at rest, reclining against a lamp or awning post; the precise angle of the ever-present cigar; the tone of voice, something between a falsetto and a growl; the unwritten slang which constituted his vocabulary cannot be described.[42]

A revivified version of the working-class dandy and the Irish "jackeen," the Bowery Boy, like the blood several decades before, depended on the backdrop of the streets to set off his self-consciously dashing presence; unlike the blood, however, he defied respectable conventions of dress.[43]

The social identity of the Bowery Boy—his presence on the streets—both contributed to and depended upon his presence in commercial culture. There he figured prominently in the 1840s, as a quaint "sight" in numerous journalistic ramblings about town and as the heroic "Mose" of an enormously popular series of melodramas staged at the Bowery Theater beginning in 1848 and subsequently exported to the national circuit. The depiction of the type became inseparable from the type himself: "His appearance on the street and his arrival in print were part of the same social transformation," observes historian Peter Buckley. While popular journalism heightened the oddities of dress and demeanor observable on the Bowery and in the Bowery melodramas, workingmen refined their perceptions of how to be a Bowery Boy through watching delightfully recognizable characterizations acted out on the stage of the Bowery Theater.[44]

Bowery culture, for all its masculinism, its celebration of the virtues of physical prowess and pugnacity, grew out of different associations than those of traditional workingmen's leisure. Although the Bowery Boy was an aggressively working-class character, he drew his identity from an awareness of a set of cultural images rather than from a common workplace experience. His class consciousness was distinct from that of the organized labor movement. The Bowery flowered after the Panic of 1837, when New York's assertive labor organizations of the 1830s had collapsed. The Bowery Boy did not spin out his associations with his fellows on the basis of common membership in a trade union or an ethnic group or even an organized gang; rather, he defined himself through his use of his leisure time. In an after-hours world, he created commonalties through dressing, speaking and acting in certain ways, always (as one former Boy remembered) holding himself "ready for excitement." In other words, he was a member of youth culture, a milieu characterized by a symbiotic relationship to its own symbolic elaboration.

This youth culture, connected to but not contingent upon the masculine camaraderie of the workplace, offered women some part in its process of imagining itself. One of the accoutrements of the Boy's persona was "his girl hanging on his arm"—in journalistic and theatrical treatments, the "Lize" to the brave "Mose." When thus fully equipped, "it would have been injudicious to offer him any obstruction or to utter an offensive remark."[45] "Lize" was a young workingwoman: a factory girl, shopgirl, milliner, dressmaker, book folder, map colorer, flower maker, or seamstress. Wage work and the loosening of domestic obligations that wages purchased

made her presence possible. George Foster, the would-be Dickens of the
New York scene, noted how such young women emerged in a crowd at
the end of the workday, streaming toward the east side: "all forming a
continuous procession which . . . loses itself gradually in the innumerable
side-streets leading thence into the unknown regions of Proletaireism in the
East End." Many of them ended up on the Bowery, sashaying up and down
the avenue with crowds of girlfriends or on the arms of their young men.
For women, the allure seems to have been exclusively heterosexual. Although the beginnings of a gay male subculture were just visible—Whitman, for one, was part of it—the social conditions for a lesbian milieu seem
to have been absent in what was still a heavily masculine culture. Still, the
young women of the Bowery, decked out in fancy clothes, beckoned to
every newly arrived country girl, a collective symbol of certain pleasures
of city life.[46]

The streets offered a panoply of places for the sexes to mingle. The
Bowery promenade was a main attraction, dazzling in the array of costumes
paraded there; for those with a little money in their pockets, there were also
more elaborate amusements. The theaters offered melodrama, burlesque
and blackface minstrelsy at cut-rate admission; dime museums and eating-
places served as meeting grounds for trysts and flirtations. Ice cream, in the
1790s a delicacy reserved for the likes of Harry Bedlow, had become cheap
enough to make the ice cream parlor a democratic resort; oyster shops also
provided inexpensive fare—all the oysters you could eat for six cents a
customer. Vauxhall Gardens, founded in 1798 and taken over by the vir-
tuoso showman Phineas Barnum in 1840, featured "variety shows"—the
precursors of vaudeville—skits, dancing, singing and comedy.[47] Balls, held
at nearby Tammany Hall, firehouses or dance halls, were the high festivals
of Bowery life. In these "high-flyer stampedes," dancing was a matter of
acrobatic strength as well as dexterity and grace, with results that moved
George Foster to a characteristic moment of metropolitan pride: "New
York is undoubtedly the greatest place for dancing in all Anglo Saxdom,"
he ventured in relation to a Bowery dance. The balls drew "the folding-
girls and seamstresses, the milliners' apprentices, the shopgirls," by the
scores: "All unmarried womanhood" from the lower east side came, it
seemed to Foster, dressed in their finest clothes. Indeed, sometimes young
women sponsored dances of their own, clubbing together for food and
liquor, while male guests provided the music.[48]

Like other youth cultures, this one was mobile. On Saturday nights and
Sundays in warm weather, the Bowery went to the country. The migration
was a vastly expanded version of earlier pleasure rides like the one Rose
Butler had taken in 1819. Steamboats, streetcars and carriages transported
working-class crowds to New Jersey, Staten Island and Long Island for

picnics and more extravagant holidays at cheap boardinghouses. "The civic scum ebbs and flows on Sundays and holidays to infest Long Island and Richmond County," observed diarist George Templeton Strong, an especially misanthropic spokesman for the prejudices of the affluent. "All conveniently accessible hotels and boarding houses are overrun by the vermin that hot weather roasts out of its homes in towns."[49]

The workingwomen who took part in these pleasurable times created a striking public presence. They were distinguished by their self-conscious "airs," a style of dress and manner which was a studied departure from ladyhood, an implicit rejection of bourgeois female decorum. Genteel rules of gender dictated that "womanly" women minimize what they saw in public of others and what others saw of them. The respectable woman on the street deflected rather than drew attention to her physical presence; her dress and demeanor might excite admiration, but should discourage overtures. Muted colors, a costume that covered the flesh except for the face (including obligatory gloves and hat), and an aloof manner were the hallmarks of a lady. Differences in the public presentation of the self became in nineteenth-century genteel culture an important means of distinguishing the "true" woman from her imitators or counterfeits. Thus popular perception identified her antithesis, the prostitute, as much by her demeanor in public as by her actual sexual behavior: A prostitute was, in common parlance, a woman "on the town," recognizable by her brightly colored dress, the comparative absence of coverings (most tellingly, the omission of a hat) and her open, searching gaze.[50]

The young workingwomen of the Bowery developed a style different from either of these feminine modes, one that allowed them freedoms similar to those of the prostitute, but that nonetheless advertised their own singularity. Bowery girls—or "Gals"—presented themselves not as streetwalkers on the prowl but as members of a high-spirited peer group, reveling in their associations with each other. Their carriage on the streets was one expression of this self-conscious boisterousness: "Her very walk has a swing of mischief and defiance in it," George Foster wrote of the Gal; Abram Dayton, another contemporary, remembered that "her gait and swing were studied imitations of her lord and master, and she tripped by the side of her beau ideal with an air which plainly said, 'I know no fear and ask no favor.' "[51]

Dress was another expression of class and sex pride. Fancy clothes were the visual reflection of women's wages, freed from family obligations. "The pretty book-folder and the pale seamstress, the buxom housemaid and the ambitious laundress, slave cheerfully all the week in the dreariest and most monotonous occupations, that they may obtain the means of making a handsome appearance at the Saturday night dance," surmised Foster.[52] Like all high fashion, Bowery styles were strange to the eyes of outsiders. The costumes of the avenue eschewed the traditional garb of the laboring classes —leather breeches and aprons for men; refurbished secondhand fancy clothes for men and women: The democratization of fashion was just beginning in the 1840s, with the expansion of men's ready-made clothing and cheap dressmaking. Bowery fashions also repudiated genteel principles of harmonious dress for their own internal logic of color, pattern and accessories. Women wore startling combinations of colors, a sharp contrast to the modest pastels, grays and browns of ladies' street wear.

> Her dress is "high," and its various ingredients are gotten together in utter defiance of those conventional laws of harmony and taste imposed by . . . the French mantua-makers of Broadway. The dress and shawl are not called upon . . . to have any particular degree of correspondence or relationship in color—indeed, a light pink contrasting with a deep blue, a bright yellow with a brighter red, and a green with a dashing purple or maroon, are among the startling contrasts which Lize considers "some pumpkins."[53]

While ladies' dress emphasized the bosom and waist and veiled other contours, Bowery styles accented the hips and thighs as well. And while the lady shielded her face with a bonnet or veil from the gaze of passersby, the fashionable workingwoman called attention to her face with her ornate hats and left herself free to look about, "the face entirely exposed, and the eyes at full liberty to see what is going on in every direction."[54] The respectable found the Lizes of the Bowery laughable in their "airs," but the eccentricities and excesses were no more bizarre than those of any other mode of high fashion—that of the old Federalist elite, for example, with its weirdly shaped wigs, rainbow hues and artificial contours, padded and corseted.[55]

A special mentality underlay these various expressions of youthful pleasure. It was this mentality—the way that the laboring people of the Bowery understood themselves in social and aesthetic terms—that made the avenue a coherent cultural milieu rather than just a place for good times. "Boweriness," a later New Englander would label it.[56] "Boweriness," for both men and women, signified a celebration of the possibilities of working-class life. A unique blend of high-spiritedness and decorum, Boweriness was fundamentally mannered, enforcing its own standards of courtesy and polite conduct: The "airs" that so amused upper-class observers were the Bowery's rendition of urbane deportment. To be sure, there was still plenty of rowdiness. In the Bowery Theater, pandemonium reigned. George Foster, journalist about town, observed that "compared with the performances in the audience, the ranting and bellowing and spasmodic galvanism of the actors on the stage, are quite tame and commonplace."[57] But the theater uproar was also ritualized, a patterned response to cues from the actors and the audience and quite different from the besotted jollity of the bawdy houses. Outside the theater, pleasure seekers in the promenade, at the pleasure gardens and in the oyster shops contained their exuberance within a self-consciously dignified civility. Down by the seamier environs of the waterfront, workingmen could still spend an evening of blood sports at the terrier and rat fights at "Sportsmen's Hall," and at Five Points, they could make the rounds of the dives. The Bowery catered to different tastes. Its most successful establishments created an aura of modishness by minimizing the presence of drinking, brawling and prostitution. Harry Hill's popular concert hall and saloon, for instance, gave free admission to women dressed in fashionable street wear, but banished anyone caught soliciting.[58]

Much of this sense of decorum was associated with a rough courtesy toward women, a mingling of a minimal respect with men's own sense of class pride. The Bowery was not egalitarian in its gender relations, but Bowery style did repudiate some kinds of antagonisms toward women, primarily those that were bound up with blatant class exploitation. While voyeuristic "aristos" had found some welcome at turn-of-the-century bawdy houses, gentlemen looking for liaisons with working girls ran into frank hostility on the Bowery. "The b'hoys are little inclined to disguise the open contempt and hatred he inspires," Foster reported of the gentleman intruder. "Should he become at all demonstrative in his attention to any of the ladies," he was likely to come to blows with her protectors. Abram Dayton, who himself had once been a gentleman looking for a good time on the avenue, remembered how risky flirtations could be. "The Broadway exquisite who ventured 'within the pale' was compelled to be very guarded in his advances towards any fair one . . . any approach to familiarity either by word or look was certain to be visited by instant punishment." Women joined in. "The g'hals themselves despise him," Foster noted of the "aristo." If a fight developed, Dayton recalled, the women rallied to the Boys' side, cheering them on as in a faction fight in Ireland or a street fight in New York.[59]

The Boys' antagonism to the prowling outsider was a way by which they defined exclusive rights to "their" women. The workingmen's own sense of the widening distance between rich and poor, Broadway and the Bowery, employer and employee, colored their perceptions of working-class women. The rise of the Bowery was inseparable from the growth of working-class consciousness between 1830 and 1860. In this context, the rough version of republican ideology that the Bowery Boys inherited—the celebration of the virtues of manual labor and physical prowess, the virile patriotism, the truculence toward outside authority—promoted a change in republican views of women. Like their eighteenth-century predecessors, Bowery men saw public life—in their case, working-class life—as a place where men were the main show and women the supporting cast. But in contrast to earlier attitudes, theirs was a paternalist stance that stressed the protective rather than antagonistic elements of their involvement with women. The visibility of the Bowery Gals must have contributed to this shift. As independent wage earners, women themselves cast off some symbolic associations with dependency.

The Boys' defense of their female guests was certainly not egalitarian or comradely, but neither was it overtly misogynist. For all the limitations of working-class paternalism—and we will see there were many—this paternalism still granted working-class women a greater ability to lay claim to some respect. On one level, the Boys, in delineating their turf, laid claims to territory in women. But on another, they challenged the unabashed sexual predation of the gentleman. In doing so, they acknowledged some obligations to their female companions, albeit in a fundamentally patronizing way.

The expansive heterosexuality of the Bowery, however, also competed with the rougher side of its working-class republicanism: the bellicosity, the masculinism (women on the sidelines), the localism and the insular loyalties. In the 1830s, the Boweryites' pugnacious defense of their rights against interfering outsiders erupted not only in melees with rival fire companies and gangs but in antiblack, antiabolitionist riots and the first stirrings of anti-immigrant nativism; in 1849 it led some of the Boys to a bloody showdown with the police at the elite Astor Place Theater over the appearance there of the British rival of "their" actor, the American Shakespearean Edwin Forrest of the Bowery Theatre.[60] A culture so concerned with vaunting its male insiders—the true American boys—at the expense of everyone else (the Irish, the English, the blacks, the wealthy and genteel) must often have cast women as parasitic outsiders.

Thus while working-class consciousness undermined some features of eighteenth-century misogyny, still others persisted. Sexual hostilities may have gone underground, but they did not disappear, either from the Bowery or from the wider working-class world around it. The abuse of women, especially sexual abuse, remained a male prerogative; for some, it became a form of recreation. Group rapes, virtually unknown in the court records of the early nineteenth century, appear occasionally in court proceedings after 1830. "Getting our hide" was one perpetrator's term for a gang rape.[61] The assailants were the same sorts of young workingmen who frequented the Bowery; their victims might have been, in other circumstances, their companions at the dance halls or oyster shops. Thus Mary Galloway, the young seamstress I introduced earlier, whom Bridget Clarke presumed upon, was on her way home from work and a visit to a friend one evening when six men attacked her, crying "Choke the Goddamned vagabond!"[62]

The term of opprobrium, "vagabond," is worth noting. As young workingwomen created within the city's public life an imaginative presence of their own, others interpreted this presence in their own ways, not always with the *esprit* of the Bowery at its most amiable. Dressed up for an evening out, Mary Galloway could hardly have looked like a vagabond, yet for the particular workingmen she encountered, it was this image, with its evocations of sexual profligacy and prostitution, that shaped their perceptions of a young woman out alone.

Indeed, in a culture where women "on the town" retained deep associations to prostitution, the working girl who made known her independence or even her aloneness could still be interpreted as issuing a sexual invitation. For this reason, even asking directions—seemingly a straightforward business in a big city full of recent immigrants—could be charged and risky. Ann Murphy, out walking early one Saturday night in 1842, stopped a man to ask directions. He offered to show her the way if she would wait for him a moment at his sister's nearby; he then took her there and promptly raped her. Similarly, the Scots immigrant Ann Stuart, nineteen years old, got lost in the streets one afternoon when she was looking for work in 1850. Two men offered to help her, took her to a porterhouse, bought her a drink and raped her. In these cases and others, accepting help from a man when searching for lodgings turned out to be rife with ambiguities. It could conjure up the sort of casual liaisons so common in New York: John Lynch, who had helped the newcomer Mary Ann Casey find a room, protested, when she resisted his advances, that the two of them "were the same as if we were married." It could also evoke the promise of an attraction consummated at a house of assignation, another situation in which men and women went together to search for rooms. It was against this interpretation of her behavior that Ann Stuart defended herself in court against the defendant's countercharges: "When you met me I did not tell you I was looking for lodgings & would go with you if you would take me to a place where I could stay all night. I asked you where Oliver Street was . . . I told you I was going home to my sister's house."[63]

One analysis of these events might argue that the men were engaged in profoundly wishful thinking, or that the women were feigning their innocence after the fact. But the uncertainties of these working-class encounters make them more complex and interesting. A woman alone on the street might really just be asking for directions—but then again, she could be looking for some kind of sexual adventure. Many women who lived on their own were prostitutes—but by the 1840s, such young women could be otherwise employed. Some girls new to the city did willingly enter into liaisons with men they met by chance—but others meant to set up housekeeping on their own. Young women out to enjoy themselves might be open to sex or might not be, depending on the terms of the encounter and the partner. In a city where women were taking new territory for themselves, the intentions of both parties in a heterosexual encounter could be murky. What these episodes reveal is neither a case study of male trickery nor of female provocation. Rather, they show the ambiguities of a situation rich in veiled meanings at a moment when interpretations of those meanings, tied to changing gender relations, were very much in flux.

Insofar as sex retained its associations to exchange and money, women's presence in a *commercial* culture of leisure, based on the purchase of pleasures, could in itself imply sexual willingness. Companionship of the kind in which Boweryites reveled could easily turn into sex, either granted by women or exacted from them by men. When women accepted men's largesse, they could conjure up the kind of transactions that went on in both prostitution and in courtship. When a young Irish coal heaver, for example, raped the young woman he was accompanying home from a ball, he took no more than what he may have considered his due. The farther afield a woman ventured with a man into the territory of amusements, the more obliged she might become. Caroline Wood, who charged a suitor with rape in 1858, seemed to have drifted—perhaps knowingly, perhaps unwittingly —into widening circles of erotic commitment. She had met the young man at a "place of amusement" and agreed to a rendezvous late one afternoon. As the pleasures he provided expanded from ice cream to an omnibus ride up Broadway to a boat trip to Newark to an excursion to the Jersey countryside, so did his sense of his sexual rights. By the time they left Newark he had raped her, and by the time they returned to New York he was introducing her as his wife. From the defense of another rape victim, we can read backwards this chain of associations, of amusements provided and obligations incurred. Of her relation to her assailant, she protested to the court, "I never went with him to any place of public amusement. He never made me presents of the value of anything."[64]

While urban youth culture provided women with a great deal of independence in courtship, it also furthered the breakdown of traditional courtship codes. Places like the Bowery were largely removed from the kinds of pressures that even city neighborhoods could bring to bear on young men. In the milieu of commercial leisure, men and women formed their liaisons out of a shifting constituency of available partners rather than from personal relationships embedded in family and community networks. As a consequence, the line between courtship and casual seduction became increasingly blurred. As working-class youth culture gave a wider scope for the exchange of pleasure and obligations between the sexes, men also gained a greater purchase over their female companions. Young men had long taken the sexual favors they believed women owed them; if necessary, they did so by force. The difference in a commercial milieu lay in what men viewed as a courtship. In household and neighborhood settings, women built up a sense of sexual obligation over a period of time and in a series of encounters. But when they met their partners in the hurly-burly of the dance halls and pleasure gardens, they could find themselves sexually accountable for just one night's round of beers and oysters.

Thus among the men of New York's working-class youth culture, older kinds of sexual exploitation and misogynistic abuse survived, albeit in new forms. While class-conscious notions of respect and protectiveness toward workingwomen could mitigate their harshest behavior, men continued to prey upon women outside the dance halls. Forced sex in courting became, if anything, more omnipresent as courting itself became more attenuated. Women alone on the streets continued to be targets for seduction and rape. The Boweryites may have despised gentlemen rakes, but the working class itself had plenty of seducers and rapists within its own ranks.

Still, while the Bowery marginalized rather than eradicated male predation, it also encouraged greater reciprocity, sexual and social, between young men and women. As was the case elsewhere in New York life, men took more than they gave. But a commercial culture that depended on the exchange of money for amusement and pleasure at least had this effect: Its practices of heterosexual exchange implied a more contingent notion of men's rights over women. Commercial culture promoted the assumption that women owed sexual favors in return for men's generosity. From women's perspective, this was hardly egalitarian, but it was an improvement on the view that women were legitimate targets for sexual coercion simply by virtue of their sex. Young women themselves probably played an active part in promoting this sexual code. Although the evidence reveals little on this point, we can speculate that youth culture allowed *female* peer groups to exert some pressure on young men by delineating their own ideas of when it was acceptable for girls to acquiesce to male demands. If indeed this was the case, such collectivities might have replaced neighborhood sanctions on courting with their own ways of protecting young women from sexual abuse and illegitimate pregnancy.[65]

Certainly, the Bowery and all it embodied of young working people's lives was a source of some kind of collective consciousness for workingwomen. The pride of the Bowery Gal was not just the reflected glow of her escort. In Bowery styles of dress and decorum, the workingwoman elaborated a presence distinct from that of the Victorian lady. It was a presence, moreover, of considerable imaginative and symbolic power. To be sure, it gave women very little of a foothold in formal institutions of working-class life—trade unions, benefit societies, party politics—but this is no surprise; women in public were, after all, still only a scant step removed from prostitution. We shall see, however, that the new sense of women as part of a working-class public presence would bring about important, if tentative, changes in trade union organizing. Most important, the possibilities of the Bowery Gal would continue, throughout the rest of the nineteenth century, to pose an alternative mode of feminine self-realization to the bourgeois ideal of true womanhood.

Life in the antebellum city entailed great hardships for most laboring people; women's difficulties, however, were especially severe. Economic dependency on men became a shaky proposition in all but the more fortunate families. Immigration and the search for work outside New York separated some men from their families and provided escape routes for others. Yet while the economic basis of the patriarchal family deteriorated, the ideology of female dependency retained force in household patterns of authority. Married men assumed their rights to deference and domestic services and used violence to enforce them. Single men continued to look on young women as fair game for sexual exploitation on the streets and in the dance halls and eating places of a nascent leisure culture. The *absence* of patriarchal protections could weigh painfully on young women, vulnerable to illegitimate pregnancy, male desertion and the ensuing problems of child support.

At the same time, the city opened up new resources. The change was most marked in the lives of young women. Urban migration and wage earning brought them a respite, however momentary, from familial regulation and purchased some measure of sexual and social independence, however paltry. As soon as women married, of course, these benefits disappeared. But even within the male-dominated structures of tenement life, married women found in the urban neighborhoods a female milieu that offered help in their dealings with men.

In contrast to the history of genteel women, no explicit feminist politics emerged from the changed circumstances of working-class women. Nor did they create a political rhetoric of female experience analogous to the masculine rhetoric of the trade unions and working-class political movements. As formal expression, the female politics of sociability remained submerged within the demands and grievances of the working-class community, a political community largely delimited by patriarchal expectations. Still, these urban workingwomen, if an inchoate presence in organizational life, pressed their claims. In doing so, they helped to change laboring men's understanding of class from a masculine entity to a heterosexual one and thus, we will see, they contributed to changes in working-class political discourse.

Part Three

Wage Work

Chapter 6 Harrowing Truths: Manufacturing Work

Laboring women found new resources within the great transformations in New York life between 1820 and 1860. But they also confronted harsh difficulties as industrial wageworkers. Women, social commentators commonly acknowledged, were the lowliest antebellum workers, subject to the worst wages and most brutal labor practices. "The great disproportion which exists between the prices of labour of men and women," conceded a charity as early as 1817, "is a matter of serious regret." Labor reformer Matthew Carey in 1830 termed women's working conditions "harrowing truths."[1] Subsequent observers concurred that of all those pulled into the wage relations of metropolitan industry, women workers were the most precariously situated.

Sex segregation in the labor force was the source of their problems. Women were a distinct group of workers, concentrated in a few "female" employments. By 1860, three or four dozen industries employed more than 90 percent of the city's workingwomen; conversely, within most of these industries, most workers were female.[2] Crowded into this segregated part of the manufacturing system, women suffered from a competition for work even keener than that which men endured in New York's overstocked labor market. The result was low wages (often below subsistence), frequent bouts of unemployment and severe overwork when employed.

The "outside system," precursor to New York's sweatshops and notorious for its starvation wages and appalling working conditions, grew directly from the sex-divided labor market and further institutionalized it.

The outworker's wage *"does not decently support life,"* the ladies of the
SRPW charged with uncharacteristic vehemence in 1859.[3] Outwork consisted of piece-rate tasks performed, mostly by hand, outside factories or
central workplaces, usually in the worker's own lodgings—lodgings that
were usually tiny and badly lit and ventilated. Outwork was synonymous
with women's work. Although men sometimes worked in the outside system, they did so only in those trades that employed women. The outside
system originated in garment and shoe manufacturing, but by the 1850s
employers in other women's industries had also adopted it, and even employers of women *inside* factories used patterns imported from the outside
system to structure work. By dispersing female workers among thousands
of individual workplaces, outside employers made it virtually impossible for
women to combat the low wages and exploitative conditions which set the
terms of their employment.[4]

Yet sex segregation and its associated forms of exploitation were consequences, not causes, of women's inferior position in the labor market.[5] Sex
segregation grew out of a deeper political economy of gender, founded in
the sexual division of labor in the household. It resulted from the incorporation of patterns of female subordination within the family into those of
capitalist exploitation. The development of the outwork system demon-
strates with particular clarity how a gender system tied to the household
economy helped to divide, or segment, the work force into a sexual hierarchy that bestowed privileges upon men. Outside work mediated the requirements of the two great employers of women's labor—families and
manufacturers. For married women and mothers, tied to the demands of
children and households, it provided a means of earning a living without
leaving the tenements, a viable way of working a double shift as housewife/
mother and wageworker. For single women, too, the outside system
offered a readily accessible way to earn a living, albeit a meager one. More
generally, the outside system, by strengthening women's ties to household
labor, minimized the cultural disruptions caused by women's wage earning
and at the same time shored up crumbling family economies with female
contributions.

Outwork and the Clothing Trade

Historians and economists have usually viewed outwork as a transition, a
precursor to the prototypical industrial form of the factory.[6] The dispersed
work force and handicraft technology intrinsic to outwork made the system

too cumbersome to allow capital accumulation, so the argument goes; as soon as technological innovation occurred and it became possible to centralize the labor force, such wasteful and irrational forms of production disappeared. By this logic outwork was marginal to "real" industrialization, and women outworkers comprised only an auxiliary to the industrial proletariat.

But if outwork was only a precursor to the factory system in some settings, it was crucial to the industrializing process in many great cities. In New York, the outside system flourished through the nineteenth century and into the twentieth with the infamous sweatshops whose horrors Jacob Riis, among others, publicized. A similar process occurred in London, Paris and other metropolitan manufacturing centers in Europe.[7] While employers in some places utilized outwork only until they overcame cultural resistance to women working outside the home, New York employers capitalized upon and strengthened that resistance.

In New York, material conditions inhibited the rise of factories. By 1815, ground rents were already high, and they spiraled throughout the next decades. There was, moreover, no readily available source of waterpower.[8] But given the enormous supply of cheap labor in the city, another course of development was possible. Rather than superseding the artisan system with large, highly mechanized factories, employers transformed it from within, avoiding high overhead costs through the proliferation of smallscale, labor-intensive enterprises. This happened in many trades, but the clothing trade was especially amenable.

Before 1812, there had been virtually no ready-made clothing in America. Except for the poor, who bought their clothes secondhand, Americans had their garments made by artisans—tailors and seamstresses—and by wives, daughters and female servants. There was a rough division of labor between the household and the artisan shop. Women at home did the plain sewing; artisans, the garments that required more skill and fitting.[9] When tailors were involved rather than tailoresses (seamstresses) and dressmakers, there was a stricter division of labor. Tailors would not touch most women's work—shirts, dresses, children's clothes and mending. They worked on those men's garments that were closely fitted, like breeches and vests, or cumbersome to sew, like coats and capes.[10] The division of labor between women and men would have important ramifications in the nineteenth century, since industrialization occurred first in the making of men's clothes—which tailors had traditionally monopolized—thus introducing female wageworkers as competition. The only ready-made clothing in the eighteenth century was for sailors and soldiers. "Slop work" was the tailors' term for these cheap garments made with little care and no fitting. The small but steady trade in slops provided journeymen tailors work in the winter, the slack season for custom orders, while masters put out some of the plainer slop work—shirts and pantaloons—to women they employed the year round.[11]

Cheap labor, not new technology, transformed the slop trade into a booming industry. By 1820, the old putting-out system was in serious decline; after the War of 1812, British manufactured goods "dumped" at low prices had driven many American handicrafts off the New York market. Because of the advent of the New England textile mills as well as the continuing progress of the British factories, hand spinning, the staple of given-out work, all but disappeared after 1815; women like one "Widow Hammel," who applied to a charity in 1817 for funds to repair her spinning wheel, would have had a hard time finding work.[12] The New England mills provided their owners with the means to utilize female labor beyond the given-out system, but in Manhattan, employers had no such resources at hand. Recall that even the stern gentlemen of the Society for the Prevention of Pauperism had allowed in 1821 that there was "a defect of profitable employment" for poor women.

The outside system opened up this labor market for profitable employment. After the War of 1812, conditions for other manufacturing besides textiles were beneficial. Because of the thriving port, the city was already a major center of capital, its prosperous merchants on the prowl for new investments. The advent of regular trans-Atlantic and coastal shipping lines put New York producers in a favored position over competitors elsewhere to buy raw materials and sell finished goods, and the federal Tariff of 1816 gave domestic industry much-needed protection from British goods. The postwar wave of immigration brought to the city an army of poor workers.

Master and merchant tailors were the first in these advantageous circumstances to hire large numbers of women. The outside system allowed them to cut costs to the bone. There were minimal expenses for overhead, and they could easily hold down wages by taking on and letting go workers according to their needs of the moment. By 1860, the federal census reported 25,000 women working in manufacturing—one-quarter of the entire labor force—and two-thirds of them worked in the clothing trades.[13] The garment trades began to prosper in the 1820s, as city merchants captured the lucrative Southern trade in slave clothing. With an assured market for slops, employers began to take on more women to sew the work that journeymen preferred to do only in the slow season. By the 1830s, some shops employed as many as 500 women, and coarse Negro cottons, as they were called, were regular cargo on southern-bound packets. From slave clothing, the trade diversified into a luxury trade in fine linen shirts and vests for Southern planters, and firms also began to keep high-quality ready-mades in stock for local customers, travelers and gentlemen visiting the city on business.

When the Erie Canal connected the city with Midwestern and upstate New York customers, a Western trade developed in dungarees, flannel drawers, and hickory and flashy figured shirts; in 1849, the gold rush gave the impetus for a California trade in overalls and calico shirts for the thousands of miners/adventurers who had no women to outfit them.[14] By 1860, two-thirds of the garments made in New York went south and the rest were shipped to a nationwide market. "Scarcely a single individual thinks of having his shirts made at home," averred an observer of fashion.[15] He neglected the farm families who continued to make their own clothes well into the late 1800s, but he was right about city people and townsfolk, whose sense of style in men's clothes was already attuned to New York ready-mades by the 1840s.

The clothing trade was one New York business that offered working-men and immigrants a path from waged employment to proprietorship. The market was usually dependable and the profit margin often high.[16] Most important, a man needed very little money to set up shop. Even the largest employers combined work on the premises with outwork, thus holding down their expenses in high downtown rents. By 1860, the re-nowned Brooks Brothers, for instance, employed 70 workers inside and 2,000 to 3,000 on the outside. The smallest proprietors, tailors themselves, did not keep shop at all but contracted out goods from the large shops, cut them at home and put them out, thus passing along all the costs of space, light, fuel, needles and thread to their home workers.[17]

If the trade offered the journeyman an entrée to entrepreneurship, how-ever, it did not necessarily bring him affluence. By midcentury, the eco-nomic pressures on employers were heavy. The trade operated on a dense network of credit, and the search to maximize credit was the driving force behind operations at every level. Profits could be high, but they seldom appeared in ready cash. At its most complex, the trade involved a jobber or merchant, a master tailor, his inside workers, one or even two levels of subcontractors, and their outworkers. Since profits at every level came from the difference between the fixed payment received and costs paid out for labor and overhead, there was heavy pressure to cut wages. All down the line, goods were passed along on credit and payment was postponed until the finished work was returned. As a result, there was little cash on hand at any given moment at any level of the trade. This was the reason that the business depressions of 1837 and 1857 were calamitous for employers large and small. Dependence on credit was also the factor that above all others bred some of the worst labor practices in the North. "The period was hardly known for its sentimentality in business, but even the hardest-boiled contemporaries acknowledged that the sewing trade was unscrupulous."[18]

The economic pressures on small shop owners at midcentury played into a plethora of complaints about rate cutting, underpayment and withholding wages. "The worst features," maintained New York *Tribune* editor Horace Greeley of employment in the trade, "are its hopelessness and its constant tendency from bad to worse."[19] Women living with a man's support were not so adversely affected, but single women and their dependents could suffer terribly. Women's charities and urban writers reacted to this situation by absorbing the figure of the seamstress into the traditional category of the "worthy" poor. Like other philanthropic constructions, the sentimental seamstress, solitary, pallid and timid, embodied bourgeois aspirations and prejudices, but there can be no doubt she also represented, however distortedly, real situations.[20] Two stories make the point, both from 1855, a depression year. "When flour was so high last winter as to place it beyond the reach of the provident poor," the secretary of the Society for the Relief of Poor Widows related, "One of the managers visited a respectable Widow, who had maintained herself and her three little girls by sewing." The eldest had just died from starvation, which the ladies delicately termed "disease aggravated by improper food," and the second child was also sick with the same malady. When the visitor inquired about the family's needs, the woman asked for flour: " 'But you have thought before that meal would answer,' said the Manager, 'and you know we hardly think it right to give flour at its present price.' 'Yes,' said the woman, bursting into tears, 'we have lived on meal this winter, but the Doctor says it killed Mary and now Katy is getting in the same way, and I cannot let her die, too.' " The response of a second mother in the same situation—one of her eight children sick with a chest complaint—was less suited to the conventions of Victorian pathos. "Perhaps it will please the Lord to take him," she replied matter-of-factly to the manager's solicitude: "If it would please the Lord to take them all, I should be glad, then I'd know they were well off; but how I shall support them all another year in this world I am sure I can't tell."[21] These were extreme cases, but they embodied the hardships not of isolated individuals but of a class of single mothers.

The outworkers' most pressing problem was underpayment. Like employment in many metropolitan trades, seasonal work peaked in October and April, when shops rushed out orders for winter and summer stock. The pattern was sufficiently predictable for women to meet the slack seasons with some forethought, by turning to other kinds of work. But there were also fluctuations week to week that were impossible to foresee; to be out of work one or two days every week was common for outside workers. There was no guarantee that when a seamstress returned her sewing to the shop she would get more, and if she did, it was not necessarily a full week's work. This meant that self-supporting women had to shift about from one shop to another for employment, a feature of the trade that workingwomen protested bitterly. For women on their own, labor time was precious, and they keenly felt the wasted hours spent seeking work, waiting for work and returning work.[22]

"Small as are the earnings of these seamstresses, they constantly tend to diminish," Horace Greeley observed. Clothing manufacturers, especially the small employers, were notorious for vicious rate cutting.[23] Because there were so many women competing for work, there was little that needlewomen could do about it. "I have heard it said, and even by benevolent men, in justification of this hideous state of things, that these women do not complain," wrote a nettled Matthew Carey in 1830. "True. It would answer no purpose. If the price of shirts were brought down to six cents (as it sometimes is . . .), they would accept it, and thankfully too. Their numbers and their wants are so great, and the competition so urgent, that they are wholly at the mercy of their employers."[24] Between 1820 and 1860, observers generally estimated wages at between 75 cents and $1.50 a week, with an increase in the 1850s at the upper end of the scale to $3.50. (See Table 2, p. 226.) In 1853, when a workingman with a family of four needed to earn $600 a year, the *Tribune* contended that a needlewoman with full employment—an uncommon enough situation—could at best earn $91.[25] These were subsistence wages for a young woman on her own or for a woman living with an employed man, but not for a single mother—and many New York workingwomen were indeed supporting households without any male assistance. (See Table 3, p. 227.) In 1855, 355 of 599 wage-earning women in two New York census districts were doing so.

Was it the unskilled nature of the work rather than the sex of the workers which accounted for the seamstresses' low wages? It is difficult to answer, since women have often been paid as "unskilled" workers by virtue of the fact of their sex. In New York, for instance, vest making was skilled work that required training and expertise, yet female vest makers' wages were far lower than those of tailors.[26] Even if we define seamstressing as "unskilled" work, however, we can still see a significant differential between the seamstresses' earnings and those of unskilled male day laborers. Throughout the period, day laborers managed to enforce a customary wage of around a dollar a day—if necessary, through informally organized "turnouts," or strikes—while outworkers earned anywhere from a shilling to 25 cents per day (the highest figures cited put the needlewomen's wages at 50 cents per day).[27]

The most unscrupulous practice of employers in the light of the antebellum moral code, and the one which outside workers protested most vehemently, was that of withholding wages. It was not uncommon for employers, especially small proprietors and subcontractors, to postpone paying a woman when she returned her work, to require alterations before they paid her, to refuse to pay her at all, or to hold back the deposits that they required for taking out work. A visitor to New York described one of these transactions between a seamstress and an employer in 1852: "He takes the bundle, unrolls it, turns up his nose, as if he had smelt a dead rat, and remarks, in the crossest manner possible, 'You have ruined the job,' makes the whole lot up together, and contempuously throws it under the counter. . . . She then asks for her money back, but only receives a threat in return, with a low, muttering grumble, that 'you have damaged us already eight or ten dollars, and we will retain your dollar, as it is all we shall ever get for our goods, which you have spoilt!' "[28]

In 1855, the outworker Margaret Byrnes took her grievances to the mayor's court when she encountered this treatment. She had taken finished shirts back three times to Davis & Company, suppliers to the Western and Southern trades; on each occasion the proprietors demanded more altera-tions, refused to pay for the shirts they did accept, held back her deposit, and finally tried to coerce her into paying them for the sewing they re-jected. Soon after Byrnes went to court, Mary Gilroy of Five Points joined the fray with her own charges against the Davises, who had also refused to settle with her and had fleeced her out of a deposit. Clearly not a woman to take foul play sitting down, Gilroy had retaliated by taking out a dozen Davis shirts to hold for ransom. While the trial shows that the nonpayment of women's wages was an open scandal, neither woman secured much satisfaction despite all the favorable publicity as well as testimony from the Davises themselves that could hardly have been more damning. Margaret Byrnes won back her deposit but not her wages, and Mary Gilroy, as far as the record shows, may have taken her hostage shirts to the grave.[29]

Proprietors like the Davises provided the material from which social investigators and journalists sympathetic to the seamstresses fashioned the figure of the villainous employer, a stock figure in fictional renditions of the outside system and a foil to the timid, pitiable seamstress of the sentimental imagination. "There sat the proprietor in his shirt-sleeves, a vulgar-looking creature, smoking a cigar." "He can browbeat, and haggel with, and impose upon a poor, weak, sickly, industrious work-girl to more purpose, and more to his own advantage than any body else."[30] These images of iniquity so dominate the historical evidence that it is difficult to look at the situation analytically: Why should these employers have been so particularly abusive and dishonest? From the small employer's point of view, what seemed villainy to others was a way to cope with the cutthroat economics in which he operated. "The clothing makers for the southern trade are generally the target of popular hostility on account of low wages, and there can be no doubt that many of them are gripers," the Tribune acknowledged. The paper was the self-proclaimed champion of the needlewomen, but its editor,

Horace Greeley, was never a man to get his mind around the imperatives of capitalism, and here his paper pointed out simple economic fact: "If they were all the purest philanthropists, they could not raise the wages of their seamstresses to anything like a living price. . . . They can only live by their business so long as they can get garments made here low enough to enable them to pay cost, risk and charges and undersell. . . . If they were compelled to pay living wages for their work, they must stop it altogether."[31] Thus when proprietors put off paying a workingwoman as the Davises did, they were not always lying when they claimed they had no cash on hand. Nor was the issue of flawed work necessarily a sham. For all the extraordinary advantages the outside system gave employers, it was not the most techni- cally efficient and rational organization of work, and one of its drawbacks was nonstandardized work—that is, garments sewn too differently from each other to be sold for a unit price.[32]

In the 1850s, employers hard pressed by growing competition introduced the sewing machine, which standardized the stitch, and began to put out detail work instead of whole garments. Home workers sewed pieces of the garment—cuffs, buttonholes, sleeves—which were then assembled in inside shops. In the shops, employers could maximize their supervision of the assemblage, the step in production at which the mark of individual workers could be most conspicuous.[33] The new methods of production increased the pressure on small employers, who did not have the resources to shift to such an organization but still had to offer standardized merchandise in order to compete. Consequently, when these men niggled over alterations, they could be genuinely concerned with the quality of their stock as well as covertly engaged in driving down the wage.

For seamstresses, wage cutting and underemployment bred overwork. When piece rates fell, they could only do more work for the income they needed.[34] Since work was not always available, they had to work as much as they could when they did find employment. In the 1830s, Matthew Carey found that seamstresses without male support worked from sunrise to nine or ten at night; in the 1850s, the sewing machine drove piece rates so low that fifteen- to eighteen-hour workdays were not uncommon. "Those who make at the lowest prices appear to have no other mission on earth but to sew up bleached muslin into shirts," maintained Virginia Penny. "In some instances we have been informed, that where there are two or three or more women or girls engaged in this enterprise of making shirts . . . they abso- lutely divide the night season into watches."[35]

To comprehend fully the hardships of outside workers, we must under- stand the nature of the labor itself. Hand sewing strained the eyes and cramped the back and neck so much that a practiced observer like Virginia Penny could recognize a seamstress on the street by her peculiar stooped carriage: "the neck suddenly bending forward, and the arms being, even in walking, considerably bent forward, or folded more or less upward from the elbows."[36] The curvature came from bending over and sewing in badly lit rooms: Most tenement lodgings were dark in the daytime, and seamstresses had to economize in their use of candles. The tiny backstitch they used was painstakingly slow; it took about twelve hours to make one shirt. There was, moreover, a multitude of chances to make mistakes. A shirt bosom could be too full, the sleeves too short and the wristbands too long, and the man who examined the garments—the employer or his "piece master," as the foreman of outside workers was called in large shops— might return the work for alterations on any of these counts. Even a clearheaded woman could easily botch the piecing, but a tired one who had been working for hours was much more likely to make a mistake that would cost hours to repair—sewing in a sleeve backwards or embroidering a buttonhole out of line.[37]

The sewing machine, as it was used in the context of nineteenth-century capitalism, did little to lighten the labor. Machine sewing was as taxing as hand sewing; it only shifted the strain from the arms to the lower torso. Women working the machines suffered chronic pain in their hips, nervous disorders from the jarring of the mechanism and eyestrain from following the long lines of stitching.[38]

In their appeals for help, seamstresses and their supporters stressed the high rate of mortality and disease associated with their trade, what we could call the biological experience of class. A doctor in 1860 guessed that a thousand women a year died of causes related to sewing in the outside system. Malnutrition, fatigue, cold and bad ventilation in the tenements bred pneumonia and consumption, the major killers of nineteenth-century cities. A newspaper investigator in 1853 heard that the hardest-working women could squeeze as much as double the average earnings out of the piece rates, but the extra money usually went to medicines. "Will the men of New-York allow the unfortunate Shirt Sewers to stitch their own shrouds?" a seamstresses' broadside rhetorically inquired.[39]

Who were the outworkers? The only systematic information comes from the New York state census for 1855, the first to record women's employments. A sample from two census districts, both neighborhoods of the laboring poor, gives us some bare facts about the "outside" seamstresses, who comprised 242 of the 599 workingwomen sampled.[40] The statistical profile is more varied than the sentimental picture of the solitary widowed seamstresses. (See Table 4, p. 227.) Many outworkers were lodgers living on their own—most likely as young, unmarried women. Daughters in the households of workingmen were also represented in significant numbers—about three in ten workers.

The outworkers, it seems, were a heterogeneous and mobile group. Workers moved in and out of the system in accordance with their situations —as self-supporting workingwomen, as daughters, as breadwinning wives and widows. In terms of historians' paradigms of female industrial forces, there are several models relevant here. The largest group of women was similar to the girls of the Lowell, Massachusetts, textile mills (who are often taken as the prototypical American case): daughters looking to improve their fortunes, living away from their families. Daughters living within male-headed family economies, the kind of households that some scholars believe to have predominated in the nineteenth-century working class, made up the next largest group. Finally, women from all-female households and women supporting children or kin each comprised about one-tenth of the outside workers.

These statistics tell nothing about the evolution of the outside system, since by 1855 it was already well in place. My guess is that in the first two decades of the century, when the sex ratio was more balanced in New York and the pool of single women smaller, the outwork system primarily employed married women. By midcentury, however, the census evidence shows that the system had come to capitalize upon a variety of female situations. The paucity of factory and workshop employments (aggravated by sexual segmentation) and the widespread distaste for domestic service pushed single women as well as housebound married women into outside work. As immigrants poured into New York, the outside system, a mesh of work reaching out through the tenements, easily pulled in new arrivals.

The Familial Relations of Outwork

Since the late eighteenth century, manufacturing entrepreneurs had integrated patterns of family industry into commodity production. The expansion of outwork in the countryside depended on the labor of wives and (especially) daughters; indeed, the assumption that families were the foundation for manufacturing labor was so widespread that when Samuel Slater set up America's first textile mill in Rhode Island in the 1790s, he routinely went about recruiting entire families to work there. The adaptation of household forms to manufacturing is hardly surprising in a society where employers hired their workers directly off family farms.[41] But in the city, too, entrepreneurs absorbed household labor into wage labor; here, in contrast to New England, the popularity of the family form as a way to organize manufacturing was not necessarily an extension of the fact that workers were already living in families. With a pool of single women at their disposal, New York employers might have organized work in other ways—in small all-female shops like those of male craftworkers, for instance, where they could more effectively enforce standards of production; for that matter, they might have set women to work alongside men in workshops. That they instead expanded the outside system of individual households indicates the power of family patterns as a model for women's proper role in industrial development.

For women, this adaptation had ambiguous consequences. On the one hand, household forms allowed them to turn cooperative family traditions, based in mutual need and common labor, to the business of surviving in the cutthroat labor market. Children, cousins and sisters helped women earn a living wage. On the other, female subordination within households allowed employers (and sometimes male heads of working groups) to reproduce especially severe forms of exploitation, underwritten by familial custom, within metropolitan industry. The outside system bolstered up older forms of patriarchal supervision and curtailed the ways in which single women could turn manufacturing work to the uses of independence. For good and ill, the household organization of work reinforced women's associations with family labor and thus inscribed a particular construct of gender relations into the manufacturing system.

By 1860, employers of women in other New York industries besides clothing had also turned to outwork. The 1840s saw the emergence of a new middle-class market for a panoply of consumer goods: embellishments and adornments to grace the Victorian home and person. Artificial-flower making, fringe and tassel making, embroidery, mantua making, fancy bookbinding and parasol making flourished, along with all manner of other fancy stitched, burnished and gilded manufactures. Light and easily transported, most of these goods could be put out. Requiring deftness and delicacy in their assemblage, they were considered suitable for female hands. Shoe binding, the female employment that had been second to sewing at the turn of the century, also continued to provide work for women. In all these industries, the organization of outside work was similar to that of the clothing trade.

The outside system promoted female dependence on the family, both because of the low wages outworkers earned and the form their labor took. Family work could be crucial in combating the effects of wage cutting. Women with children assigned home work to their children just as they did domestic chores. In box making, children helped with the easier parts of cutting and gluing; in matchstick making, the lowliest of put-out employments, young children dipped the matchheads while mothers and older siblings cut out the sticks. In families of seamstresses, children as young as five could do the simple task of pulling bastings, and at ten years or so, daughters were nimble-fingered enough to sew straight seams and attach buttons. Most important, children who knew their way about the streets could save their mothers valuable time by carrying work back and forth from the shop.[42] Female kin and younger siblings provided help to single women and daughters.

In the households of some immigrant craftworkers—tailors, shoemakers, fur workers—family industry existed as the "family shop." In their work relations, these operations resembled the cooperative groups of farms and eighteenth-century craft shops. The men did the most skilled work, nego-tiated with employers and supervised the different operations; women and children worked at the preparatory and subsidiary tasks.[43] In the 1855 census of one poor neighborhood in the Fourth Ward near the waterfront, 16 percent of seamstresses were living with male kin who worked in the tailoring trade; such households were probably family shops.[44] By the 1850s, piece rates were so low that a journeyman tailor had difficulty making a living without a family to help him: "A tailor is nothing without a wife, and very often a child," went a maxim of German craftsmen.[45]

The family shop was a unit laboring for its own subsistence, dependent on the help of all. Men and women, however, occupied different positions within this cooperative group, just as they did in the family, with men at the top and children at the bottom. The hierarchical structure may not have been especially important when families labored on farms or in craft shops, each person working for the common good and sharing more or less equally in the earnings. But hierarchy did become significant when each individual earned wages, for as wage differentials developed between men, women and children, it became profitable for adults, especially men, to replicate familial arrangements among non-kin as well as kin. In other words, in the nineteenth century, traditions of family labor became a means of exploiting women and children as well as a way for working people to support themselves cooperatively.[46]

Forms of outside work that replicated the family hierarchy thus devel-oped among unrelated men and women. Women on their own were well situated to work in these groups. Women and girls began to work in the 1850s for unmarried journeymen in the same capacities as wives and daugh-ters who assisted tailors in their own homes. The journeymen mediated between piece masters and the home shop and took the largest portion of earnings. Poor as these men were, they were still employers and women were their workers. They paid the women fixed wages and took the small profits for themselves.[47] Women also put themselves at the top of this type of arrangement in the "learning" system. Learning was a debased form of apprenticeship that corresponded to the relation of parents and children in family labor. In exchange for the crudest training, girls worked for tailors, seamstresses, dressmakers and milliners either for their keep or for a few pennies a day. Journeymen also used this system: Adults made their profit by taking out work at regular piece rates and paying learning girls either lower rates or nothing at all to make it up. Learning proliferated in the 1850s along with the family shop and its variants as a way for individuals to combat the effects of the sewing machine. Like all child laborers, learners were the humblest of the trade, but since their employers themselves were so poor, the learners' condition was especially lowly. In 1853 a *Herald* reporter found a learners' garret near the waterfront where four teenage girls worked for an Irish seamstress every day except Sunday in exchange for their board; they paid for rent, clothes and Sunday's food by prostituting themselves to sailors.[48]

All forms of outside work merged with "sweating," whereby a subcontractor exacted his profits from the "sweat," or highly exploited labor, of his outworkers. Sweating spread through the poor districts in the 1850s. It combined all varieties of family labor. There were many levels of sweaters: journeymen tailors, piece masters themselves (who contracted work from their employers), garret masters and mistresses. The journeymen who took out work for their wives were engaged in a kind of sweating, although in the sweating system proper, the contractor invested no labor of his own.[49] The use of the sewing machine, made practicable in 1850 with Isaac Singer's invention of the foot treadle, encouraged the spread of sweated labor. Very few women workers (and few tailors, too) could afford their own machines, but neither could they afford to do without them.[50] Employers could impose the sewing machine relatively easily upon a system in which small-scale production predominated and workers were used to absorbing overhead costs. A German-born New York tailor told the story well. "The bosses said: 'We want you to use the sewing-machine, you have to buy one,'" he recalled. "Many of the tailors had a few dollars in the bank, and they took the money and bought machines. Many others had no money . . . so they brought their stitching . . . to the other tailors who had sewing machines, and paid them a few cents for the stitching. Later, when the money was given out for the work, we found out that we could earn no more than we could without a machine."[51] Since seamstresses were less able to save money than tailors, few could purchase their own machines, and the shift to machine work made it more necessary for them to work for some kind of sweater.

There is no evidence about how laboring people felt about the comparative merits of outwork and other kinds of employments—whether, for instance, parents preferred their daughters to work in sweatshops rather than in factories, because close family or family-like supervision made it more difficult for girls to stray. In the New England countryside, the outwork system allowed farmers to patch up disintegrating family economies with women's earnings and at the same time to keep their daughters at home.[52] Similar dynamics may have been at work in the city, where outside work may have helped to ensure the cooperation of children—especially daughters—in family wage economies. Married women, of course, were already tied to families; the incorporation of domestic patterns into the manufacturing system greatly weakened their position in the labor market, but it was consonant with the actualities of their everyday lives. For single women, especially those on their own, the situation was different. Here a comparison with Lowell is helpful. Both the Lowell system and the New York outside system imposed household forms on women living away from their families. When the Boston Manufacturing Company set up shop at Lowell in 1814, the employers created a system of boardinghouses alongside their factories, a system that required their young female employees to live under strict supervision.[53] Although the New York outside system was not consciously crafted by one group of men, it had similar effects. In a city where people of all classes feared the adverse effects of city pleasures and wage earning on young women, outwork quieted anxieties about female independence by reintegrating young women into household dependencies. For single women, outside work reinforced economic pressures toward dependency at just the historical moment when their ties to family life were weakening.

The submersion of women wageworkers in private households did a great deal to make a large part of the female work force invisible. Employers capitalized upon a construction of women as "outside" the economy, lacking acumen about the world outside their doors. "Our employers set up the most frivolous pretexts for reducing our wages," a former seamstress remembered. "Some of them were so transparently false that I wondered how any one could have the impudence to present them." She concluded that they could because they "considered a sewing-woman as either too dull to detect the fallacy, or too timid to expose and resent it."[54] This was a psychology of heterosexuality as well as one of class; likewise, when a piece master used derision in order to drive down a woman's wage.[55] Employers were writing a language of women's sphere—working-class version—into industrial capitalism.

Inside Work

After 1850, a small but growing number of factories began to employ women. In the sewing trades, the introduction of the sewing machine encouraged employers to centralize their work in "inside" shops, and in other consumer manufactures, employers installed light machinery that women could tend. These developments were significant enough that by 1860, the Children's Aid Society could hail the expansion of factory work for women as one of the most hopeful signs of progress in the city.[56]

It was this sector of employment that must have provided the readiest recruits to working-class youth culture. Inside workers were overwhelmingly young and single. The factory "girls" were just that, late adolescents and young women sixteen to twenty-five years.[57] The wages for inside work were much better than payments for outside work, high enough to finance fine clothes and leisure pursuits. This was partly because piece rates were higher on the inside (the pool of available workers was probably smaller than it was in the outside system), partly because employment was steadier: Factory hands did not have to piece together a full week's work from different shops. (See Table 5, p. 228.) Although inside workers could experience seasonal unemployment, their employers would have had to consider the depreciation of machines and buildings and so would have engaged in a less capricious pattern of production than those who depended on outside work.

In inside shops where there was no machinery, the camaraderie of workmates could resemble that of earlier artisans. This was the case in a straw-sewing manufactory which a reporter sketched in a newspaper article on female labor in 1853. Straw sewing, an old put-out female trade, had once been the source of straw hats and bonnets for Northeasterners. In the 1830s New York straw shops found a new market in the Southern and Western trades, producing hats for farmers across the country.[58] The sewing was as wearisome as any waged needlework, but the straw sewers the reporter met, "a lively, intelligent class of women," did not fit the popular image of the victimized sewing woman. Mingling amusement with labor, the straw sewers' working time was more like that of artisans in the early 1800s. As the journalist reported it, they talked the whole day through, touching on politics, theology and metropolitan affairs. They were great newspaper readers, and from their knowledge they argued about elections (although they could not vote) and zealously expounded their views on the prospects of American expansion. There were "rowdy girls" who might have frequented the dance halls after hours. There was also a more respectable set. The latter, devoted like so many male artisans to self-education, frequented lecture halls in their leisure time and on the particular day of the reporter's visit were discussing a physiology lecture one of them had heard. Sermons, too, furnished material for talk from the churchgoers. For the less serious, there were pastimes like those of the Bowery. The theater was a favored recreation, mimicry a worktime diversion. The reporter watched them entertain each other with imitations of local electioneering candidates, just as Bowery habitués might have done on an evening when the talk turned to Tammany politicos. At the dinner hour some talked and others danced and later, back at work, all joined in singing, directed by a leader they all had elected. A few who were taking voice lessons also rehearsed what they had learned for the benefit of the others.[59]

The straw sewers were a singular lot, whose workplace culture was sufficiently strong to sustain other, more formal associations. Eight years before the reporter's visit, they had called a meeting of all workingwomen in the city in an attempt to create a federation of women's trade unions. In 1851, they were again in the forefront of efforts to organize the sewing trades. Here was a female workplace network which, like that of the Lowell girls in the 1830s and 1840s, could foster consciously militant collective action. This is not to romanticize their work, which was as tedious and tiring as any task work.[60] Working away from home, however, did bring chances for thinking and acting that were less available to outside workers or women engaged in domestic labor, who were more entangled in ubiquitous household concerns. The sixty straw sewers pried open for each other a world in which their imaginations could roam from Canada to Cuba, from theology to physiology, and even venture into the male sanctum of electoral politics.

The Familial Relations of Workshops

The workshops, the domain of single women, would seem to have been quite separate from family households. But there, too, household relationships and patterns of domestic authority proved extraordinarily adaptable to women's employment. Inside as well as out, employers translated familiar forms of gender relations into the organization of factories and workshops.

Structurally, the line between inside shops and the outside system was blurred. Employers seem to have drawn quite specifically on their experiences and successes with outside work when they set up workrooms. Many shops that employed women, for instance, put out work not only to home workers but to inside hands as well. Evening outwork helped inside girls increase their earnings and allowed them to supplement their own energies with family labor. The practice was possible in most women's trades, since materials tended to be light, portable and workable by hand. Mantilla makers, for example, took sewing home after hours; hat makers took linings home to stitch; cap makers, who worked in an especially low-paid trade, took work home at night.[61]

On the shop floor itself, work might also replicate outwork patterns. When employers hired children, for example, they lessened the trouble children caused by placing older hands over them in a kind of parental arrangement. Children increased problems of work discipline greatly, and in New York, adult labor was so cheap there was no real incentive to employ them. Nonetheless, some shops set children up as learners, trading off the problems they caused for their nearly gratuitous labor. In the outside system, parents, masters and mistresses mediated between children and employers; employers transferred this arrangement to the factory, where the incentive for older hands to keep children in line was their own piece-rate payment.[62]

The position of the factory foreman was often analogous to that of the outworkers' piece master, and in all but the largest businesses he was the same person; in small shops, employers themselves did both jobs. The distinguishing feature of the foreman, like the piece master, was his ability to make arbitrary decisions which, when they concerned women workers, were often based on heterosexual concerns. He had considerable power. The inside hands received their materials from him, as did the outworkers; he decided who could do the best paid work; he collected finished goods and tallied up the piece-rate payments. It was often the foreman (or foreman/employer) who set the piece rates and hired and dismissed workers. The superimposition of outwork onto the workshop regime enlarged the area in which women depended on his discretion. He chose the women who could take work home. In umbrella factories, it was only the "best" girls who could take home extra work, lest they damage the silk; in a belt manufactory, only those women the foreman knew. During slow seasons, workingwomen were also especially dependent on his favors, for then there was not enough work to go around and he divvied it up according to his own preferences.[63]

There was a psychology of gender at work in the foreman's determinations. Intent on opening new fields of employment for her sex, the indefatigable Virginia Penny wondered why there were not more fore*women* and fewer fore*men* in New York. William Sanger, a physician commissioned by municipal authorities in 1855 to investigate the causes of prostitution, noted the same phenomenon, and went on to criticize the extraordinary power these men wielded over a workingwoman. "If she finds that a smile bestowed upon her employer or his clerk will aid her in the struggle for bread, she will not present herself with a scowling face; or if a kind entreaty will be the means of procuring her dinner as a favor, she will not expose herself to hunger by demanding it as a right," contended Sanger, who knew something about the trades from his female working-class patients at the hospital for venereal disease.[64]

Of course, foremen also wielded power over male workers. In the early inside shops, the structure of work gave foremen far more leeway than their descendants in the twentieth century would know. Work was not yet minutely subdivided or highly mechanized. The antebellum workrooms lacked the systematization that the assembly line and scientific management, which diminish the play of individual judgment, were later to establish. In this sense, the foreman's position resembled that of a master craftsman; he gained his power over both men and women in the give and take of production. New York printers in 1850, for instance, protested their foreman's favoritism in distributing copy: "The certain men who are noted for their amenity of manners, and plasticity of sentiments, to the Foreman, always get the fat, while others, men who think civility is preferable to servility, have to take the refuse."[65] While the printers chafed under a debased workplace authority, however, workingwomen negotiated with their foremen within extraneous but firmly rooted patterns of family and gender hierarchies. As in the household, women never supervised male workers, although they did sometimes oversee children and other women. Masculinity continued to be a more desirable attribute than femininity for those whose job it was to discipline others in work.[66]

Still, transplanted sexual hierarchies were a less effective means of labor discipline in the context of factories and workshops than they were in the outside system. Female workers found plenty of ways to circumvent the dictates of deference. Women were "more apt to get in trouble among themselves" when employed in large numbers, complained one shop owner.[67] With their own knowledge of workroom standards, precedents and procedures, factory girls must have been able to confront the foremen with their own expertise; in their very numbers, they offered each other some degree of mutual protection. They may have brought to the workroom some of the same skills in limiting male caprice which their mothers exercised in the neighborhoods or they themselves used in the dance halls. Certainly they do not seem to have been an especially "pliant and docile" labor force, to use the patronizing characterization Marx made of women workers in *Capital.* [68] Rather, the same sociability that expanded in evenings on the Bowery sprung up during the day at all sorts of odd moments to disrupt the pace of work.

Like all people when they first experienced industrial work discipline, New York workingwomen would not recognize the importance of time and steady work in the owner's balance sheet. "They do not feel the interest in their work they should," an employer complained to Virginia Penny. "If a procession is passing, they think it very hard if they cannot have ten or fifteen minutes to look out the windows . . . they forget that three minutes lost by twenty girls amounts to an hour."[69] In the now-famous terms E. P. Thompson explicated, the employer had to *use* the time of his workers;[70] to him, time was money, and when his employees idled, they were not passing their own time but wasting his. Women would "laugh and talk and 'carry on' half the time" with each other. The straw sewers' pleasures, so appealing to the journalist who spent the day with them, may not have amused an employer trying to cut costs and stabilize production. From another point of view, those women's diversions were simply the "habits of levity and idleness" which annoyed so many overseers of female labor: talking, gossiping, joking, singing, bickering.[71]

Similar problems afflicted any factory owner in the early years of industrialism, when capitalists struggled to inculcate workers with a discipline of time and regular work that went against the grain of centuries of human "nature." But the "habits of levity and idleness" must have run especially deep in young women, whose interests in men, amusements and courting could be more pressing than their worries over hungry children at home. The girls in a gunnysack manufactory were always late, their employer attested, and absented themselves so often that he had to employ more hands than he wanted so that he would "not get out of a supply" of workers on any given day. When shoe binders had earned enough on piece rates to get by for the next few days, they took a day or two to rest whether or not they were due for a holiday. Women wire workers in one factory were such habitual absentees that for a while the proprietor had to stop his machinery altogether; they wanted days off on the flimsiest of pretexts, he complained—to help their mothers, to go on a picnic, to get ready for a party.[72]

Since most inside shops employing women also employed men as either foremen or workers, the workroom became a place where, to some extent, the preoccupations of pleasure could be played out. The powers of desire could slip into the daily routine. When men and women worked together, they smuggled into the rigorous and dreary workday some of the same pleasures of bantering and flirting that blossomed after hours. A journalist charged in 1851 that the prospect of fraternizing with men was luring young women away from female trades to the printing houses—although it is likely that the high wages there were as important as the attractions of mixed company. Working with men posed all too many opportunities for "trifling" young women—a favorite disparagement used by employers of women. "When men and women are employed in the same department, they talk too much," claimed one of Penny's informants. In a candy manufactory, the "girls make so much noise, laughing and talking with men, and waste so much time" that the exasperated proprietor separated them in different rooms. Another employer's strategy was to forbid conversation; Penny deduced this rule in operation at Brooks Brothers when she heard not a word spoken in a mixed workroom in the half-hour she was there.[73] These sociable, often high-spirited workers were difficult to incorporate into the popular figure of the mournful workingwoman. Rather, they provided the material for a competing image, the factory girl, an image that embodied a recognition, however muted, of the challenges to women's customary place that inside workers might pose.

The Factory Girl

The factory girl first materialized in social commentary in the 1830s, then more noticeably in the 1850s. This urban woman bore little resemblance to the factory girls at Lowell, with their spotless reputations, nor was she anything like the stereotype of the sewing woman, the quintessential victim. The factory girl was, in her own way, an emblem of female self-assertion: impudent rather than timid, sociable rather than retiring, robust rather than thin and pale. She was close kin to Lize of the Bowery, but while Lize was a comic figure, laughably feminine in her adulation of boyfriend Mose, the factory girl signified a more disturbing kind of female independence. She appeared in urban journalism and reform literature not in connection with poverty or popular culture but with the problems of sexual immorality and prostitution.

At issue was female work culture and the inducements it gave to sexual and social adventuring. "The crowding of young girls in large factories and shops is always perilous," warned the Children's Aid Society in 1860.[74] Journeying to and from work, factory girls were liable to all sorts of temptations from strangers and workmates. The mixing with men, the after-hours amusements and the encouragement young women gave to each other's "trifling" concerns supposedly undermined female morals.

"The daily routine goes very far toward weakening that modesty and reserve which are the best protectives against the seducer," argued William Sanger. "Women contract acquaintance for the sake of having an escort on their holiday recreations, or because some other woman has done so, or as the mere gratification of an idle fancy; but all tend in the same direction, and aim to undermine principles and jeopardize character."[75]

Denunciations of the supposed low morals of factory girls had been common in British and American condemnations of the factory system since the 1830s; Engels fell right into line in 1844 with his imputations in *The Condition of the Working-Class in England* that female factory workers were too uppity and sexually wanton to make good wives.[76] But not only reformers or allies of the labor movement were worried. Workingmen, too (and possibly mothers, although we don't hear from them), saw the factory girl as threatening to the kind of working-class community they were fighting for, a community based (at least in aspiration) on family cooperation and women's submersion within it. Radical English artisans through the 1820s and 1830s denounced the destruction of female morals the textile mills supposedly effected, and the association between prostitution and factory employment was pivotal to the discussions of female labor in the National Trades' Union of the American Northeast in the early 1830s.[77]

We have one detailed account of the problem from a workingman. James Burn was an English hatter who lived and worked in New York during the Civil War. Young women in general, and factory girls in particular, were among the things about New York Burn really did not like. He would have been familiar with the already well-worn discussion of the domestic failings of English factory girls when he set about recording the perfidies of their New York counterparts. At work and in the boardinghouses where so many lived, he observed, the gathering of young women in itself wreaked havoc. Like the Lancashire factory girls, few made good wives. "They are neither fitted for wives by a due regard for the feelings and wishes of their husbands, nor a knowledge of the simple rudiments of housekeeping." Although many did marry, they remained lamentably independent. "They will not be instructed by their husbands; and as proof of their obstinacy, one of their common remarks to each other when speaking of their husbands is that they would like to see a man who would boss them." This was all reminiscent of Manchester, bad enough, but the metropolitan context made things worse. The range of "out-door temptations" was wider; indulgence all too readily available for "the passion for amusement, or the impulse for vanity." The New York incarnation of the factory girl presented her particular difficulties.[78]

Burn's comments are especially interesting because he was one of the few workingmen to register his personal opinions on female independence in the historical record. He was a crotchety fellow who looked gloomily on most of the lighter side of life, and he also had an ax to grind. By the time Burn was living in New York, the intractable masculinism of working-class consciousness had been shaken a bit; Burn, with his authoritarian patriarchalism and his baleful portrayals of women's pleasures and women's self-regard, seems a throwback to another era. Yet in his own dyspeptic way he was complaining about what concerned other people as well. For if the working class, as men imagined it, now granted women a respected place, just what that place was and who was to define it were matters of considerable disagreement. One understanding, which enjoyed strong support from skilled men like Burn, flowed from the labor movement's vision of a reconstituted working-class family, where wives and daughters would derive their social worth from their households, and where both their labor and their sexual conduct would be subject to the authority of husbands and fathers. The factory girl, who worked outside her household, carried on flirtations and liaisons away from parental scrutiny, circumvented the family wage economy and used her wages to indulge her "vanity"—this low, loose character was anathema to such hopes and ambitions.

Exactly what were the "low" morals of inside workers, the "trifling concerns" that threatened to degrade their characters? Sexual freedom seems to have been the issue: not the *fact* of premarital sexual activity, but young women's freedom from parental control over their erotic ventures. Sexuality was both a consequence of social autonomy and its metaphor. The real sin of the factory girl lay not in premarital sex, but in advertising, with her fancy clothes and assertive ways, the possibilities of a life for women outside the household just at the moment when great numbers of working people were beginning to look on the rejuvenation of that household as a primary political goal.

The factory girl was, of course, the creation of a discourse, a representation of experience refracted through political concerns. She was not, however, sheerly a contrivance of the imagination. Her "passions" and "vanity" were others' renditions of her life in a new kind of milieu of work and leisure, a life which grew out of the conjuncture of immigration patterns, youth culture and women's manufacturing work. To be sure, the factory girl represented only an evanescent moment in any one woman's experience, an identity embraced (if at all) for a few years before marriage and motherhood. Moreover, while many young women must have indeed taken advantage of the distance from their families, others were dutiful daughters who went right home from work. Still, the women who learned the benefits of "outdoor temptations" as opposed to indoor duty, meager and short-lived as was their independence, stood outside a centuries-old order of female dependency. No wonder James Burn the hatter found them deplorable.

In its first phase in New York, capitalist manufacturing turned the household into its own kind of workplace. Domestic work and family relations mediated employers' requirements and women's obligations. The household organization allowed small entrepreneurs to cut overhead costs drastically and promoted the translation of family relationships of authority and subservience into the idiom of employer and employee. In outwork, the translation was direct, since wage labor actually incorporated domestic labor. The process was more striking in factories, which were structurally removed from the household. There the importation of family or family-like arrangements served to heighten the contradiction between women's independence as wage laborers and their continuing connections, psychological and economic, to family economies and male authority.

In both the tenements and the factories, family labor helped working-women survive on wages that were often below subsistence. But the persistence of family relationships in female manufacturing labor also tied women to particular kinds of exploitation. The development of the outside system as the dominant structure of female wage labor in America's leading industrial city deeply divided the work force along gender lines. Outside work, partly sanctioned by its resemblance to household relations, limited women's means of redress through collective action. The sexual divison in the labor force made it less feasible for men and women to organize together. Structurally, socially and psychologically, family relations circumscribed women's position as individual wageworkers whether or not their work spilled over outside the family economy. By 1860, great numbers of workingwomen were laboring for their own subsistence or working as primary breadwinners for their families; they were neither temporary wage earners nor contributors to households headed by male breadwinners, and they were certainly not working for pin money. Yet these were the terms in which the manufacturing system engaged them.

In other ways, however, the logic of wage relations worked *against* women's consignment to the family. In the factories and workshops, some possibilities for a transformed female identity opened up, consonant with those that appeared in the milieu of leisure. But female workshop employment, while economically functional in a city with a surplus population of single women, also touched off cultural anxieties. The starving seamstress was an object of pity and concern and her distress was a spur to reform efforts, but she was assimilable to those efforts precisely because she was the kind of working-class woman, housebound, deferential and meek, that genteel people liked, a version of the "true" woman of the bourgeoisie. The factory girl, better off economically, was more venturesome and disturbing. In her antidomesticity, she conjured up threatening possibilities in a society ideologically moored to separate sexual spheres. However efficient work-shop production might have been, employers must have found outside work—and the set of cultural dependencies it invoked—a stabilizing force in the manufacturing system. Employers might yet find common ground with workingmen in agreeing that a wage-earning woman's place was in the home.

Chapter 7 Women and the Labor Movement

Beginning in 1825, wage-earning women in New York took to the assembly halls—and on occasion, the streets—to protest and remedy conditions in the female trades. The integration of female wage work with family life certainly curtailed the disruptions that ensued from women's entrance into manufacturing. But the conservatizing elements of women's work did not eliminate opposition or militance among female workers themselves. While bourgeois women began their struggles for an enlarged share of a dominantly masculine public life in the reform movements and churches, so workingwomen pressed their own needs upon a male labor movement.

The women who led these organizing efforts were, by all accounts, the same sort of working girls who appeared on the Bowery: daughters and independent wage earners. These women distinguished their particular problems from those of workingmen and articulated a specifically working-class experience of womanhood. Except for a few brief moments, however, their male counterparts proved unable to grasp the distinctions of class and gender the women tried to make. Instead, the men rejuvenated the ideology of the republican family within the terms of the antebellum labor movement —an ideology that subordinated women to their breadwinning patriarchs. In the process, the men greatly weakened their abilities to help both the young women activists and the entire class of female wage earners, both married and single. Cut adrift by the men, the women's cause turned into a loose fish in labor politics, an easy catch for reformers. By the 1850s, the promising beginnings of cooperation between men and women in the 1830s had disappeared, and the labor movement had almost completely excluded women. Laboring women's tentative expressions of their particular dilemmas in supporting themselves had dissolved amidst a masculine rhetoric that posed marriage as the answer to their problems.

From one perspective, the women's trade unions seem unimportant. The women who were directly involved represented only a small proportion of the female work force. They had no great successes in raising wages or improving working conditions. They did not establish any continuous tradition of women's labor organizing: After 1845, there would be no replication of their efforts on so broad a scale until the great shirtwaist makers strike of 1909.

Yet from another perspective, the very evanescence of the women's trade unions makes them interesting—especially since it would be such a long time before women again took such independent initiatives. Although the number of women militants may have been small, their activity still testifies to how volatile relations of class and gender were in the 1830s and 1840s. The trade union women asked, albeit in disconnected and tentative ways, why they were oppressed, what they could do about it and who could help them in their struggles. Their questions were fresh and direct, partly because their situation as manufacturing wageworkers was new, partly because the other interested parties—working-class men and middle-class reformers—had not yet monopolized the answers. After the Civil War, it would be different. The air would be too thick with pronouncements on women's proper place for working-class women to speak much for themselves.

For the moment, however, much about workingwomen's relations to the public life of the city, to the men of their own class and to the women of the privileged classes was in flux. The old gender system of household dependencies was disintegrating, but the new one—which would eventually bring about an uneasy reconciliation between women's wage-earning abilities and their subordination to men—had yet to emerge fully. For the time being, all the talk going round New York about republican rights and the tyranny of some over others made a few workingwomen think that they, too, might have earned a rightful place in the republic of labor.

Early Departures

Before the 1820s, men and women workers probably never considered the possibility that they might cooperate in any organized way. Skilled men belonged to the craft societies that had long been the basis of association in the artisan trades.[1] These societies did not include wives and daughters trained in the crafts; if female craft associations existed, they would have been only for those few journeywomen and mistresses who worked in the women's trades of millinery and mantua making.

The strict exclusion of women from craft associations was not based on an *actual* division of labor (women had long been skilled workers in the crafts), but on an *ideological* division: Men were the keepers of the arts and mysteries of ancient skills, women the perpetual apprentices in family workshops.[2] These assumptions were, of course, congruent with other eighteenth-century views of women as outsiders and parasites. The earliest discussion of female labor we have from workingmen in New York draws its imputations from such notions. It comes from a journeyman tailor in 1819. Seamstresses were apparently garnering the slop work on which the tailors depended for their meat and potatoes, and the tailors in retaliation were threatening a strike. The irate journeyman summed up the men's grievances in a letter to a newspaper: "Is it reasonable that the best of workmen should be unemployed half of the year," he demanded irascibly, "and calmly submit to reiterate privations by the empiricism of women, many of whom have served but a few months at the business, aided by the mercenary supports of their employers, merely because women work cheaper than men?" The tone is exasperated and derisive. "Nothing can be offered in justification of women asking, or employers giving work to women, other than the long continuance of an unwarrantable practice." It was against all reason for women to sew vests and pantaloons, a "preposterous and truly ridiculous idea." "It is an indisputable fact, that women are very inadequate to perform the work of a Tailor."[3]

As people often do when their prerogatives are attacked, the tailor invoked higher principle and supposedly self-evident truth to defend the men's monopoly. But the form the invocation took is interesting, since it resonated with ideas about separate sexual spheres and women's abilities that were also beginning to come from genteel quarters in 1819. The journeymen reified a customary eighteenth-century division of labor—tailors sewed vests, women didn't—into a law of gender: Women *could not* sew vests properly, by virtue of reason and nature. Although the argument ultimately rested on the superior talents of the skilled over the unskilled, it derived its emotional energies from expectations at work elsewhere in laboring men's relations with women. For what is most striking in the tailor's assertions is his utter neglect of the fact that the seamstresses needed this work in order to live. "They ought to disclaim all right and title whatever to the avocation of a tailor," he insisted; they were simply the pawns of the masters. Unlike the journeymen, the women had, apparently, no virtues to uphold, no privations to endure, no injustices to denounce. They were dependents—supposedly—expected to set aside their own requirements in order to defer to men's skills and men's anger, yet ultimately reviled as parasites for the very subordination that men like this one demanded from them.

Women themselves were to help change the terms of the discussion in the next fifteen years. By 1834, when the journeymen's National Trades' Union began to examine the question of women's wage labor, it did so in the context of a wave of female labor activism up and down the Eastern Seaboard. Lynn women shoe binders, Baltimore seamstresses and Lowell factory girls had all organized; Philadelphia shoe binders and women and child cotton spinners would soon do so. New York workingwomen— umbrella makers, seamstresses, shoe binders, and bookbinders—were especially prominent in the activity.[4] In 1825 the first all-women's strike in the United States had occurred among New York seamstresses ("What next?" a Philadelphia paper expostulated).[5] Throughout the 1830s, as many of the city's journeymen were caught up in militant thought and activity, a few New York workingwomen also took up the fight for themselves.

Of the women active in New York, we know little except about the tailoresses in 1831, who turned out (went on strike) to enforce a price list.[6] They were singular, not so much in their militance and tenacity—qualities that would recur in women's organizing—as in their feminism. For a brief moment, the woman question and the labor question were linked in a plain speaking, straightforward workingwoman's feminism. The tailoresses set forth a conception of their role in the labor movement that matched the much-prized republican "manliness" of the artisans with a republican "womanliness" based on the solidarity of sex and capable of defending its own rights and virtues. It was a considerable feat, which involved overcoming well-learned lessons of submission, as the women themselves were well aware. "It needs no small share of courage for us who have been used to impositions and oppression from our youth up to the present day, to come before the public in the defence of our own rights," one Sarah Monroe stressed to her sisters. One "imposition" was the assumption that they were born to be imposed upon. But, she asked, "if it is unfashionable for the men to bear oppression in silence, why should it not also become unfashionable with the women? or do they deem us more able to endure hardships than they themselves?" The questions were not just rhetorical. In general, men expected just that.[7]

The tailoresses probably owed something to Frances Wright, who had created a great stir in New York two years before. To a city already alive with free thought and political radicalism, Wright brought from Britain the ideas and energies of a class-conscious European feminism, the tradition of

Mary Wollstonecraft and the female militants of the French Revolution who had agitated in women's interests. It was a tradition that linked the interests of the popular classes with those of women; Wollstonecraft's own enthusiasm for the French Revolution was partly what gave fire to her *Vindication of the Rights of Women,* first published in 1792. After 1794, the gathering anti-Jacobin reaction excoriated all advances for women outside the domestic sphere as part and parcel of popular anarchy and drove self-conscious feminism outside the pale of genteel opinion in Europe and America. In England, however, Jacobin feminism found a refuge among utopian socialist thinkers, who continued to raise questions about the position of women as part of their project to transform all social relations. In the 1830s, Jacobin feminism was still very much alive in the Owenite movement of English workers, and both Wright and Robert Dale Owen, her companion in New York, were familiar with feminist agitation in Owenite papers and cooperatives.[8] They brought these ideas to New York. In a series of immensely successful lectures, Wright urged her following—comprised largely of radical workingmen—to see that there were other kinds of tyranny besides that of priests, kings and monopolists. "Fathers and husbands!" Wright cried. "Do you not see how, in the mental bondage of your wives and fair companions, ye yourselves are bound?"[9]

Wright had left New York by the time the tailoresses turned out in the spring of 1831, but her ideas must have still reverberated throughout the Northeast. Three years later in Lowell, they may have been at work in a woman's turnout: A Boston paper reported that "one of the leaders mounted a pump, and made a flaming Mary Wollstonecroft speech on the rights of women and the iniquities of the 'monied aristocracy' which produced a powerful effect on her auditors."[10] New York workingwomen were never such rabble-rousers as the Lowell girls, but the speaker at the first meeting of the Tailoresses Society began in a Wollstonecraft kind of way by putting their difficulties with employers in the context of woman's subordination in *all* social relations: "That females are imposed upon, and oppressed in almost every stage of action to which the circumstances of their existence render them liable, is a fact, that . . . requires only the reiteration of cases." Another speaker declaimed against discrimination against women in education, a favorite topic of Fanny Wright, and against women's exclusion from politics.[11]

By the second month, the strike was faltering, and the tailoresses' initial elation had disappeared. Their feminism, however, had developed from the first exhilaration at denouncing "impositions" into a graver appraisal of the liabilities of their sex. They continued to be convinced that whatever the odds, independent action was their best hope. "After all, my friends, who is to stand between us and oppression?" Sarah Monroe somberly inquired in a remarkable address.

> If we do not come forth in our own defence, what will become of us? . . . Need I ask what is to become of us—let us bring back to our recollection the scenes of distress that have been exhibited in this city during the past winter. . . . Long have the poor tailoresses of this city borne their oppression in silence; until *patience* is no longer a virtue. . . . High time is it, my friends, that we awake—high time is it that we were up and doing . . . let us unite—let us organize ourselves— let us do all in our power to increase our members; for on that the success of our cause depends.[12]

Although the strike ended and the society folded soon thereafter, scraps of evidence suggest that a commitment to female action persisted beyond its demise. Striking New York bookbinders in 1835 drew a similar picture of women cut off from a system of male support and anticipating a lifetime of earning their own and others' bread: "Consider how many of us are without parents—several have the care of younger brothers and sisters, and many have aged parents depending on them," they appealed to the public. Developments elsewhere, too—the formation of a federation of Philadelphia workingwomen from a number of trades in 1835, another Lowell strike in 1836—may reflect the influence of early feminist ideas beyond New York.[13]

The articulation of the importance of female self-reliance is startling in a context where women were routinely expected to defer to men. It is even more surprising when we consider how little even genteel women, who had by 1831 already given some thought to matters of gender, had to say about the possibility that women could act together *without* masculine help. Even though they actively organized women's prayer groups and women's charities, respectable ladies only did so with some kind of male patronage (from ministers or men's associations). The rudiments of public life—public assemblies, public speaking—were prohibited for women unless men accompanied them. Frances Wright was the first woman in America to ascend a speaker's platform before a mixed audience, an act which (along with her unorthodox sexual life) earned her the epithet Priestess of Beelzebub. Eight years later, the high-born Grimké sisters incurred vitriolic condemnation for daring to speak to antislavery audiences that included men. Even the militant ladies of New York's Magdalene Society, engaged in what was in 1831 the quite daring reform work of reclaiming prostitutes, still asked men to chair their meetings.[14] But here, with the tailoresses, we have poor

g women voicing a well-developed awareness that women must
on themselves to advocate their interests and that there were serious
es, internal and external, to doing so. This was nearly two decades
before antislavery and reform women would put forth similar sentiments
at the first women's rights convention at Seneca Falls, New York.

Frances Wright can provide only a partial explanation of the sources of
the tailoresses' independent behavior and talk. Wright tossed off her remarks about women amidst long abstruse speeches on education, political
economy and free thought; she never developed any sustained analysis of
gender and did not speak explicitly about the problems of laboring women.
She almost always addressed herself to men. But women did go to hear her
—at her last New York address, more than half the audience was female,
according to one surprised observer.[15] Wright's simple point, that power
structured the relations between men and women, must have had some
influence on laboring women, whose own experiences might well have
made them receptive to what she had to say.

The other factor in the seamstresses' activities was the radicalism of the
New York labor movement. The growing militance of workingmen, in
conjunction with Wright's influence, gave some women workers the means
to examine their relations with employers in a new light. For the female
working class 1831 was a complex political moment. In 1829 the Working
Men's movement, comprised of journeymen and small masters, had
emerged in New York to put forth political candidates at the polls and to
debate a number of propositions on the injustices of private ownership.[16]
The original "Workies" popularized a far-reaching critique of the exploitativeness of property relations, but despite the influence of the *Free Enquirer*
group, they had little to say about women. Even amidst the surge of radical
ambitions and solidarities, views of women as an intolerable presence in the
trades had yet to be explicitly challenged.

How, then, did the women benefit? The tailoresses were probably aware
that men, even radical men, considered them outsiders to their own community of interest. Certainly some of the women's more acerbic asides
suggest so. But if wage-earning women had long known that others com-
prehended little about "the circumstances of their existence," the new ideas
in the air in 1830–31 about working-class action still gave them a way to turn
that knowledge around, the means to transform the debilities of exclusion
into the resources of self-reliance. Perhaps it was the very antipathy toward
women, rooted in a plebeian culture in decline, that allowed women to
confront workingmen's lack of support and to look to themselves for their
own "defence." The tailoresses, by their own account family breadwinners,
were in an especially strong position to comprehend the limitations of male
protection in improving their lot. In a few years' time, organized working-

men would be talking about women as frail partisans in the labor struggle, under their benevolent care. Once that ideology of protectionism was in place, it would be more difficult for women to voice their own distinct needs.

The National Trades' Union and Male Benevolence

The activity of the tailoresses and other organized women in the early 1830s must have impressed some workingmen that women workers could no longer be simply dismissed. The first sustained discussion of female labor occurred at the conventions of the National Trades' Union (NTU) between 1834 and 1836. The NTU was a convocation of delegates from the General Trades' Union affiliates, federations of journeymen from different cities, mostly in the Northeast. The NTU included a strong contingent of radical workingmen from the New York City General Trades' Union (GTU); a few of its leaders were from the now-defunct Working Men's Party. The New York men had been the moving force in forming the organization and figured prominently in the NTU's leadership and its discussions.[17] For these men, too much had happened to working people to support the old presumption that wage-earning women were simply the cause of their own ills.

In the NTU deliberations, an attitude of concern and responsibility overshadowed any explicit hostility toward women. There was, however, deep if unacknowledged confusion over how concern should be expressed. Certainly the men assumed that whatever was to be done, it was their job to do it. "Who shall reform the system but the workingman?" the delegates inquired in 1834, despite the considerable evidence of women's own activism. "The natural weakness of the sex—their modesty and bashfulness—their ignorance of the forms and conduct of public meetings and of the measures necessary to enable them to resist the oppression under which they labor—will ever prevent their obtaining any melioration or improvement of their condition."[18] Women, by virtue of their nature and their upbringing, were unfit to organize themselves in their own defense.

Given this assessment, one logical response to women's problems was to keep them out of the labor force altogether. In 1835 the NTU convention (held in New York) voted to oppose "the multiplying of all description of labor for females" and the next year declared women's manufacturing work "highly injurious to the best interests of the working classes."[19] The reasoning was substantially different from that employed by the irascible tailor in 1819. In the NTU deliberations—as on the Bowery a decade later—women were presumed to be members of the workingmen's community, not troublesome aliens. Indeed, the delegates implicitly acknowledged women's domestic labor to be central to the welfare of all, so much so that the interests of the class as a whole were served when men supported women at home. Under these auspices, the NTU could even discuss the unpleasant question of women's competition with men in a sympathetic spirit. Competition, the men agreed, was not a matter of conflicting interests between the sexes but rather a choice between short-term solutions and long-term improvement. When women undercut men's wages, "the parent, the husband, or the brother is deprived of a sufficient subsistence to support himself and family, when without the auxiliary aid of the female, by his own labor alone he might have supported himself and family in decency, and kept his wife or relative at home, to perform the duties of the household."[20] Families might temporarily solve their problems of subsistence by sending wives and daughters to work, but in the long run women damaged their interests and those of the entire working class by undercutting men.

Thus gender entered working-class politics, woven into a vision of a working-class home supported by men's wages, where women could be free "to perform the duties of the household." The family that the NTU men wanted was a corporate body capacious enough to serve the needs of all, something that harked back to the eighteenth century, a thrifty and productive household supervised by an energetic and prudent manager skilled in the domestic arts. Nonetheless, contemporary conceptions of gender also shaped the ideal. A kind workingman—woman's "natural protector, Man"—not a stern patriarch would rule there, and women would find it a refuge for their "natural weakness."[21] In other words, the workingmen envisioned a nineteenth-century home not unlike the bourgeois ideal, a repository for women's "true" nature as well as a refuge from the miseries of wage labor.

But it would be too simple to see the workingmen as emulating genteel ideals of domesticity. Rather, we need to place the treatment of female labor in the context of their other views. These men were radicals: They offered a fiery critique of the entire system of capitalist wage relations. They sought working-class dignity, not bourgeois respectability. True, their formulations at times echoed those of evangelicals and ladies' magazines. Their opposition to women's labor, however, was not a capitulation to bourgeois society but a protest against it: "It is not enough that freemen have sunk below the level of humanity at the shrine of Mammon, but their wives and daughters must be offered at the pyre. Is not Avarice satisfied with a nation of Fathers and Sons, but our Wives and Daughters, the loved ones of our hearts and affections, shall be thrown into the spoilers' arms?"[22]

Nonetheless, as a guiding propensity in the labor movement, this species of radical paternalism had its limits. Insofar as women's interests were tied up with those of male-headed families, the NTU was right on target. The men's views, after all, came from firsthand knowledge of the effects of manufacturing work on women; they knew its debilitating effects well enough, having seen their sisters and wives and neighbors work themselves to the bone. But there was something else at issue here than simply women's well-being: Workingmen raised no protests, after all, when they watched women work themselves to the bone in other ways, keeping their houses, bearing and raising their children. Women's particular difficulties, in fact, made no major appearance in these deliberations.

The limits were especially evident in the NTU's discussion of the factory girl, who made one of her earliest appearances here. The attention the men devoted to her tells more about their own anxieties than about women's troubles. Sexual immorality was to them the crux of the problem. When women worked in factories, "their morals frequently depart before their health, in consequence of being often crowded in such large numbers, with all characters and sexes."[23] But sexual immorality only epitomized a deeper failing of character, an absence of virtue which, in the logic of republicanism, made women susceptible to all sorts of tyrannies. When women worked away from their households, the pernicious authority of the employer could easily usurp the beneficent rule of husbands, brothers and fathers. And on the crucial point of virtue, the supposed problem of sexual immorality converged with women's supposed inability to organize. Women quite simply lacked the strength of character to sustain themselves in the struggle against tyranny in the workplace.[24] Through the images of the seduced factory girl and the lascivious employer, the men translated the eighteenth-century figures of the bawd and her aristocratic patron into the setting of industrial capitalism.

These republican-minded workingmen cared about nothing so much as they cared about "liberty." Their belief in the duty of freeborn Americans to uphold the legacy of the Revolution was central to their conception of labor politics as a struggle of the independent producer to guard the fruits of his labor from the tyranny of employers. They were less sure, however, about what it meant for women to love liberty. They knew well enough that women could also defend their liberties against the domination of the masters: In 1836 the NTU wasted no time in passing a resolution of sympathy for the Lowell girls whose strike had been defeated, regretting the women's failure but applauding their meritorious conduct in defending their rights.[25] Like eighteenth-century republicans, however, they tended to see the household as a necessary restraint on women's otherwise wild, corrupt nature. The republic to which the workingmen were committed was, in the end, a republic of men, and they had difficulty in conceiving of a polity in which women could also maintain a virtuous independence in consort with their peers. If women belonged in the home, it was not to shed their sacred "influence," a genteel view of female nature still alien to the unionists, but to submit to the benign authority of a republican patriarch. In raising the family wage as a cardinal demand, the men reinvoked, within a nineteenth-century idiom, older feelings about the rightful places of the sexes.[26]

Artisans' associations in the early nineteenth century had also protested the erosion of the family wage, but they primarily directed their denunciations of employers at wage cutting, the devaluation of skilled craftsmanship and the changing character of the workplace itself. With the NTU, the language of grievance reached out beyond the workplace to encompass the sexual order as well. "Female labor, when carried beyond the necessities of the family" could only undermine the republic of labor; the family was the place where the working-class independence and decency so damaged by the wages system might once again flourish. For it to do so, however, required a transformed social organization, where custom and family needs, not employers, dictated the disposition of women's energies.[27]

The inadequacies of this paradigm of family labor to women's circumstances did not always escape the workingmen. The men generally recognized that the neediest women workers lived without male support. Their proposals, however, hinged on some abstract, future attachment to men, which these women would acquire in the course of fighting for the workingmen's republic. Somehow, if women stepped aside, men could resume their places as their natural protectors. The NTU proposed that women should actively campaign against their own employment ("the present state of society . . . must be destroyed by gradual means, and by the active co-operation of the female operatives"); short of that, the committee on female labor advocated legislation that restricted the factory employment of girls (but not boys!) to arrangements "under the care and supervision of a parent." The radical shoemaker William English, leader of the Philadelphia branch of the NTU, pragmatically acknowledged that women could not simply stop working, "for then you would have no means of subsistence," he pointed out perspicaciously. He advised them instead to organize —*not* in order to improve their wages or working conditions, but to limit the amount of work they did so that men might have a greater share and thus make more money! Once everyone was back in place in the family, wives could practice a virtuous maternity, and single women would have the free time to learn the "sober duties of wives, mothers and matrons."[28]

That these were mostly solutions to men's problems, not women's, eluded the workingmen, however self-consciously sympathetic they might be.

Certainly the unionists' pronouncements left behind, in most respects, the old language of open sexual antagonism. To assume responsibility for women's economic situation was also to repudiate a frank hostility toward women—shared with men of other classes—in favor of a respect rooted in a common working-class experience. In place of the derision for women as nags and bawds, the NTU voiced an attitude of care and an unprecedented acknowledgment of the importance of women's domestic labor. Rather than stressing the intrusion of wage-earning women into a male collectivity of craft, the journeymen redrew the boundaries of class to include women, recognizing women's exploitation at the hands of their employers and emphasizing the interdependence of the sexes. The assumption of benevolence at least allowed the men to posit one role for women in the labor movement—as members of an auxiliary of equal rights, valued for their role in their households. It blinded them, however, to the alternative possibility: that women might organize themselves along with men.

Cooperation

Some workingmen saw things differently. While their fellows stressed the importance of solidarity within the working-class household, these men found it possible to support women workers in their own trades. There is too little evidence to explain how and why workingmen's perspectives diverged, why some men sought to revive the verities of the old family labor system while others sensed there was something to be gained elsewhere. Different factions within the labor movement may have fostered different views of women workers; disparate attitudes may have coexisted in the minds of the same people. The 1830s were a volatile period in New York, not the least in relations between men and women. The "woman question" was relatively new. Along with the patriots of the French Revolution (forty years earlier) and workingmen and radicals in Britain (in their own time), American workers were the first group of men to grapple with it. It is not surprising that their responses were muddled.

Instances of men's cooperation with organized women are few but important. In 1835, the journeymen bookbinders supported striking women in the trade, vowing to "use all honorable means to sustain them in their difficulties" and expressing their "utter contempt" for the employers who worked the women at starvation wages while "fattening on the sweat of their brow." The New York journeymen also organized careful, ward-by-ward support that year for the striking women and children of Paterson. More substantive incidents of cooperation occurred elsewhere. In 1833–34, the men of Lynn vowed in support of striking women shoe binders to boycott any employer who did not accede to the women's demands. In Philadelphia, male and female textile workers went on strike together in 1834; in 1836, women shoe binders turned out to join striking men and the men pledged to "flourish or sink" with their sisters.[29]

These actions were part of a general expansion of the journeymen's sense of fellowship in the mid-1830s, as they interested themselves in strikes and movements around the country and began in the New York GTU to discuss the problems of unskilled laborers. But there was a logic to their sympathies. Their interest in helping any group of organized women greatly depended on how much, in a given trade, a customary sexual division of labor legitimated the women's presence. The journeymen tended to support women in those trades with a strong tradition of family-based production and in those where a rigid sexual division of labor protected men from female competition. For example, in cordwaining (a trade where men were active in aiding the women) female employment had been associated with family labor since the late eighteenth century. Shoemaking was often organized along family lines in New York and wholly so in Lynn, where more dramatic instances of cooperation occurred. Shoe binding had been work for artisan wives and daughters since the late eighteenth century, and the customary sexual division of labor found in family industry survived intact even in those sectors of the trade where women worked independently of their households: Men sewed the "uppers," women bound the shoes together.[30] The Paterson spinners to whom the New York GTU gave strike support were also working within a family context. Silk spinning had been a family domestic industry in the eighteenth century; cotton spinning had long been organized along family lines in American factories. Whether or not Paterson employers hired men (the evidence is murky on this point), traditions of family labor continued to shape the industry, as the employers gave work to the wives and children of men who worked in the town's machine shops. In book manufacture, a strong sexual division of labor still held: Folding and sewing were traditionally women's tasks, and women had not yet encroached upon the more skilled tasks of binding.[31]

The sewing trades, crucial to the New York situation, were a more complicated case. Women did work in the trade as family members in family shops, and they worked within a family context as helpers to journeymen who lacked families. At the same time, however, a class of independent female wageworkers emerged quite early in the century who breached the sexual division in the trade to take on various kinds of men's work. The weakness of sexual segmentation in the sewing trades and the continuing threat of female intrusion must partly account for the well-organized tailors' continuing disinterest in organizing workingwomen.[32] By the 1830s, the journeymen seem to have lost the rancor of their predecessors in 1819, but the Tailoresses Society could still allude to their determined indifference and hostility. The women's cause, Sarah Monroe noted, was so dire that even "the tailors themselves dare not openly slander, nor I think they would be ashamed openly to oppose." When seamstresses subsequently organized a cooperative in 1836, they made a bid for the journeymen's interest, but despite the high-minded benevolence of the NTU that year, none of the men seem to have responded. The women were left to the mercies of bourgeois male patrons, whose factionalism eventually destroyed the organization. In 1844, when Boston tailors and tailoresses turned out together in a sensational strike, two thousand New York tailors followed suit, but no published account mentions they gave any consideration to inviting the New York women to join in.[33]

The 1830s distilled conflicts and issues that ran through the entire antebellum period. Women's wage work, however bound to customary household relations, still threw open a series of possibilities for change within the family. Women's labor organizing played an important role in putting these questions on the agenda of the labor movement. When we know more about the history of gender among laboring people, we may discover that America as a whole in the 1830s was as volatile, as laden with possibilities for change between the sexes as was working-class England. To some extent New York City, at least, bears out Barbara Taylor's characterization of the 1830s in Great Britain: "All was plastic, all was possible."[34]

But not *all*. Even the most open-minded journeymen used the customary expectations of the household as standards against which to judge the situation of women in manufacturing. This inclination to see the family as the determinant of women's lives could lead the journeymen in several directions, from adamant opposition to female wage work to solidarity in common labor struggles. Overall, the labor movement's elevation of family relations to one of its primary concerns benefited women in ruling out explicit misogyny in trade union discussions and in recognizing women as important contributors to the decency of working-class life. It was no accident that as the New York chair maker John Commerford, veteran of the Working Men's movement and president of the New York GTU, searched over time for the words to describe the commonalty of wage earners, he tried (first) mechanics and workingmen, (then) operatives, and finally fastened on the "family of labor," the "working classes."[35] The family had become a controlling metaphor of class consciousness.

At the same time, by installing the family at the center of their vision of a just social order, the men began a subtle process by which eventually their domestic aspirations for the women would come to override all else. Even the champions of women's trade unionism tended to act from modified assumptions about male authority and privilege, advocating women's interests so long as women worked within a sharp sexual division of labor. The support they gave to organized women was one indication of the openness of the gender system in a period of political radicalism and of the seriousness of discussions of women's place in the 1830s. But ultimately, the terms of cooperation did not differ greatly from the premises of those journeymen who opposed female labor. The sympathetic journeymen, like their more recalcitrant fellows, oriented themselves within the "family of labor," leaving sexual divisions in work and women's economic and social subordination to men unchallenged, and condemning their attempts at heterosexual solidarity.

Throughout the nineteenth century, union men tended to think of themselves in the paternalist terms the NTU first defined, as breadwinners for women at home or, at best, as supporters of women at work, lending aid from a more authoritative position. The wider possibilities of the 1830s —a time of temporary suspension, when the old plebeian rules of gender were challenged and reshaped—would persist only as an undercurrent in the labor movement. Trade unionists would generally see further reconsiderations of the gender system as distractions from their manly undertaking. It would take more women like the young tailoresses to reopen questions of female self-reliance which the family of labor saw as better left alone.[36]

The Ladies' Industrial Association

The Panic of 1837, a calamity for New York's manufacturing economy, leveled the radical artisan milieu in which both working-class feminism and working-class paternalism had grown. When working people began to regroup in the 1840s, a sense of caution predominated. The journeymen's militant denunciations of their employers' lack of scruples had abated. Associations for self-improvement and mutual benefit were for the moment more appealing to people badly hit by unemployment and wage cutting.

Yet the shifts in men's consciousness of women as fellow members of the working class proved permanent. Both the urban populist Mike Walsh and the land reformer George Henry Evans, for example, addressed themselves to "workingmen and women" in the newspaper they edited in the 1840s (while slighting all specifically female concerns).[37] Twenty years earlier, even such a rhetorical recognition of women would have been inconceivable. Moreover, workingwomen themselves carried on something of the ideas and strategies of the previous decade as they launched (in a period generally devoid of militant activity from men) a major organizational effort, the Ladies' Industrial Association (LIA) of 1845.

The women who led the LIA based their task on the assumptions of female self-reliance laid out by their predecessors. In March, the straw sewers, ever independent-minded, called a meeting of all workingwomen in the city to combat the wage cuts women had continually suffered since the panic. They addressed themselves specifically to "young women" in manufacturing work. In what seems to have been a bid for autonomy from both workingmen and more privileged patrons, they initially barred men from the meeting, "as those for whose benefit it is called prefer to deliberate by themselves." Except for a few journalists, men obliged, and several hundred women convened in City Hall Park in early March.[38] In itself, this was extraordinary—meeting in such a highly public place was sure to draw taunts and jeers. In previous efforts women had convened in the respectable precincts of churches; when the lady shoe binders met at a hotel in 1835, they used a "private entrance" of their own.[39] In fact, on the meeting day, city hall authorities precluded any insults to the women by offering them a room inside. Women from all ranks of the trade assembled: shirt sewers, plain sewers, tailoresses and dressmakers, fringe and lace makers, straw workers, the comparatively prosperous book folders and stitchers and the lowly cap makers and shoe crimpers.[40]

They proceeded with dispatch. The elected chairwoman, Miss Elizabeth Gray, impressed all observers with her self-possession, intelligence and skill at presiding over 700 women unaccustomed to collective deliberation on a large scale. They constituted themselves into a federation and quickly discussed and passed several resolutions, one setting price scales in all the female trades, another stating their intention to form trade unions and strike if their demands were not met.

They were confident about their organizational abilities, so much so that they rebuked one well-meaning man who offered to help them write an address for their next meeting, "saying that they were competent to manage their own affairs."[41] This is surprising, given how little laboring women seem to have been involved in organizational efforts since 1831. Although poor women were hardly retiring when it came to expressing their grievances on the streets and in the tenements, they could not have known much about the formal usages of political life in which antebellum workingmen could be so adept: voting, writing up notices, debating, circulating petitions, and composing rules and constitutions. Sarah Monroe of the Tailoresses Society had acknowledged this handicap in 1831: "That we are not in the practice of pleading our own cause, our employers are well aware."[42] It seems—it is often the case in women's labor organizing—as if organizational sophistication had materialized out of thin air. Perhaps the generation of the 1830s had managed after all to pass on their skills; perhaps some women's trade societies had quietly struggled on as mutual benefit societies through the panic (the shoe binders did this), teaching a new generation of women something of the arts of organizing.

The images of struggle certainly hearkened back to the women of the early 1830s. At first, the LIA presented its members as self-reliant and independent of male support, responsible for "aged fathers and mothers, young brothers, helpless sisters" as well as for each other. Whatever men might have thought about women's natural infirmities, these women implied they could shoulder their own burdens. The golden day of the family wage was remote from their concerns, which touched on the ability of women to earn their living rather than on their eventual return to the home. As Elizabeth Gray declared of the impending turnout, "we know it to be our duty, and that of every female who wishes to earn an honest livelihood."[43] Their language also echoed the republicanism of the 1830s. "The boon we ask is founded upon RIGHT alone," the women averred, and vowed "to take upon themselves the task of asserting their rights against the unjust and mercenary conduct of their employers."[44]

There were many varieties of republicanism in antebellum America; different groups—masters and journeymen, for example—could invoke republican ideas to justify directly competing social interests. The workingwomen's version was quite distinct from the other major female appropriation of republicanism, the ideology of republican motherhood, which stressed the role of mothers in inculcating in their (male) children the virtue and reason necessary to a strong citizenry. Later domestic writers applied republican motherhood to the cult of domesticity and assigned to the female inhabitants of the home a critical role in the enterprise of American nationalism and the expansion of republican institutions. This version, which was current among antebellum ladies, emphasized women's mediated relationship to republican virtue; it also downplayed the language of rights and struggle critical to men's usages, focusing rather on women's moral superiority and their role in exercising an improving influence on society.

In contrast, the workingwomen, like the Lowell girls and the New York tailoresses before them, laid a direct claim to virtuous independence and declared themselves willing to enter into the fray.[45] The straw workers led off the strike, and immediately met with obdurate resistance from most of the employers. "Don't give up the ship," Elizabeth Gray urged at the next meeting. She invoked the labor theory of value, keystone of the artisans' political economy, and called upon the women to resist their employers' injustices. "The time has now come," Gray vowed, "for us to stand up for our rights, and to let our employers see that we can do more than they think we can."[46]

At the same time, Gray hedged her bets. In a recognizably feminine manner of appeasement, she assured the public that the women were not striking for higher wages from motives of "extortion" but so that they could be better workers: "more cheerful at their work and still more earnest and willing to serve their employers."[47] Such an advertisement of concern for employers was not as singular as it might seem. The old artisan ideal of the mutuality of interests between masters and men, undercut by the radicalism of the 1830s, was again gaining ground in New York, especially in the mutual benefit societies that had regrouped after the panic. Yet there was another layer of associations to the phrases. "Cheerful," "more earnest and willing"—these were idealizations of female nature popular in the writings of domesticity, descriptions of the selfless nature of the "true" woman.

The sudden appearance of the virtues of domestic womanhood may have had something to do with an influx of bourgeois supporters at this point in the strike. The LIA took a new turn in amalgamating workingwomen's efforts with those of genteel reformers. In the 1830s, outside interest in women's efforts had been small. Male moral reformers had been briefly involved in the Tailoresses Cooperative of 1836, but otherwise, women's organizing went unnoticed by the middle-class public. By the 1840s, however, Matthew Carey, George Henry Evans, Horace Greeley and the women's charities, all from their different viewpoints, had widely publicized the plight of the needlewomen; the popular literary figure of the starving seamstress also drew sympathetic attention from a middle-class audience to the actual plight of female workers. Accordingly, the workingwomen of 1845 attracted far more attention than had their predecessors. City politicians, sentimental novelists, labor reformers and well-to-do ladies— "strong-minded women" (including a "woman's rights auxiliary") and "political demagogues," as the *Herald* described them retrospectively— flocked to help the "distressed needlewomen."[48]

Support, however, had mixed results, as the priorities of the federation shifted from conducting a strike to attracting public sympathy, a task for which professions of womanly virtue were better suited than declarations of republican rights. The initial determination of the workingwomen bogged down in a welter of schemes offered by the patrons, who quickly came to dominate the proceedings. Of the three women delegated to write an address on female labor, probably only one (Elizabeth Gray) was a wage earner; the others were Ann Stephens, a popular women's writer, and a Mrs. Storms, an advocate of the wages-fund theory, a favored bourgeois panacea for laborers' ills. A benefit performance at Palmo's Opera House flopped; a meeting was postponed because the woman who was to address it fell ill (seemingly there were not enough workingwomen who would brave the terrors of public speaking to provide a substitute from the ranks). At a subsequent meeting, Mrs. Storms cautioned the strikers against the ineffectuality of unions—only when the surplus of labor in the city was dispersed, she argued, would wages rise, and accordingly proposed the association should devote its energies to sending workingwomen to the West and ousting men from retail clerkships in the city.[49] As the strike faltered, the search for sympathy became more urgent, leading someone to propose (with no results) a meeting to publicize the women's situation at the Broadway Tabernacle, Charles Finney's old church and seat of evangelicalism in the city. The turn toward the Broadway Tabernacle and all it represented was, by any lights, a strange one for a labor organization.

Ladies like Mrs. Stephens and Mrs. Storms would have been especially interested in drawing out the connections between the workingwomen's struggle and the universal plight of womanhood, in promoting a "womanliness" among women fated to exist outside woman's proper place. The strike's working-class leaders may have found gender prescriptions a useful means to attract support. Elizabeth Gray, for instance, agreed with Mrs. Storms that men should be banished from clerkships, on the grounds that the work was "more fitting for women."[50] But as the women cited contemporary beliefs about women's proper place, so did their employers. Each side called up gender expectations to legitimate itself. The most obdurate employers, playing on images of the factory girl, treated the strikers like prostitutes, taunting them with abusive and obscene language and threatening them with incarceration in the Tombs (where arrested prostitutes awaited trial). The equation of prostitution with any form of women's public life was not new. In the shoe binders' strike of 1835, for instance, employers had alleged "that the Society was got up by prostitutes" and had used language against the strikers "not fit for public print." This time, however, the strikers used notions of propriety to counterattack by charging the employers with "ungentlemanly" behavior.[51]

The strike fell apart in the late spring. As was the case with the Tailoresses Society, nothing more was heard subsequently from the organization. Elizabeth Gray, its spokeswoman, must have married and settled down in the tenements or, being a singularly self-assured and determined young woman, perhaps she migrated out West, as Mrs. Storms had advised (to try her luck where the wages fund was higher!). The women she had exhorted to republican battle retired into obscurity. Support from polite society had been a mixed blessing (as it was again to prove in the ensuing years). Beginning with assertions of self-reliance, the workingwomen ended up relying almost entirely on public sympathy. In the process, they diluted their initial declarations of rights with assurances that they were really only acting as "true" women, concerned not with their own problems of under-payment but with how better to serve their employers. Earlier organized women had to some extent also addressed these issues. The influx of sup-porters into the LIA, however—people who were interested in mitigating women's victimization rather than securing them their rights—made these considerations far more important.

Allusions to "true" womanhood also undercut the female republicanism that had given women the impetus to strike in the first place. In elaborating their identity not just as wage earners but as wage-earning *women*, the LIA members had shown themselves capable of decisive, even bold action. The abandonment of this specific, class-based gender identity for one of univer-sal womanhood, beckoning across class lines, gained them little in the next great metropolitan insurgency.

The Industrial Congress

Workingmen's own consciousness that women shared their difficulties waned in the 1840s. When men again entered the committee rooms in 1850 to form the Industrial Congress, any serious considerations of the place of workingwomen were gone. The mutualist, egalitarian strains of union thought in the 1830s were missing, and paternalism had hardened into rigid notions of woman's place. It was as if the LIA and all it revealed about women's capabilities had never existed. When workingmen did turn to organizing women in 1851, they did so in the patron's role developed by supporters in 1845. Within the field of action the workingmen helped to define, workingwomen entered as victims, to be helped by the more power-ful, rather than as protagonists of their own struggle.

The Industrial Congress represented all the city's labor reform groups: benevolent societies, protective unions, trade unions, land-reform associa-tions and cooperatives. As a federation encompassing day laborers, semi-skilled craftworkers, trained journeymen, immigrants and native-born workers, it was the most inclusive body of workingmen that existed in New York before the Civil War. The congress had grown out of a wave of strikes and organizing activity that began in the early part of the year; by the summer, the congress had demanded (and secured) space in City Hall for its meetings and was primarily engaged in supporting a tailors' strike against police violence. In addition, the congress coordinated other strikes in the city, debated the causes of industrial distress and considered a wide variety of proposals for alleviation and reform.[52]

The size of the Industrial Congress, its heterogeneous membership and the seriousness of its debates and activities make it all the more surprising that neither women nor women's issues played any substantive part in its proceedings. There were certainly problems to consider, as the LIA had amply demonstrated five years before. The men occasionally mentioned women. But there was no sustained deliberation on the place of women in the labor movement, and the only extended discussion of women seems to have been a "thorough" debate on whether female associations would be allowed representatives, with inconclusive results.[53]

The pronounced indifference to women workers may have had something to do with the immigrants who played an important part in the organization. In contrast to the New York GTU, the Industrial Congress was heavily immigrant. Recall that by 1855 an estimated three-quarters of the city's workers were foreign born. Although both German and Irish immigrants could speak incisively about the needs of workers, their lives in the Old World had done little to press the "woman question" upon them. All the issues that New York journeymen debated in the 1830s—the role of women in the family, the mutual oppression of men and women in manufacturing work, the propriety of women engaging in public life—were new matters to men and women who came from the countryside. Immigrant artisans and peasants were accustomed to family-based labor, and the problems and possibilities that arose between the sexes in an urban family wage economy did not as yet occupy their attention. Perhaps something of the proliferation of family shops and sweatshops in the 1850s can be attributed to the ways in which those forms transformed the unfamiliar issues of the family wage economy into the familiar ones of family-based labor. Indeed, in at least two trades in which immigrants were heavily involved, basket making and shoemaking, craftworkers in the 1850s tried to ensure the continuance of family shops. The Journeymen Cordwainers Society, whose members were mainly Irish, resolved in 1850 to ban the employment of any woman in the trade "unless she be a member's wife or daughter, and he shall be held responsible for her acts." Similarly, the German basket makers union refused to work for any shop employing women who were unconnected to the union men's families.[54]

This is not to lay the blame solely on immigrants, with their supposedly backward, feudal ways. The immigrants' highly familial and patriarchal view of women easily squared with the paternalism that had been developing among native New York men since the 1830s. Like the analogous body of the GTU, the Committee on Female Labor of the congress concluded peremptorily that female wage work was "a mode of life incompatible with the true dignity and nature of woman"; unlike the GTU, however, the Congress let the matter go there, with no vows to do anything about it.

In this climate, organizing female wage earners took on the cast of charity. If the men conceived of the women's situation as having little to do with them *systematically*, then helping them was a moral, not a political matter. In 1851, as the Industrial Congress faltered, workingmen helped to found the Shirt Sewers' Cooperative, a cooperative store for needle-women's products. Producers' cooperatives in all the consumer finishing trades had come out of the movement of 1850; the women's cooperative, however, was organized along distinct lines, not on the principle of inde-pendence for producers but on that of sympathy for the downtrodden. The cooperative was run like a charity, with men acting as the stewards of organizational resources.

The workingmen conducted the first meeting of the cooperative; the indefatigable straw sewers helped, but did not take any formal role in the proceedings. The men opened with avowals of commitment to the women's cause and urged the women to fight as the straw workers had in earlier years. Then they asked those present to speak about their grievances. A woman stood up, and her stricken appearance immediately touched the hearts of many in the audience. When she had heard that morning about the meeting, she said, she had put down her sewing, "as it was an ease to her long sufferings to hear their case taken up." Her scrap of speech, however the *Tribune* reporter may have distorted it in transcribing his notes for the paper, carried a simple statement of her sense of her place in the world. "Their case," she called it: She saw herself as part of a group of fellow sufferers. But it was a group waiting to be helped, to be "taken up" by others more powerful. When a tailoress two decades earlier had urged her sisters to shed the conviction that they could not act without the help of men, she must have had in mind women just like this one—a woman waiting.[55]

Whatever others at the meeting might have had to say, this woman, timid and passive, occupied center stage, at least in the *Tribune*'s construction of the event. The frail and trembling seamstress of popular literature had entered the arena of labor organizing. In previous efforts, other sorts of women had articulated the seamstresses' plight—the forthright Sarah Monroe, the resourceful Elizabeth Gray. If such women were present at the 1851 meeting among the very capable straw sewers, the reporter did not think their comments important enough to record. The representatives from the Industrial Congress formed themselves into a committee to pre-pare resolutions and a constitution for the cooperative, and to invite other friends of labor reform to help. The beginning, colored by such a dramatic profession of female need, had been auspicious for both workingmen and reformers, to whom the figure of the helpless seamstress was familiar and inviting. When the Shirt Sewers' Cooperative was formally constituted, it was as a benevolent society with a board of managers composed of twice as many men as women.[56]

There was little room within such a structure for independent action from the workingwomen involved. The cooperative drew its sustenance from the donations of patrons, not from the energies of its workers. There was a scant handful of women involved—forty or fifty at most, compared to the hundreds who had participated in the LIA. The cooperative's appeals were directed toward charity; in the major address of its short-lived existence, the managers solicited the public's benevolence in terms similar to those of charity associations. The centerpiece of the address was Thomas Hood's "Song of the Shirt," the sentimental sensation current on both sides of the Atlantic which, as Frederick Engels had drily remarked, "drew sympathetic but unavailing tears from the daughters of the bourgeoisie."[57] Trade union energies mingled with literary rhetoric, and the defense of the sewing woman, a wageworker in capitalist manufacturing, merged with comfort to the "defenseless" and "friendless" orphan and widow, applicants for traditional charitable relief.

The cooperative store hung on until 1853, but always under the management of its patrons, who were waiting to relinquish control until the workers could repay the original loan that capitalized the business. Sometime thereafter, it quietly folded.[58] The experiment, such as it was, prefigured the peculiar amalgam of benevolence and female associationism that would play a major role in women's labor organizing in the next half century.

By 1860, the possibilities of women's trade unionism, evident in the 1830s, had disappeared. The short-lived, fragile tradition of female labor organizing was buried in reformers' well-intentioned efforts and in workingmen's rhetoric of the working-class home. Whatever resources of eloquence and organizational skill the straw sewers in 1851 might still have possessed, the men from the Industrial Congress ignored them. Whatever professions of female rights the women might have made, their patrons were more interested in testimonies to female victimization. A strain of female dissent, nourished by popular republicanism, had dissolved.

In the 1850s, women's labor activity narrowed to a few flurries in family-based trades: a strike of handloom weavers in 1850, an organizing effort by German women shoe binders in 1859. By 1865, when the National Labor Union first met to try to expand upon the kind of national solidarity the NTU had represented thirty years earlier, only three national unions admitted women. Of the three, shoemaking and cigar making were, as we have seen, family-based trades. Only in the third, printing, had women outside familial networks succeeded in pressing their claims on the men.[59] Admittedly, in places like Lynn, where family-based work persisted into the late nineteenth century, the tradition of female republicanism continued without interruption.[60] When women expressed their workplace griev-ances in the voices of wives and daughters (as they did there), echoing the sentiments of a tightly knit community, it was easier for men to reconcile female claims to rights with their own sense of themselves as the women's protectors. But the female working class in New York encompassed a far wider range of women's situations. It was this female heterogeneity, this metropolitan variety in women's relations to the family, that New York workingmen had such difficulty in recognizing.

Unlike the insurgencies of the 1830s, the 1850–51 crisis in labor relations stirred up no new thoughts on women. Even the paternalism of the Indus-trial Congress was less developed, less considered than that of its predeces-sors. By 1851, working-class paternalism leaned more heavily on genteel formulations of women's nature than on elucidations of women's place in working-class life. A "true womanhood" for the working class had ap-peared, clothed in meekness and fragility.

Eventually, the conflation of bourgeois and working-class women's ex-perience in the imagery of universal womanhood would prove useful for both groups, at least within the late nineteenth-century women's move-ment. The notion that similar oppressions affected women of all classes was eventually to enrich all women's comprehension of gender experience, and was to provide working-class women with important allies in labor bat-tles.[61] But New York labor politics in the 1850s were largely detached from the women's rights movement, and laboring women there gained little from linking their troubles to sentimental renderings of women's sorrows. The construction of the meek, impoverished seamstress, bearing in silence "suf-ferings and trials that would chill the sternest heart," did legitimate work-ingwomen's problems within the discourse of antebellum reform. More-over, it introduced to a broad popular audience the perception that there was a systematic relationship between gender oppression and wage work. But sentimentalism also undercut workingwomen's greatest resource, their comprehension of their problems within the framework of a female legacy rooted in their class experience. It also obliterated part of that experience. The solitary seamstress was a denuded realization of the real-life urban wage earner, with her special problems and preoccupations. Could such a friendless, defeated creature invoke her rights as a breadwinner? Could she, for that matter, ever dance on the Bowery or fight with her neighbor?

Workingwomen had enough trouble in articulating their particular problems and aspirations; in the future, they would find it far more difficult to elucidate those parts of their lives that lay outside the imaginative arena which sentimentalist language claimed as properly female. If they were no longer quite outsiders, either to their own men's community or to the ideological community of women, they had also given up the immediate possibility of a language of their own.

Chapter 8 Domestic Service

Even as the manufacturing system extended its reach, domestic service, that most traditional of female employments, remained the largest paid occupation for women in New York. Since the early nineteenth century, service had increasingly tended to be women's work; by 1840 it was entirely so in bourgeois homes. But it was also work that women did not much like, and they abandoned it whenever they had the chance. Manufacturing employments, outside and inside, brought their own hardships, but women often preferred them to domestic service, with its relatively high wages but claustrophobic conditions. As other female employments opened, the women who knew where to seek them did so, and domestic service increasingly became work for those just off the boat. Once the Irish Famine immigrants began pouring into Manhattan, domestic service became even more sharply defined as immigrant women's work.

Domestic service dramatized the problems that poor immigrant women presented to the cult of domesticity. Nowhere was the contest between two modes of womanhood more evident than between the Irish immigrants and the ladies who employed them. Service had always been full of difficulties for both parties involved; in antebellum New York, however, those difficulties worsened into what commentators commonly observed was "a general servile war."[1] Some conflicts were over wages and working conditions. Although the Irish girls and young women were fresh from the countryside, they nonetheless held strong opinions about what their employers owed them, opinions that differed considerably from their mistresses' convictions of what their servants owed *them* as ladies. Other tensions arose over issues of gender, as mistresses imbued with the evangelizing message of true womanhood encountered servants whose yearnings for metropolitan recreations lay well outside the province of what their mistresses deemed to be female propriety. By midcentury, the "servant problem" in New York involved an attempt by mistresses to reform immigrant women *as* women, as well as to discipline them as workers, to change the way they dressed, courted and carried on their social lives.

Like the women of the city's charity and reform associations (who were employers of servants themselves), mistresses believed that the working-class women who entered their sphere could only benefit from an experience of properly feminine ways. Because Victorian women saw moral reform in the home as their particular social responsibility, the task of helping domestics to better themselves as women became for the mistresses a mission of their own womanly influence. As the New York novelist Catharine Sedgwick wrote in 1856 about the servant problem, "We know it requires great virtue, conscientiousness, efficiency, and, above all, patience on the part of the mistress; but let her think of the missionary . . . who brings the ignorant to the light of her home, and makes that the field of her *mission*."[2]

Servants' Work

In the early nineteenth century, New York servants were a heterogeneous group: the country-born and the city-bred, natives and immigrants, blacks and whites, freeborn and slaves. Although most were women, a substantial minority of men worked as butlers, coachmen and footmen in the retinues of the wealthy.[3] Some servants were children, like the poor little Dutch girl charged with attempted arson in 1805; she purposefully left live coals scattered about, hoping that when her employers discovered her carelessness they would send her back to her parents in Amsterdam.[4] Aside from children, most female servants were teenagers, whatever their origin or race. It was usually impossible for mothers and wives to work in service, which was a live-in employment, and older women stayed away from servants' work because it was too arduous physically for those beyond the prime of life.[5]

By midcentury the servant class was far more homogeneous, comprised of young Irish women in their teens and early twenties. By 1855, 74 percent of New York's domestics were Irish; only 4 percent were native-born whites.[6] The transformation had begun with the immigration from the British Isles in the 1820s; in the same period, white native-born women began to turn aside from service as manufacturing work became an alternative. American-born women considered domestic service degrading. "The unwillingness of the poorer classes of Americans to hire themselves out as servants" was proverbial in the 1820s, and in the 1830s, British travelers found that domestic servants were "a subject of incessant complaint with the wealthier and more aristocratic families."[7] The practice of hiring children also declined; as was the case in manufacturing, there was little need for employers to take on girls when young women were so easy to come by. The availability of the Irish pushed black women, who, in the early nineteenth century, had often worked as general household servants (as free laborers and as slaves) into specialized situations in the retinues of the wealthy and in brothels as laundresses, charwomen and maids. In 1855, only 3 percent of the city's servants were black. German immigrants in the 1840s would also work cheaply, but the language barrier made them less desirable employees; although 14 percent of domestics were German in 1855, they would have mostly worked in German households.[8]

Many of the young Irish women were in comparatively advantageous circumstances, although their wages were as low as those of any other women workers.[9] The difference lay in the live-in situation: Since room and board were free, servants had no necessities to purchase except clothes. Compared to outside work, their employment was also steadier, probably about as reliable as factory work. To be sure, a word from a mistress could throw a woman out of work within the hour, and unemployment was common during the summer when the prosperous left New York for the country. Still, service was not casualized work, and there was no week-to-week threat of unemployment. Consequently, most Irish domestics lived a little above the hand-to-mouth regimen so common to women of their class.

With their wages, servants built up dowries, brought over kin from Ireland and helped their families make ends meet. Servants were, in fact, the only women workers who saved money. From 1819 to 1847, they accounted for one-half to two-thirds of the unskilled workers, male and female, who opened accounts each year at the New York Bank for Savings.[10] Their wages, however, did not always go to such prudent concerns. Servants spent liberally on fancy dresses and evenings at the theater, manifesting a predilection for working-class leisure culture that constantly irritated their mistresses.

In the 1820s, servants' work was mostly unchanged from the eighteenth century. The material setting of the prosperous household was much the same. From the 1790s until the Greek Revival fashions of the 1840s, the four-story brick row house, Federal style, was the favored architecture of the families of prosperous tradesmen and master artisans, merchants and professionals.[11] As in the households of the poor, there were no utilities. Street pumps provided water; fireplaces provided heat; candles and kerosene lamps gave light and cooking was done on an open hearth. Compared to later Victorian styles, the decorations and furnishings of these Federal households were restrained, but the residents did take house-proud pleasure in what ornamentation there was. Street fronts, for instance, were adorned with plain brass railings which were always shined to a high polish despite New York's corrosive weather, and a servant girl who "could not clean brasses to suit" could lose her situation.[12]

Service in these households was a demanding occupation. The work load was heavy and the day long. It began at 4:30 or 5 a.m., an hour before the family rose, and ended at 9 or 10 p.m.; when there were young children a servant was on call all night.[13] The chores of any one domestic depended on how many others the family employed; prosperous households divided up the work among a cook, waiter and maid, but more modest people would employ one maid-of-all-work. No matter how many domestics there were, there was certain work that always fell to them rather than to family members. Cooking, serving and washing up for three meals and an afternoon tea were their duties, as well as all the menial labor that women and children did in the tenements and that utilities would later make unnecessary. Charles Haswell, a lifelong New Yorker born in 1816, described the routine of the antebellum years in some detail:

> Domestic service . . . until the introduction of illuminating gas, hot-air furnaces, and Croton water, and the construction of street sewers, was much more onerous than at this time. Oil lamps required trimming and filling; candlesticks, the fronts of grate-fenders, and frequently the shovel and tongs of brass, were to be cleaned; wood and coal to be brought from the cellar to all the fires, and the absence of hall-stoves rendered fires necessary in all sitting rooms. All water required for the kitchen, or bedrooms, or for baths, was drawn from the nearest street pump, and all refuse water and slops were carried out to the street and emptied into the gutter. . . . The street, for half its width in front of each building, was to be swept twice a week.[14]

Along with this round of housekeeping and provisioning, there were also the chores of tending children, laundering, sewing and mending the family's garments.[15]

Between roughly 1780 and 1820, the involvement of mistresses in this domestic routine changed as the skilled work of domestic production— candle making, soap making, spinning and weaving—began to decline in the city. Some household crafts were yet alive: In the 1820s women still hurried back from the country in September to lay in preserves, sausage and head cheese, and Harriet Martineau found on her tour a decade later that wives of business and professional men still supervised the sewing, baking and preserving.[16] Nonetheless, with the commercialization of many domestic crafts, there was a diminution of actual labor in the lives of the prosperous and a new emphasis on their role as consumers rather than producers in the household economy. Being a lady, in fact, meant *not* doing certain kinds of housework. "It is not genteel for mothers to wash and dress their own children, or make their own clothing," observed Lydia Maria Child, who arrived in New York in 1841.[17] Neither did a lady scrub her own floors, do her own washing, make fires or empty slops. "Women might work, but not ladies; or when the latter undertook it, they ceased to be such," a contemporary explained.[18]

The disengagement of mistresses from household labor gave them a great deal of leisure for shopping, entertaining, making calls and working for evangelical and charity associations. Maria Todd is a case in point. A merchant's wife, she supervised her domestics at home in the morning and spent the afternoons visiting about among the households of her married children. She was a deeply devout Baptist, her evenings usually taken up with some kind of Christian endeavor: tract society meetings, her women's prayer group, church services or her own private devotions.[19] Julia Lay, married to a head bookkeeper in a bank, had five children whom she left with her servants while she went out to shop, distribute tracts, visit the poor and attend reform lectures.[20] Women like Julia Lay and Maria Todd were not the idle Victorian ladies of cultural convention: Both were purposeful and industrious women, burdened by frequent pregnancies, the tasks of nursing sick children and the obligations of extensive and intimate kin networks. Nonetheless, they were not involved in the daily business of producing for and maintaining a household, as middling women had been in the late eighteenth century.

Those eighteenth-century households had required "helps," as servants were called then, apprentices and assistants in domestic production. The homes of antebellum ladies required servants, "domestics," for different sorts of duties.[21] Less involved in the productive and caretaking tasks of domestic labor, mistresses in the 1840s and 1850s came to concentrate on housework as the creation and maintenance of comfort and appearance. Cleanliness, tidiness and the care and arrangement of possessions replaced domestic production as housewives' preoccupations. The homes of the urban bourgeoisie became a means of elaborating a class and gender identity, one which for many people, newly arrived from the ranks of middling tradesmen and craftsmen, was still tenuous. In New York, the tendency to

make the home a display of "woman's place" dominated the sensibility of
the upwardly mobile ladies of the stratum that George Foster in 1850
sarcastically labeled "the Upper Ten Thousand."[22] These were the women
who read ladies' magazines and the counsels of domestic advice manuals on
the arrangement and decoration of rooms. They were the customers for the
city's burgeoning ready-made furniture industry. They ornamented their
houses with knickknacks and plants; they worked doilies, netted curtains
and embroidered cushions for their parlors.[23] These decorations emblema-
tized their talents at acquiring, arranging and fashioning things that expressed, within an aesthetic of interior design, their love and care for their
families. Feminine genius delighted in "decorating life," wrote Ralph
Waldo Emerson;[24] servants became adjuncts to the process of feminine
self-expression by helping their mistresses to maintain the tranquil and
orderly tone and embellished decor of the home.

A more defined geography of class distinguished the town houses these
families built in New York from those of the old merchant and professional
elite. A separation of work and leisure between downstairs and upstairs
advertised both the social distance between the two sets of residents and the
power of one set to make the other climb stairs. If a lady's place was in the
home, it was also upstairs in the home. When a servant had "high words"
with her mistress in 1819, it was in the kitchen,[25] but in the 1840s the scene
of domestics' confrontations shifted upstairs to the parlor, where they were
literally "called on the carpet." The position of the dining room is the most
telling indication of the altered topography. In Federal row houses, the
dining room and kitchen adjoined each other on the ground floor. In Greek
Revival brownstones, the informal dining room remained below, but the
back room on the parlor floor became the formal dining room, so that when
there were guests for dinner, servants climbed the stairs to serve the meal.
In the great five-story houses built in the 1850s in the most fashionable
neighborhoods, dumbwaiters put an end to carrying food up and down, but
they also allowed residents to move their dining rooms up to the third floor,
and servants climbed four flights instead of one between kitchen and table.
Differences in living conditions between family rooms and servants' quarters further dramatized class distinctions. There were two very different
standards of living within the same four walls. The servants' bedrooms on
the top floor were low-ceilinged, ill ventilated, badly heated and shabbily
furnished. When the first modern utilities became available in the 1840s,
they eased the work servants did for their employers, but they did not
change the servants' own living conditions. Water closets and bathtubs
appeared on the second and third floors where the family slept, but not on
the top floor where the servants' bedrooms were located. Domestics con-

tinued to use chamber pots and backyard privies and to take their baths in the kitchen. The family drew water for washing in their rooms, but servants still carried their own basins up the stairs and their slops back down.[26]

While servants were still responsible for the menial work that had been their province in the eighteenth century, by the 1840s they also had new obligations in fulfilling their mistresses' developing conceptions of the home. Much of the servant's labor was in service to her mistress's imagination—a situation that, given the Irish women involved, was highly abrasive. It was these new duties that aggravated endemic tensions between employers and servants into the notorious nineteenth-century servant problem, widely discussed in the feminine popular press and among New York ladies themselves. "The incapacity of servants is a constant theme," testified Dr. Sanger; the query "have you good help?" according to one writer in a ladies' magazine was a staple of feminine parlor conversation.[27] Serving girls were "universally complained of" and "generally and unhesitatingly denounced, even in their very presence [as] pests and curses."[28] In one sense the servant problem was an element of class-consciousness: One could not really *be* a lady if one did not have a problem with servants. For ladies who were not entirely confident of their own class identity, asserting judgment over the immigrant poor affirmed their position and status.

Tensions between employers and servants were certainly nothing new; there had always been room for trouble in the gap between what mistresses thought should be done and what domestics could or would do. As Rose Butler, whom we met before, recounted in 1819, her mistress "was always finding fault with my work, and scolding me"; this was why she had struck back by trying to burn the house down. Her response was extreme, but the vexations which prompted it were common. "I never did like her," she replied matter-of-factly to questions about her motives.[29]

Ideally, a domestic served as an extension of her mistress's sensibility, but in actuality she constantly made her own judgments about housework. Despite its reputation as unskilled labor, service required some skill and logic. A domestic did not work by rote, but made her own determinations about methods and standards. Should she polish a door knob to a high shine, or the highest? Was her dishwater too greasy for the remaining dishes, and should she bother to heat more? The household crafts of the eighteenth century—soap and candle making, brewing, preserving—were serial processes with their own logic to direct workers, but nineteenth-century housework was a set of discrete operations, each with its own potential for error. As mistresses came to invest more care and significance in the appearance of their homes, this contradiction became more stressful. Each task carried the potential for dispute. It was the mistress alone who was the judge of what was dirty and what was clean. Insofar as a domestic replicated her employer's sense of order, she succeeded; insofar as she diverged from it, she failed.[30]

The particular kind of housework required in Victorian rooms increased the opportunities for disagreements. These houses presented a denser material setting to servants than had the simple interiors of the Federal style; Victorian *horror vacui* was already asserting itself in New York interiors by the 1840s—an "epidemic of humbug and sham finery and gin-palace decoration," George Templeton Strong called it.[31] Objects multiplied: bric-a-brac, memorabilia, furniture, pictures. Detail proliferated in the popular Gothic and rococo styles: scrolls, fluting, carving, fretting, gilding, japanning and edging.[32] From the perspective of domestics, the profusion of detail and carving meant more surfaces to polish and cracks to dust. Possibilities for disorder increased with the number of objects. There were more possessions to be kept in place, more ornaments that could be broken. "Broke lid of butter crock, Joan of Arc lampshade, range cover & c—in three weeks," an aggrieved diarist noted of her new servant.[33] Doilies had to be set right, mementoes placed correctly, pictures straightened, crystal polished. Fashionable appointments called for special care. Cushions had to be plumped up, houseplants watered and vases filled with flowers. Brussels carpets, *de rigueur* for the parlors of all women with a love for domestic niceties, were brushed several times a week on hands and knees.[34] Ladies sedulously guarded the emblems and effects of "elegance" (a favored accolade of the ladies' magazines) they had acquired, and exacted the labor of their Irish girls accordingly.

The households in which rural Irish women had been raised did not prepare them for the demands of Victorian housekeeping. Although domestic service was the major paid occupation for young women in Ireland, employers there were likely to be farming people who trained their help in domestic crafts rather than in the kind of caretaking necessary in American homes. Even so, many Irish women had never worked outside the smallholders' cabins in which they lived. In the 1840s, about one-tenth of the female population in Ireland was employed as servants, an indication that many immigrants would have come to New York with no experience at all.[35] They had grown up in huts furnished with stools, pots and pans, sometimes bedsteads and tables or, lacking these amenities, straw pallets. Most Irish women were unfamiliar with the standards and techniques of Victorian housework and had little empathy with a sensibility that linked feminine virtue to the appearance of the home.[36]

"The principal difficulty a newcomer had to contend with is that of getting fairly initiated into, what is to her, a new system of housekeeping," advised the English hatter James Burn.[37] The employer's watchfulness and the servant's incompetence embroiled the two parties in a constant, fretful contact that was the bane of domestic service for both sides. "The girls do not work to her satisfaction unless she is over them all the time," a diarist remarked of a friend and her servants at spring cleaning time. The effort, she added, left the friend tired and fretful. "Wearied in body and mind after cleaning a large house," Maria Todd penned in her journal one Saturday night at the same time of year. "I have been much tryed with domesticks through the day but will try to write a few lines of prayer." The *Nation*'s editor Edwin Godkin, who lived in the city from 1856 to 1875, remarked on this "nagging of the employer" and the constant "presence of an exacting, semi-hostile, and slightly contemptuous person" as the reason that service was an employment "extraordinarily full of wear and tear."[38] The middling housewife of the eighteenth century had worked alongside her servants in a relationship approximating that of masters and apprentices. With the antebellum lady, the cult of domesticity and its attendant notions of the "womanly" became forms of labor discipline.

Private Affairs

The scrutiny of mistresses went beyond matters of work discipline. As they linked the home and its effects to their own gender identity, they associated standards of housekeeping with the vocations of womanhood: To be a lady was to enforce tidiness and cleanliness around one. In this context, they saw the sloppiness of their domestics as something more than the notorious idleness and laziness of the poor. Supervising servants became in itself something of a reforming vocation.[39] Servants were not only recalcitrant, they were unwomanly, and like charity visitors, female employers especially disapproved of working-class feminine deficiencies. "They turn her [the domestic] round and round, and look at her in all sorts of cross lights, so that if there be a spot or blemish in her they never fail to discern it."[40] The servant's social life, personal affairs, dress and appearance came under examination. "Do not people feel at liberty to question servants about their private affairs; to comment on their dress and appearance, in a manner which they would feel to be an impertinence, if reciprocated?" Catharine Beecher and Harriet Stowe remarked in their household manual.[41] The *Tribune* described similar attitudes toward servants' relations with men. "What a sneer runs the family circle of faces at the idea of Sally the cook or Betty the chambermaid having a beau! How impossible it is thought that either should be allowed to go out two evenings in succession after working

thirteen good hours during the day!"[42] Thus "Bridget, out in the evening
. . . though her beau had spent Wednesday evening with her," complained
a mistress in her journal in 1857. A week later: "Man to see Bridget, staid
till after 10." These were not offenses against work discipline so much as
violations of feminine propriety. A week later this mistress forbade the
servant to receive any male callers at all—and Bridget departed.[43]

Dress took on significance in this context. Like other single workingwomen, servants were notorious for spending their money on fancy
clothes. In 1822, for instance, the Society for the Relief of Poor Widows had
attributed as much importance to dress as a cause of women's thriftlessness
as the ladies did to drink for men.[44] Of the deposits made by workingwomen in a Baltimore savings bank in the same period, the director proudly
reported to his New York associates in the Society for the Prevention of
Pauperism that the money was "saved from luxury and dress."[45] But not
as much was saved as philanthropists might have wished. By the 1840s,
domestics provided enough business to support a large group of slop dressmakers in the city. The dresses cost two to three dollars—just about a
month's wages—and according to the Tribune's sources, some servants
ordered as many as eight a year.[46] "Outlandish, hot-looking dresses,"
George Foster described the clothes of women in an intelligence office—
an employment agency for servants. When one walked by, the dark interior
gave off "an intolerable glare of crimson and scarlet shawls, ribands, and
faded bonnet-flowers, with a sultry sense of yellow calico past all endur-
ance."[47] Irish girls, as soon as they could, shed their clogs and shifts—so
different from New York styles that one guidebook warned they were apt
to be "laughed out of use"—for hoopskirts and flowered bonnets.[48] An
employer exclaimed at her servant's presumptuousness: "New girl wanted
early tea that she might go to a dressmaker!"[49]

Employers had not always moralized about dress. In the eighteenth-
century world of urbane English fashion, employers of rank had encouraged their domestics to dress well, even sumptuously, by giving them their
cast-off clothes, a practice which the Anglophilic New York elite probably
shared. A well-dressed servant was an emblem of the employer's own
status.[50] There was, however, a countervailing belief that high dress among
the poor would erase class distinctions and increase insubordination, a
perspective which came to prevail in nineteenth-century America. The
democratization of fashion in America after 1820 conflicted with the desires
of an emerging urban bourgeoisie, who, themselves bereft of high origins,
liked to keep signs of rank to themselves. In New York, a city where
everyone had ambitions to stylishness, employers suffered particularly from
the cheeky dress of the lower orders. "Dress in a manner becoming your
station," the Society for the Encouragement of Faithful Domestic Servants

counseled its subjects in 1828. "Silks and satins put out the kitchen fire."[51]

By midcentury, clothes had become a highly charged issue between mistresses and Irish servants. The female editor of a ladies' magazine voiced a common criticism in 1861:

> Where is the servant girl who wears a costume adapted to her duties and position in life, or who would mark herself as a menial by the assumption of the style enforced eighty years ago upon every domestic . . . which differed in make and material diametrically from the "robe" or "gown," worn by the lady mistress.[52]

At first hand in their own households, New York ladies encountered the presumptions of working-class feminine fashion that offended them from afar on the streets. "The washerwoman's Sunday attire is now as nearly like that of the merchant's wife as it can be, and the bootblack's daughter wears a bonnet made like that of the Empress of the French." "The girls generally imbibe from their mistresses the worst and most pernicious of all domestic follies—love for finery," a male critic remarked.[53] Mistresses did not take imitation as flattery; they resented it. Fancy dress ran too close to their own sense of distinctiveness and what they felt to be their monopoly on womanly airs. Mistresses pressed servants to dress plainly and sensibly, as befitted the women who, in their view of things, were born to labor so that other women might be freed to exercise the influence of their sex. When domestics dressed in their own fashion to slip out for an evening on the Bowery, they asserted their claims to a womanhood incompatible with the silent suffering that was, in theory, the true working-class woman's lot. The stylish dress of working-class women, with its elaborated code of feminine physicality, implicitly challenged the ladies' designation of themselves as chief proprietors of womanly gratification. It was a sign that servants as well as mistresses could aspire to the finery of life.

"Unreasoning Habits"

Against their mistresses' pressure to put themselves under their scrutiny and at their disposal, Irish domestics succeeded, on the whole, in guarding a certain independence, grounded in both a sense of themselves as wage-workers and as women with their own prerogatives of sex. In the 1820s, too, the laments of the Society for the Encouragement of Faithful Domestic Servants in New York show that servants had resisted employers' attempts to impose paternalist obligations upon them. By the 1840s, however, Irish-women seem to have been especially adept at cutting through such trappings to the heart of the wage relation. Virginia Penny heard from employers that "most are raw Irish girls, who think when they come to this country, everybody is equal."[54] Unlike their mistresses, who liked to look on their help as extensions of themselves, servants themselves looked at service as an exchange of a given amount of labor for a wage rather than a moral obligation to a benevolent overseer. Insofar as they could, they stated the limits to their side of the exchange in the agreement they made when they were hired. "Difficulties arise from labor being required . . . that they have not stipulated to perform," Penny reported. "Many of them are very exacting."[55]

Despite the numbers of immigrants who sought work in service, the demand was high enough for young women to negotiate terms with some success. Some emigrated knowing something about the terms and pitfalls of domestic service, having worked as servants in Ireland. Others were familiar with the arts of tough bargaining from bartering and selling garden and dairy products, a common women's occupation in Ireland.[56] City life and the milieu of the intelligence offices, however, quickly socialized even inexperienced girls into the tricks of the trade. A journalist who visited an intelligence office was amused and affronted to see the immigrants meet potential employers with skeptical queries: "One might naturally suppose that, under the circumstances, some degree of gratefulness would be manifested. But there is not a bit of it." Instead, they asked " 'how many children have yees?' 'Shure yees don't expect a girral to stay in doors on Sundays?' —'Do yees give the washin' out?' " "The next question is the wages," he continued, "and they will not infrequently refuse a good home and reasonable pay for the doubtful contingency of securing half-a-dollar per month more, after waiting a long time unemployed."[57] The contacts that young women made with each other in the intelligence offices and the policies of the agencies themselves fostered informal collective agreements about reasonable terms of employment, collaborations that Penny complained about. "Another thing that makes some so trifling, is that such swarms come, and they are so ignorant, and many of them so corrupt, that they instigate each other."[58] Domestics brought to their situations strong opinions about the limits to their duties, and they often left when those limits were transgressed. "Whenever one thinks she is imposed upon," wrote Horace Greeley, "the invariable plan is to threaten to leave the situation at once, instead, as in other kinds of employment, of being fearful of losing it."[59] "We endeavoured to reconcile Nancy the cook to her situation which she considered quite laborious," the secretary of a charity asylum wrote in the minutes in 1840. "The washing and baking from the increase of inmates, was too much for her."[60] Nancy agreed to stay, providing the ladies hired more help for her. She bargained on the probability she could find another position and on the ladies' reluctance to spend time finding and training a new cook, as did many of her fellow workers when they bridled at being "imposed upon."

Time off was another area where servants bargained for formally stated terms. Victorian mistresses were more parsimonious in this regard than employers had been in the eighteenth century, when time off on Sundays and holidays and for parties and the theater was a perquisite of employment.[61] This is not to say that masters and mistresses always granted the time happily, since time off was always an area of struggle for employers and domestics. But by the mid-nineteenth century, the balance of power on this count had so shifted that domestics had to wrangle for time off on Sunday alone. "Where is the family with half a day's work on Sunday?" Horace Greeley inquired. "In how many families is not Sunday as hard a day for servants as any in the week?" He went on to argue that the absence of time for a personal life caused respectable women to look on service as demeaning; some mistresses, in fact, tried to limit or forbid their servants receiving company in the house.[62] Penny also found that "girls prefer mechanical labor to domestic service, because they have the evenings to themselves. . . . They think it more honorable, and it secures to them more time—in short, they are more their own mistresses."[63] A highly critical Southern visitor to the city observed with gleeful malice that servants in the metropolis of free labor had to beg for the time to attend mass.[64]

Domestics were at a particular stage of life: sexually mature but not yet constrained by marriage and children. They were not tied to households of their own, and insofar as life ever bloomed for them, it did so at their age, in courting, lovemaking, dancing, drinking at places like the Bowery resorts. The social lives of young women were insistent and urgent: Chances had to be taken or lost forever. It is significant that despite the reputation of the factories for setting girls on the road to ruin, the ostensibly respectable employment of domestic service far more readily propelled girls into prostitution. Of all working girls, servants were the most likely to engage in the sex trade, Dr. William Sanger found. Proprietors of brothels often recruited girls at intelligence offices.[65] The freedom and high living that prostitution promised were all the more compelling to young women constrained in service.

The prying of mistresses as well as their demands for time interfered with the pursuits of unmarried women. A factory, for all its oppressions, set a standard work routine and hours that were more or less limited, and outside workers, for all their hardships, could still mingle wage work with their own concerns and social relations. But "in domestic service all of a chambermaid's time is expected."[66] An immigrant who had just arrived in New York might acquiesce for a time, like the young woman lauded for her exemplary behavior in the annals of the Society for the Encouragement of Faithful Domestic Servants in 1828. "She has little or no company," her employer testified warmly, "and never wishes to go out, except to church on Sunday. . . . She has no idea of poor girls either going to or giving parties, and has never been to one since she has been here."[67] But most young Irishwomen in the 1840s were not so pliable. Even a new arrival who had no kin or friends could make acquaintances on the way to market. Once she felt the pull of a place like the Bowery, a rule against receiving company in the house became an aggravation, and a mistress's questions about her reasons for wanting to go out in the evening became an imposition. Then half a day on Sunday or an hour stolen away on an errand was not enough time, and she could bridle, "with all the unreasoning habits and prejudices of the Celtic blood."[68]

"We are continually harrowed with tales of the sufferings of distressed needle-women," Beecher and Stowe remarked, "and yet women will en-counter all these chances of ruin and starvation rather than make up their minds to permanent domestic service. Now, what is the matter with domes-tic service?"[69] It was hard menial labor, but so were other kinds of paid employment that women chose over service when they had the chance. But added to the hardships of domestic service were the close quarters with employers, the personalized and irregular work routine and the curious set of pressures that mistresses brought to bear on their domestics concerning their conduct as women. These strains made the Victorian servant problem different from the perennial conflict between employee and employer. The incursions that moral reformers made into the lives of poor women were necessarily limited, but mistresses had a wider field in which to teach their domestics the lessons of gender. Despite their poverty, however, these young immigrant women, with their gaudy costumes, promenades and evenings at the theater, had their own notions of where to seek the makings of womanhood.

Part Four

The Politics of the Streets,

1850–1860

Chapter 9 Women on the Town: Sexual Exchange and Prostitution

As urban reformers and writers told it, no tale of working-class life was more chilling in its revelations of vice than the prostitute's. From the 1830s on, prostitutes flitted wraithlike across the pages of urban social commentary, a class of women rendered human only by the occasional penitent in their ranks. Prostitutes had long been familiar to New Yorkers, but between 1830 and 1860 women "on the town" became the subject of a sustained social commentary. By the 1850s, urban prostitution was troubling enough to lead city fathers to lend the services of their police force in aiding William Sanger in conducting a massive investigation. Dr. Sanger's report, the compendious *History of Prostitution*, represents the coming of age of prostitution as a social "problem" in America, and its integration into the new discourse of secular urban reform.

The very fact that reformers in the 1850s were thinking about prostitution had to do with tensions over gender relations and female sexuality. To them, prostitution was simply a verifiable empirical reality synonymous with the degradation of morals and public health. But between the lines of their considerations ran another discussion, barely delineated, about the dangerous impulses of girls and young women. In New York culture, the image of the Bowery Gal was one side of the coin of youthful pleasures; that of the hardened girl on the streets was the other. The alarm over prostitution was one response to the growing social and sexual distance that working-class women—especially working-class daughters—were traveling from patriarchal regulation.

The problem of prostitution as reformers defined it had no necessary relation to the experience of the women involved. For laboring women, prostitution was a particular kind of choice presented by the severities of daily life. It was both an economic and a social option, a means of self-support and a way to bargain with men in a situation where a living wage was hard to come by, and holding one's own in heterosexual relations was difficult. The reasons girls and women went into prostitution, the uses they made of it and the relation it bore to the rest of their lives varied greatly. The reformers' image of prostitution as an irreversible descent into degradation obfuscated more of this complex reality than it revealed.[1]

The Problem

In 1818, when the city watch published its latest statistics on crime, the authorities took a complacent view of prostitution. Although the numbers of known prostitutes and bawdy houses in the city had doubled in a dozen years, they reported, the women and their patrons had never been more quiet and law-abiding.[2] In subsequent years, an offensive against urban vice put an end to such laissez-faire attitudes. After 1831, when the evangelical women of New York's Magdalene Society first took up the battle to banish prostitution from the city, denunciations of what was purported to be an urgent problem became common currency among moral reformers and public authorities. "We have satisfactorily ascertained the fact that the numbers of females in this city, who abandon themselves to prostitution is not less than TEN THOUSAND!!!!!" announced John McDowall, agent for the Magdalene Society, in its first annual report in 1832. McDowall's figure was up by more than eight times from the 1818 estimate, a supposed increase which should give us pause.[3] Whatever number reformers picked, however, they used it to stress the reason for alarm. The National Trades' Union in the 1830s, the Ladies' Industrial Association in 1845, reformers Matthew Carey and later Horace Greeley all promoted a similar view that prostitution was making heavy incursions into the female poor.[4] By 1855, public concern was sufficiently strong to move the aldermen to commission William Sanger to conduct a statistical investigation in New York of the kind Parent-Duchâtelet had published for Paris in 1836. Sanger's researches confirmed to him and to his public (as such researches often do) that the city was indeed prey to an "enormous vice." It was, he gravely concluded, "a fact beyond question that this vice is attaining a position and extent in this community which cannot be viewed without alarm."[5]

Was, indeed, prostitution on the rise, expanding along with the manufacturing system, as many people believed? Given the fragmentary statistics, it is hard now to answer conclusively, but the reformers' and officials' estimates tend (contrary to their own conclusions) to disprove the argument. In fact, prostitution seems only to have increased along with the population, at the rate one would expect in a city that multiplied in size more than six times between 1820 and 1860. There was certainly an increase in the absolute number of prostitutes. Police Chief Matsell estimated there were 5,000 women on the town in 1856, as compared to the watch's 1,200 in 1818.[6] But these figures, tenuous as they are, actually indicate a slight *decrease* in the numbers of prostitutes proportional to the urban population. On the level of numbers alone, then, it seems there were more prostitutes simply because there were more people.

Of course, this does not mean there were no problems. The increase in absolute numbers had important effects. Commitments of women to prison for vagrancy, the statutory offense under which prostitution fell, more than doubled between 1850 and 1860; imprisonments for keeping disorderly houses, often the rubric under which houses of prostitution fell, multiplied by more than five times between 1849 and 1860.[7] These statistics cannot tell us how many women were convicted for prostitution, since the police could arrest women in the streets simply because they were homeless. But since the majority of female arrests were of girls and young women ten to thirty years old, the age bracket into which the majority of the women Sanger interviewed fell,[8] it seems likely that prostitution played some role in the increase in vagrancy arrests from 3,500 in 1850 to nearly 6,500 in 1860. In itself, this spectacular rise must have convinced New Yorkers they were living amidst an epidemic of female vice, insofar as they closely associated female homelessness and poverty with depravity.

The urgency of the discussion, however, was also a response to the changing character of the trade. What disturbed observers was not just the number of women who bargained with men for sex, but the identity of those women. For if the numbers of known professional prostitutes were not growing disproportionally, those of casual prostitutes—girls or women who turned to prostitution temporarily or episodically to supplement other kinds of livelihoods—probably were. Moreover, the entire context of the transaction was changing, as prostitution moved out of the bawdy houses of the poor into cosmopolitan public spaces like Broadway. "It no longer confines itself to secrecy and darkness," lamented Sanger, "but boldly strikes through our most thronged and elegant thoroughfares."[9]

Prostitution was becoming urbane. The trade was quite public in the

business district as well as in poor neighborhoods, a noticeable feature of
the ordinary city landscape. Since prostitution was not a statutory offense,
there was no legal pressure to conceal it. By 1857, William Sanger could
catalogue a wide range of establishments catering to prostitution. "Parlor
houses," clustered near the elegant hotels on Broadway, were the most
respectable, frequented by gentlemen; the second-class brothels served
clerks and "the higher class of mechanics."[10] In some theaters, prostitutes
solicited and consorted with patrons in the notorious third tier, reserved for
their use, although the high-toned Park Theater had closed its third tier in
1842, and Sanger noted that other theaters patronized by the genteel were
following suit. Except for the parlor and bawdy houses, however, the trade
was informal rather than organized; that is, a woman could easily ply it on
her own outside a brothel. Prostitution was still a street trade of independent workers; pimps were a phenomenon of the early twentieth century,
a consequence of the onset of serious police harassment.[11] The places where
"street-walkers" resorted served other erotic functions as well. Houses of
assignation, where much casual prostitution took place, were private establishments where a couple could rent rooms by the hour; illicit lovers used
them for trysting places. There was a hierarchy of houses of assignation:
the respectable brownstones off Broadway, where ladies carried on affairs
during the hours of the afternoon promenade; the shabby-genteel houses,
where shopgirls, milliners and domestic servants went with gentlemen
"sweethearts" with whom their work brought them in contact; and the
cheap houses where working-class couples and prostitutes resorted and
where fast young men set up their working-class mistresses to live. Around
the waterfront were the lowest class of establishments, basement dramshops
with rooms in the back frequented by sailors, immigrants and poor transients, and better-kept dancing houses with adjoining rooms for girls and
their clients.[12] In the same working-class neighborhoods, prostitution also
went on in the tenements themselves. In the district near City Hall, where
there was a lively interest in commercial sex from the many men of all
classes doing business there, an investigating commission found that "it is
a well-known fact that in many of the tenant-houses of this district such
persons [prostitutes] occupy suites of apartments interspersed with those of
the respectable laboring classes, and frequently difficult to be distinguished
from them." In the lowest neighborhoods, near-destitute residents sometimes rented out corners of their rooms to prostitutes.[13]

There were specialized services as well. In the 1840s, a nascent commercial sex trade began to offer variegated sexual experiences beyond the
prostitute's bed, mostly to gentlemen. The sex trade was centered in the
area between City Hall Park, the commercial heart of the city, and the Five
Points. There, crime and amusement rubbed elbows, laboring people mixed

with gentlemen and the quick scam flourished. Visitors and men about town could, within an easy walk from most places of business, gain entrance to dance halls featuring naked performers, brothels with child prostitutes, eating places decorated with pornographic paintings, pornographic book shops and "model artist" shows, where naked women arranged themselves in edifying tableaux from literature and art (Susannah and the Elders, for example)—as well as a variety of facilities for having sex. The network of sexual experiences for sale was certainly troubling evidence of the centrality of sex to metropolitan life; indeed, its presence in the most cosmopolitan areas of the city was one indication of just how closely a particular kind of sex (bourgeois men with working-class women) was linked to an evolving mode of sophisticated urbanity.[14]

In a city so concerned with defining both women's proper place and the place of the working class, the alarm over prostitution stemmed in part from general hostilities to the milieu of laboring women from which prostitutes came. "Prostitution" evolved in the nineteenth century as a particular construction, the grouping of a range of sexual experiences which in actual life might be quite disparate. The discourse about prostitution was embedded in genteel preoccupations; while working-class people had their own concerns about prostitution, they remained marginal to the developing public discussion. Bourgeois men and women, who understood female sexuality within the terms of the cult of true womanhood, tended to see any woman who was sexually active outside of marriage as a prostitute. While their judgments were not inherently class bound ("true" women who strayed were equally liable to condemnation), they obviously weighed more heavily on poor women, who did not adhere to standards of premarital (or sometimes even extramarital) chastity. Although working-class men and women could judge and condemn with the same severity as reformers, they did so by the standards of a sexual morality with more fluid definitions of licit and illicit, good and bad, respectability and transgression.

Going to Ruin

For laboring people as well as bourgeois moralists, prostitution was closely linked to "ruin," a state of affairs to be avoided at all costs. But while bourgeois men and women viewed ruin as the consequence of prostitution, working-class people reversed the terms. It was ruin, occasioned by a familial or economic calamity (for women the two were synonymous), that precipitated the "fall" into prostitution. The disasters that afflicted women's lives—male desertion, widowhood, single motherhood—propelled adult women into prostitution as a comparatively easy way to earn a living. The prospect of prostitution was, like the possibility of these other misfortunes, a part of everyday life: a contingency remote to the blessed, the strong and the fortunate, right around the corner for the weak and the unlucky. Prostitution was neither a tragic fate, as moralists viewed it (and continue to view it), nor an act of defiance, but a way of getting by, of making the best of bad luck.

Prostitution was indeed, as reformers liked to point out, tied to the female labor market. Women on their own earned such low wages that in order to survive, they often supplemented waged employment with casual prostitution. There is a good deal of information on this practice in the 1850s because William Sanger asked about it. "A large number of females," he observed, "earn so small wages that a temporary cessation of their business, or being a short time out of a situation, is sufficient to reduce them to absolute distress."[15] A quarter of Sanger's subjects, about 500 of the 2,000 women interviewed, had worked in manufacturing employment, mostly in the needle trades. More than a quarter again had earned wages of a dollar or less a week; more than half earned less than three dollars. Some 300 were still working at a trade; 325 had only left their work within the six months previous.[16]

From this information, we can infer something about the earning patterns of young women on their own. Their wages alone could not have financed nights on the Bowery. Casual prostitution, exchanging sexual favors with male escorts for money or food and drink (what a later generation called "treating"[17]), may have been one way young women on the town got by. The stories Sanger collected from his errant subjects, however, also chronicled the grimmer side of female employment, when there was no money to buy food, let alone theater tickets. "M. M., a widow with one child, earned $1.50 a week as a tailoress." "E. H. earned from two to three dollars a week as tailoress, but had been out of employment for some time." "M. F., a shirt-maker, earned one dollar a week." "S. F., a widow with three children, could earn two dollars weekly at cap-making, but could not obtain steady employment even at those prices."[18]

Many of the women with whom Sanger and his police interviewers talked had turned to prostitution as the closest employment at hand after suddenly losing male support. Many had been left alone in the city by husbands or family: 471—almost one-fourth—were married women who had become single and self-supporting through circumstances beyond their control. Eight percent had been deserted by their husbands; fifteen percent widowed. Fifty-seven percent had lost their fathers before they reached the age of twenty.[19] In themselves, such statistics tell us nothing about the role that destitution played in prostitution. Taken together, however, they do reveal the forces that made prostitution a reasonable choice in a society in which economic support from a man was a prerequisite for any kind of decent life. "No work, no money, and no home," was the succinct description one woman gave of her circumstances. The stark facts that others recited illuminate some of the urgent situations which pushed women out onto the streets. "My husband deserted me and four children. I had no means to live." "My husband eloped with another woman. I support the child." "I came to this city, from Illinois, with my husband. When we got here he deserted me. I have two children dependent on me."[20] These were the painful female actualities from which popular culture would fashion its own morality tales of sexual victimization and depravity.

Sanger veered away from the blanket moral condemnations of early reform literature toward the more dispassionate and environmentalist perspective of early British and French social science. While moral categories entered into his analysis, he preferred to focus on exterior forces and social solutions rather than on the spiritual transformation of the working class that the evangelicals sought.[21] Women were victims of poverty, the wage system, orphanage, abandonment and seduction. For Sanger, even their "passion" became a kind of environmental factor, divested of moral choice and existing apart from their conscious agency.

Yet ultimately Sanger's survey yields a very different picture than his own preferred one of the victim of circumstance, the distressed needle-woman and the deserted wife at starvation's door. His exhaustive queries revealed a great deal about the roots of prostitution in economic desperation, but they also produced compelling evidence about more complex sources. When Sanger asked his subjects their reasons for taking up prostitution, over a quarter—a number almost equal to those who cited "destitution"—gave "inclination" as their answer. "Inclination," whatever its moral connotations, still indicated some element of choice within the context of other alternatives. "C. M.: while virtuous, this girl had visited dance-houses, where she became acquainted with prostitutes, who persuaded her that they led an easy, merry life." "S. C.: this girl's inclination arose from a love of liquor." "E. C. left her husband, and became a prostitute willingly, in order to obtain intoxicating liquors which had been refused her at home."[22]

The historical issues are complicated. One can imagine a sullen woman trapped in the virtual jail that was the Blackwell's Island venereal disease hospital, flinging cynical answers—"drink," "amusement"—to the good doctor's questions as those most likely to shock him or to appeal to the preconceptions she sensed in him. But although this may have been true in some encounters, the dynamic between the doctor and his subject is an unlikely explanation of why so many women rejected a paradigm of victimization (which, if anything, Sanger himself promoted) for answers that stressed their own agency in entering prostitution. Altogether, 918 of the subjects implied motives other than hardship. Sanger classified their responses as: "too idle to work," "persuaded by prostitutes," "an easy life," "drink, and the desire to drink," "ill-treatment of parents, relatives or husbands."[23] Whatever the ways in which the women constructed their stories in consort with Sanger, there seems to have been some common self-understanding, widely enough shared to seem independent of the doctor, that one might choose prostitution within the context of other alternatives.

Of course we cannot separate such answers from the economic difficulties laboring women faced. But structural factors alone cannot clarify why some women took up prostitution and others in similar straits did not. Nor can they illuminate the histories of women who entered prostitution from comparatively secure economic positions. Almost half of Sanger's subjects, for instance, were domestic servants; servants were long notorious (at least since 1820) for turning to prostitution not because they were desperate for work but because they longed for a change.[24] And although the poorest New Yorkers, new immigrants, were well-represented in the 1855 sample —35 percent of Sanger's subjects were Irish, 12 percent German—there were also significant numbers of the native-born: 38 percent, or 762 of the total. Daughters of skilled workers were also present to a surprising extent —30 percent—surprising, since one would suspect their family's prosperity would protect them.[25] True, divisions between immigrant and native-born, skilled and unskilled in themselves mean little. Plenty of native-born laboring people found themselves in distressed circumstances by 1855, and the economic distinction between skilled and unskilled broke down in many trades. The point is more general, however. It is possible to see from Sanger's statistics that while a substantial proportion of prostitutes came from the ranks of unskilled immigrants, as one might expect, a large number did not. Even more significantly, a sizable group of women (73) had fathers in the elite artisanal trades—ship carpentry, butchering, silversmithing—and a scattering (49) claimed to be daughters of professional men— physicians, lawyers and clergymen. Still others came from small property-owning families in the city and country, the daughters of shopkeepers, millers and blacksmiths.

Sanger threw up his hands over an array of data that defied his preconceptions. "The numerous and varied occupations of the fathers of those women who answered the question renders any classification of them almost impossible."[26] But the range of family circumstances is confounding only if one assumes that indigence was the major cause of prostitution. In fact, a variety of factors led women into the trade. The daughter of a prosperous ship carpenter could end up on the streets because she was orphaned and left to support herself; she could also use prostitution as a way to escape a harsh father's rule. A country girl, abandoned by a suitor, might go on the town because she knew no other way to earn her bread, or because she was determined to stay in the city rather than return to the farm. A married woman might even hazard the prospects of a hand-to-mouth independence, supported in part by prostitution, rather than submit to a drunken and abusive spouse.

Prostitution as an economic choice dictated by extreme need cannot be understood apart from women's problems in supporting themselves and their consequent forced dependency on men. Prostitution as a social choice, an "inclination," cannot be separated from the entire fabric of that dependency. Sexual mores must have varied among Catholics and Protestants, immigrants and native-born, country and city folk (the evidence is silent on this point). Whatever the differences, however, by the 1850s urban culture exposed all working-class women to modes of sexual exchange which, in certain situations, easily merged with casual prostitution. Sexual favors (and, for wives, domestic services) were the coin with which women, insofar as they could, converted that dependency into a reciprocal relation. Sexual bartering, explicit and implicit, was a common element in relations with men from the time a girl became sexually active. Girls and women traded their sexual favors for food, lodgings and drink. This is not to say that all sexual relations with men were coterminous with prostitution; there were boundaries. Working-class women seem to have known when their daughters and peers threatened to slip over the line into "ruin." Mothers, we shall see, sensed when their girls were approaching "trouble," and "whore" was an insult that women flung about in neighborhood quarrels.

But while middle-class people clearly demarcated opposing erotic spheres of darkness and light, working-class people made more accommodating distinctions. Some women who had "gone to ruin" could find a way back before they became too old to marry. Of all that went on the town, one out of five sooner or later left prostitution, reported the Almshouse commissioners. "They find some way of earning an honest livelihood."[27] The parents of Sarah Courtney, an Irish serving girl, sent her to the House of Refuge in 1827 for having "yielded her virtue for gain"; six years later, the warden noted, Sarah had married a respectable workingman. Sarah Freeman, detained a year earlier, had taken up prostitution after the man who kept her died; she was contrite when she entered, the superintendent noted, and some years later he appended the information that she had married respectably.[28] One wonders about these women. Were there difficulties with their husbands? Was there atonement, and what was its price? What was the nature of repentance? The answers remain veiled. Perhaps for the minority of working-class Protestant churchgoers, the boundaries between licit and illicit sex were more rigid, the road back to propriety a difficult one. Christian observance, however, did not necessarily entail strict condemnations of female transgression. It is likely, for example, that free blacks, a highly devout community, held to the permissive views of premarital female sexuality that characterized Afro-American culture throughout the nineteenth century. And even Irish Catholics, whom one would guess to be subject to strict interdictions from the church, seem generally to have been immune to the conception of irredeemable female transgression (perhaps because the American church had not yet embarked on the surveillance of sexual mores for which it later became so well known). In general, laboring people seem to have made their judgments of female vice and virtue in the context of particular situations rather than by applying absolute moral standards.

For working-class women, the pressures of daily life took the form both of need and desire: the need for subsistence, the desire for change. Either could be urgent enough to push a girl or woman into that shady zone not too many steps removed from the daily routines in which she was raised. The resemblance of prostitution to other ways of dealing with men suggests why, for many poor women, selling themselves was not a radical departure into alien territory.

Girls

It was in large part the involvement of young girls in prostitution—or more important, the relationship to the family that juvenile prostitution signified —that brought prostitution to public attention in the 1850s.

Indeed, the discourse of prostitution expressed and deflected popular anxieties about what happened when daughters ventured out on the town. Adolescents and young women found casual prostitution inviting as metropolitan life made it an increasingly viable choice for working girls. Casual prostitution bordered on working-class youth culture; both provided some tenuous autonomy from family life. Of course, there were other reasons for widespread public concern about this kind of youthful sex. Prostitution was inseparable from venereal disease, economic distress, unwanted pregnancy, the sexual degradation of women and class exploitation. The public discourse about prostitution, however, also addressed deeper changes in gender relations within the working class.

Prostitution was by no means a happy choice, but it did have advantages that could override those of other, more respectable employments. The advantages were in part monetary, since prostitution paid quite well. The gains could amount to a week or even a month's earnings for a learner, a servant or a street seller; for girls helping their mothers keep house or working in some kind of semi-indentured learning arrangement, money from men might be the only available source of cash. As a thirteen-year-old in the 1830s tartly answered the moralizing warden of the House of Refuge when he insisted on the point, she would, indeed, sell herself for a shilling if she could get no more, and she would prefer to do so (or "play the Strumpet," as he interpolated) to her usual work, scrubbing up in public houses in exchange for food for her family.[29] Earnings could be far more substantial than this culprit's shilling. In 1825, for example, fifteen-year-old Jane Groesbeck, who also ended up in the House, earned a glorious five dollars (a poor girl's fortune) when she went to the races and met Mr. G., a merchant storekeeper, who hired Jane and her girlfriend to spend the night with him. Ten years later, Mary Jane Box made between twenty shillings and three dollars every time she slept with a man at a bawdy house; the serving girl Harriet Newbury, a country girl from Pennsylvania, came into a windfall of luck in 1828 when a navy captain gave her ten dollars each time they had intercourse.[30] These were gentlemen's prices. Prostitution with workingmen yielded smaller gains, "trifling things"—a few shillings, a meal or admission to the theater. But even to sell oneself for a shilling was to earn in an hour what a seamstress earned in a day in the 1830s.

The lively trade in juvenile prostitution is one of the most striking—and least explored—features of the Victorian sexual landscape. Who were the men who created the demand for young girls' sexual services? It is easy to assume they were bourgeois gentlemen. Certainly gentlemen had money for such pleasures, and Victorian men could use sex with prostitutes to satisfy longings they could not express to their supposedly asexual wives. What we know most about in this regard, the illicit sexuality of the British late Victorians, tends to bear out the assumption that pedophilia was a gentleman's vice that grew out of the bourgeois eroticization of working-class life and depended upon the availability of poor girls for purchase. Dickens's deliciously vulnerable Little Nell was an early, less self-conscious representation of an erotic interest that Lewis Carroll—to take a well-known example—pursued in private photographic sessions with naked little working-class girls, and that fueled a London trade in child prostitutes which became by 1885 a national scandal.[31]

Contrary to this parable of bourgeois (male) depredation, however, the erotic sensibilities of workingmen were also involved. Juvenile prostitution stemmed not just from class encounters but from the everyday relations of men and girls in working-class neighborhoods. Rape trials, one source of information about illicit sexuality, show that sex with girl children was woven into the fabric of life in the tenements and the streets: out-of-the-ordinary, but not extraordinary.[32] Child molestation figured significantly among reported rapes between 1820 and 1860.[33] Poor girls learned early about their vulnerability to sexual harm from grown men, but they also learned some ways to turn men's interest to their own purposes. Casual prostitution was one.

The men who made sexual advances to girls were not interlopers lurking at the edges of ordinary life, but those familiar from daily routines: lodgers, grocers (who encountered girls when they came into their stores on errands) and occasionally fathers. Sometimes the objects of their attentions could be very young. For the men, taboos against sexual involvement with children seem to have been weak; in court, they often alluded to their actions as a legitimate and benign, if slightly illicit, kind of play. A soldier, for example, charged with the rape of a five-year-old in 1842, claimed that he had only done what others had. "It is true I lay the child in the Bunk as I often have done before as well as other men in the same company. I did not commit any violence upon the child."[34] This man and others accused seem to have respected a prohibition against "violence," or actual intercourse, while they saw fondling, masturbation and exhibitionism as permissible play. "He then pulled my clothes up," seven-year-old Rosanna Reardon testified of her assailant in 1854, "and carried me behind the counter . . . he unbuttoned his pantaloons and asked if I wanted to see his pistol." "I did not intend to hurt the girl," a grocery clerk protested of his four-year-old victim. He had only taken her on his lap and petted her. "I will never do it again and had no wish to hurt her."[35] Episodes like these did not necessarily involve severe coercion; rather, child molestation often involved child's play. "He danced me about," remembered Rosanna Reardon. Michael O'Connor, another girl's assailant, claimed he had merely come visiting on a summer's night—as he said, "took off my hat coat and shoes and went to the front door and sat down with the others"—when two girls out on an errand "commenced fooling around" in the doorway "about which would go upstairs first." He gave one a push and told her to go upstairs and the other to stay. Soon thereafter the mother of the remaining child charged downstairs "and accused me of having put my hands under her Daughter's clothes."[36] Whatever really happened, the mother thought there were grounds for suspicion when a grown man took to tumbling about with two girls. Roughhousing, teasing, fondling and horseplay were the same tokens of affection that men gave to children in the normal course of things. Similarly, the favors men offered in exchange for sexual compliance—pennies and candy—were what they dispensed in daily life to garner children's affection. Men's erotic attention to girls, then, was not a discrete and pathological phenomenon but a practice that existed on the fringes of "normal" male sexuality.

Child molestation could blur into juvenile prostitution. The pennies a man offered to a girl to keep quiet about his furtive fumblings were not dissimilar to the prostitute's price. Adult prostitutes were also highly visible throughout the city, and their presence taught girls something about sexual exchange. A baker's daughter in 1830 learned about the pleasures of the bawdy houses in carrying sewing back and forth between her mother and the prostitutes who employed her to do their seamstressing.[37] John McDowall was shocked in 1831 to see little girls in poor wards playing unconcernedly in the streets around the doors of dramshops that served prostitutes; two decades later, Charles Loring Brace observed packs of girls on Corlears Hook hanging about the dance saloons prostitutes frequented and running errands for the inhabitants and their customers.[38] For the great majority of girls, however, it was not the example of adult prostitutes that led them into "ruin" but the immediate incentive of contact with interested men. Laboring girls ran across male invitations in the course of their daily rounds—street selling, scavenging, running errands for mothers or mistresses, in walking home from work, in their workplaces and neighborhoods and on the sophisticated reaches of Broadway. Opportunities proliferated as New York's expanding industry and commerce provided a range of customers extending well beyond the traditional clientele of wealthy rakes and sailors. Country storekeepers in town on business, gentlemen travelers, lonely clerks and workingmen were among those who propositioned girls on the street.

Men made the offers, but girls also sought them out. "Walking out" in groups, hanging about corners, flirting with passersby, and generally being "impudent & saucy to men" (as parents committing a girl to the House of Refuge described it) could lead to prostitution.[39] The vigilant John McDowall at watch on fashionable Broadway observed "females of thirteen and fourteen walking the streets without a protector, until some pretended gentleman gives them a nod, and takes their arm, and escorts them to houses of assignation."[40] Catharine Wood, fifteen years old in 1834, was a girl with two trades, stocking making and book folding, and thus more advantaged than an ordinary servant or slop worker. Still, when a girlfriend took her out walking on the Bowery, she could not resist the prospects of nearby Five Points, and began to take men to houses of assignation there. Sarah White, a fur worker in 1840 and likewise from respectably employed working folk, took to walking out at night with her workmates from the shop and soon left her parents to go "on the town."[41] Girls actively sought out other girls, tempting friends and acquaintances with the comparative luxuries of a life spent "walking out" to places like the Bowery Theater, where Sarah White's brother found her, stressing such pleasures to the still-virtuous as, in the words of one reprobate "how much better clothes she could wear who worked none."[42] By the 1850s, respectable New Yorkers were appalled at the eroticization of public space girls like these had brought about. "No one can walk the length of Broadway without meeting some hideous troop of ragged girls," an outraged George Templeton Strong reported.[43]

As witnesses to men's sexual initiatives to adult women, and occasionally objects themselves of those advances, girls must have learned early about the power—and danger—of male desire. As they grew up, however, they could also learn to protect themselves; even more, to bargain for themselves. Girls saw older women trade sex for male support, lodgings, drink and dress; these lessons in exchange educated them about sexual bargaining. As a result, adolescents could sometimes engage in it with considerable entrepreneurial aplomb. The testimonies of a gang of girls committed to the House of Refuge in 1825 for prostitution and pickpocketing give some insight into the mentality and mechanics of sexual bargaining on the street in the early part of the century. Eleven to fifteen years old, the girls had all worked off and on in service but at the time of their apprehension were living at home. They went out during the days street scavenging for their mothers and eventually went for higher stakes, first by prostituting themselves with strangers on the streets, next by visiting a bawdy house behind the Park Theater "where they used to accommodate the men, for from two to twelve shillings." The series of episodes that finally landed them in the House of Refuge began one day when, along with a neighbor boy, they fell into company with a country merchant on Broadway. They took him to a half-finished building near City Hall, where two of the girls went down to the basement with him. While he was having intercourse with one, the other picked his pocket. Their next client was an old man they also met on Broadway. The transaction with him took place right on the street, in a dark spot under the wall of St. Paul's churchyard. While one "was feeling of him," another took his money. Finally apprehended at the theater, where they were spending their spoils, the girls were taken to the House where most of them remained intractably unrepentant: one, put in solitary confinement to soften her heart, "singing, Hollowing, and pounding," pretending to be beaten by the discomfited warden and screaming "Murder."[44]

City life allowed such girls to find a wide range of customers and to travel far enough to thwart their mothers' vigilance. Early experiences with men, which girls may have shared round with their peers, perhaps bequeathed a bit of knowledge and shrewdness; perhaps the streets taught them how to turn sexual vulnerability to their own uses. To be sure, there were no reliable means of artificial contraception; only later, with the vulcanization of rubber, did condoms become part of the prostitute's equipment. Any sexually active girl would have risked an illegitimate pregnancy, attended by moral and financial burdens that could bring her to the edge of "ruin." Nonetheless, there were ways to practice birth control. Most likely, a girl engaging in sexual barter stopped short of sexual intercourse, allowing the man instead to ejaculate between her legs, the client's customary privilege in the nineteenth century. Recipes for abortifacients and suppositories, I have already noted, probably circulated among young women. If other measures failed, abortions, provided by midwives and "irregular" physicians (as those outside the medical establishment were called), were widely available in American cities. Indeed, ferreting out abortions—both medically induced and self-induced—was a major task of the city coroner. In 1849, the chief official of public health in the city reported that stillbirths were increasing at an alarming rate, and he concluded darkly that the role of "crime and recklessness"—that is, abortion—in this phenomenon "dare not be expressed."[45]

To us now, and to commentators then, selling one's body for a shilling might seem an act imbued with hopelessness and pathos. Such an understanding, however, neglects the fact that this was a society in which many men still saw coerced sex as their prerogative. In this context, the prostitute's price was not a surrender to male sexual exploitation but a way of turning a unilateral relationship into a reciprocal one. If this education in self-reliance was grim, the lessons in the consequences of heterosexual dependency were often no less so.

"On the Town"

Prostitution offered more than money to girls. Its liaisons were one important way they could escape from or evade their families. For young girls, the milieu of casual prostitution, of walking out, could provide a halfway station to the urban youth culture to which they aspired. For older girls, casual prostitution could finance the fancy clothes and high times that were the entrée to that culture. For all ages, support from lovers and clients could be critical in structuring a life apart from the family.

Prostitution and casual sex provided the resources for girls to live on their own in boardinghouses or houses of assignation—a privilege that most workingwomen would not win until after the First World War.[46] Before factory work began to offer a more respectable alternative, sex was one of the only ways to finance such an arrangement. The working-class room of one's own offered a girl escape from a father's drunken abuse or a mother's nagging, the privilege of seeing "as much company as she wished" and the ability to keep her earnings for herself.[47] Sanger touched on this aspect when he identified "ill treatment" in the family as one of the primary reasons girls went into prostitution. The testimony he collected bears witness to the relationship between youthful prostitution and the relations of the household: "My parents wanted me to marry an old man, and I refused. I had a very unhappy home afterward." "My step-mother ill-used me." "My mother ill-treated me." "My father accused me of being a prostitute when I was innocent. He would give me no clothes to wear." "I had no work, and went home. My father was a drunkard, and ill-treated me and the rest of the family."[48] Sexuality offered a way out. For this reason, while petty theft was the leading cause of boys' commitments to the House of Refuge, the great majority of girls were there for some sexually related offense. Bridget Kelly was the daughter of a dock laborer who drank and beat his children, making her (in the experience of the House of Refuge warden) "an easy prey for Care less persons who persuaded her from home." A washerwoman's daughter made the acquaintance of a young man in 1845 on the Bowery and began meeting him regularly without her mother's knowledge, sometimes at a house of assignation. Her mother found out and put a stop to the courtship, afterwards upbraiding the girl so relentlessly that she finally ran away to live in the house of assignation where she had already lost her virtue; from there it was only a short step to incarceration. A foundry worker brought his daughter to the House in 1850 because, he claimed, she had gone to live in a bad house; the girl said she had left because her parents beat her.[49]

The inducement was freedom from domestic and wage labor. From the parents' point of view, running about the streets went hand in hand with laziness and idleness at home and abnegating one's obligations to earn one's keep. Elizabeth Byrne, her father claimed in 1827, thought he "should support her like a Lady"; he sent her to the House of Refuge to save her from ruin. Other families took the same step. Mary Ann Lyons, a "hard" girl given to singing vulgar songs, had been living with her mother for several months in 1830 "doing little or nothing." "Her brother undertook to punish her for not bringing chips [scavenged wood] to help her Mother in Washing Clothes." Amelia Goldsmith, daughter of a cartman, expected more help from her family "than she ought and because she did not get it, she left her trade" in 1840 for an all-female lodging house.[50]

For many young girls the most immediate restraint on sexual activity was not the fear of pregnancy but rather family supervision. A girl's ability to engage quietly in casual prostitution or sexual bartering depended largely on whether she used streetwalking openly to defy her obligations to her family. She might earn a little money now and then from casual liaisons; as long as she hid the luxuries she gained thereby and continued to earn her keep at home, she might evade suspicion. But part of the allure of prostitution was precisely the chance it offered to break free of work and authority. The "ruin" working people feared for their girls was not sexual activity alone, but sex coupled with irresponsibility; the defiance of the claims of the family went hand in hand with working-class conceptions of immorality. Parents became alarmed and angered, for example, when their girls moved about from one servant's position to another without consulting them. They saw such independent ways as a prelude to trouble. Sometimes the girl had changed to a place in a "bad house," a dance hall or house of assignation where the temptation to dabble in prostitution would have been nearly irresistible. Sometimes, however, the girl provoked her parents' wrath simply by shifting from one place to another. Mary Galloway, for instance, fifteen in 1838 and a shoemaker's daughter, had been enamored of walking the streets since she was thirteen. She left home to go into service "thinking that then she would have a better opportunity to walk out evenings," but this led her continually to change places in search of a situation where she would have more time to herself, and she changed so often that her mother finally thought it best to send her for "correction" to the House of Refuge, where incarceration and the strictest of daily routines would presumably set her straight.[51]

Fancy dress also played into prostitution. As in the cases of domestic servants and factory girls, fancy dress signified a rejection of proper feminine behavior and duties. For the girls who donned fine clothes, dress was an emblem of an estimable erotic maturity, a way to carry about the full identity of the adult, and a sign of admission into heterosexual courting. Virtuous girls, who gave over their wages to their families, had no money to spare for such frivolities; from a responsible perspective, fancy dress was a token of selfish gratification at the expense of family needs. The longtime warden of the House of Refuge, who had seen plenty of girls come and go, declared in the 1830s that "the love of dress was the most efficient cause of degradation and misery of the young females of the city."[52] Sarah Dally is a case in point. Her involvement in prostitution stemmed from a set of circumstances in which fine clothes, freedom from work and resentment of her mother were all combined. In 1829 she was the fifteen-year-old daughter of poor but respectable Irish people. In one of her places at service she befriended another serving girl who was in the habit of staying privately with gentlemen. In walking out with her friend "in pursuit of beaux," Sarah met a Lawyer Blunt and stayed with him several times. In return, Mr. Blunt liberally set her up with ladies' clothes: a silk coat and dresses, a chemise and lace handkerchief, a gilt buckle (all which she put on to go out walking with him) and a nightgown and nightcap for their private meetings. Sarah successfully concealed the new clothes from her family, but her mother's watchfulness began to chafe. When she complained, her friend convinced her to accompany her to Philadelphia, where Sarah would be free to go out fully on the town. To pay for the trip, the pair tried to rob a house, failed and ended up in jail. The journey back to virtue, however, was far more possible than it would have been for a girl from polite society who had similarly chosen "ruin." Eight years later, Sarah was reported to be respectably married and doing well. She had presumably renounced the delights of ladies' clothes.[53]

Country girls from New England and upstate New York were also open to the inducements of prostitution in the city. Refugees from the monotony and discipline of rural life, they were drawn by the initial excitement of the life, its sociability and novel comforts. Rachel Near, for instance, came from Poughkeepsie to New York in 1835 to learn the trade of tailoressing from her sister. About three months after she arrived she ran into another Poughkeepsie girl on the street whom a man was supporting in a house of assignation. "She persuaded her to go into her House, which was neatly furnished by her ill gotten gain, and asked her to come and live with her, and persuaded her until she consented to do so." There Rachel met a Dr. Johnson, visiting the city from Albany, who supported her in style for six weeks, and she supplemented her earnings from him with visits to a bawdy house "where she used to get from 5 to 7 $ pr night, some weeks she used to make 40 & 45$." Rachel's kin found her and sent her back home, but the next summer she ran away from Poughkeepsie and "fully turned out again." Fifteen-year-old Susannah Bulson also followed a well-trodden path. She was an Albany girl who had been "seduced" by a young cabinetmaker. For a few weeks after they began their liaison in 1835, he supported her in a room across the river in Troy, but she did not want to disgrace her family by her presence, so the two left for New York, where he took a room for them in a boardinghouse. A number of the other boarders were single women who came and went as they pleased, and after seeing this kind of life, Susannah "felt she should prefer this kind of pleasure" to living with her young man and left for a house where she set up on her own. Several months later, the man who would have played the part of heartless seducer in a melodramatic rendition of their story was still trying to persuade Susannah to come back to him.[54]

Rural courtships often played a part in urban prostitution. Some young women had sex with their suitors, were "kept" by them and eventually married: They make no appearance in the historical record. For others, the adventure ended badly; unlike Susannah Bulson, they were the ones left behind, not the ones who did the leaving. It was from such experiences that nineteenth-century popular culture would eventually create the seduced-and-abandoned tale. A virtuous country girl succumbs to her lover's advances; he persuades her, against her better judgment, to follow him to the big city. Once there he cruelly deserts her, leaving her penniless, alone, shamed before her family and the world. William Sanger gave an early version of this plot in his interpretation of the category "seduced and abandoned" that 258 of his subjects had cited as the reason for their fall. "Unprincipled men, ready to take advantage of women's trustful nature, abound, and they pursue their diabolical course unmolested," Sanger explained. The woman, "naturally unsuspicious herself . . . cannot believe that the being whom she has almost deified can be aught but good, and noble, and trustworthy."[55] Women's generous and undiscriminating nature made them an easy mark.

In truth, it was a bad bargaining position, not a too-compliant nature, that made women a mark for "unprincipled men." Courtship was a gamble; elopement, the possibility of rape and male mobility made it all the more treacherous. Country girls were especially vulnerable to the process whereby desertion led to prostitution. Sanger found that 440 of his subjects were farmers' daughters.[56] Left alone in the city, often without friends to help them, country girls sometimes had no choice but to turn to the streets for their bread. The sanctions of rural communities gave some protection to young women, but once they isolated themselves from neighbors, family and other women, they could find themselves caught in an escalating series of circumstances in which intercourse, voluntary or involuntary, led to prostitution.

Once again, however, we should avoid interpreting prostitution as a desperate measure. It could also be an act of shrewdness, prompted by a woman's comprehension of the power relations in which she found herself. Once a farm girl perceived the possibilities the city held out, to sell her favors for money was a logical countermove in a sexual system in which men might take what they could get—sometimes through rape—and turn their backs on the consequences. To exact a price from a man, hard cash, must have held some appeal to a woman whose last lover had just skipped off scot-free.

But it would also be wrong to cast prostitution as a deliberate bid for control; mostly, farm girls—like their urban peers—just wanted to live on their own. Once abandoned by a suitor, a young woman could easily want to stay away from the family she had deserted or defied. Cornelia Avery ran away from home in Connecticut in 1827 with a stagecoach driver her father had forbidden her to marry; when the man deserted her, she took up prostitution instead of going back. And what else could Marian Hubbard do, tired of the farm, and taken in by a scoundrel? Marian's second cousin Joe Farryall from New York, visiting his kin in Vermont in 1835, convinced her to return with him to the city. Although she knew nothing of his character, he persuaded her—or so she later recounted—that she worked too hard, and that he would make a lady of her if she came to New York. Halfway there she slept with him, only to find on arriving that he was the keeper of a brothel inhabited by a dozen other country girls he had lured there under similar pretenses. When the warden of the House of Refuge, where Marian ended up, inquired about Farryall, the watchmen told him that the man made three or four such recruiting trips to the countryside each year.[57]

The money and perquisites from casual prostitution opened up a world beyond the pinched life of the tenements, the metropolitan milieu of fashion and comfort. Every day girls viewed this world from the streets, as if in the audience of a theater: the elaborate bonnets in shop windows, the silk dresses in the Broadway promenade, the rich food behind the windows of glittering eating places. Bonnets, fancy aprons, silk handkerchiefs, pastries were poor girls' treasures, coveted emblems of felicity and style. There were serious drawbacks to prostitution: venereal disease, physical abuse, the pain of early intercourse and the ever-present prospect of pregnancy. While the road back to respectable marriage was not irrevocably closed, it must have been rocky, the reproaches and contempt of kin and neighbors a burden to bear. Still, casual prostitution offered many their best chance for some kind of autonomy—even for that most rare acquisition for a poor girl, a room of her own.

In this context, the imagery of unregeneracy served to interpret a particular kind of adolescent female rebellion. The debauched juvenile would become central to the bourgeois construction of a pathological "tenement class." "Hideous and ragged" girls and young women moved attention away from other villains—capitalist exploitation, deceiving seducers, deserting husbands, the ordinary and sometimes cruel nature of erotic experience between the sexes—to the supposedly pitiable nature of working-class childhood and the supposedly disintegrating moral standards of working-class families.

The urgency that discussions of prostitution took on in the 1850s indicates just how disturbing youthful female independence could be in a society structured culturally on women's dependence on the household. In the public spaces of New York, as well as in domestic service and on the Bowery, the evidence of girls' circumvention of family discipline was deeply troubling, especially (but not exclusively) to people who saw the family as woman's *only* proper place and asexuality as a cardinal tenet of femininity. The stress on the female reprobate's active pursuit of her appetites was the reformers' rendition of an obvious fact of youthful prostitution: It was not solely the resort of hopelessness and misery.

Antebellum Victorian culture generated two opposing images of the prostitute. One was the preyed-upon innocent, driven by starvation's threat or by a seducer's treachery to take to the streets. Women reformers—especially the ladies of the Female Moral Reform Society—played an important role in popularizing this construction. The prostitute-as-innocent was a sister to the familiar figure of the downtrodden sewing woman and similarly allowed genteel women to stretch their sexual sympathies across class lines. The other image was the hard, vice-ridden jade, who sold her body to satisfy a base appetite for sex or, more likely (such was the difficulty of imagining that women could have active sexual desires), for liquor. This creature was almost wholly beyond redemption, certainly forever cast out from the bonds of womanhood. The prostitute-as-reprobate depended upon older conceptions of the vicious poor, but the figure also assimilated moral "viciousness" into the new environmentalist thought promoted by the secular reformers of the 1840s and 1850s.

In the 1850s it was the "abandoned" female, not the betrayed innocent, who captured public attention. Her popularity reflects the generally hardening tone social commentators were taking toward the poor, as an emerging "scientific" comprehension of urban problems gripped their imagination. The ascendancy of the abandoned woman may also signify a weakening of women's influence in urban reform movements. Women had drawn their reforming energies from evangelicalism. As reformers moved away from a religious to a secular orientation, women's evangelical language of the heart and their empathy with the "fallen" of their sex may have seemed less than relevant to the new breed of scientific philanthropists concerned with environmental solutions to problems of public health and disorder.

We are still too much influenced by the Victorians' view of prostitution as utter degradation to accept easily any interpretation that stresses the opportunities commercial sex provided to women rather than the victimization it entailed. Caution is certainly justified. Prostitution was a relationship that grew directly from the double standard and men's subordination of women. It carried legal, physical and moral hazards for women but involved few, if any, consequences for men. Whatever its pleasures, they were momentary; its rewards were fleeting and its troubles were grave. But then, the same could be said of other aspects of laboring women's relations with men. Prostitution was one of a number of choices fraught with hardship and moral ambiguity.

Charles Loring Brace, who labored to redeem girls from New York's streets, spoke to the heart of the issue. By the time he began his mission in 1853, poor girls knew enough about the politics of interpretation to invoke the sentimentalist imagery of prostitution in their own defense when dealing with reformers and police. "They usually relate, and perhaps even imagine, that they have been seduced from the paths of virtue suddenly and by the wiles of some heartless seducer. Often they describe themselves as belonging to some virtuous, respectable, and even wealthy family." "Their real history," scoffed the streetwise Brace, "is much more commonplace and matter-of-fact. They have been poor women's daughters, and did not want to work as their mothers did."[58] In the 1850s, the opportunities for girls to repudiate their mothers' lot in this way were greater than ever.

Chapter 10   The Uses of the Streets

On a winter's day in 1856, an agent for the Children's Aid Society encountered two children out on the street with market baskets. Like hundreds he might have seen, they were desperately poor—thinly dressed and barefoot in the cold—but their cheerful countenances struck him favorably, and he stopped to inquire into their circumstances. They explained that they were out gathering bits of wood and coal their mother could burn for fuel, and agreed to take him home to meet her. In a bare tenement room, lacking heat, furniture or any other comforts, he met a "stout, hearty woman" who, even more than her children, testified to patient perseverance in a crushing situation. A widow, she supported her family as best she could by street peddling. Their room was bare because she had been forced to sell off her clothes, furniture and bedding to supplement her earnings. As she spoke, she sat on a pallet on the floor and rubbed the hands of the two younger siblings of the pair from the street. "They were tidy, sweet children," noted the agent, "and it was very sad to see their chilled faces and tearful eyes." Here was a scene that seemingly would have touched the heart of even a frosty Victorian soul. Yet in concluding his report, the agent's perceptions took a curious turn. "Though for her pure young children too much could hardly be done, in such a woman there is little confidence to be put . . . it is probably, some cursed vice has thus reduced her, and that, if her children be not separated from her, she will drag them down, too."[1]

Home visits like this one had been standard practice for thirty years. But why the indictment, seemingly so unsupported? Philanthropists cus-

tomarily parlayed harsh judgments about, but in the 1830s such a devoted
mother surely would have won approbation as "deserving" and "virtuous."
What, then, accounts for the distinction between her and her "innocent"
children?

The answer lies in a curious place—the streets where the agent from the
Children's Aid Society first met the children. Their presence there was to
him *prima facie* evidence of their mother's vicious character. Between
roughly 1846 and 1860, this association between the streets, children and
parental depravity crystallized in bourgeois thought into a dramatic imagery of the fearful pathology of the "tenement classes." The problem of the
streets generated a discourse and a politics which engaged some of New
York's ablest, most energetic and imaginative reformers. Like the earlier
evangelicals, they aimed to eradicate poverty itself. Their aims shifted,
however, from the redemption of souls to the transformation of the material conditions of the city. Although Christian zeal inspired many of
them, salvation was only an incidental byproduct of their efforts. Urban
social geography, not the landscape of the soul, engaged their ardor for
exploration.[2]

The Reformers

The ascendancy of the problem of the streets to paramount importance on
the reform agenda in the 1850s can be attributed to two men, George Matsell
and Charles Loring Brace. Matsell, New York's first chief of police,
sounded the call for action in 1849, when he used the forum of his office's
semiannual report to alert the public to "a deplorable and growing evil" of
which, he insinuated, they did not know the half. Poor children were
overrunning New York's streets, spreading crime, disorder and disease into
every thoroughfare, every cranny. "I allude to the constantly increasing
number of vagrants, idle and vicious children of both sexes, who infest our
public thoroughfares," the chief solemnly warned.[3]

Matsell was a man who liked to take himself seriously. Son of a tailor and
a printer by trade, he had worked himself up through the Tammany ranks,
garnering the plum of the chief's spot when the city established its first
professional police force in 1845.[4] On his inauguration (according to his
inveterate enemy, the labor journalist Mike Walsh) the chief promptly
commissioned a bust of himself for the office and saddled his subordinates
with the cost. Walsh held Matsell and Matsell's face in utter contempt: "It
is difficult to conceive why a fellow so revoltingly ill-looking and stupid

should desire to give publicity to that which other ugly people take pains to conceal." The question of the man's looks and the man's figure aside (he weighed more than 300 pounds and was, in Walsh's words, a "degraded and pitiful lump of blubber and meanness," a "Beastly Bloated Booby"⁵), the anecdote of the bust reveals an unabashed drive toward self-aggrandizement which was also to play into the report of 1849.

On one level, the report was Matsell's bid for a place in the ranks of New York's most distinguished reformers, alongside such men as the learned John Griscom and the well-born Robert Hartley. Matsell cast himself as a heroic sentry who cried the news to his fellow citizens of a threat to the very survival of their city. He made the case for himself at the expense of the city that employed him by casting the police (and their chief) in a bold, noble light against a dark and menacing background.

There had been strong opposition to the creation of the police, and their participation in the bloody Astor Place Riot in 1849 intensified public protest. In the context of this political battle, the report, published in the aftermath of the riot, functioned as a sensational advertisement for the necessity—the indispensability—of the police as an army standing between civilized life and a criminal invasion. It is difficult to convey fully the report's inflammatory effect; a few phrases will have to do: "Their numbers are almost incredible," Matsell said of the street children. The danger was so great, yet so concealed, that those whose "business and habits do not permit them a searching scrutiny" of the city around them (i.e., everyone except the police) could only be dimly aware of the threat. "The degrading and disgusting habits of these almost infants" were such that "it is humiliating to be compelled to recognize them as a part and portion of the human family." "Clothed in rags" and "filthy in the extreme," "cunning and adroit," habitués of "the lowest dens of drunkenness and disease," one looked in vain for vestiges of childhood innocence in them.⁶

Weird and paranoid as the text seems now, it was rapidly reprinted, widely circulated and quoted all over the newspapers. No one seems to have taken issue (Mike Walsh had left off publishing his paper for a career in professional politics). The wide acceptance shows how much a particular narrative mode had come to structure perceptions of the working class. Matsell's alarmist exposé of high crime seemed true because he packaged his observations within the rhetoric and conventions of an established genre of reportage about the city, the urban sketch. Dating from Pierce Egan's *Life in London,* published in 1821, the sketch was a fictional tour of the city in which a cosmopolitan man-about-town, the author/narrator, conducted his readers through the metropolis, chiefly the spots of vice and poverty respectable people would never otherwise visit. In New York, the penny presses, which began publishing in the 1830s, serialized sketches for a mass audience; in the late 1840s, journalists like Ned Buntline, George Foster and Solon Robinson began packaging their sketches as books: Buntline's immensely popular *Mysteries and Miseries of New York,* Foster's series *New York in Slices, New York by Gas-Light* and *New York Naked,* Robinson's *Hot Corn: Life Scenes in New York Illustrated.* [7] The short sketches in reform literature—the accounts of home visits—developed in parallel with these literary sketches and also appeared in the penny newspapers as news-about-town. Reports from home visitors likewise presented their ramblings about the poor quarters of New York in graphic and lurid detail, and the two forms played off each other. Reformers derived some of their imaginative zest from the literary accounts and began publishing sketches themselves in the 1850s, and the journalists drew on reformers for their details of low life. Robinson, for example, centered his "narratives of misery" on encounters of fictional characters with the real-life reformer Louis Pease of the Five Points House of Industry. While the sketch writers could create animated and sympathetic portrayals of working-class life, they also peopled their most exotic and titillating pictures of urban poverty with depraved creatures who bore a strong resemblance to the "vicious" poor.

The lines of literature and reform converged in Matsell, who used the role of venturesome cosmopolitan to heighten his credibility as reformer. As chief of police he posed as the official man-about-town, the hardy narrator who in the people's service gallantly strode into those fearful regions where genteel readers feared to tread. If, in the end, he was only dramatizing mundane (if unpleasant) encounters with little scavengers, peddlers and child prostitutes—encounters that many middle-class people had on the streets—then all the more compelling. This was the best kind of exposé, the one that recast the familiar within the conventions of suspense, one that electrified the ordinary with the excitement of the titillating, the significant and the grand. Literary convention as much as social reality created the urban horror in which ordinary working-class people, going about their daily business, came to figure as an almost subhuman species.

One of Matsell's readers was Charles Loring Brace, a new graduate of Yale seminary and scion of a distinguished Connecticut family of declining fortunes. In 1852 Brace had just returned from a European tour, inspired but also vaguely shaken by what he had seen in the aftermath of the revolutions of 1848. Looking for meaningful ways to help the laboring classes with whose aspirations he had sympathized in Europe, he immersed himself in New York in city mission work. Matsell's observations echoed what Brace was coming to learn in his work with boys in the mission. Moved to act, in 1853 Brace founded the Children's Aid Society (CAS), a charity that concerned itself with all poor children but especially with street "orphans," as the society was wont to call its beneficiaries. [8]

Throughout the 1850s, the CAS carried on the work Matsell had begun, documenting and publicizing the plight of street children in vivid prose. Together, Matsell and Brace laid out the parameters of the problem of the streets that gripped the socially conscious in the 1850s. Although the *problems* of the streets—the fights, the crowds, the crime, the children—were nothing new, the "problem" itself represented altered bourgeois perceptions and a broadened political initiative. An area of social life that had been taken for granted, an accepted feature of city life, became visible, subject to scrutiny and intervention.

Matsell's report and the writing Brace undertook in the 1850s distilled the particular way the genteel had designated themselves arbiters of the city's everyday life. Clearly, the moment had been long in the making. Since the 1820s moral reformers had conceived their task as refashioning the cultural milieu of the poor; the campaign against the streets was one episode in a long offensive. Nonetheless, that offensive reached a new pitch in the 1850s. Never had New York faced social problems of such magnitude; never had bourgeois fears of the poor been so intense. In the face of this crisis, reformers moved out with unprecedented energy and confidence, buoyed by a conviction of their abilities to change the very face of the city.

The reasons for the consolidation of bourgeois consciousness in the 1850s are complex. The recovery in the 1840s from the prolonged depression that followed the Panic of 1837 was one factor, a signal proof that capitalism— what New Yorkers knew as "commerce and trade"—was capable of regenerating itself. A new breed of entrepreneurs rode the tide of recovery, often men who had risen from humble stations to positions of wealth and power: the clothiers, the broker-speculators, ex-artisans like the publisher and mayor (1844–45) James Harper or, for that matter, Matsell himself. More generally, the great outpouring of domestic ideology in this period, in advice books, sermons, novels and ladies' magazines, widely disseminated conceptions of a genteel cultural identity. This identity still incorporated Protestant piety—certainly the observance of Protestant forms—but its ties to evangelicalism were looser than they had been in the 1820s and 1830s. In the 1840s, domesticity had become a social program as much as a religious one, devoted to what Catharine Beecher, a preeminent exponent of true womanhood, called "the building of a glorious temple" to democracy.[9] Domestic ideology, not religious ardor, allowed reformers to expand their support beyond the circles of zealots of the 1830s; it also gave them the impetus and the popular interest to begin translating reform measures into the law.

The Crisis of the 1850s

New York in the 1850s contained extremes of wealth and poverty. There was an elegant downtown of expensive shops and residences, mostly serene. In the poor parts of town, wretched new arrivals stumbled about, ragged and gaunt. There were shanties on the outskirts, and here and there, sights of shocking filth and poverty. Many, of course, beginning in 1847, were refugees from the Irish Potato Famine. Melville's hero Redburn need not have traveled to the British Isles to confront the terrors of human misery; in the city from which he sailed he could have found ragged women and children crouching in basement entryways, if not in holes in the ground as he did in Liverpool.

The crisis was evident in the sight of homeless indigents who roamed the streets. Although real-estate developers built blocks and blocks of new tenements in the northern wards, the construction could not absorb the flood of immigrants. New York's population increased by 300,000 over the decade, to a total of about 813,000. The more resourceful of those who could not afford or could not find lodgings threw up shacks in empty lots outside the built-up districts and squatted there; others, disoriented and at wit's end, wandered through the streets looking for housing, kin, work or, at least, a spot to shelter them from the elements. A small newspaper notice from 1850 reported an occurrence that was atypical enough to be newsworthy, but certainly not rare: "Six poor women with their children, were discovered Tuesday night by some police officers, sleeping in an alleyway, in Avenue B, between 10th and 11th streets. When interrogated they said they had been compelled to spend their nights where ever they could obtain any shelter. They were in a starving condition, and without the slightest means of support."[10] This was uptown and east of the Bowery, in a poor neighborhood. But homeless people also appeared in more prosperous locales like the business sections around City Hall. Police Inspector William Bell, in his laconic and monumentally phlegmatic fashion, described one desperate case he attended there: "I found a woman and Girl about 7 or 8 years of age sitting on the coping in the rain. I asked her where she lived. She appeared not to understand English. I told her I would give her her choice —to go home or to go to Blackwell's Island for 6 months—She appeared to understand me as she got up and went away."[11]

Although most indigents managed eventually to double up in other people's rooms, overcrowding took its toll. Entire families crowded into sublet small back bedrooms. In some pockets of what is now the Lower East

Side, population densities approached those of London's worst neighborhoods.[12] Public health deteriorated drastically. When cholera struck in 1849,
it raced through the tenements like fire and fanned out over the rest of the
city. By fall, more than 5,000 people had died. Typhus, an immigrants'
disease of dirt and overcrowding, was endemic and, in some sections of the
city, became epidemic in 1852. Deaths from consumption also rose sharply,
especially in the small black community and among immigrants, who were
the principal victims of overcrowding. General mortality climbed, peaking
in 1849 and 1853 but through 1860 remaining far above the stable level of the
forty years before the Famine migration. In 1859, the mortality rate was 1
in 27, far higher than that of Paris (1 in 37) or London (1 in 40). Deaths of
children also increased alarmingly: In 1820, 38 percent of children under the
age of five died; in 1850, the figure was 52 percent and remained the same
in 1860, a proportion equal to the infant mortality rates of the worst English
factory districts. "The infants and children die in fearful ratios," one investigation acknowledged.[13]

Economically, the post-Panic upswing of the 1840s continued until the
depression of 1853–54, which anticipated the Panic of 1857. The surge of
impoverished laborers into the city, apart from the social perils they posed,
meant high profits for trade and industry. Many workingmen, we have
seen, wanted things to be different. In 1850 associated craftworkers had
taken to the streets and to the committee rooms of the Industrial Congress
to combat the "trickish system of speculators that makes use of us like
machines," as the window shade painters put it so eloquently.[14] The employment of immigrants exacerbated the processes of sweating and de-
skilling already proceeding apace in the crafts. But good times for the city's
employers came to an end with the downturn in the business cycle and then
the far more serious Panic, which approached in its gravity the catastrophe
of 1837. Unemployment soared. In 1857, when businesses first began to fold
in the fall, an estimated thousand people a day were discharged; by the end
of October, some 20,000 workers in the clothing trade (out of a total of
30,000) were out of work. In response, laboring men organized a movement
of the unemployed that reached out beyond the crafts to any man (but not
woman) by virtue of his lack of work. In 1854–55 and again in 1857, thousands
of workingmen marched to demand jobs and relief from the Common
Council. Troops and militia were called out to protect the Sub-Treasury
and the Custom House. To one visitor from Britain, this all had the familiar
ring of class warfare, despite all one had heard of American equality: Even
in America, he wrote in 1858, "bands of men paraded in a menacing manner
through the streets of the city demanding work and bread."[15]

It was this sense of impending catastrophe that animated a second generation of reformers to formulate a wide-ranging program of social renewal.

activists reoriented themselves away from the familiar categories of
m—virtue and vice—toward a surveillance of the material conditions
of city life. Public health, mortality rates and housing conditions became
their chief concerns. They pursued a pietist science of poverty, based on
utilitarian premises of standardization and efficiency but also on a consideration of the moral properties of the environment. This group included the
leaders of the Association for the Improvement of the Condition of the Poor
(AICP), especially the influential Robert Hartley, the public health expert
John Griscom, William Sanger, Charles Loring Brace, the women of the
American Female Guardian Society and Louis Pease of the Five Points
House of Industry.[16]

Women were not prominent among these philanthropists. The American Female Guardian Society, descendant of the Female Moral Reform
Society, did turn to environmentalist measures with a shelter for homeless
women opened in 1847, vocational programs and a "placing-out" program
for destitute children to rural foster homes. But most of the female associations that survived were not inclined toward the new analysis, with its
emphasis on medical language and its arrays of statistics. Rather, they held
onto the familiar methods of moral reform, to be belittled by some male
reformers as "unscientific."[17]

The common enemy of the tenement classes brought these men together. A precursor to the "dangerous classes" (a term not used widely in
America until after the Civil War), the tenement classes were conceived as
a source of both moral and physical contagion—agents, not victims, of
social distress, active allies of "sickness and pauperism." In 1842, when John
Griscom published his influential report on public health, the phrase had
not yet materialized. He referred to his subjects as the laboring population.
In Griscom's writing, laboring people were products of their environment,
fading back into the material squalor that was his main focus—shadows on
crumbling walls, ghosts in garbage-strewn hallways. Still, they did carry on
as active, coping human beings, objects of pity if not of sympathy.[18] With
the invention of the tenement classes, however, the distinctions between
people and their surroundings began to blur, and humanitarian sentiment
faded away. The tenement classes and the tenements themselves appeared
equally loathsome.

An official investigation of the tenement house problem in 1857 enlarged
the scope of the discussion.[19] This "scientific" undertaking assimilated the
conventions of the urban sketch to produce an account far outstripping in
its sensationalism the productions of the 1840s. The police force contributed
to the genre by shedding light on a milieu that had been, except for the
incursions of tract visitors, mostly closed to the genteel. The popularization
of the idea of the tenement classes after 1850 was partly due to publicized

police investigations like Matsell's and to accounts written by journalists who accompanied policemen on their rounds—or, conversely, by urban explorers who ventured into the dark places of the city under police escort (Dickens's visit to Five Points, chronicled in his *American Notes* of 1842, is a case in point). The lurid narrative of the Tenant House Report of 1857 vied with the detective stories of the (deceased) New Yorker Edgar Allan Poe in its allusions to unspeakable horrors. In the report, a pack of state legislators became men-about-town. Braving what the "mere theorist in political economy"—pantywaist!—could only picture to himself, these daring men steeled themselves to sights that they could not have imagined. The intrepid explorers plunged into Corlears Hook as if it were a remote African settlement on the Congo, its "mysteries" and "horrors" tucked away from civilized knowledge. "Though expecting to look upon poverty in squalid guise, vice in repulsive aspects, and ignorance of a degraded stamp," they assured their readers, "we had not yet formed an adequate conception of the extremes to which each and all of these evils could reach."[20] The parallel between fact and fiction was not lost on the committee members, who claimed they had visited scenes that, "if portrayed in the pages of romance, might be regarded as creations of diseased fancy."[21] These were voyeuristic journeys into the heart of darkness, the enthralling, "unimaginable" sinfulness of working-class life hidden away behind the facade of bourgeois society.

> Why attempt to convey to the imagination by words the hideous squalour and deadly effluvia, the dim, undrained courts oozing with pollution, the dark, narrow stairways, decayed with age, reeking with filth, overrun, with vermin; the rotted floors, ceilings begrimned and often too low to permit you to stand upright; the windows stuffed with rags? or why try to portray the gaunt, shivering forms and wild ghastly faces, in these black and beetling abodes?[22]

In contrast to Griscom's characterizations in 1842, the poor of the Tenant House Report never did anything. They did not converse, or cook, or do laundry, or discipline their children; mostly they just peered out from their "fever-nests," an exhausted and depleted species. Crowded together, the pathologies of the "pariah inhabitants" fed on each other. The festering cancer threatened to contaminate the whole body social:

> Narrow alleys, dark, muddy, gloomy lanes, courts shut in by high walls, and dwellings, into the secrets of which the sun's rays never penetrate, are a portion of the veins and arteries of a great city; and if they be disregarded, the heart and limbs of the city will sooner or

later suffer, as surely as the vitals of the human system must suffer by
the poisoning or disease of the smallest vehicle.[23]

Family life was one of the principal sources of infection. A view of
familial patterns as the preeminent source of poverty moved to the center
of the reformers' etiology, displacing the evangelical belief in the defective
moral character of the individual as the fundamental cause. In the web of
images of blight and disease the reformers used, the family emerged as a
recurring motif. The tenement house itself was "the parent of constant
disorders, and the nursery of increasing vices."[24] This attention to the
importance of the family came from bourgeois men's and women's own
preoccupations with domesticity. When reformers entered tenement
households, they saw a domestic sparseness which contradicted their deep-
est understanding about what constituted a morally sustaining household;
material effects and domestic morality were closely connected. "[Their]
ideas of domestic comfort and standard of morals, are far below our own,"
observed the AICP. The urban poor had intricately interwoven family
lives, but they had no *homes*. "Homes—in the better sense—they never
know," declared the 1857 investigating committee. The AICP scoffed at
even using the word: "homes . . . if it is not a mockery to give that hallowed
name to the dark, filthy hovels where many of them dwell." The children,
who should be protected within the domestic sphere, were instead encouraged to labor in the streets, where they "graduate in every kind of vice
known."[25]

Children's presence on the streets was thus not a *symptom* of poverty but
a cause. In opposition to the ever more articulate and pressing claims of
New York's organized workingmen, these first scientific experts on urban
poverty proposed that family relations, not industrial capitalism, were responsible for the massive distress which anyone could see was no transient
state of affairs. Low wages, unemployment, even the crisis of overexpansion
of the city's population might be irrelevant to the problem of poverty: As
the AICP claimed, families were "more deteriorated by the defects of their
habitations, corrupting associations, and surrounding nuisances, than by
the greatest pecuniary want to which they are subjected."[26]

Two lines of social thought, then, came together in the interest in the
streets. One was the concern with public health, which grew stronger after
the cholera epidemic of 1849. The street was the path whereby the malign
energies of the tenement spread outward; "the multitude of half-naked,
dirty and leering children" carried contamination from the "fever-nests."[27]
The other was the absorption in domesticity as the paramount mode of
civilized life. The presence of children on the streets, besides being morally
and epidemiologically dangerous, was proof of how tragically lacking the

working poor were in this respect. From both standpoints, a particular geography of sociability—the engagement of the poor in street life rather than in the home—became in itself evidence of a pervasive urban pathology.

"Idle and Vicious Children"

New York's streets, we have seen, in large part belonged to its working-class people. Family economies bridged the distance between public and private to make the streets a sphere of domestic life. For poor children, the streets were a playground and a workplace. Street life, with its panoply of choices, its rich and varied texture, its motley society, played a central role in their upbringing, part and parcel of a moral conception of childhood that emphasized early independence contingent on early responsibility.

George Matsell was in part reacting to a great expansion of children's presence on the streets that took place after 1846. The crowds of ragged urchins, which both appalled and fascinated him and his contemporaries, were in part a consequence of the population explosion in that decade, in part a result of changes in hiring practices. In the crafts, the use of apprentices had long been declining, but in the 1840s apprentices virtually disappeared from artisan workshops, as masters rearranged work to take advantage of a labor market glutted with impoverished adults. Where apprenticeship did survive, the old perquisites, room and board and steady work, were often gone: The "halfway" apprenticeships which did remain provided only irregular and intermittent work to boys. Small girls, too, found themselves replaced by young Irishwomen in the service positions that had traditionally been theirs. In New England industrial centers, children shifted from apprenticeships and domestic service into the factories. New York, however, lacked the large establishments that elsewhere gave work to the young, and the outwork system was limited in its abilities to absorb child workers.[28] Thus while New York's streets had always been a domain for children, they took on a new importance in the 1850s as a major employer of child labor.

Huckstering was the most reliable legitimate employment for children on the streets. The resurgence of huckstering (or street peddling) in the 1850s took place right alongside the debut of such modern institutions of marketing as A. T. Stewart's department store; the efflorescence of this ancient form of urban trade is one index of the strains which children's rising unemployment in other sectors placed on family economies. Musing in 1854 on a collection of New York sketches entitled *Hot Corn Stories* (after

the indigenous Manhattan delicacy), George Templeton Strong wonder-
fully evoked the way in which the street sellers' presence tinged the metropolitan atmosphere: "*Hot Corn* suggests so many reminiscences of sultry
nights in August or early September, when one has walked through close,
unfragrant air and flooding moonlight and crowds . . . and heard the cry
rising at every corner, or has been lulled to sleep by its mournful cadence
in the distance as he lay under a sheet and wondered if tomorrow would
be cooler."[29] Hucksters, both adults and children, sold all manner of necessities and delicacies. Downtown, passersby could buy treats at every corner:
hot sweet potatoes, baked pears, tea cakes, fruit, candy and hot corn itself.
In residential neighborhoods, hucksters sold household supplies door to
door: fruits and vegetables, matchsticks, scrub brushes, sponges, strings and
pins. Children assisted adult hucksters, went peddling on their own and
worked in several low-paying trades that were their special province: cross-
ing sweeping for girls, errand running, boot blacking, horse holding and
newspaper selling for boys. There were also the odd trades in which children were particularly adept, those unfamiliar and seemingly gratuitous
forms of economic activity which abounded in nineteenth-century metropolises: One small boy whom Virginia Penny found in 1859 made his
living in warm weather by catching butterflies and peddling them to canary
owners.[30]

The growth of the street trades meant that large numbers of children,
who two decades earlier would have worked under close supervision as
apprentices or servants, spent their days away from adult discipline. This
situation magnified children's opportunities for illicit gain, the centuries-
old filching of apprentices and serving girls—the thieving which Matsell
argued was reaching epidemic proportions. When parents sent their children out to the streets to earn a living, the consequences were not always
what they intended. We have already seen how chores like scavenging
could lead to theft. While robbing people—pickpocketing and "baggage
smashing"—seems to have been limited to professional child thieves (properly trained by adult sponsors), appropriating random objects was another
matter. Child peddlers were not averse to lifting hats, umbrellas and odd
knickknacks from the household entryways they frequented in their
rounds, or snatching shop goods displayed outside on the sidewalks as they
roamed about.[31] Indeed, children skilled in detecting value in the seemingly
inconsequential could as easily spot it in other people's loose ends. As the
superintendent of the juvenile asylum wrote of one malefactor, "He has
very little sense of moral rectitude, and thinks it but little harm to take small
articles."[32] A visitor to the city in 1857 was struck by the swarms of children
milling around the docks, "scuffling about, wherever there were bags of
coffee and hogsheads of sugar." Armed with sticks, "they 'hooked' what

they could."[33] The targets of such pilfering were analogous to those of scavenging: odd objects, unattached to persons. The booty of children convicted of theft and sent to the juvenile house of correction in the 1850s included, for example, a bar of soap, a copy of the *New York Herald* and lead and wood from demolished houses. Pipes, tin roofing and brass door-knobs, Chief Matsell warned, were likewise endangered.[34]

The police often made scavenging synonymous with theft when defining crime and vagrancy. A vagrancy charge depended on whether or not an officer considered a child to be engaged in legitimate activity. It is possible, then, that the increase in juvenile commitments (from 475 in 1851 to 936 in 1860) came partly from the tendency of the police to see a child on the streets as inherently criminal.[35] Charles Loring Brace noticed the ongoing confrontation between children, police and mothers in Corlears Hook. The streets teemed with "wild ragged little girls who were flitting about . . . some with baskets and poker gathering rags, some apparently seeking chances of stealing. . . . The police were constantly arresting them as 'vagrants,' when the mothers would beg them off from the good-natured Justices, and promise to train them better in the future."[36] The journalist George Foster thought that many arrests of children for petty larceny were due to the police's narrow view of what constituted private property. The city jail, Foster wrote, was filled, along with other malefactors, "with young boys and girls who have been caught asleep on cellar doors or are suspected of the horrible crime of stealing junk bottles and old iron!"[37] As children's presence in the public realm became criminal, so did the gleaning of its resources. The distinction between things belonging to no one and things belonging to someone blurred in the minds of propertied adults as well as propertyless children.

So when reformers accused working-class parents of encouraging their children to a life of crime when they sent them out to the streets to earn their keep, they were not always wrong. Parents were not necessarily concerned with whether or not their children took private property. Some did not care to discriminate between stolen and scavenged goods; the very poorest could not afford to quibble with their children about whether or not a day's earnings came from illicit gain. One small boy picked up by the CAS told his benefactors that his parents had sent him out chip picking with the instructions "you can take it wherever you can find it"—although like many children brought before the charities, this one may have been embroidering his own innocence at his parents' expense.[38]

But children also took their own chances, without their parents' knowledge. We have seen how girls gambled with prostitution, another lure of street life. This is why an upstanding German father tried to prevent his fourteen-year-old daughter from going out scavenging after she lost her place in domestic service. "He said, 'I don't want you to be a rag-picker. You are not a child now—people will look at you—you will come to harm,' " as the girl recounted the tale. The "harm" he feared was the course taken by a teenage habitué of the waterfront in whom Inspector Bell took a special interest in 1851. After she rejected his offer of a place in service, he learned from a junk shop proprietor that, along with scavenging around the docks, she was "in the habit of going aboard the Coal Boats in that vicinity and prostituting herself." Charles Loring Brace claimed that "the life of a swill-gatherer, or coal-picker, or chiffonier in the streets soon wears off a girl's modesty and prepares her for worse occupation," and Matsell claimed that huckster girls solicited the clerks and employees they met on their rounds of countinghouses. Petty theft, too, could be lucrative for children. By midcentury, New York was the capital of American crime, and there was a place for children, small and adept as they were, on its margins. Its full-blown economy of contraband, with the junk shops at the center, allowed children to exchange pilfered and stolen goods quickly and easily. Anything, from scavenged bottles to nicked top hats, could be sold immediately.[39]

The self-reliance that the streets fostered through petty crime also extended to living arrangements. Abandoned children, orphans, runaways and footloose boys made the streets their home, sleeping out with companions in household areas, wagons, market stalls and saloons. In the summer of 1850, the *Tribune* noted that the police regularly scared up thirty or forty boys sleeping downtown along Nassau and Ann streets. They included boys with homes as well as real vagabonds.[40] Prostitution was the only way girls could get away from home, but boys were less constrained: "Sleeping out" was a permissible sort of boyhood escapade. Chief Matsell reported that in warm weather, crowds of roving boys, many of them sons of respectable parents, absented themselves from their families for weeks. Such was Thomas W., who came to the attention of the CAS; "sleeps in stable," the case record notes. "Goes home for clean clothes; and sometimes for his meals." Thomas's parents evidently tolerated the arrangement, but this was not always the case. Boys as well as girls could strike out on their own to evade parental discipline. John Lynch, for example, left home because of some difficulty with his father. His parent's complaint to the police landed him in the juvenile house of correction on a vagrancy charge.[41]

Reformers like Matsell and the members of the CAS tended to see such children as either orphaned or abandoned, symbols of the misery and depravity of the poor. Their perceptions, incarnated in the waifs of sentimental novels, gained wide credibility in nineteenth-century social theory and popular thought. Street children were essentially "friendless and homeless," declared Charles Loring Brace. "No one cares for them, and they care for no one."[42] His judgment, if characteristically harsh, was not without truth. Orphanage was far more frequent among all classes in the nineteenth century than it is today. Last-born children could easily see both parents die before they reached adulthood. Poor people were more adversely affected than their well-housed contemporaries by contagious diseases, unhealthful work and unsanitary living conditions and thus often died at earlier ages. If children without parents had no kin or friendly neighbors to whom to turn, they had to fend for themselves. This is what happened to the two small children of a deceased stonecutter, who had been a widower. After the father died, the pair "wandered around, begging cold victuals, and picking up, in any way they were able, their poor living." William S., fifteen years old, had lost his parents when very young. After a stay on a farm as an indentured boy, he ran away to the city, where he slept on the piers and supported himself by carrying luggage off passenger boats: "William thinks he has seen hard times," the CAS agent recorded.[43]

But the evidence reformers garnered about the "friendless and homeless" young should also be taken with a grain of salt. Just as reformers were more sympathetic to those women who claimed that seduction or starvation had driven them to prostitution, the CAS, a major source of these tales, favored those children who came before the society's agents as victims of orphanage, abandonment or familial cruelty. Accordingly, young applicants for aid could present themselves in ways pitched to gain favor. Little Johnny the street seller, a great favorite with the society, confessed that he had used the ploy of orphanage to gain admission to their Newsboys' Lodging House. The truth he admitted, however, was a melodramatic tale as appealing as the original to the hearts of the charity agents. His drunken parents, he explained, had sent him to the streets to steal and beg to support their vices. Whatever the veracity of his story, it meshed nicely with the beliefs about working-class parents that he must have sensed in his benefactors.[44] In reality, there were few children so entirely friendless as the CAS liked to believe. The reformers' category of the street orphan concealed a variety of circumstances. In the worst New York slums, families managed to stay together and to take in those kin and friends who lacked households of their own. Orphaned children as well as those who were temporarily parentless —whose parents, for instance, had found employment elsewhere—typically found homes with older siblings, grandparents and aunts.[45]

Working-class families, however, were often far from harmonious. Girls and young women, we have seen, sometimes took considerable risks to escape them. Interdependence, enforced cooperation and obligatory sharing in the family wage economy bred conflicts that weighed heavily on the young. In response, children sometimes chose—or were forced—to strike out on their own. Relations with stepparents often generated tensions which eventually pushed a child out of the household. Two brothers whom a charity visitor found sleeping in the streets, for example, explained that they had left their mother when she moved in with another man after their father deserted her. If a natural parent died, the remaining stepparent could be indifferent to the fate of the stepchild; a stepmother, facing dismal prospects for herself and her own offspring, might reject the burden of additional children. "We haven't got no father nor mother," testified a twelve-year-old wanderer of himself and his younger brother. Their father, a shoemaker, had remarried when their mother died; when he died, their stepmother moved away and left them, "and they could not find out anything more about her."[46]

The difficulties experienced by all, children and adults, in finding work in these years also contributed to a kind of halfway orphanage, as family members traveled about seeking employment. Parents seeking work elsewhere could leave children in New York in situations that subsequently collapsed and cast the children on their own. The parents of one boy, for example, left him at work in a printing office when they moved to Toronto. Soon after they left, he was thrown out of work; to support himself he lived on the streets and worked as an errand boy, newsboy and bootblack. Similarly, adolescents whose parents had placed them in unpleasant or intolerable situations might simply leave. A widow boarded her son with her sister when she went into service; the boy ran away when his aunt "licked him." Because of the estrangements and uncertainties such arrangements entailed, parents sometimes lost track of their children. The widower Mr. Pangborne, for example, put his little girl out to board when he signed on to a whaling ship in 1849; when he returned, he found that the woman in charge had lost the child in the streets. He finally located his daughter in the municipal orphanage, where she had been placed as an abandoned child.[47]

What reformers portrayed, then, as a stark tableau of virtue and vice was in actuality a complicated geography of family life, invisible to men and women who believed a child's place was in the home, under the moral tutelage of a woman. Children were expected to earn their keep, and when they could not, they took to the streets. To reformers, this response was *de facto* proof of parental depravity.

Although reformers included both parents in their condemnations of working-class families, the indictments affected women more than men. Women dealt with the charities more often than did men: In 1858, for instance, the AICP aided 27 percent more women. And mothers were more directly involved than fathers in the domestic labor that was the cause of all the alarm. Single mothers, in particular, relied on their children's casual employment in the streets. In general, poor women were more responsible for children, both from the perspective of reformers and within the reality of the working-class household: Like other women, motherhood was central to their adult lives. Yet as genteel society saw it, mothering was an expression of an innate "womanly" nature which took the particular psychological and material forms of emotional nurturance and a comfortable home. The very different patterns of working-class motherhood, shaped by social factors reformers were ill prepared to understand, could only be construed as unwomanly neglectfulness, reflecting badly not only on their character as parents but on their very identity as women. In reform annals of the 1850s working-class mothers frequently take on the character of a subhuman species: bestially drunken and abusive, indifferent, "sickly-looking, deformed by over work . . . weak and sad-faced." If, as in the case of the mother we encountered at the beginning of this chapter, a woman's appearance did not fit the bill, reformers deduced a hidden depravity from the facts of her situation. Like prostitutes, working-class mothers became a kind of half-sex, by virtue of their inability or refusal to conjure up the "natural" abilities of the "true" woman.[48]

The Children's Aid Society and Corrective Domesticity

Charles Loring Brace shared the alarm and revulsion of reformers like Matsell at the "homelessness" of the poor, but he also brought to the situation an optimistic liberalism, based upon his own curious and ambiguous uses of domesticity. In his memoirs of 1872, looking back on two decades of work with the New York laboring poor, Brace took heart from his belief that the absence of family life so deplored by his contemporaries actually operated to stabilize American society. In America, immigration and continual mobility disrupted the process by which one generation of the working class taught the next a cultural identity, "that continuity of influence which bad parents and grandparents exert." Brace wrote this passage with the specter of the Paris Commune before him; shaken, like so many of his peers, by the degree of organization and class consciousness among the Parisian poor, he found on native ground consolation in what others condemned. "The mill of American life, which grinds up so many delicate and fragile things, has its uses, when it is turned on the vicious fragments of the lower strata of society." In New York, families were constantly broken up, Brace continued cheerfully. "They do not transmit a progeny of crime."[49]

It was through the famed placing-out system that the CAS turned the "mill of American life" to the uses of urban reform. Placing out sent poor city children to foster homes in rural areas where labor was scarce. It was based on the wages-fund theory, the popular scheme that, a few years before, Mrs. Storms had urged the workingwomen of the Ladies' Industrial Association to adopt. "If, owing to the peculiarity of our country," the CAS argued, "we have, in the families of our farmers, institutions scattered all over our fields, which will take this very burden . . . which need the labor whereof we have an abundance . . . is it not the better part of economy and wisdom to make use of them?" This was the argument whereby the CAS defended itself against critics' quite plausible charges that "foster parents" were simply farmers in need of cheap help, and placing out was a cover for the exploitation of child labor. At first, children went to farms in the nearby countryside, just as did those the city bound out from the Almshouse, but in 1854 the society conceived the more ambitious plan of sending parties of children by railroad to the far Midwest, to Illinois, Michigan and Iowa. By 1860, agents had placed out 5,074 children.[50]

At its most extreme, the CAS only parenthetically recognized the social and legal claims of working-class parenthood. The organization considered the separation of parents and children a positive good, the liberation of basically innocent, if somewhat tarnished children from the tyranny of irredeemable adults. The legacy of childhood innocence was ambiguous. Socially liberating in many respects, the idea also provided one basis for class domination. Since the CAS viewed children as innocents to be rescued and parents as corruptors to be displaced, its methods depended in large measure on convincing children themselves to leave New York, generally, but not necessarily, with parental knowledge or acquiescence. Street children were malleable innocents in the eyes of the charity, but they were also little consenting adults, capable of breaking all ties to their class milieu. Many parents did bring their children to be placed out, but the society also at times worked directly through the children.[51] In 1843, the moral reformer and abolitionist Lydia Maria Child had mused that the greatest misfortune of "the squalid little wretches" she saw in the New York streets was that they were not orphans.[52] The charity visitors of the CAS tackled this problem directly: Where orphans were lacking, they manufactured them.

It is difficult to discern much about the actual experience that lay behind the society's paeans to the placing-out scheme. On the one hand, agents inquired into the family circumstances of potential emigrants and sought out the consent of those parents who could be located. On the other, CAS visitors alluded to opposition to children's emigration from parents and acknowledged that their "orphans" were sometimes runaways with fictitious histories. Brace lamented the fact that mothers would rather see their sons "ruined" in New York than send them to salvation out West. Parents, he complained, were known to follow emigrating parties to recover their children. Priests supposedly propagated rumors among the Irish that the CAS sold their children into bondage, converted them to Protestantism, and renamed them: "that thus even brothers and sisters might meet and perhaps marry!"[53] We can wonder retrospectively how carefully the society inquired into stories of orphanage, and how thoroughly agents for the emigrating parties searched for living parents. We can also conjecture about the expectations the poor themselves—children and parents—held about the trip West. The Irish, in particular, were accustomed to the seasonal migrations of adolescents as farm laborers and domestic servants.[54] Sending one's son to Iowa may not have initially appeared much different from sending him on a harvest gang. For similar reasons, emigration may have seemed ordinary to children. Certainly the CAS appealed to the street child's enterprising nature with its tales of Western opportunity and fortune.

The domestic ideology that underlay placing out gave a liberal like Brace the theoretical basis for constructing a persuasive rather than a coercive program to reform the tenement classes. Placing out was based on the thoroughly bourgeois belief in the redeeming influence of the Protestant home in the countryside. "The great duty . . . of the Visitor," the CAS declared, "is to get these children of unhappy fortune utterly out of their surroundings, and to send them away to kind Christian *homes in the country*. No influence, we believe, is like the influence of a *Home*."[55] There, the morally strengthening effects of labor, mixed with the salutary influences of domesticity, could remold the child's character. Standards of desirable behavior could be internalized by children rather than beaten into them, as had been the practice with the CAS's most important forerunner in the field of juvenile reform, the House of Refuge. Like other early nineteenth-century asylums, the House had been based, in theory, on the power of geometrically ordered architecture and strictly regimented routines to reorder inmates' habits; in practice, its staff freely used solitary confinement and corporal punishment to force the recalcitrant into compliance with the forces of reason.[56] Home influence, however, could bypass the use of force by deploying subliminal persuasion instead. The foster home, with its all-encompassing moral influence, could be a more effective house of refuge than the genuine article. "We have wished to make every kind or religious family, who desired the responsibility, an Asylum or a Reformatory Institution . . . by throwing about the wild, neglected little outcast of the streets, the love and gentleness of home." The home was an asylum, but it was woman's influence rather than an institutional regimen that accomplished its corrections.[57]

. . .

Gender divisions were marked in the CAS. Male and female reformers did different work, the men as paid agents who supervised the society's main ventures, the women as volunteers who staffed the more marginal girls' projects. The latter—a lodging house and several industrial schools—were less novel than the programs the men operated and thus less well described in the organization's literature. The women volunteers were accordingly much less visible.

The society also gave different kinds of help to boys and girls. Placing out was mostly for boys, who seem to have been more allured by the journey than were girls. Parents were less reluctant to place out sons, who were likely to roam away from home anyway, than daughters, whose contributions to the household were more reliable and more easily enforced.[58] Sexual considerations may have also entered in. Sending girls away, unlike boys, was courting sexual danger.

Brace's own imagination was more caught up with boys than girls, his most inventive efforts pitched to them. Alone among his contemporaries, Brace sensed something of the creative energies of street culture. His writings are sweeping, animated and brimming with detail precisely because he was so fascinated by the vitality and hardihood of the street boys. His absorption in the Western scheme came partly from the hope that emigration would redirect their toughness and resourcefulness, "their sturdy independence," into hearty frontier individualism.[59] Brace activated male sympathies to enliven the society's much-touted Newsboys' Lodging-House, a boardinghouse where, for a few pennies, newsboys could sleep and eat. The Lodging-House was, in fact, a kind of early boys' camp, where athletics and physical fitness, lessons in entrepreneurship (one of its salient features was a savings bank), and moral education knit poor boys and gentlemen into a high-spirited but respectable masculine camaraderie.[60]

This approach had little to do with the female side of things—heading for the territories was very much a masculine adventure—and so the women were left mostly to their own devices with their girls. Mixing Brace's critique of the city with the understanding of domesticity they drew from their own experiences, they developed the rudiments of a parallel, yet distinctly female, strategy of secular urban reform.

In their efforts, the women drew sustenance from the sentimentalist imagery of virtuous working-class women that had long inspired their most sympathetic work with the poor. Rather than limiting themselves to separating the virtuous from the vicious, however, the women of the CAS took as their task the creation of a plebeian womanliness from the materials at hand. The domestic arts, not prayer and repentance, were their agents of transformation. In the industrial schools and lodging house, girls recruited off the streets learned the arts of plain sewing, cooking and housecleaning. The precepts of domesticity guided their education: "Nothing was so honorable as industrious *housework*," the ladies insisted. The goals were partly vocational—outfitting the students for work as seamstresses and domestic servants—but they were also familial. Many students, the ladies proudly attested, went on to enter respectable married life as well as honest employment. Marriage was the vehicle of reform. "Living in homes re-formed through their influence," these women carried on as emissaries of domestic womanhood.[61] Energized by their mission, properly understood through learning from their social betters, and equipped with the proper skills, "true" working-class women need not retire into timid and tearful solitude, but could enter into the effort to transform their class milieu.

The women reformers also instituted meetings to convert the mothers of their students to a new relationship to household and children. Classes taught the importance of sobriety, neat appearance and sanitary housekeeping, the material bases for virtuous motherhood and proper homes. Most important, the ladies stressed the need to keep children off the streets and send them to school. Their pupils were not always willing. Mothers persisted in keeping children home to work and cited economic reasons when their benefactresses upbraided them. Such rationales the ladies considered a mere pretense for the exploitation of children and the neglect of their character training. "The larger ones were needed to 'mind' the baby," volunteers sarcastically reported, "or go out begging for clothes . . . and the little ones, scarcely bigger than the baskets on their arms, must be sent out for food, or chips, or cinders."[62] The Mothers' Meetings tried to wean away laboring women from such customary patterns to what the ladies believed to be a moral geography of family life: men at work, women at home, children inside.

The CAS was to prove immensely influential in the subsequent history of nineteenth-century reform.[63] In the 1850s, its ideas were already compelling because they gave coherence to diffuse but widely felt discomforts with city life. Between the lines of Brace's writing, we can catch glimpses of what a comfortable bourgeois city might look like. The regenerated metropolis would be far better ordered, as one might expect, its streets free for trade and respectable promenades, emancipated from the inconveniences of pickpockets and thieves, the affronts of prostitutes and hucksters, the myriad offenses of working-class mores. The respectable would dominate public space as never before, and the city itself could become something of an asylum, an embodiment of the eighteenth-century virtues of reason and progress, the nineteenth-century virtue of industry.

The women's approach was at first only a minor strain within the CAS vision. It was, however, their far more prosaic version of domestic reform, not Brace's, that would eventually predominate within American reform and social work. The thrust of Brace's program—promoting the disintegration of families—ran counter to the ladies' faith in the importance of a strong domestic life. Rather than encouraging girls to break away, then, the ladies sought just the opposite—to create among the urban working class an indigenous domestic life, thereby transforming urban social space.

In short, the women viewed domesticity and true womanhood as a means to regenerate a class-divided city. What they understood to be common sense, we can see as a hegemony of gender. Properly established gender norms could realign the social geography of the city, strengthening boundaries between public and private and circumscribing the riotous energies of working-class children and the promiscuously sociable lives of working-class women. While Brace looked to the past, to a rural republic, to solve the problems of the modern city, the women worked from a different angle. Their own understanding of domesticity led them to focus on the power of a new kind of working-class woman to abolish class conflicts. Still marginal in the secular reform movement, the CAS women stuck close to their girls' schools. Yet they were onto something.

Family Law

State involvement in child raising increased dramatically in the nineteenth century. The key to the great intervention—what Jacques Donzelot has termed "the policing of families"—lay in changes in the common law. In the colonial and early national years, the legal identity of children (like that of women) had been wholly subsumed, within a strictly patriarchal logic, under male heads of families. But American courts, in a line of child custody cases beginning right after the turn of the century, began to chip away at the principle of absolute paternal rights by advancing a doctrine of "the best interests of the child." To accomplish the separation of the child's legal identity from the patriarchal unit, judges invoked the state's sovereign authority over children's welfare—*parens patriae*, literally, the state is the parent.[64]

Parens patriae legitimated state intrusion into the once inviolable domain of the father. The doctrine affected a wide range of legal disputes over apprenticeship, custody and adoption in which bourgeois as well as working-class people were involved. Its main *social* consequences, however, lay with the child-saving agencies and institutions it spawned, and were borne by the poor who were their chief clients. We have encountered two child-saver organizations in New York, the CAS and the House of Refuge. By the end of the century, there were 250 such agencies nationwide.

There is a persuasive argument, however, that judicial law does not initiate change but codifies changes already in the works. Taking this tack, we can return to the social history of the urban poor and see its importance in transforming legal doctrine. The problems—and the "problem"—of the poor were the material from which, in large measure, judges fashioned their reconsiderations of authority and power within the family. Apart from individual cases of custody contested between spouses and kin, it was the reformers' involvement with poor children which raised, in the first place, questions of child welfare. In the context of prevailing antebellum strategies of reform, a broad reading of *parens patriae* made a great deal of sense: Reformers as early as the 1820s had seen their task to be removing children from vicious, corrupt "associations." The seminal antebellum decision on institutional custody, indeed, involved a suit against the Philadelphia House of Refuge, a replica of its New York progenitor. The court was only approving established practice when it ruled that state guardianship could supersede that of natural parents "unequal to the task of education." Since its establishment, the New York House of Refuge had assumed the power to alienate custody from parents; in the Philadelphia case the courts followed suit.[65]

More broadly, changes in the law bore a relationship to changes in urban working-class families. Into the causal sequence of reform movements and legal transformation we must insert the actions of children. Strict legal notions of patriarchy broke down, in part, because they no longer made sense in a society where some of its most troublesome members so often defied patriarchal control. In cutting loose from their families, children themselves raised the question of their distinct legal identity, as they began in large numbers to slip through the family networks of regulation which in the eighteenth century had served as an informal judicial system for the young.

New York's first school truancy law, passed in 1853, brought the doctrine of *parens patriae* to bear directly on the problem of street children. The framers of the act, the AICP, saw the law as an extension of their work. With far more clout than "mere Moral influence," it made children's school attendance a condition of family relief. In essence, the law banned school-age children from the streets. Those found "wandering" there were to be taken before a magistrate, then either released on parents' assurance (to be sent to school, to some lawful employment or kept at home) or, if orphaned, to be taken on as wards of the state. Moreover, whatever the family circumstances, the state could assume custody of habitual wanderers. "Our State

. . . by assuming the place of a parent to its helpless children . . . raises them from the degradation of their present condition to one of equality." "Degradation" was a cultural, not an economic term; the abrogation of parental rights depended not (as it had in the eighteenth century) on whether parents were providing a livelihood for their children, but on the social context in which they were raising them. "If the parent is intemperate, incompetent, or indifferent to the education of his children, the law should take his place."[66]

His place? It was to take thirty more years, and an active women's movement in the city's settlement houses which insisted that working-class mothers, properly trained, could undo the worst effects of poverty, before women would become fully visible in the discourse of the working-class family. Nevertheless, considerations of women were *inscribed* early on in that discourse, and a politics of gender was implied in this nascent politics of the family.

In a period that so idealized maternal influence (the courts themselves increasingly cited it as a reason to award children to mothers in contested custody cases), the alienation of children from their "natural" ties required seeing the mothers in those cases in a different light. Domesticity, with its overwhelming thrust toward universal standards of womanhood, provided the means to do so. Authorities could not have gained such wide powers to intervene in parental rights had it not been for assumptions in the making since the 1820s about the depravity of poor women as mothers. Certain kinds of mothers, by their social behavior, denied the womanly nature which gave them their claim to their children. Gender was on its way to becoming public policy.

Conclusion

In 1789, New York's laboring women lived and worked primarily within the sphere of the family. Submerged within domestic production, women depended on household members—fathers, husbands, children and (as servants) on masters—for their livelihoods. To a great extent, families—and the patriarchal order of power on which families were based—absorbed conflicts between the sexes: Women and the problems women posed went largely unnoticed in the policies and actions of the municipality and the new federal government. The system of household production, although under considerable stress, was still sufficiently stable to accommodate most women; single women living completely on their own were virtually absent in eighteenth-century American society.

In the next half century, metropolitan industrialization was to strengthen many elements of this gender system, particularly women's economic dependence on men. But neither did capitalism simply mesh with patriarchal relations. By 1860, both class struggle and conflicts between the sexes had created a different political economy of gender in New York, one in which laboring women turned certain conditions of their very subordination into new kinds of initiatives. Collectivities of laboring women—a city of poor women—spilled out of family households to stake out a presence in New York's economy, culture and its ideological conflicts. A female working class labored at the very center of the manufacturing economy, including women living outside families as well as those within. In the context of paid work that denied most women a living wage, they con-

tinued to depend on family ties to men as the most secure means of livelihood. But immigration, widespread misery and the casualization of male
labor made those dependencies all the more precarious and forced women
to seek other means of support. They did so by becoming family heads
themselves and utilizing their children's labor, by depending on other
women and by pressing their needs upon the municipality. The problems
of supporting women and the problem of controlling them overstripped the
boundaries of the family and entered into formal politics, to be taken up
by city officials, social reformers and trade unionists.

The terms of accommodation and struggle between men and women of
the emerging working class were in flux. The transformation of productive
households into family wage economies had proved to be more than simply
an adaptation to the hardships of proletarian life. Although family cooperation did serve the needs of employers looking for efficient and profitable
ways to exploit labor, wage earning in the industrial city also put considerable strain on corporate family forms, especially in the case of young women.
Daughters worked to help their families, but they also used their wages
to distance themselves from parental authority. The independence they
fashioned for themselves was slight and existed only at the margins of
working-class life; nonetheless, it represented an important challenge to a
gender system predicated on the control of daughters' labor and daughters'
sexuality.

Working-class women helped to modify the masculinist culture of the
city into one in which, by the Civil War, they played an acknowledged,
if peripheral role. In the daily life of the neighborhoods, mothers and wives
developed a style of life that reconciled anonymity with intimacy, an order
that served as a basis for neighborhood community and fostered a peculiarly
urban ethical mixture of watchful generosity and communal judgment.
Young women's presence in the milieu of commercial leisure contributed
to a cultural imagery betokening a prideful working-class female independence distinct from the imagery of female virtue produced by bourgeois
culture. The image of the Bowery Gal was quite different from the contemptuous depictions of laboring women that had haunted masculine lore
since the eighteenth century; similarly, it transcended the dichotomous
depictions of female vice and virtue used by Victorian sentimentalist writers, male and female, in their renditions of workingwomen's lives. The Gal
of commercial culture signified a female presence where once existed only
others' projections of the female; as such, she represented for laboring
women a break with misogynistic culture something like that which the
"true" woman represented for middle-class women.

One response of workingmen to the heightened presence of women was
an ideological paternalism, associated in New York with growing labor

radicalism. The new protectionism, most clearly expressed in the labor movement's call to remove women from wage labor, was in one sense an attempt to preserve male prerogatives, but it also embodied the success of workingwomen in pressing some of their own claims on men. In working-class commercial culture, too, men's paternalist views of women as members of their own class to be protected pushed to the margins earlier views of laboring women as fair game for all.

As gender identity became a contested issue in conflicts of class, reformers drew part of their own sense of mission from combatting this expansion of working-class female culture. Especially on the streets, both the sexual culture of daughters and the domestic culture of mothers were antithetical to the terms of home life and womanhood developed and championed by urban ladies. Sympathy for their working-class sisters and a rudimentary perception of the debilities they shared with them did motivate female charity workers and reformers. Ultimately, however, the bonds of womanhood depended on notions of "true" gender identity based on a particular class experience, and sympathy for the "virtuous" working-class woman—she who conformed to the ladies' standards—was conferred at the expense of all the "vicious" who did not. The vision of universal sisterhood elevated bourgeois women and their imitators above misogynist ideology, but left unchallenged—indeed perpetuated—misogynist views of the mass of working-class women.

The idea of sisterhood was thus inextricable from the ascendancy of the bourgeoisie in New York to cultural and political dominance. By the 1850s, the reform of the working-class gender system had become a programmatic goal of many municipal leaders. A movement largely dominated by men institutionalized domesticity into laws which sought to enforce genteel family practices among working-class people, laws that implicitly sought to transform the character of working-class womanhood into one resembling more closely the female identity that the cult of domesticity celebrated.

The 1850s set the terms of both female struggles and female accommodations across class lines for the next half century. In the new school attendance law and the work of the CAS female volunteers lay the roots of the Americanization campaign which at the end of the century reshaped the lives of so many working-class immigrants to New York. Then, the settlement houses and public schools were to expand the antebellum mothers' classes and girls' housekeeping lessons into a vast program of nativist assimilation as well as female self-help. Women social workers and teachers, many of them inspired by feminist impulses to help their poorer sisters, would assure immigrant mothers and daughters that the key to decent lives lay in creating American homes within the immigrant neighborhoods—homes

that aspired to a particular bourgeois configuration of possessions,
housekeeping practices and family relations. As in the 1850s, the effort to
domesticate the plebeian household would be linked in the Progressive era
to a campaign to eradicate a ubiquitous and aggressive working-class
culture.

The women's rights movement before the Civil War was too absorbed
in middle-class women's dilemmas in marriage, work and property relations to learn much from working-class women. Only in the 1870s did Susan
Anthony begin to turn away from abstract, sentimentalist images of workingwomen popular in her social milieu to begin learning about the concrete
debilities of working-class women's lives. Even then, Anthony mostly had
to do the investigating for herself; working-class women still lacked a
collective language in which to articulate publicly their particular grievances. Male-dominated trade unions, increasingly committed to the family
wage, provided few ways for women to express either the troubles they
endured or the desires they might conceive in the social terrain outside the
male-headed family. Even the Knights of Labor, which actively sought out
women's participation, did so under the beacon of a higher working-class
domesticity, to be achieved when (male) workers finally earned the full
value of their labor. The family wage—and the ideology of gender that
encompassed it—served well enough for women attached to men. For
them, it meant a liberation from the double shift of wage earning superim-
posed on household work. And certainly when the labor movement at its
most radical mobilized entire communities—as in the great railroad strike
of 1877, the eight-hour day strikes of 1886 and the IWW strikes of the early
twentieth century—it incorporated many concerns of wives and mothers.
Nonetheless, what Sally Alexander has written of the Chartist women in
England in the 1830s and 1840s was also true of the militant wives in the
small Ohio railroad towns on strike in 1877, the German women who
cheered the May Day demonstrators in Chicago, 1886 and the Italian mill-
worker mothers who marched for bread and roses in Lawrence, 1912:
"Women could only speak as active subjects at selective moments, and
within the community."[1] The language of feminism subsumed working-
class women's experience into categories of victimization, and the language
of class struggle blurred the particularities of their lives into the unified
interests of the working-class family.

Only with the historic rising of the daughters in the great women's strike
of shirtwaist makers in 1909 did the possibilities of a distinct workingwomen's feminism in New York, so briefly kindled in the 1830s, take fire.
The young women's hopes and their militance grew out of the socialist and
anarchist ideas of their Italian and Eastern European Jewish families, and
they drew their collective strength from the solidarities of the immigrant

neighborhoods. But something of their aspirations came as well from a collective imagination nourished by the urban culture of the young of which they were a part.

At first glance, that shabby milieu of cheap cafés, tacky clothes and shady negotiations with men seems a world away from the high-minded rhetoric of the rebel girls. And in some ways it was. Its sexual latitude and material delights, in cutting working girls adrift from the family ties that had sustained as well as oppressed them, could certainly numb the soul. In the 1890s, the city's sexual opportunities and fancy clothes had completed the transformation of the farm girl Sister Carrie into an amoral demimondaine; and there must have been many more like her. But in the same years, New York culture also provided another newcomer, a young Russian Jew named Emma Goldman, the materials to turn the fleeting experience of the undutiful, pleasure-seeking daughter into a political vision of women's freedom.

All through the nineteenth century, working-class New York was like that. It led women astray; then again, it made something new of the ones who had gone bad. It was a place where the dialectic of female vice and female virtue was volatile; where, in the ebb and flow of large oppressions and small freedoms, poor women traced out unforeseen possibilities for their sex. Therein lies the importance of its tenements, sweatshops, promenades and streets for the history of American women.

Appendix: Tables

Notes

A Note on Sources

Index

Appendix: Tables

TABLE I

Women's Occupations in New York City, 1805

OCCUPATION	TOTAL PERSONS LISTED IN OCCUPATION	NUMBER OF WOMEN	PERCENTAGE OF WOMEN
Boardinghouse keepers	141	79	56
Mantua makers and milliners	59	51	86
Teachers	107	32	30
Seamstresses	31	31	100
Nurses	25	25	100
Tailors and tailoresses	188	22	12
Grocers	793	18	2
Midwives	11	11	100
Tavern and coffee-house keepers	113	7	6
Fruiters	27	5	19
Other occupations with women	455	10	2
TOTAL	1950	291	14.9

Source: *Longworth's American Almanac . . . and City Directory for 1805.*

TABLE 2
Wages in the Clothing Trade—Outworkers

YEAR	WEEKLY WAGE (6-DAY WEEK)	TYPE OF WORK	SOURCE
1830	$ .72	Trousers	*Working Man's Advocate*
	.42	Shirts	
1831	1.25	Seamstress	Matthew Carey
1844	1.25	Southern work	*Working Man's Advocate*
1845	.75	Common shirts	*Tribune*
	1.50	Linen-bosomed shirts (skilled work)	
	.72	Trousers	
	2.00	Heavy coats (skilled work)	
	.84–1.50	Caps	
	.60–1.25	Outworkers	*Working Man's Advocate*
1849	.75	Shirt-sewer ("good hand")	Foster
	1.50	Linen-bosomed shirts	
1853	1.20 (maximum)	Shirts	*Herald*
	1.00–2.00	Coarse shirts	
1857	3.00	Shirts	*Herald*
	2.50	Outworkers	
(post-Panic)	.72	Shirts	
1858	12 shillings –$2.00	Caps, pantaloons, good shirts (lowest rates)	*Times*
1859	.75	Shirts	SPRW
	3.50	Caps (with sewing machine)	Penny*

*Penny noted the evidence of wages as high as this was "mixed." *Employments of Women,* pp. 342–43.
Sources: *Working Man's Advocate,* September 11, 1830, July 27, 1844, March 8, 1845; *Tribune,* August 14, 1845, June 8, 1853; Foster, *New York in Slices,* p. 51; Carey, "Report on Female Wages," *Miscellaneous Essays,* p. 267; *Herald,* June 7, 1853, October 21, 25, 1857; *New York Daily Times,* November 11, 1858; Penny, *Employments of Women,* pp. 342–43; Minute Books, November 1859, SRPW.

TABLE 3
Household Situations of Female
Primary Wage Earners*—All Trades

	4TH WARD	17TH WARD	TOTAL
Lodgers	131	45	176
Supporting dependents (children or kin)	67	27	94
Pooling wages with female kin	29	33	62
Single household heads without dependents	13	10	23
	240	115	N = 355

*No male wage earner over 16 years of age in household.
Source: New York State Manuscript Census, 1855, Fourth Ward, Election District (E.D.) 2, Seventeenth Ward, E.D. 3.

TABLE 4
Household Situations of Female Outworkers

	4TH WARD	17TH WARD	TOTAL
Lodgers	59	17	76
Daughters or sisters in households with employed men	44	28	72
Pooling wages with female kin	13	13	26
Primary wage earner supporting dependents (children or kin)	18	7	25
Living with employed sons, uncles, brothers-in-law, cousins	14	6	20
Wives in households of employed men	17	1	18
Single household heads without dependents	1	4	5
	166	76	N = 242

Source: New York State Manuscript Census, 1855, Fourth Ward, E.D. 2, Seventeenth Ward, E.D. 3.

TABLE 5
Women's Wages—Inside Workers

DATE	WAGES	OCCUPATION	SOURCE
1845	$1.50–3.50	Bookbinding	*Young America*
	2.50–3.50	Umbrella sewing	
1851	1.00–2.50	Type rubbing	Burns
1853	2.50	Straw sewing	*Herald*
	6.00–7.00	Straw plaiting	
1857	5.00–6.00	Shirt sewing (machine)	*Herald*
	4.00–5.00	Shirt sewing (hand)	
1859	4.00–6.00	Sewing (machine)	Penny
	2.00–3.00	Basting	
	4.00	Booksewing	

Sources: *Young America*, September 13, November 29, 1845; Burns, *Life in New York*; *Herald*, June 7, 1853, October 25, 1857; Penny, *Employments of Women*, p. 111.

Notes

ABBREVIATIONS

AALW Association for the Asylum for Lying-In Women
AICP Association for the Improvement of the Condition of the Poor
CAS   Children's Aid Society
CGS   Court of General Sessions
DCC   Documents of the Common Council
HRCH House of Refuge Case Histories
MCC   Minutes of the Common Council
NYCTS New York City Tract Society
NYHS New-York Historical Society
NYMA New York Municipal Archives
NYPL New York Public Library
SPP   Society for the Prevention of Pauperism
SRPW Society for the Relief of Poor Widows

INTRODUCTION

1   Many books and articles have developed this view. I have in mind Bruce G. Laurie, *Working People of Philadelphia, 1800–1850* (Philadelphia, 1980); Gary John Kornblith, "From Artisans to Businessmen: Master Mechanics in New England, 1789–1850" (Ph.D. diss., Princeton University, 1983); Sean Wilentz, *Chants Democratic: New York City & the Rise of the American Working Class, 1788–1850* (New York, 1984); Alan Dawley, *Class and Community: The Industrial Revolution in Lynn* (Cambridge, Mass., 1976); Paul G. Faler, *Mechanics and Manufacturers in the Early Industrial Revolution* (Albany, N.Y., 1981); Herbert G. Gutman, *Work, Culture, and Society in Industrializing America* (New York, 1977); Paul E. Johnson, *A Shopkeeper's Millennium: Society and Revivals in Rochester, New York, 1815–1837* (New York, 1978).
2   I refer to a rich store of work, of which the best known books are Nancy F. Cott, *The Bonds of Womanhood: "Woman's Sphere" in New England, 1780–1835* (New Haven, Conn., 1977); Mary P. Ryan, *Cradle of the Middle Class: The Family in Oneida County, New York, 1790–1865* (New York, 1981); Kathryn Kish Sklar, *Catharine Beecher: A Study in American Domesticity* (New Haven, Conn., 1973). A sophisticated and perceptive treatment of domesticity as a mode of class identity is Barbara

Leslie Epstein, *The Politics of Domesticity: Women, Evangelism and Temperance in Nineteenth-Century America* (Middletown, Conn., 1981).

CHAPTER I: FEMALE WORK AND POVERTY

1   I am indebted to a paper by Peter Linebaugh for my sense of the importance of the picaresque mode in seaports of the Atlantic basin, "The Picaresque Proletarian in Eighteenth Century London" (Paper presented at the Conference on Proletarianization, Rutgers University, April 1983). General descriptions of New York in the years 1789–1820 are in Bayrd Still, *New York City: A Students' Guide to Localized History* (New York, 1965), pp. 6–8 and *Mirror for Gotham: New York As Seen by Contemporaries from Dutch Days to the Present* (New York, 1956); Sidney I. Pomerantz, *New York, an American City 1783–1803* (New York, 1938); Frank Monaghan and Marvin Lowenthal, *This Was New York: The Nation's Capital in 1789* (New York, 1943); James Grant Wilson, ed., *The Memorial History of the City of New-York*, 4 vols. (New York, 1892); Thomas E. V. Smith, *The City of New York in the Year of Washington's Inauguration* (New York, 1889); Typescript, I. N. Phelps Stokes Collection on New York City Slums, Manuscript Room, New York Public Library (NYPL).

2   Pomerantz, *New York*, pp. 147–93; Robert Greenhalgh Albion, *The Rise of New York Port 1815–1860* (New York, 1939), pp. 7–8.

3   J. P. Brissot de Warville, quoted in Still, *Mirror for Gotham*, p. 46. On fashionable New York see also John Lambert, *Travels Through Canada and the United States*, 3rd ed., 2 vols. (London, 1816), 2:50–60; Wilson, *Memorial History*, 3:21–22, 109–110.

4   Howard B. Rock, *Artisans of the New Republic: The Tradesmen of New York City in the Age of Jefferson* (New York, 1979), pp. 151–82; Wilentz, *Chants Democratic*, pp. 35–42; David Montgomery, "The Working Classes of the Pre-Industrial American City, 1780–1830," *Labor History* 9 (Winter 1968): 3–22.

5   Raymond A. Mohl, *Poverty in New York 1783–1825* (New York, 1971), pp. 17, 24–25; David M. Schneider, *The History of Public Welfare in New York State, 1609–1866* (Chicago, 1938), pp. 133–39.

6   Richard Varick to James Duane, 1788, quoted in Mohl, *Poverty*, p. 17.

7   Linebaugh, "The Picaresque Proletarian," p. 5.

8   On the prostitutes, Roi Ottley and William J. Weatherby, *The Negro in New York* (New York, 1967), pp. 40–41; the "Banditti" are mentioned in *Minutes of the Common Council (MCC)*, 1:49, 115. On the migratory poor, often categorized in the literature as vagrants, see Mohl, *Poverty*, pp. 21, 31–33; Schneider, *History of Public Welfare*, pp. 148–52; also, Douglas Lamar Jones, "The Strolling Poor: Transiency in Eighteenth Century Massachusetts, *Journal of Social History* 8:28–54. On the seasonal migration to the city to take advantage of its relief policies, see also the letter from a "friend in the country," *Evening Post* (New York), February 11, 1805.

9   Gary B. Nash, "Urban Wealth and Poverty in Pre-Revolutionary America," *Journal of Interdisciplinary History* 6 (Spring 1976): 575; Pomerantz, *New York*, pp. 201–209; the literature on land shortages and rural/urban migration is ably summa-

rized in Richard L. Bushman, "Family Security in the Transition from Farm to City," *Journal of Family History* 6 (Fall 1981): 238–44. See also the synthetic interpretation by Allan Kulikoff, "Class, Gender and Race in Early America, 1650 to 1900" (Paper presented at the Philadelphia Center for Early American Studies, May 1985).

One group of poverty-stricken newcomers had once been winners in the Atlantic sweepstakes, the Santo Domingans who arrived, black and mulatto sympathizers in tow, with little more than the clothes on their backs. In these respects New York was a great leveler: The white aristocrats settled down to the *déclassé* life of the expatriate, with its shabby boardinghouse life and dreams of the *revanche;* the blacks melted into the community of free blacks. Ottley and Weatherby, *The Negro in New York,* pp. 47–48.

10   Report of the Commissioners of the Almshouse and Bridewell, February 1, 1796, Documents of the Common Council (DCC), New York Municipal Archives (NYMA).

11   Nash, "Urban Wealth"; Nash analyzes in detail the pre-Revolutionary economic situation as it affected the laboring classes in *The Urban Crucible: Social Change, Political Consciousness and the Origins of the American Revolution* (Cambridge, Mass., 1979), pp. 3–25, 54–75, 102–128, 233–63, 312–38. See also Billy G. Smith, "The Material Lives of Laboring Philadelphians, 1750 to 1800," *William & Mary Quarterly,* 3rd ser., 38 (April 1981): 201–202.

12   Nash, "Urban Wealth," pp. 575–79; Jackson Turner Main, *The Social Structure of Revolutionary America* (Princeton, N.J., 1965), p. 41. Billy G. Smith's estimate for Philadelphia in "Material Lives," p. 201 concurs with Main's; Nash's figures in "Urban Wealth" also lend support.

13   The figures can be read as showing as much as a 63 percent increase. Donald R. Adams, Jr., "Wage Rates in the Early National Period: Philadelphia, 1785–1830," *Journal of Economic History* 28 (September 1968): 404–17. Adams underestimates, however, the extent of periodic unemployment.

14   Between 1789 and 1815 in the quintessentially plebeian Fourth Ward, the taxable property of the journeymen dropped by 20 percent. In the same period, the wealthiest 10 percent of the ward's residents owned the same proportion of the district's personal property (three-fourths) as the top 30 percent had twenty-five years earlier (personal property included capital and personal goods, but not real estate). Examined more closely, even the master craftsmen (on the face of things a "propertied" group) reveal important discrepancies among themselves: In a sample from an 1816 tax list, a handful (5 percent) owned nearly 40 percent of their total assessed wealth. In some of the largest crafts, between one- and two-thirds of the masters owned less than $500 worth of personal property. Rock, *Artisans,* p. 254; Wilentz, *Chants Democratic,* pp. 35, 42–48. See also Bruce Martin Wilkenfeld, "The Social and Economic Structure of the City of New York, 1695–1776" (Ph.D. diss., Columbia University, 1973), pp. 203–13.

15   Thomas F. De Voe, *The Market Book* (New York, 1862), p. 379; Albion, *Rise of New York Port,* pp. 30–31; Wilson, *Memorial History,* 3:307.

16   The budgets are reprinted in Rock, *Artisans,* p. 253; Thomas is in *Trial for Murder . . . 1811 . . . The People v. George Hart* ([New York], c. 1811), pp. 14–15;

journeymen quoted in Alfred F. Young, *The Democratic Republicans in New York: the Origins, 1763–1797* (Williamsburg, Va., 1967), p. 471.

17   Smith, "Material Lives," p. 202. See Main, *Social Structure of Revolutionary America*, pp. 131–35 for a corroborative discussion; see also the tailor's petition in Committee on Charity, April 26, 1813, DCC. Fincher is in ibid., September 1785, December 13, 1786, April 1, 1816. See also the petitions of Elijah Wedge, July 20, 1785, Anthony Tiebout, February 15, 1796, the rigger Gershom Piercy, April 1, 1816 and passim. These petitions give graphic testimony to the precarious livelihoods of the laboring classes.

18   Schneider, *History of Public Welfare*, pp. 45–60, 109–40, 150. Figures for the Almshouse population can be found in Committee on the Almshouse and Bridewell, 1797–1813, File Papers, DCC, and in *MCC* thereafter. See also the chart in Mohl, *Poverty*, p. 86.

19   Committee on the Almshouse and Bridewell, letter January 16, 1809, Annual Report, April 1, 1814, DCC; Ezra Stiles Ely, *Visits of Mercy . . . the Second Journal*, (London, 1816), p. 5. For the war period see also Mohl, *Poverty*, pp. 110–14. For 1817, see ibid., pp. 114–17; Elaine Weber Pascu, "From the Philanthropic Tradition to the Common School Ideal: Schooling in New York City, 1815–1832" (Ph.D. diss., Northern Illinois University, 1980), p. 57.

20   Nash stresses that widows, especially in periods of war, posed one of the colonies' greatest problems of poor relief. *Urban Crucible*, p. 65 and passim for the sources of colonial poverty. See also Schneider, *History of Public Welfare*, pp. 75–88; David J. Rothman, *Discovery of the Asylum: Social Order and Disorder in the New Republic* (Boston, 1971), pp. 164, 169–70, 290–92. On outdoor relief, see Committee on the Almshouse, Annual Report, April 1, 1814, DCC; *MCC*, 7:424 (April 5, 1813); 8:204–205 (May 8, 1815).

21   Duc de La Rochefoucauld in 1797, quoted in Still, *Mirror*, p. 67.

22   On the development of the post-Revolution market in housing, see Elizabeth Strother Blackmar, "Housing and Property Relations in New York City 1785–1850" (Ph.D. diss., Harvard University, 1980), pp. 95–101; on residential patterns, ibid., pp. 245–49, 275, and Rock, *Artisans*, pp. 2–3, 254–55; also I. N. Phelps Stokes, *The Iconography of Manhattan Island, 1498–1909*, 6 vols. (New York, 1915), 3:520–21; M. L. Davis, *A Brief Account of the Epidemic Fever* (New York, 1795), pp. 6–7. Carl Abbott points out that some class segregation in residential patterns was already evident before the Revolution. "The Neighborhoods of New York, 1760–1775," *New York History* 55 (January 1974): 35–53. Quote is from Richard Bayley, *An Account of the Epidemic Fever . . . In the City of New-York* (New York, 1796), p. 90.

23   Smith, *The City of New York*, p. 9; John Duffy, *A History of Public Health in New York City 1625–1866* (New York, 1968), pp. 78–82, 176–231; Rock, *Artisans*, p. 2.

24   Jonas Smith Addoms, *An Inaugural Dissertation on the Malignant Fever* (New York, 1792), p. 7; Duffy, *History of Public Health*, pp. 135–41. Cf. the observations of the Society for the Relief of Poor Widows (SRPW): "The yellow fever had so increased the number and misfortunes of Widows, that none but eye-witnesses could have imagined the sufferings of many respectable, industrious

women. . . . House rents were going on, while every kind of industry was at a stand. . . . No provision made for the winter.—the Landlords, many of whom were nearly as poor as their tenants, clamorous for their rent—complaint of the want of employment universal. . . ." Minute Books, April–November 1798, New-York Historical Society (NYHS). At the height of the epidemic of 1798, the soup kitchen established to help the indigent served 1,600–2,000 people daily, and the Almshouse supported 800 people on indoor relief: There were roughly 2,500 people on charity out of a population of about 60,000. Schneider, *History of Public Welfare*, p. 163.

25   The classic accounts of domestic production and its decline are Edith Abbott, *Women in Industry* (New York, 1924), pp. 10–47 and Rolla Milton Tryon, *Household Manufactures in the United States, 1640–1860* (Chicago, 1917). More recent analyses can be found in Cott, *Bonds of Womanhood*, pp. 36–44; Alice Kessler-Harris, *Out to Work: A History of Wage-Earning Women in the United States* (New York, 1982), pp. 3–31; Mary Beth Norton, *Liberty's Daughters: The Revolutionary Experience of American Women, 1750–1800* (Boston, 1980), pp. 3–39; Mary P. Ryan, *Womanhood in America: From Colonial Times to the Present*, 3rd ed. (New York, 1983), pp. 27–32, 73–85. Norton also stresses that domestic manufactures *increased* after 1700, as rural areas became more thickly populated and trading networks made better household goods available and increased the incentives for women to engage in barter. She cautions, however, that "the classic image of the colonial housewife as a woman who normally engaged in a full range of domestic manufactures has been exaggerated." Rather, women produced some items themselves, bartered for others and (I would add) bought still others when they were near enough to shops. "The Evolution of White Women's Experience in Early America," *American Historical Review* 89 (June 1984): 604–605. In an intervention in a broader debate about the extent of the capitalist market in eighteenth-century America, Carole Shammas likewise argues against the image of the totally self-sufficient colonial housewife. Her evidence does not disprove, however, the important role of *some kinds* of domestic production in most eighteenth-century households. "How Self-Sufficient Was Early America?" *Journal of Interdisciplinary History* 13 (Autumn 1982): 247–72. For a comparative dimension see Olwen Hufton's precisely drawn picture in "Women and the Family Economy in Eighteenth-Century France," *French Historical Studies* (Spring 1975): 1–22.

26   My argument about urban household production is based on evidence from several sources and similar observations from other scholars. Duffy discusses the sustained battle over pigs in the New York streets from the late eighteenth century to the 1850s in *History of Public Health*, pp. 191, 216–18, 376, 385–86. The *Independent Mechanic* (New York), published for an artisanal audience, included in its pages recipes for domestic manufactures—butter, wine and beer making, dying wool— and advice about raising turkeys. Issues for June 22, 1811, July 18, 1812 and passim.

Grant Thorburn, who arrived in New York c. 1800, laments the passing of the domestic crafts once practiced there in his *Fifty Years' Reminiscences of New-York* (New York, 1845), pp. 151, 205, 280. As late as 1808, the city marshal complained about cows pastured on the Battery: Committee on Police, petition of David Joslin, May 23, 1808, DCC. See also Bushman, "Family Security," p. 247. Bushman stresses the transference of rural patterns of domestic production to the city in nineteenth-century migrations.

27   On the difficulties women experienced throughout the eighteenth century in supporting themselves outside the family economy, see Alexander Keyssar, "Widowhood in Eighteenth-Century Massachusetts: A Problem in the History of the Family," *Perspectives in American History* 8 (1974): 81–119. Male desertion was "lamentably extensive," a Philadelphia-based charity announced in 1817. Quoted in the *Commercial Advertiser* (New York), August 19, 1817; Society for the Prevention of Pauperism (SPP), *Report of a Committee on the Subject of Pauperism* (New York, 1818), p. 14. On widowhood and its ruinous consequences, see Committee on Charity, passim, DCC. The Hallam petition is in ibid., July 24, 1815.

28   Faye E. Dudden, *Serving Women: Household Service in Nineteenth-Century America* (Middletown, Conn., 1983), p. 46 and passim; *The Only Correct Account of the Life, Trial and Confession of John Banks* (New York, 1806), pp. 5–7.

29   Blackmar points out that while women had provided for boarders in their homes since the seventeenth century, the character of lodging changed; no longer necessarily employees to the family, lodgers brought in cash, not labor, to the household. Thus, as lodgings became a commodity, taking in boarders became one way women entered the market economy as producers. "Housing and Property Relations," pp. 176–79; George Daitsman, "Labor and the 'Welfare State' in Early New York," *Labor History* 4 (Fall 1963), p. 254 refers to seasonal farm labor.

30   Richardson Wright, *Hawkers & Walkers in Early America* (Philadelphia, 1927), p. 234; *The Cries of New-York* (New York, 1814); Charles H. Haswell, *Reminiscences of New York By An Octogenarian* (New York, 1896), p. 444.

31   Ely, *Visits of Mercy; Being the Journal of the Stated Preacher to the Hospital and Almshouse* (New York, 1812), p. 21.

32   Pomerantz, *New York*, p. 176 stresses women's strong part in the market trade, dating back to the colonial period; see also the many petitions from and concerning market women throughout the *MCC*. Occupational list is in *Longworth's American Almanack, New-York City Register, and City Directory* (New York, 1805).

33   Minute Books, August 8, 1817, October 1804, SRPW. Hundreds of complaints about bawdy houses can be found in the New York City Court of General Sessions (CGS), File Papers, NYMA. Sometimes bawdy houses catered to interracial sex as well. This may have simply been an early version of the kind of interracial prostitution between black women and white men that would become a staple of nineteenth-century American life, but fragments of evidence indicate that poor whites mingled with free blacks on a common footing in bawdy houses—although not without racial tensions—and that white women, too, sometimes consorted sexually across race lines. See, for example, CGS, People v. Colris, August 6, 1802; also Allen v. Allen, 1826, Records of Divorce and Separation, New York County Clerk's Office; also the *Independent Mechanic*, July 27, 1811.

34   Natalie Zemon Davis has described women's involvement in the crafts as wives and widows in early modern Europe. "Women in the Crafts in Sixteenth-Century Lyon," *Feminist Studies* 8 (Spring 1982): 47–80. Davis shows that widowhood was the most common route to female proprietorship. An example from New

York: In 1793 Ann Kip, the widow of an upholsterer, announced she was carrying on her husband's business in the *Daily Advertiser* (New York), October 16, 1793. See also Joan Scott and Louise Tilly, *Women, Work and Family* (New York, 1978), pp. 47–51. Claudia Goldin's exhaustive analysis of the Philadelphia city directories in the 1790s likewise turns up only a handful of craftswomen in male trades, all apparently widows. "The Changing Status of Women in the Economy of the Early Republic: Quantitative Evidence" (Paper presented at the Weingart/Social Science History Association Conference on Quantitative Methods in History, California Institute of Technology, 1983). My thanks to Claudia Goldin for sharing her work with me.

35   Abbott, *Women in Industry*, pp. 19–20, 42, 70–78; Cott, *Bonds of Womanhood*, pp. 25, 39–40; Minute Books, January 10, February 21, 1803, SRPW.

36   Mohl, *Poverty*, pp. 44, 49, 141; *New-York Gazette*, or *Weekly Post Boy* (New York), June 13, 1765; Smith, *City of New York*, p. 109.

37   Mohl, *Poverty*, p. 223; *Evening Post*, July 5, 1814, October 27, November 29, 1819.

38   Textile handicrafts did continue after the War of 1812, although they were of decreasing importance. U.S. Congress, Senate, *History of Women in Industry in the United States*, by Helen L. Sumner, p. 43. *Report on Condition of Women and Child Wage-Earners in the United States*, v.9, S. Doc. 645, 61st Cong. 2nd Sess., 1910 (hereafter cited as Sumner, *History of Women in Industry*); Victor S. Clark, *History of Manufactures in the United States*, 3 vols. (New York, 1929), 1:563–64. On the collapse of the House of Industry, see *Evening Post*, November 29, 1819. On the insufficiency of put-out work, see Minute Books, January 23, 1815, SRPW. Mothers with children were "incapacitated from going into service," the House of Industry noted. *Evening Post*, October 27, 1815.

39   Ely, *Visits of Mercy*, p. 76. Billy G. Smith finds that from 1750 to 1800, women's wages at the Philadelphia Hospital were about half those of the unskilled men who did the same work. "Material Lives," p. 188. The Pennsylvania Society for the Promotion of Public Economy noted in 1817 that "the great disproportion which exists between the prices of labour of men and women, is a matter of serious regret." *Commercial Advertiser*, August 19, 1817; Minute Books, November 16, 1815, SRPW.

Not all women had the skills for put-out work, having grown up in households so makeshift that domestic crafts were irrelevant to housekeeping. The Society for the Promotion of the Arts, contemplating its efforts to set up the city's first manufactory, had noted this problem in 1765: "There are a great Number of poor children in Town, whose Parents are incapable, or not in a Situation to teach them Flax-Spinning." *New-York Gazette, or Weekly Post Boy*, June 13, 1765.

40   CGS, People v. Wallace et al., August 6, 1820. Ely alludes to the seasonal uses the poverty-stricken made of the Almshouse in *Visits of Mercy*, pp. 53–54, 78.

41   Committee on Charity, petition of May 16, 1803, File Papers, DCC; Ely, *Visits of Mercy; Being the Second Journal*, p. 61.

42   The first available statistics show there were always more women than men in the Almshouse. The ratio varied from slightly more than even (during the years

when male unemployment was singularly high) to 2.0 in 1815, when male absence reached crisis proportions during the war.

Numbers of Persons in the Almshouse

YEAR	MEN	WOMEN	RATIO OF WOMEN TO MEN
1806	178	291	1.6
1808	230	296	1.3
1809	356	391	1.1
1813	252	468	1.9
1814	241	408	1.7
1815	207	405	2.0
1818	300	372	1.2
1819	343	369	1.1

Source: Reports, Committee on the Almshouse, DCC.

The story is recounted in Ely, *Visits of Mercy*, pp. 91–92, 188–89; *Visits . . . the Second Journal*, p. 171.

43   Livingston's letter to James Warner, published in the *Evening Post*, February 24, 1803. Similarly, Shammas notes the paucity of employments for women in Philadelphia, "Female Social Structure," p. 75. See also SPP, *Fifth Annual Report* (New York, 1821), p. 12; *Report of a Committee on the Subject of Pauperism*, p. 14.

CHAPTER 2: THE PROBLEM OF DEPENDENCY

1   Laurel Thatcher Ulrich, *Good Wives: Image and Reality in the Lives of Women in Northern New England, 1650–1750* (New York, 1982); Carol Karlsen, *The Devil in the Shape of a Woman: Witchcraft in Seventeenth Century New England* (New York, forthcoming). Antonia Fraser catalogues English views in *The Weaker Vessel* (New York, 1984), pp. 1–6.

2   Janet Wilson James, *Changing Ideas About Women in the United States, 1776–1825* (New York, 1981), pp. 40–42; Patricia Jewell McAlexander, "The Creation of the American Eve: the Cultural Dialogue on the Nature and Role of Women in Late Eighteenth-Century America," *Early American Literature* 9 (Winter 1975): 252–66; Philip Stanhope Chesterfield, *Letters*, ed. John Bradshaw, 3 vols. (New York, 1892), 1:296. The first American edition of the *Letters* was published in 1779. See also Mary Sumner Benson, *Women in Eighteenth Century America: A Study of Opinion and Social Usage* (New York, 1935), pp. 27–40 and passim.

3   Ibid., p. 206. These writers, although widely differing in their political orientations, voiced a common concern for female education, respect for women in marriage, and the cultivation of women's moral faculties rather than the ornamental frivolities of society ladies.

4   For a synthesis of the extensive literature on republicanism, see Robert Shal-hope, "Republicanism and Early American Historiography," *William & Mary Quarterly*, 3rd ser., 39 (April 1982): 334–56.

5   *Women of the Republic: Intellect and Ideology in Revolutionary America* (Chapel Hill, N.C., 1980), p. 31; see also Norton, *Liberty's Daughters*, pp. 110–17.

6   Adams's letter is reprinted in Alice Rossi, ed., *The Feminist Papers* (New York, 1973), pp. 10–11.

7   Norton, *Liberty's Daughters*, pp. 155–299; Kerber, *Women of the Republic*, pp. 189–231, 269–88; Ruth H. Bloch, "American Feminine Ideals in Transition: The Rise of the Moral Mother, 1785–1813," *Feminist Studies* 4 (June 1978): 101–26.

8   Quoted in Young, *Democratic Republicans*, p. 347. According to the French consul in 1793, New York was "the town of the United States in which the aristocracy and what is here called the British *influence* most prevail." Ibid., p. 346.

9   On aristocratic pastimes and blood sports, including fox hunting, cock fighting, dueling, gambling and bear baiting, see Pomerantz, *New York*, pp. 460–64, 497–99; Esther Singleton, *Social New York Under the Georges 1714–1776* (New York, 1902), pp. 259–71 and Wilson, *Memorial History*, 2:458–59. A Russian traveler as late as 1823 observed that "in maritime cities, and even in the metropolis, libertinism is carried to a great length by the young men." Quoted in James, *Changing Ideas*, p. 135. As late as 1815, a butcher in the plebeian district of Corlears Hook kept a bison in his cellar for bull and bear baiting. De Voe, *The Market Book*, pp. 388–89.

10   James suggests the double standard *flourished* after the Revolution and notes that libertinism was an admired male identity. *Changing Ideas*, pp. 51–52. Kerber notes the criticisms and attacks directed against women's education and the advo-cates of an enlarged role for women in the public sphere. *Women of the Republic*, pp. 198–99, 226–31, 279–88. Eve Kornfeld mentions the vitriolic attack the writer Susanna Rowson incurred from William Cobbett on his American tour, and stresses how Rowson publicly backpedaled from her private sympathies with Woll-stonecraft's positions. "Women in Post-Revolutionary American Culture: Susanna Haswell Rowson's American Career, 1792–1824," *Journal of American Culture* 6 (Winter 1983): 56–62. In this Rowson was typical of other literate American women. See, for example, Eliza Southgate's exchange with her male cousin about the *Vindication*, reprinted in Eve Merriam, ed., *Growing Up Female in America: Ten Lives* (New York, 1971), pp. 33–39.

On the English situation, see Barbara Taylor, *Eve and the New Jerusalem: Social-ism and Feminism in the Nineteenth Century* (New York, 1983), pp. 1–15; the quotation from Burke is on p. 11. On Wollstonecraft's reception in America, see Norton, *Liberty's Daughters*, pp. 251–52; Kerber, *Women of the Republic*, pp. 222–25. McAlex-ander lends support to my view of a conservative reaction after 1790. "Creation of the American Eve," especially pp. 257–58.

11   Elizabeth Fox-Genovese, "Property and Patriarchy in Classical Bourgeois Political Theory," *Radical History Review* 4 (Spring–Summer 1977): 36–59; Kerber, *Women of the Republic*, pp. 15–32.

12   *Report of the Trial of Henry Bedlow for Committing a Rape of Lanah Sawyer* (New York, 1793).

13   Ibid., p. 40.
14   James, *Changing Ideas,* pp. 48–51; Fordyce, quoted in ibid., p. 49. *Female Policy Detected* was published in London in 1695 and ran through five American editions, the last two in 1795. Benson, *Women in Eighteenth Century America,* p. 27.
15   Chesterfield, *Letters,* 1:143.
16   James Fordyce, *Sermons to Young Women* (Philadelphia, 1787), quoted in James, *Changing Ideas,* p. 49.
17   *Report of the Trial of Richard D. Croucher . . . for a Rape on Margaret Miller* (New York, 1800). Interestingly, Croucher's attorney was Brockholst Livingston, who had also been a defense lawyer in the Bedlow case. Further research might uncover deeper political connections in the Croucher and Bedlow trials and the riot following the latter, since several of the lawyers in these cases were notables in the Clintonian-Federalist battles of the early 1790s.
18   *Report of the Trial of Henry Bedlow,* pp. 40, 22. I am indebted here to Marybeth Hamilton's subtle analysis in " 'The Life of a Citizen in the Hands of a Woman': Sexual Assault in New York City, 1790–1820," forthcoming in a collection of essays presented at the New-York Historical Society Conference on New York City History, Spring 1983. See also Ryan, *Womanhood in America,* 2nd ed., p. 57.
19   Accounts of the crowd action can be found in the *Columbian Gazetteer* (New York), October 17, 1793; *New York Journal & Patriotic Register,* October 16, 19, 1793; *Daily Advertiser,* October 16, 1793. See also the reminiscences of Philip Hone (a neighbor of Sawyer's who as a boy watched the crowd from his perch in a tree), Hone Diary, Manuscript version, August 9, 1838, NYHS; the contemporary account of John Drayton, quoted in the Stokes Collection Typescript, p. 154; and Alexander Anderson Diary, October 14, 1793, Manuscript Room, Columbia University. Much more research needs to be done on crowd actions against houses of ill repute to understand the gender as well as class dynamics involved. There is a brief discussion of these so-called antiprostitution riots in John C. Schneider, *Detroit and the Problem of Order* (Lincoln, Neb., 1980), pp. 26–29, and they are also mentioned in Pauline Maier, "Popular Uprisings and Civil Authority in Eighteenth-Century America," *William & Mary Quarterly,* 3rd ser., 27 (January 1970):15 and Edward Countryman, "The Problem of the Early American Crowd," *Journal of American Studies* 7 (April 1973):86.
20   Young, *The Democratic Republicans,* pp. 349–53.
21   *Columbian Gazetteer,* October 17, 1793; *New York Journal,* October 16, 1793.
22   The "Justitia" letters appear in *The Diary; or Loudon's Register* (New York), October 24, 25, 1793. It is interesting in light of the convergence of anti-Jacobinism and antifeminism, and the events in France of 1793, to note that Justitia, the bluestocking, was accused of allying herself with the mob—"anarchy and misrule"— that had attacked and sacked the bawdy houses in the Bedlow affair.
23   *Report of the Trial of Henry Bedlow,* pp. 9, 44.
24   Diatribes against the bloods can be found in the *Independent Mechanic,* May 11, 18, 25, 1811. Ellen Moers elucidates the European elements of dandyism in *The Dandy: Brummell to Beerbohm* (New York, 1960). Carole Shammas notes that in

eighteenth-century Philadelphia, ladies did not wander unaccompanied outside their households. "Female Social Structure," pp. 78–79.

25   CGS, People v. Buchanan and Wilson, March 13, 1821.

26   *The Amorous Sailor's Letter to His Sweetheart and the Jolly Orange Woman* (Worcester, Mass., 1781).

27   *Evening Post,* February 9, 1808.

28   *Merry Andrew's Pocket Almanac* (New York, 1775).

29   Bracken v. Bracken, 1816, Records of Divorce and Separation, New York County Clerk's Office. See CGS, People v. Scrouder et al., for a case where a man demonstrated his patriarchal proprietorship by stripping his former household— that of his estranged wife—of all its goods. November 14, 1820.

30   *Trial for Murder . . . George Hart,* pp. 2, 15; *The Only Correct Account . . . of John Banks,* p. 12.

31   M. J. Heale, "From City Fathers to Social Critics: Humanitarianism and Government in New York, 1790 to 1860," *Journal of American History* 63 (June 1976): 23, 27–29; idem, "Humanitarianism in the Early Republic: The Moral Reformers of New York, 1776–1825," *Journal of American Studies* 2 (October 1968): 161–69; Sydney V. James, *A People Among Peoples: Quaker Benevolence in Eighteenth-Century America* (Cambridge, Mass., 1963), pp. 322–23; Clifford S. Griffin, *Their Brothers' Keepers: Moral Stewardship in the United States, 1800–1865* (New Brunswick, N.J., 1960), pp. 6–7; Mohl, *Poverty,* pp. 121–58. On the origins of elite benevolence in New England as an opportune alliance between the clergy and the merchant class, see Christine Leigh Heyrman, "The Fashion Among More Superior People: Charity and Social Change in Provincial New England, 1700–1740," *American Quarterly* 34 (Summer 1982): 107–24.

32   *Forlorn Hope* (New York), May 3, 1800.

33   Carroll Smith Rosenberg, *Religion and the Rise of the American City: The New York City Mission Movement 1812–1870* (Ithaca, N.Y., 1971); Mohl, *Poverty,* pp. 160–61.

34   Sermon for the Presbyterian Charity School, November 6, 1791, John Rodgers Papers, NYHS.

35   Quoted in Schneider, *History of Public Welfare,* 1:196.

36   For similar patterns throughout America, see David Brion Davis, "The Emergence of Immediatism in British and American Antislavery Thought," *Mississippi Valley Historical Review* 49 (September 1962): 209–30.

37   Quoted in Mohl, *Poverty,* p. 160.

38   Gary Nash, for example, stresses the punitive quality of eighteenth-century poor relief practices. *Urban Crucible,* pp. 184–85.

39   The New York Dispensary, for example, explained in 1800 why it had removed any restrictions on admission: "No questions are asked to wound the sensitiveness of poverty, and no reproofs offered to drive away the vicious. This is not our business. They suffer or they would not come for aid; and while we do not measure out our beneficence with a censorious hand, we know that we are doing good." Quoted in Schneider, *History of Public Welfare,* 1:196.

40   Quoted in M. J. Heale, "The New York Society for the Prevention of Pauperism, 1817–1823," *New-York Historical Society Quarterly* 55 (April 1971): 156.

41   *MCC,* 7:585 (October 18, 1813); see also Report of Commissioners, April 1, 1809, Committee on the Almshouse, DCC, where the prevention of street begging is seen only as a matter of civic pride. On expenses see Mohl, *Poverty,* p. 91.

42   *MCC,* 7:172 (June 15, 1812), 660–61 (January 10, 1814). On the scope of the crisis of poverty during the war, see Alexander C. Flick, ed., *History of the State of New York,* 10 vols. (New York, 1933–37), 5:243–44; Mohl, *Poverty,* pp. 143–44.

43   See, for example, the correspondence between Thomas Eddy and the British reformer Patrick Colquhoun in Samuel L. Knapp, *The Life of Thomas Eddy* (New York, 1834). "Rumford," in a series of letters to the *Evening Post* in 1817, modeled himself on Count Rumford, the peripatetic British poor-law reformer and supporter of cheap soup as a relief measure. Mohl, *Poverty,* pp. 165–66. See also Heale, "New York Society for the Prevention of Pauperism," p. 164.

44   The original petition is in Committee on Almshouse, January 4, 1808, DCC. See also Daitsman, "Labor and the 'Welfare State,' " p. 254.

45   Ely, *Visits of Mercy,* pp. 53–54, 78; *MCC,* 12: 158–59 (December 24, 1821).

46   *MCC,* 9:360–61 (November 17, 1817).

47   Report of the Superintendent, Commissioners of the Almshouse, October 30, 1805, DCC.

48   Heale, "New York Society for the Prevention of Pauperism," p. 156; for the general shift in philanthropic practices from meliorism to reform, see also Mohl, *Poverty,* pp. 159–70 and 241–58 (on the SPP); Smith Rosenberg, *Religion and the Rise of the American City,* pp. 36–40.

49   SPP, *Report to the Managers . . . on Idleness and Sources of Employment* (New York, 1819), p. 5.

50   Mohl, *Poverty,* pp. 159–70; Smith Rosenberg, *Religion and the Rise of the American City,* pp. 4–5; for an overview of this change across America, see Rothman, *Discovery of the Asylum.*

51   SPP, *First Annual Report* (New York, 1818), pp. 14–16.

52   SPP, *Report to the Managers,* pp. 4–5.

53   *MCC,* 9:236 (July 14, 1817); see also 12:158–59 (December 24, 1821) and 13:89–90 (May 26, 1823) where the councilmen's terminology and formulations of the problem of poverty directly borrow from those of the SPP.

54   Rock, *Artisans,* p. 196; *MCC,* 12:158–59 (December 24, 1821).

55   *MCC,* 12:158–59 (December 24, 1821); Heale, "The New York Society for the Prevention of Pauperism," p. 170.

56   Colden quoted in Pascu, "Philanthropic Tradition," p. 75; *MCC,* 10:466 (June 28, 1819).

CHAPTER 3: WOMEN IN THE NEIGHBORHOODS

1   Cott, *Bonds of Womanhood,* pp. 63–100; Ryan, *Cradle of the Middle Class,* pp. 14–15.

2   For images of a strange and alien world, see New York Assembly, *Report . . . to examine into the condition of Tenant Houses in New-York and Brooklyn,* Assembly doc. 205, 80th Session, 1857; Ned Buntline [E. Z. C. Judson], *The Mysteries and Miseries of New York* (New York, 1848), p. 84.

3   Blackmar, "Housing and Property Relations," pp. 226–385, 448–49; Richard
Stott, "The Worker in the Metropolis: New York 1820–1860" (Ph.D. diss., Cornell
University, 1983); Robert Ernst, *Immigrant Life in New York City, 1825–1863* (New
York, 1949), pp. 40–42.
4   Carl N. Degler, "Labor in the Economy and Politics of New York City,
1850–1860; A Study of the Impact of Early Industrialism" (Ph.D. diss., Columbia
University, 1952), pp. 3–4.
5   *The Diary of George Templeton Strong*, ed. Allan Nevins and Milton Halsey
Thomas, 4 vols. (New York, 1952), 2:24 (entry for October 27, 1850).
6   For discussions of economic change in the city, see Albion, *The Rise of New
York Port;* David T. Gilchrist, ed., *The Growth of the Seaport Cities 1790–1815; Proceedings of a Conference Sponsored by the Eleutherian Mills-Hagley Foundation* (Char-
lottesville, Va., 1966); Ernst, *Immigrant Life;* Flick, *History of the State of New York,*
5:327–28.
    Economic changes in New York did not simply replicate those in other industri-
alizing American cities. In particular, New York's high rents, lack of ready coal
supplies and abundant cheap labor force made the expansion of divided handicrafts
more practicable than the use of capital-intensive machinery and the establishment
of large factories. This process of protoindustrialization remained the dominant
pattern of the city's industrial growth throughout the nineteenth century. For an
excellent study of the role of handicraft technology in industrial growth, see Ra-
phael Samuel, "The Workshop of the World: Steam Power and Hand Technology
in Mid-Victorian Britain," *History Workshop* 3 (Spring 1977): 6–72.
7   John M. Duncan, *Travels Through Part of the United States*, 2 vols. (New York,
1823), 1:25.
8   Wilentz, *Chants Democratic*, pp. 117, 120–22, 126–27. Printers are another example of these developments. Printers, who epitomized the prideful, self-respecting
artisanate, were subjected after 1820 to both technological innovation and competition from semiskilled hands. Wages were so low, the union noted in 1850, that it
was the rare man who could save for times of sickness or debility, or "provide for
his family when he shall be removed from among them." "Report of the Printers'
Union on the State of the Trade," reprinted in John R. Commons et al., eds., *A
Documentary History of American Industrial Society*, 10 vols. (New York, 1958),
7:109–31. At the same time, the earnings of journeymen at work in the large newspaper and book printing establishments were high enough to lift them, when employment was secure, above the hand-to-mouth regimen of the struggling proletarian
to a life of shabby—if precarious—gentility. Wilentz, *Chants Democratic*, pp. 129–32.
9   Ernst, *Immigrant Life*, pp. 23, 192–93; Stott, "Worker in the Metropolis," pp.
54–60.
    I should note that the sources on New York women in the first half of the
nineteenth century yield little systematic information about race and ethnicity: the
specific situations of black women compared to white women, the differences
between the experiences of Irish and German-born, immigrant and native. I have
done what I can to bring to light these distinctions. The female laboring poor was
certainly not a unified and homogeneous collectivity.

10　　Another estimate places the number of foreign-born in the *nonclerical* work force at 85 percent in 1855. Stott, "Worker in the Metropolis," pp. 58–60.

11　　On Germans, see Ernst, *Immigrant Life*, pp. 84–92. On blacks, see Leo H. Hirsch, Jr., "The Negro and New York, 1783 to 1865," *Journal of Negro History* 16 (October 1931): 382–473; Ottley and Weatherby, *The Negro in New York*, 1–91.

12　　Richard Stott stresses that the city's male labor market was *regionally* based, thus necessitating that men travel frequently outside the city for work. "Worker in the Metropolis," p. 101. Contemporary testimony about the mobility of male laborers can be found in the Society for the Reformation of Juvenile Delinquents, *Fifteenth Annual Report* (New York, 1850), p. 9; Matthew Carey, "Essay on the Public Charities of Philadelphia," *Miscellaneous Essays* (Philadelphia, 1830), pp. 172–73.

Both Sally Alexander in "Women's Work in Nineteenth Century London; A Study of the Years 1820–50," in *The Rights and Wrongs of Women*, ed. Juliet Mitchell and Ann Oakley (Harmondsworth, Eng., 1976), p. 80, and Barbara Taylor in *Eve and the New Jerusalem*, pp. 203, 244, 336, note the growing instability of male support among British laboring people. See also the general comments on the numbers of women in New York bereft of male support in the Association for the Asylum for Lying-In Women (AALW), *Sixth Annual Report* (New York, 1829) and Commissioner of the Almshouse, *Annual Report* (New York, 1847), p. 39. On male mortality see Carol Groneman Pernicone, " 'The Bloody Ould Sixth': A Social Analysis of a New York City Working-Class Community in the Mid-Nineteenth Century" (Ph.D. diss., University of Rochester, 1973), p. 29.

13　　The best account of tenement development is Blackmar, "Housing and Property Relations," pp. 169–492. Richard Stott points out that by 1864, 70 percent of New York's population lived in multiple family dwellings; in 1859, two-thirds of the city's families lived in buildings occupied by three or more other families. "Workers in the Metropolis," p. 305.

14　　Association for the Improvement of the Condition of the Poor (AICP), *Fourteenth Annual Report* (New York, 1857), p. 18. Blackmar gives an interesting account of the evolution of multiple occupancy. "Housing and Property Relations," pp. 184–88.

15　　City Inspector, *Annual Report of the interments . . . in New York . . . and a Brief View of the Sanitary Conditions of the City* (New York, 1843), p. 163; AICP, *Sixteenth Annual Report* (1859), p. 46; Ernst, *Immigrant Life*, p. 49.

16　　A sensational account of the Old Brewery and similar tenements is in Herbert Asbury, *The Gangs of New York* (New York, 1927), pp. 12–17; the *Daily Tribune* (New York), June 19, 1850 contains a contemporary account. See also Groneman Pernicone, "The 'Bloody Ould Sixth,' " pp. 39–40.

17　　New York City Tract Society (NYCTS), *Thirteenth Annual Report* (1839), p. 25.

18　　*Daily Tribune*, September 9, 1845.

19　　Blackmar, "Housing and Property Relations," pp. 436–37; Smith Rosenberg, *Religion and the Rise of the American City*, pp. 176–77.

20   Blackmar, "Re-Walking the 'Walking City': Housing and Property Relations in New York City, 1780–1840," *Radical History Review* 21 (Fall 1979): 131–48.
21   Ernst, *Immigrant Life*, pp. 49–51; Stokes Collection Typescript, passim,
NYPL; New York Assembly, *Report.*
22   Ibid., p. 13; AICP (1862), quoted in Groneman Pernicone, " 'The Bloody
Ould Sixth,' " p. 15.
23   George C. Foster, *New York Naked* (New York, 1850), p. 118.
24   James Dawson Burn, *Three Years Among the Working Classes* (London, 1865),
p. 15; see also Stott, "Worker in the Metropolis," pp. 313–14.
25   George B. Arnold, minister-at-large, in 1834, quoted in Stokes Collection
Typescript, p. 593.
26   Catharine Maria Sedgwick describes the interior of a respectable artisan
household where pawning had not taken its toll in *The Poor Rich Man, and the Rich
Poor Man* (New York, 1839), p. 105, and in *Clarence; Or, a Tale of Our Own Times*
(New York, 1849), p. 320. See also Stott, "Worker and the Metropolis," pp. 311–13
for the cheap furniture market.
27   Arnold, quoted in Stokes Collection Typescript, p. 593; *Working Man's Advocate* (New York), September 10, 1831. A shoemaker's family budget published in a
trade union journal estimated the annual cost of living at $648.00, and a journey-
man's annual wages at $416.00, working six days a week, fifty-two weeks a year at
$6–$8/week. Such full employment, of course, was infrequent. *National Trades'
Union*, June 6, 1835.
28   Minutes of the Visiting Committee, October 21, 1828, Papers of the AALW,
NYHS; AALW, *Eleventh Annual Report*, p. 6. See also the cases of January 18, 1827
and January 26, 1830 in the Minutes of the Visiting Committee.
29   This account of tenement conditions is drawn chiefly from John H. Griscom, *The Sanitary Condition of the Laboring Population of New York* (New York,
1845); New York Assembly, *Report;* Citizens' Association of New York, *Report of
the Council of Hygiene and Public Health . . . Upon the Sanitary Condition of the City*
(New York, 1865).
30   *Poor Rich Man*, p. 176.
31   Asa Greene, *A Glance at New York* (New York, 1837), p. 163.
32   Sarah Mytton Maury, *An Englishwoman in America* (London, 1848), p. 162.
For the changes in housekeeping brought about in English cities by the new
industrial dirt, see Leonore Davidoff, "The Rationalization of Housework," in
Dependence and Exploitation in Work and Marriage, ed. Diana Leonard Barker and
Sheila Allen (London, 1976), p. 128.
33   Susan Strasser, *Never Done: A History of American Housework* (New York,
1982), pp. 6, 67–72, 85. On the absence of utilities, see Duffy, *History of Public Health*,
pp. 209, 275, 524; New York City Inspector, *Annual Report . . . and a Brief View of
the Sanitary Condition of the City*, p. 201; New York Assembly, *Report*, p. 35;
Citizens' Association, *Report*, passim.
34   Griscom, *Sanitary Condition*, p. 8; [Sedgwick], *Poor Rich Man*, pp. 99, 157;
Foster, *New York in Slices; By an Experienced Carver* (New York, 1849), p. 82;

Matthew Carey, *A Plea for the Poor* (Philadelphia, 1837), p. 12. The reference to Godfrey's Cordial comes from Records of the County Coroner, case #414 (1855), NYMA; tea, from New York Assembly, *Report*, pp. 25–26. On throwing slops see Duffy, *History of Public Health*, pp. 361, 364–65.

35 Smith, "The Material Lives of Laboring Philadelphians," p. 188; New York City police magistrate John Wyman, quoted in Carey, "Essays on the Public Charities of Philadelphia," p. 161.

36 As early as 1823, the SPP had denounced chip picking along the waterfront. SPP, *Report of a Committee . . . on the Expediency of Erecting an Institution for the Reformation of Juvenile Delinquents* (New York, 1823), p. 17. For other references see Joseph Tuckerman's comments on similar patterns in Boston in *An Essay on the Wages Paid to Females* (Philadelphia, 1830), p. 22; Samuel I. Prime, *Life in New York* (New York, 1847), p. 87; [Sedgwick], *Poor Rich Man*, p. 87; Virginia Penny, *The Employments of Women* (Boston, 1863), pp. 122, 435, 444, 467, 484–85; Solon Robinson, *Hot Corn: Life Scenes in New York Illustrated* (New York, 1854), p. 207; *Daily Tribune*, March 16, 1850; William H. Bell Diary, NYHS; Phillip Wallys, *About New York: An Account of What a Boy Saw on a Visit to the City* (New York, 1857), pp. 43–44.

37 *New York Mirror*, quoted in Stokes Collection Typescript, p. 461.

38 There were earlier attempts to constrain the trade in scavenged goods. In 1809, a group of citizens petitioned the council to outlaw the secondhand trade in articles from "children, apprentices and others." *MCC*, 5:505 (April 17, 1809). By 1817, the council had passed the statute which William Bell was to enforce in 1850, prohibiting the secondhand dealers from trading with minors. *Laws and Ordinances . . . of the City of New-York* (1817), p. 112. Bell's observations are from the Bell Diary, November 25, 1850.

39 *Jonathan's Whittlings of War* (New York), May 24, 1854.

40 Ibid., March 27, 1854. Earlier references to pawning are in *MCC*, 9:511 (March 2, 1818); Carey, "Essays on the Public Charities of Philadelphia," pp. 160–61, wherein Carey reprints a report on pawning from the New York police. For details of pawning practices see Bell Diary, March 27, April 6, 10, 16, June 19, 1851.

41 Foster, *New York in Slices*, pp. 30, 32–33.

42 New York House of Refuge Case Histories (HRCH), cases #1495 (1835), #59 (1825), #16 (1825), New York State Archives, State Education Department, Albany, N.Y.

43

YEAR	NUMBER OF CHILDREN ADMITTED	NUMBER OF COMMITMENTS INITIATED BY PARENTS/KIN	PERCENTAGE INITIATED BY PARENTS/KIN
1825	78	9	11.5
1835	166	78	47.0
1845	181	51	28.2
1855	192	52	27.0

Source: House of Refuge Case Histories.

The decline in the proportion of family-initiated commitments in 1845 and 1855 was probably related to the establishment of the police force in 1845, which replaced the more informal and less organized city watch.

44 Letter reprinted in Diarmaid O Muirthe, *A Seat Behind the Coachman: Travellers in Ireland 1800–1900* (Dublin, 1972), p. 139.

45 M. Dorothy George, *London Life in the Eighteenth Century* (London, 1925), pp. 116–57; Eric E. Lampard, "The Urbanizing World," in *The Victorian City: Images and Realities*, ed. H. J. Dyos and Michael Wolff (London, 1973), p. 13; Jeffrey Kaplow, *The Names of Kings: The Parisian Laboring Poor in the Eighteenth Century* (New York, 1972), pp. 30–34.

46 The standard exposition of the urban breakdown thesis is Oscar Handlin, *Boston's Immigrants* (Cambridge, Mass., 1941) and *The Uprooted* (New York, 1951). A major challenge to the view of immigration as a disintegrative social experience came from Herbert Gutman in "Work, Culture and Society in Industrializing America, 1815–1919," in *Work, Culture & Society*, pp. 3–78. For a more recent study of migration patterns, see Judith E. Smith, *Family Connections: A History of Italian and Jewish Immigrant Lives in Providence, Rhode Island 1900–1940* (Albany, N.Y., 1985). On New York, see Groneman Pernicone, "The 'Bloody Ould Sixth' "; Stott, "Worker in the Metropolis," pp. 98–99.

47 Ibid., p. 366; Groneman Pernicone found that in the Sixth Ward in 1855, a little over one-half of the immigrants had traveled in two-parent families; of the rest, characteristically the husband had emigrated first. "The 'Bloody Ould Sixth,' " pp. 54, 57, 61.

48 Quoted in Citizens' Association, *Report*, p. 170.

49 Findings summarized in Stephan Thernstrom, *The Other Bostonians: Poverty and Progress in the American Metropolis 1880–1970* (Cambridge, Mass., 1973), pp. 222–23. For an analysis of the results of recent studies of migration and immigration, see A. Gordon Darroch, "Migrants in the Nineteenth Century: Fugitives or Families in Motion?" *Journal of Family History* 6 (Fall 1981): 257–77. Darroch characterizes migration from the countryside as not a "fugitive" experience but rather a "highly-organized and custom-governed practice." Ibid., p. 268. On New York, see Stott, "Worker in the Metropolis," pp. 91–95.

One reason for the high turnover within the city was the stiff eviction law, which allowed a landlord to terminate a lease immediately if the tenant did not pay the rent at the precise moment it was demanded. City Inspector, *Annual Report . . . for 1842*, p. 174. Blackmar also discusses the mobility of the tenement population. "Housing and Property Relations," p. 576.

50 Of course, statistics of mobility, taken on their own, can give a deceptive picture of flux. Scholars will have to wait for some massive computer study to tell us more about the peregrinations of those who moved about. How many of the thousands who left Northeastern cities each year soon returned? When people relocated within the city, did they tend to remain in the same neighborhoods? Even with all the moving about, it is possible that stable neighborhoods in some form persisted as centers to which people gravitated.

The question of differences—ethnic and economic—*within* neighborhoods is also difficult to answer. Overall, working-class neighborhoods tended to be mixed. There were no wards exclusively occupied by particular ethnic groups; ethnic settlements tended rather to cluster on individual streets or blocks. By 1850, ethnic segregation was diminishing rather than increasing. Stott, "Worker in the Metropolis," pp. 368–71; Paul O. Weinbaum, *Mobs and Demagogues: The New York Response to Collective Violence in the Early Nineteenth Century* (Ann Arbor, Mich., 1979), p. 137. Economic differences within the working class manifested themselves within buildings and blocks rather than *between* neighborhoods, with the very poorest residents living in sunless rear buildings, cellars and attics and the more prosperous housed in apartments on the lower floors. Stott, "Worker in the Metropolis," p. 365.

51   D. W. Mitchell, *Ten Years in the United States* (London, 1862), p. 145.

52   The court cases cited in this and subsequent chapters are drawn from the papers of the New York Court of General Sessions (CGS). Of these records, I read all assault cases for the years 1789–1820, 1831 and 1841, various other assault cases, and all rape and murder cases for the entire period 1789–1860. All told, I read several thousand cases. Because this vast collection of records was in considerable disarray for most of the time I conducted my research, it was impossible to do any systematic statistical investigation of the cases.

53   Records of the County Coroner, case #424 (1854), NYMA.

54   CGS, People v. Gunning et al., December 13, 1858.

55   Records of the New York Foundling Hospital, August 7, 1839, New York City Almshouse Indentures, NYHS; see also November 14, 1840.

Ann Marshall, in 1840, was similarly unconcerned about a strange woman's intrusion on her privacy: When a woman stepped in from the street to her room "and asked . . . the privilege of Steping in her yard a moment to answer a call of Nature," Mrs. Marshall took the baby into her room, apparently without hesitation, and showed the mother the way out back. Ibid., October 15, 1840.

56   See, for example, the cases of suspected fraud in ibid., March 24, 1840, August 11, 1838. By 1830 fraud was enough of a problem for the commissioners to institute an oath to which women bringing in putative foundlings had to swear.

57   *MCC*, 29:303 (June 9, 1845). Networks of domestic sharing were common to other working-class communities, although it seems that some measure of stability was necessary—the cessation of heavy in-migration—before the elaborate and intricate neighborhood networks of late nineteenth-century metropolises developed. See Ellen Ross, "Survival Networks: Women's Neighbourhood Sharing in London Before World War I," *History Workshop* 15 (Spring 1983): 4–27.

58   *The Subterranean* (New York), February 13, 1847.

59   CGS, People v. Corwin, October 15, 1824.

60   CGS, People v. Clements, September 13, 1830. Similarly, Elizabeth Burns promised Elizabeth Hogan she would follow her "as long as she would live" and would kill her "if she had to wait twenty years" and indeed had managed to keep at least the first part of her pledge for a year and a half when Hogan finally took her to court for violent assault in 1841. CGS, People v. Burns, July 15, 1841.

61   CGS, People v. Young, September 9, 1829.

62   A firsthand account of a faction fight in Connemara in 1834 is reprinted in O Muirthe, *A Seat Behind the Coachman,* pp. 56–58: "The women took no part in the fight; but they are not always so backward: it is chiefly, however, when stones are the weapons, that women take a part, by supplying the combatants with missiles. . . . I noticed, after the fight, that some, who had been opposed to each other, shook hands and kissed; and appeared as good friends as before."

63   On male violence in the city, see Peter G. Buckley, "To the Opera House: Culture and Society in New York City, 1820–1860" (Ph.D. diss., SUNY/Stony-brook, 1984); Paul A. Gilje, "Mobocracy: Popular Disturbances in Post Revolutionary New York City, 1783–1829" (Ph.D. diss., Brown University, 1980); Weinbaum, *Mobs and Demagogues;* Asbury, *Gangs of New York.*

The contentiousness of the Irishman was proverbial. See for example the comments on Irish canal workers in the South quoted in Eugene Genovese, *Roll Jordan Roll* (New York, 1972), p. 635.

64   Elizabeth Blackmar terms the streets of pre-Revolutionary New York a "republican forum" for the crowd. "Housing and Property Relations," pp. 250–51. See also Countryman, "The Problem of the Early American Crowd," pp. 77–90, and Maier, "Popular Uprisings," pp. 3–35. Gilje ably summarizes the extensive literature on New York popular violence, to which he adds his own findings, in "Mobocracy."

65   CGS, People v. Roach, February 4, 1828.

66   CGS, People v. Doyle et al., August 11, 1820; see also People v. Duffy et al., August 12, 1825.

67   CGS, People v. Jacobus et al., June 14, 1831.

68   CGS, People v. Hyland et al., December 7, 1821; People v. Hogan et al., December 6, 1821.

69   CGS, People v. Watson, August 14, 1827.

70   CGS, People v. Carrigan et al., September 12, 1826; see also People v. Bigley, July 15, 1837, and an interesting case in which a landlord courts a neighborhood mob that watches while he beats his lodger, whom he has locked into his room, with a broom as the latter tries to climb out of a second-story window. People v. Smith, June 16, 1827.

71   People v. Shay, August 11, 1825; People v. Brown, December 6, 1833; People v. Williams, May 13, 1820.

72   *The Subterranean,* March 27, 1847.

73   People v. Doyle et al., August 11, 1820; People v. Jacobus et al., June 14, 1831.

74   People v. Thomas, June 15, 1830, People v. Matthews, November 14, 1831, People v. Furrell, February 15, 1831.

75   Lydia Maria Child, *Letters from New York. Second Series* (New York, 1845), p. 167. Mike Walsh recounts an incident when an old Irish female street peddler, harassed by a policeman, turned on him and pummeled him unmercifully to the cheers of the crowd that had collected. The crowd then took up a collection for her on the spot. *The Subterranean,* July 19, 1845.

CHAPTER 4: PLACES OF VICE

1   NYCTS, *Ninth Annual Report* (1835), p. 8.

2   NYCTS, *Eleventh Annual Report* (1837), p. 12; *Twelfth Annual Report* (1838), pp. 5–6.

3   NYCTS, *Thirteenth Annual Report* (1839), p. 16.

4   The literature on evangelicalism is voluminous. The most helpful books on the religious reformers with whom I am concerned are Smith Rosenberg, *Religion and the Rise of the American City;* Thomas Bender, *Toward an Urban Vision: Ideas and Institutions in Nineteenth-Century America* (Lexington, Ky., 1975); Paul Boyer, *Urban Masses and Moral Order in America, 1820–1920* (Cambridge, Mass., 1978). See also Griffin, *Their Brothers' Keepers;* Charles J. Foster, *An Errand of Mercy: The Evangelical United Front 1790–1837* (Chapel Hill, N.C., 1960).

5   Many scholars have explored the shift in theology and in social attitudes embodied in evangelicalism. For a cogent summary see Smith Rosenberg, *Religion and the Rise of the American City,* p. 80.

6   Ibid., pp. 44–69; Ward Stafford, *New Missionary Field: A Report to the Female Missionary Society* (New York, 1817). The Society for Promoting the Gospel Among the Poor, founded in 1812, was one of New York's earliest evangelical associations.

7   Pascu, "From the Philanthropic Tradition to the Common School," pp. 106, 108; Smith Rosenberg, *Religion and the Rise of the American City,* pp. 56–58.

8   For the British parallel see Anne Summers, "A Home from Home—Women's Philanthropic Work in the Nineteenth Century," in *Fit Work for Women,* ed. Sandra Burman (London, 1979).

9   NYCTS, *Sixth Annual Report* (1833), p. 9.

10   Minute Books, November 16, 1820, SRPW.

11   NYCTS, *Eighth Annual Report* (New York, 1835), p. 6.

12   Smith Rosenberg, *Religion and the Rise of the American City,* p. 79.

13   NYCTS, *Thirteenth Annual Report* (1839), p. 7.

14   See *The Old Brewery, and the New Mission House at the Five Points, By Ladies of the Mission* (New York, 1854); [American Female Guardian Society], *Wrecks and Rescues* (New York, 1859); Samuel Halliday, *The Lost and Found; or Life among the Poor* (New York, 1859). Two novels whose plots derived from charity accounts of virtuous seamstresses are Charles Burdett, *The Elliott Family; or, the Trials of New York Seamstresses* (New York, 1850) and Marie Louise Hankins, *Reality; or, a History of Human Life* (New York, 1858).

15   NYCTS, *Fifteenth Annual Report* (1841), p. 9.

16   NYCTS, *Thirteenth Annual Report* (1839), p. 18.

17   For accounts of the kinds of receptions laboring people gave charity visitors, see NYCTS, *Tenth Annual Report* (1836), p. 69, *Thirteenth Annual Report* (1839), p. 32; *Advocate of Moral Reform* (1840) 6:6, 30. See also Stafford, *New Missionary Field,* pp. 10–11, 15; *Working Man's Advocate,* July 30, 1831.

18   Smith Rosenberg, *Religion and the Rise of the American City,* p. 77; Bertram

Wyatt-Brown, *Lewis Tappan and the Evangelical War Against Slavery* (Cleveland, Ohio, 1969), pp. 61–62.

19   See Wilentz, *Chants Democratic*, pp. 145–53, 271–86; Johnson, *Shopkeeper's Millennium*, pp. 136–41.

20   Boyer, *Urban Masses and Moral Order*, p. 61; see also Ryan, *Cradle of the Middle Class*, p. 128.

21   Smith Rosenberg, *Religion and the Rise of the American City*, p. 98. See also Ryan, *Cradle of the Middle Class*, pp. 60–144; Cott, *Bonds of Womanhood*, pp. 126–59.

22   Ibid.; see also Bloch, "American Feminine Ideals in Transition"; Cott, "Passionlessness: An Interpretation of Victorian Sexual Ideology, 1790–1850," *Signs: A Journal of Women in Culture and Society* 4 (Winter 1978): 219–36.

23   *Bonds of Womanhood*, p. 140.

24   Abram C. Dayton, *Last Days of Knickerbocker Life in New York* (New York, 1882), p. 98; John Kouwenhoven, *The Columbia Historical Portrait of New York* (New York, 1972), p. 138.

25   Minute Books, November 21, 28, 1814, 1825–26, January 28, 1828, December 1833, November 27, December 26, 1837, October 25, 1841, November 17, 1845, December 15, 1851, November 17, 1853, March 5, 1855, December 13, 1858, April 4, 1859, November 19, 1860, SRPW.

26   Smith Rosenberg, "Beauty, the Beast and the Militant Woman: A Case Study in Sex Roles and Social Stress in Jacksonian America," in *A Heritage of Her Own*, ed. Nancy F. Cott and Elizabeth H. Pleck (New York, 1979), pp. 197–221.

Women's forays into charity work in New York were, by 1820, systematic enough to support financially and in some cases to administer an entire network of associations for the poor. The SRPW, the Orphan Asylum, charity schools for girls, the Female Sunday School Union and the Female Missionary Society either grew directly from the revivals or were closely linked to them. Mostly the female philanthropists chose work that grew out of their maternal roles. But the societies did more than simply extend motherly impulses. The largest, like the SRPW, taught skills of organization, administration and financial management and consciously encouraged their members to enlarge women's sphere of social influence, sometimes in the face of hostile—if scattered—male opposition.

27   In the one New York women's charity (the Female Benevolent Society) for which there is an available analysis of the backgrounds of the members, the majority of women in 1835 for whom there is information came to the city from small New England or mid-Atlantic towns in the 1810s and 1820s. Of the sample of twenty-six, fourteen were married to businessmen, four to ministers and four to religious agents or missionaries. Larry Howard Whiteaker, "Moral Reform and Prostitution in New York City, 1830–1860" (Ph.D. diss., Princeton University, 1977), p. 138.

28   On letters of recommendation, see Ernst, *Immigrant Life*, p. 64. This discussion of female charities is based on the records of the AALW, *Annual Reports*, 1828–64, and Minutes of the Visiting Committee, 1828–31; SRPW, *Annual Reports*, 1833–60, and Minute Books, 1798–1870; Miscellaneous Mss., Association for the Relief of Respectable, Aged and Indigent Females—all at NYHS.

These requirements consequently favored those who could be singled out from the masses of applicants by their Protestant church affiliations or personal contacts with the privileged. See the *Working Man's Advocate*, April 6, 1844 on the obstacles to receiving charity; also Charles E. Rosenberg, "And Heal the Sick: The Hospital and Patient in 19th Century America," *Journal of Social History* 10 (June 1974): 430.

29   Minutes, November 11, 1827, June 23, 1830, AALW.

30   Ibid., December 11, 1827, December 29, 1829, January 18, June 13, 1827.

My interpretation of women's charities differs with the view that female associations transcended the loyalties of class. Cf. Barbara J. Berg, *The Remembered Gate: Origins of American Feminism 1800–1860* (New York, 1978), pp. 149, 175–270. For a more nuanced view of sisterly relations between classes, see Susan Porter Benson, "Business Heads and Sympathizing Hearts: The Women of the Providence Employment Society 1837–1858," *Journal of Social History* 12 (Fall 1978): 302–312.

For an argument implicitly closer to my own, see Smith Rosenberg's analysis of charity and class formation in *Religion and the Rise of the American City*, especially p. 117 on "worthiness" as a category of charity.

The Ladies Philanthropic Association, an apparently small and short-lived charity founded in 1838, was one exception to the attitudes I have described. The ladies of this group vowed to attend immediately to all applicants and pointedly pledged to "studiously avoid any painful inquiries." Unbelievers were to be meekly admonished, but not deprived of help. Of the three members who could be traced to city directories, two were wives of artisans (a baker and a bookbinder). Whether or not this organization represented some alternative tradition of charity among prosperous artisan families is a question for further study. Ladies Philanthropic Association of New York, *Constitution, By-Laws and Report* (New York, 1841).

31   Minute Books, November 10, 1813, SRPW.

32   Ibid., November 16, 1826; see also the comments, probably occasioned by the formation of the SPP, for November 20, 1817. At the same time, the ladies sometimes adopted utilitarian rhetoric for their own purposes. In 1824, stressing their skillfulness at separating the worthy from the unworthy, the ladies rousingly echoed the SPP: " 'If a man will not work, let him not eat!' " November 18, 1824.

33   Ibid.

34   Ibid., November 15, 1827.

35   See the consideration the SRPW gave to the issue of the disposition of children. Minute Books, December 12, 1803, January 18, 1804, December 16, 1806, January 13, 1807, April 6, October 18, 1808, November 27, 1854.

36   Ibid., November 3, 1824, October 1804, November 27, 1837, December 1, 1851, December 13, 1852, December 10, 1855, January 3, 1860, November 28, 1814, December 26, 1837, December 15, 1851, November 17, 1853, December 13, 1858.

37   Cf. Ryan, *Cradle of the Middle Class* and Epstein, *Politics of Domesticity*. Both describe domesticity as a development *internal* to the middle class, growing out of tensions and antagonisms *between* men and women. "Evangelical Christianity had

emerged in an America in which the working class had been neither numerically large nor experienced as a major threat by other classes. To the extent that women of this movement had developed a particular consciousness, it had been defined in conflict with the irreligious (men) of their own culture; issues of class, when raised, were posed in terms of the difference between aristocratic and middle class ways of life." Ibid., p. 90. Only in the late nineteenth century, Epstein argues, did domesticity come to embody class antagonisms as well. For an elegant discussion of the problem of female bourgeois identity and the construction of "alternative femininities" in women's writing, see Cora Kaplan, "Pandora's box: subjectivity, class and sexuality in socialist feminist criticism," in *Making a Difference: Feminist Literary Criticism*, ed. Gayle Green and Coppélia Kahn (New York, 1985), pp. 166–67.

38   Willis in 1846, quoted in the Stokes Collection Typescript, p. 673.

CHAPTER 5: WOMEN AND MEN

1   Nancy Cott notes the contractual, pragmatic character of marriage among the middling as well as the laboring classes in the eighteenth century and stresses that in some respects, "marriage resembled an indenture between master and servant." "Divorce and the Changing Status of Women in Eighteenth Century Massachusetts," *William & Mary Quarterly*, 3rd ser., 33 (October 1976): 611. Suzanne Lebsock dissects the economic realities underlying the romantic veneer of nineteenth-century middle-class marriage in the *Free Women of Petersburg: Status and Culture in a Southern Town, 1784–1860* (New York, 1984).

2   Laurel Thatcher Ulrich describes the tensions between strong patriarchal traditions and female assertiveness in the colonial New England countryside in *Good Wives;* for the eighteenth century, see Norton, *Liberty's Daughters* and Kulikoff, "Class, Gender and Race," pp. 22–26.

3   Hasia R. Diner, *Erin's Daughters in America: Irish Immigrant Women in the Nineteenth Century* (Baltimore, 1983), p. 13; Gearóid O Tuathaigh, "The Role of Women in Ireland under the new English Order," in *Women in Irish Society: the Historical Dimension*, ed. Margaret Mac Curtain and Donncha O Lorráin (Westport, Conn., 1979), pp. 26–36; J. J. Lee, "Women and the Church since the Famine," in ibid., pp. 37–45; Carol Groneman, "Working-Class Immigrant Women in Mid-Nineteenth Century New York: the Irish Woman's Experience," *Journal of Urban History* 4 (May 1978), pp. 255–73; Diner, *Erin's Daughters*, pp. 5–13. On family workshops, see Tilly and Scott, *Women, Work and Family*, pp. 31–60.

4   Stott, "Worker in the Metropolis," p. 298.

5   CGS, People v. Russ, 1846 [n.d.].

6   CGS, People v. Twomey, January 19, 1853.

7   *The Old Brewery*, p. 171.

8   CGS, People v. Garretson et al., July 10, 1822; People v. Twomey; People v. Carroll, October 20, 1845.

9

	MALE ASSAULTS AGAINST WOMEN	FEMALE ASSAULTS AGAINST MEN	MALE ASSAULTS AGAINST MEN	OTHER*	TOTAL	PERCENTAGE OF MALE ASSAULTS AGAINST WOMEN	RATIO MALE ASSAULTS AGAINST WOMEN: FEMALE ASSAULTS AGAINST MEN
1820	71	14	150	61	296	24	6:1
1831	74	9	170	69	322	23	8:1
1841	60	6	216	46	328	18	10:1

*Includes women's attacks on other women, attacks by mixed groups, attacks on the watch and attacks by assailants of undetermined sex.
Source: Records of the New York Court of General Sessions.

10   A general discussion of patterns of male dominance in marriage in the European working class can be found in Mary Lynn McDougall, "Working Class Women During the Industrial Revolution, 1780–1914," in *Becoming Visible: Women in European History*, ed. Renate Bridenthal and Claudia Koonz (Boston, 1977), p. 274.

11   On the Washingtonians, see Wilentz, *Chants Democratic*, pp. 306–314.

12   CGS, People v. Harrington, June 13, 1831; also, People v. McMahon, August 12, 1854; People v. Quinn, September 20, 1844; People v. King, September 23, 1854.

13   CGS, People v. Coyle, October 9, 1856. Cf. the case of Susan White, who had left her household two or three times one day to take a drink and returned to an irate husband who, while she lay in a stupor, dosed her with laudanum "to keep her off the streets" and inadvertently killed her. Records of the County Coroner, case #387 (1854), NYMA.

14   On similar patterns in London, see Nancy Tomes, "A 'Torrent of Abuse': Crimes of Violence Between Working-Class Men and Women in London 1840–1875," *Journal of Social History* (Spring 1978), pp. 328–45; for a later period, Ellen Ross, " 'Fierce Questions and Taunts': Married Life in Working-Class London, 1870–1914," *Feminist Studies* 8 (Fall 1982), pp. 580–82, 591–94. Elizabeth Pleck notes the common acceptance of wife beating among all classes in the nineteenth century. "Wife-beating in Nineteenth Century America," *Victimology* 4 (Fall 1979): 62–74.

15   CGS, People v. Quinn, September 28, 1844; People v. Harrington, June 13, 1831; People v. Molloy, April 8, 1852.

16   People v. Carroll, July 25, 1840; People v. Finley, October 7, 1860.

17   Records of the County Coroner, case #354 (1855).

18   See these infanticide cases: CGS, People v. Westerfield, July 6, 1811; People v. Winn, January 10, 1832; People v. Newport, October 10, 1833; People v. Kennedy, December 12, 1842; People v. Owens, August 8, 1842; People v. Weidemeyer, April 12, 1848.

19   People v. Stevens, January 7, 1841; People v. Buckman, January 21, 1857.

20   David Montgomery, in *Growth of the Seaport Cities*, ed. Gilchrist, pp. 100–101. In the early 1840s, Horace Greeley was already stressing the social "evil" of the

skewed sex ratio. *New Yorker,* January 2, 1841. A fascinating analysis of the importance of single young men and women in the nation as a whole in the antebellum period is Carroll Smith Rosenberg's "Davy Crockett as Trickster: Pornography, Liminality, and Symbolic Inversion in Victorian America," in her book *Disorderly Conduct* (New York, 1985), pp. 90–108.

21 Stott, "Worker in the Metropolis," pp. 60–62, 124–27.

22 Margaret McCarthy letter, quoted in O Muirthe, *Seat Behind the Coachman,* p. 140.

23 The proportion of single people rose in 1841–51 from 43 to 61 percent for men, 28 to 39 percent for women. Robert E. Kennedy, Jr., *The Irish: Emigration, Marriage and Fertility* (Berkeley, Cal., 1973), p. 150. See also Groneman, "Working-Class Immigrant Women," p. 258; Lee, "Women and the Church," pp. 38–39.

24 Interesting evidence of different mobility patterns for rural sons and daughters on the eve of the English Industrial Revolution can be found in R. S. Schofield, "Age-Specific Mobility in an Eighteenth Century Rural English Parish," *Annales de Demographie Historique* (1970): 261–74; Tilly and Scott, *Women, Work and Family,* p. 37.

25 Nash shows the proportion of single women among transients "warned out" of Boston increased from 4 to 20 percent of the total between 1747 and 1771, "Urban Wealth," p. 564. The evidence from Massachusetts supports the view that the migratory poor included a high proportion of young single people of both sexes. Jones, "The Strolling Poor," pp. 34–35. The reference to Philadelphia is in Shammas, "Female Social Structure," pp. 71, 80, 82–83.

26 My census sample from 1855 shows these household arrangements of single workingwomen:

		PERCENTAGE OF TOTAL
Independent single women	224	56
Boarders	151	67
Living with siblings or cousins	62	28
Living alone or as household heads	11	5
	224	100
Dependent single women (living with parents, aunts and/or uncles)	176	44
TOTAL	400	100

Source: New York State Manuscript Census, 1855, Fourth Ward, E.D. 2, Seventeenth Ward, E.D. 3.

27 *Daily Tribune,* August 19, 1845.

28 Penny, *Employments of Women,* pp. 112, 350–51; see also ibid., p. 403; Marie

Louise Hankins, *Women of New York* (New York, 1861), p. 196; William M. Bobo, *Glimpses of New-York, by a South Carolinian* (Charleston, S.C., 1852), p. 193; Burn, *Three Years Among the Working-Classes*, pp. 6–7.

29   CGS, People v. Gunning et al., December 13, 1858.

30   McCarthy letter, in O Muirthe, *Seat Behind the Coachman*, p. 141.

31   *An Authentic Statement of the Case and Conduct of Rose Butler . . . Who Was Tried, Convicted and Executed for the Crime of Arson* (New York, 1819), p. 9.

32   The promenade was also a European courting practice. Olwen H. Hufton, "Women, Work and Marriage in Eighteenth-Century France," in *Marriage and Society*, ed. R. B. Outhwaite (New York, 1981), pp. 200–201.

33   Wilentz, *Chants Democratic*, p. 280.

34   Ely, *Visits of Mercy*, pp. 155–56, 217–19, 221.

35   Much work remains to be done on changing sexual mores in the laboring classes in eighteenth- and nineteenth-century America. Mary Beth Norton notes that in the eighteenth century, the code of premarital female chastity had yet to be accepted by either the middling or lower orders. *Liberty's Daughters*, pp. 51–56. My research indicates that an acceptance of premarital sex—in the context of betrothal —continued among working-class people at least through the Civil War. Thus the American situation seems, at least in its rough outlines, to fit the picture that scholars have drawn for Europe in this period. See Louise A. Tilly, Joan W. Scott, and Miriam Cohen, "Women's Work and European Fertility Patterns," *Journal of Interdisciplinary History* 6 (Winter 1976): 447–76; Cissie Fairchilds, "Female Sexual Attitudes and the Rise of Illegitimacy: A Case Study," *Journal of Interdisciplinary History* 8 (Spring 1978): 627–67; and especially the superb fine-grained study by John R. Gillis, "Servants, Sexual Relations, and the Risks of Illegitimacy in London, 1801–1900," *Feminist Studies* 5 (Spring 1979): 142–67 and his definitive *For Better or Worse: British Marriages 1600 to the Present* (New York, 1985), especially pp. 114–16 and 126–28. English social observers attested to widespread premarital intercourse as a token of betrothal among young workingwomen in the textile mills. Margaret Hewitt, *Wives and Mothers in Victorian Industry* (London, 1958; Westport, Conn., 1975), pp. 54–55. McDougall summarizes much of this literature in "Working-Class Women," p. 27.

    K. H. Connell describes the powerful sanctions Irish villagers exercised over premarital sexuality to prevent illegitimate pregnancies. "Illegitimacy Before the Famine," in *Irish Peasant Society: Four Historical Essays* (Oxford, Eng., 1968), pp. 51–86.

36   *Trial of Henry Bedlow*, p. 4.

37   *Report of the Trial of Levi Weeks . . . for the Murder of Gulielma Sands* (New York, 1800), p. 20.

38   Ibid., p. 19; James Hardie, *An Impartial Account of the Trial of Levi Weeks* (New York, 1800), p. v.

39   *Miller's New York As It Is; Or Stranger's Guide-Book* (New York, 1863), pp. 23–24.

40   Asbury, *The Gangs of New York*, pp. 21–45; Alvin F. Harlow, *Old Bowery*

Days: The Chronicles of a Famous Street (New York, 1931); Foster, *New York in Slices*, p. 121; Wilentz, *Chants Democratic*, p. 257. Dickens gives a splendid description of the Bowery in *American Notes* (London, 1842; New York, 1970), p. 81.

41   Harlow, *Old Bowery Days*, pp. 190–212; Buckley, "To the Opera House," pp. 294–409.

42   Dayton, *Last Days of Knickerbocker Life*, pp. 164–65. Cf. Haswell, *Reminiscences of an Octogenarian*, pp. 270–71: "The Bowery boy of that period was so distinctive a class in dress and conversation that a description of him is well worthy of notice. He was not an idler and corner lounger, but mostly an apprentice, generally to a butcher, and he 'ran with the machine.' . . . In the evenings, other than Saturdays (when the markets remained open all day and evenings) and on Sundays and holidays, he appeared in *propria persona*, a very different character; his dress, a high beaver hat, with the nap divided and brushed in opposite directions, the hair on the back of the head clipped close, while in front the temple locks were curled and greased (hence, the well-known term of 'soap-locks' to the wearer of them), a smooth face, a gaudy silk neck cloth, black frock coat, full pantaloons, turned up at the bottom over heavy boots designed for service in slaughter houses and at fires."

43   Dayton: "They affected to look upon a Broadway swell with the most decided contempt." *Last Days of Knickerbocker Life*, p. 164. The "jackeen" is mentioned in O Muirthe, *Seat Behind the Coachman*, p. 17.

44   Harlow, *Old Bowery Days*, pp. 212–14. Buckley makes a brilliant argument about the relationships between New York journalists, the cultural imagery of the Bowery Boy, and the working-class milieu of the street. "To the Opera House," pp. 294–409.

45   Haswell, *Reminiscences*, p. 271.

46   Foster, *New York by Gas-Light* (New York, 1850), p. 107. On gay male culture, see Michael Lynch, "Urban Carnality," paper presented at the annual meeting of the American Historical Association, December 1985. On the different patterns of development of gay male and lesbian cultures, see John D'Emilio, "Capitalism and Gay Identity," in *Powers of Desire: The Politics of Sexuality*, ed. Ann Snitow, Christine Stansell and Sharon Thompson (New York, 1983): 100–113.

47   Michael and Ariane Batterberry, *On the Town in New York: From 1776 to the Present* (New York, 1973), p. 98; Harlow, *Old Bowery Days*, pp. 219, 260, 321–22; Foster, *New York by Gas-Light*, pp. 64–71; Paul Dickson, *The Great American Ice Cream Book* (New York, 1973), pp. 25–26; Dayton, *Last Days of Knickerbocker Life*, pp. 140–41; David Grimsted, *Melodrama Unveiled: American Theater and Culture 1800–1850* (Chicago, 1968), pp. 51–58.

48   Foster, *New York by Gas-Light*, pp. 95–100; Burn, *Three Years Among the Working-Classes*, pp. 90–91; Dayton, *Last Days of Knickerbocker Life*, pp. 162–63.

49   *Diary of George Templeton Strong*, 2:61 (entry for August 15, 1851). Cf. Philip Hone's more restrained indictment seven years earlier: "I do not object to an

innocent enjoyment of the pleasures of a short excursion into the neighboring country," Hone stressed primly. "I object to a concentration of hundreds of half-drunken apprentice boys and women of light character." Hone Diary, May 15, 1843, NYHS.

50   Discussions of the social conventions of nineteenth-century fashion are in Ann Douglas, *The Feminization of American Culture* (New York, 1977), pp. 70–71; Lois W. Banner, *American Beauty* (New York, 1983), pp. 72–78; Helene E. Roberts, "The Exquisite Slave: The Role of Clothing in the Making of Victorian Women," *Signs* 2 (Spring 1976–77): 554–69. On prostitutes' dress, see Judith R. Walkowitz, *Prostitution and Victorian Society: Women, Class and the State* (New York, 1980), pp. 26, 195, 208. See also Dayton, *Last Days of Knickerbocker Life*, pp. 121–22.

51   Foster, *New York by Gas-Light*, p. 107; Dayton, *Last Days of Knickerbocker Life*, p. 166.

52   Foster, *New York in Slices*, p. 111. For other references to working girls' love of fancy dress: Burn, *Three Years Among the Working-Classes*, p. 85; *Daily Tribune*, August 25, 1845. There is an interesting series of references to employers' frustrations with female factory workers who insisted on wearing hoop skirts which got in the way of machinery in Penny, *Employments of Women*, pp. 252, 362, 376; see also "Needle and Garden. The Story of a Seamstress Who Laid Down Her Needle and Became a Strawberry-Girl," *Atlantic Monthly* 15 (1865).

53   Foster, *New York by Gas-Light*, pp. 107–108.

54   Ibid.; if a middle-class girl wore anything like a Bowery costume, Foster surmised, her mother would lecture her sharply "on the proper distinction between some folks and some people—concluding with a fearful warning against the dangers of overstepping the barrier which separates persons of 'position in society' from the mere common vulgar herd," pp. 107–108. See also ibid., pp. 68–69.

55   Still, *Mirror for Gotham*, p. 46; Wilson, *Memorial History*, 3:109–110; Smith, *The City of New York*, pp. 95–98.

56   Thomas Wentworth Higginson, *Cheerful Yesterdays* (Boston and New York, 1898), p. 230, uses the term to describe Whitman.

57   Foster, *New York in Slices*, p. 120.

58   Batterberry, *On the Town*, pp. 103–105. It is unclear whether or not the Bowery Theater banned prostitutes from the third tier as had genteel New York theaters, beginning with the Park in 1842. Claudia D. Johnson, "That Guilty Third Tier: Prostitution in Nineteenth-Century American Theaters," in *Victorian America*, ed. Daniel Walker Howe (Philadelphia, 1976), pp. 111–120.

59   Foster, *New York by Gas-Light*, p. 100; Dayton, *Last Days of Knickerbocker Life*, pp. 166–68.

60   Wilentz, *Chants Democratic*, pp. 262–63, 358–59.

61   CGS, People v. Holbertson, February 1, 1852.

62   People v. Gunning et al.; another case was that of a young man escorting a girl home one night up an avenue. He asked her to go into a side street with him to have intercourse, she refused, whereupon he and two other male companions raped her. People v. Murphy et al., February 17, 1858.

63   People v. Dingler et al., December 14, 1842; People v. Meeker et al., May 24, 1850; People v. Lynch, December 12, 1855.

The number of indictments for rape in New York, proportional to the population, remained about the same throughout the period 1790–1860 (with the exception of the period 1800–20, when the proportions are much higher).

Indictments include those for rape, intent to rape, and intent to ravish.

DECADE	NUMBER OF INDICTMENTS	POPULATION AT END OF DECADE	RATE PER 100,000 POPULATION
1790–99	5	60,529	8.26
1800–09*	13	96,573	13.4
1810–19	27	123,706	21.8
1820–29	20	197,092	10.2
1830–39	32	312,710	10.2
1840–49	57	515,547	11.1
1850–59	76	813,662	9.3

*Two years of indictment papers missing.
Source: Papers of the New York Court of General Sessions.

64   CGS, People v. Sexton, September 15, 1858; People v. Brady, November 13, 1851.
65   I was unable to locate any statistics on prenuptial pregnancies in antebellum New York City; statistics on illegitimate births are lacking for the United States. Moreover, there are no class-specific statistical studies. Those numbers that do exist can be seen as consonant with my argument about the sexualization of youth culture. In a sample of New England towns, historian Daniel Scott Smith found these proportions of prenuptial conceptions to live births:

before 1701	11.1
1701–60	23.3
1761–1800	33.7
1801–40	25.1
1841–80	15.5

Source: "The Dating of the American Sexual Revolution: Evidence and Interpretation," in The American Family in Social-Historical Perspective, ed. Michael Gordon (New York, 1978), pp. 426–38.

These statistics alone cannot tell us much about working-class sexuality in New York. They certainly do not provide a convincing case for the supposed "Victorianization" of the working class argued by Smith and Hindus in "Premarital Pregnancy in America, 1640–1971; An Overview and Interpretation," Journal of Interdisciplinary History 5 (Spring 1975): 538.

Sexual prohibitions in the *middle* class might account for the decrease after 1841. It is worth noting, however, that for most of the period under consideration, prenuptial pregnancies remained quite high, never dropping below one in four live births.

If prenuptial pregnancies *did* decrease among the urban working class toward midcentury, did illegitimate births increase? That is, in the cities, were men less likely to marry after having conceived a child? In general, the trend of illegitimate births follows that of prenuptial pregnancies (Peter Laslett, *Family Life and Illicit Love in Earlier Generations* [London, 1977], p. 539), but it would be interesting to know if this indeed was the case in nineteenth-century cities.

Birth statistics should not be taken as the sole indicator of sexual activity. In cities, abortions were readily available. Young women would have had access to information about abortionists as well as to "folk" techniques of contraception (which, contrary to common belief, could often be quite effective) through networks of female workmates and fellow lodgers. See Ellen Ross and Rayna Rapp, "Sex and Society: A Research Note from Social History and Anthropology," in *Powers of Desire*, pp. 58–61.

It is also possible that working-class intercourse did decline as young women were better able to control their sexual lives; in a peer group culture where female friends helped to restrict men's sexual activity, young people might have developed other forms of sexual play. Heavy petting, for example, is often carried on when there is strong peer group supervision of courting couples. Kathy Peiss's description of working-class couples in the late nineteenth century shows that working-class girls could draw a strict line between petting and intercourse. Kathy Peiss, " 'Charity Girls' and City Pleasures: Historical Notes on Working-Class Sexuality," in *Powers of Desire*, pp. 78–79.

CHAPTER 6: HARROWING TRUTHS

1   Report from the Pennsylvania Society for the Promotion of Public Economy (Philadelphia), quoted in the *Commercial Advertiser*, August 19, 1817; Carey, "Essays on the Public Charities of Philadelphia," p. 154.

2   Degler, "Labor in the Economy and Politics of New York," pp. 105–106, 124–25. Degler found that women were prominent in 46 (14.3 percent) of 321 trades listed in the 1860 census. Ibid., pp. 125–26. He found the following industries dominated by women workers:

INDUSTRY	PERCENTAGE OF WORKERS WHO WERE FEMALE
Paper boxes	66.3
Hoopskirts	87.6
Shirts and collars	95.6
Millinery	94.8

INDUSTRY	PERCENTAGE OF WORKERS WHO WERE FEMALE
Miscellaneous millinery goods	85.7
Artificial flowers	91.7
Umbrellas and parasols	75.5
Ladies' cloaks and mantillas	95.4

3   Minute Books, November 1859, SRPW.

4   Cf. Egal Feldman: "The outside shop was almost completely dominated by female labor." *Fit for Men: A Study of New York's Clothing Trade* (Washington, D.C., 1960), p. 102. On male outside workers see Wilentz, *Chants Democratic*, pp. 113, 122–24, 126–27, 155. McDougall concurs that in the case of nineteenth-century Europe, women were especially vulnerable to outside work. "While the overall number of domestic workers declined in the process of industrialization, mainly men gave it up, leaving behind a preponderance of women." "Working Class Women," p. 266. For the same pattern in London, see James A. Schmiechen, *Sweated Industry and Sweated Labor: The London Clothing Trades, 1860–1914* (Urbana, Ill., 1984).

5   The clearest and strongest statement of this theoretical position is Heidi Hartmann, "Capitalism, Patriarchy, and Job Segregation by Sex," in *Capitalist Patriarchy and the Case for Socialist Feminism*, ed. Zillah R. Eisenstein (New York, 1979), pp. 206–47. Kessler-Harris, *Out to Work*, is a rich and sweeping historical analysis of the problem.

6   See, for example, Eric Hobsbawm, "The Formation of the Industrial Working Classes: Some Problems," *3e Conférence Internationale d'Histoire Économique, Congrès et Colloques* (The Hague, 1965), 1: 176–77. Marx speaks of domestic manufactures as peripheral to the central tendency of industrialization "to conversion to the factory system proper." *Capital*, trans. Samuel Moore and Edward Aveling (Moscow: Progress Publishers, n.d.), 1:445. See also Sidney Pollard, *The Genesis of Modern Management* (Cambridge, Mass., 1965), pp. 34–35.

An essay that maintains this focus on factory labor, and at the same time takes female employment as its central analytic problem, is Claudia Goldin and Kenneth Sokoloff, "Women, Children and Industrialization in the Early Republic: Evidence from Manufacturing Censuses," *Journal of Economic History* 42 (December 1982): 741–74.

7   For London, see Alexander, "Women's Work in Nineteenth-Century London," pp. 63, 65; for Paris, Henriette Vanier, *La Mode et Ses Metiers: Frivolités et Luttes des Classes, 1830–1870* (Paris, 1960); for Holland, Selma Leydesdorff, "Women and Children in Home Industry" (Paper presented at the International Conference in Women's History, University of Maryland, 1977); for Germany, Barbara Franzoi, "Domestic Industry: Work Options and Women's Choices," in *Ger-*

man Women in the Nineteenth Century, ed. John C. Fout (New York, 1984), pp. 256–69.

For a general discussion of the importance of hand technology in industrialization, see Samuel, "Workshops of the World."

8   Clark, *History of Manufactures,* 1: 465. On early manufactures, see the compilations for 1810–20 in Franklin B. Hough, *Statistics of Population of the City and County of New York* (New York, 1865).

9   See the eighteenth-century seamstress's notice quoted in Flick, *History of the State of New York,* 3: 297–98.

10   Abbott, *Women in Industry,* p. 217; Feldman, *Fit for Men,* pp. 1–2.

11   For sailors' slops, see Feldman, *Fit for Men,* pp. 1–2; Edwin T. Freedley, ed., *Leading Pursuits and Leading Men* (Philadelphia, 1856), p. 89. For uniforms, see Flick, *History of the State of New York,* 3:315. In 1819 the ladies of the House of Industry acquired a contract for navy blankets and uniforms to avert insolvency. *Evening Post,* November 29, 1819. For journeymen sewing slops, see Feldman, *Fit for Men,* pp. 77–78; Jesse Eliphalet Pope, *The Clothing Industry in New York* (Columbia, Mo., 1905), p. 11. For mentions of women sewing slops, see Ely, *Visits of Mercy,* p. 32; Minute Books, 1798, January 10, 1803, April 8, 1807, SRPW.

12   Ibid., November 17, 1817. On the dumping of British goods, see Albion, *Rise of New York Port,* pp. 12–13; Flick, *History of the State of New York,* 5:350.

13   Clothing manufacture was the leading manufacturing employer of women in the city well into the twentieth century. I have traced it in the United States census for manufactures as far as 1940, when it still outstripped by far any other industry.

The 1860 figures come from *Manufactures of the United States in 1860: Compiled from the Original Returns of the Eighth Census* (Washington, D.C., 1865), calculated from returns for New York County, pp. 380–85.

Precisely because of the prevalence of outwork among women wageworkers, we can only take these census statistics as rough estimates of the number of women in the labor force. Any discussion of female labor-force participation in industrializing countries must take account of this serious problem of underenumeration.

14   Feldman, *Fit for Men,* p. 3; Sumner, *History of Women,* p. 122; Freedley, *Leading Pursuits,* p. 89; Chauncey M. Depew, *One Hundred Years of American Commerce* (New York, 1895), p. 565; *New York Herald,* October 25, 1857.

15   Ibid. See John C. Gobright, *The Union Sketch-Book: A Reliable Guide . . . of the Leading Mercantile and Manufacturing Firms of New York* (New York, 1861), pp. 40–41 for the national market.

16   Sumner, *History of Women,* p. 138.

17   Penny, *Employments of Women,* p. 113; for the attractions of the clothing trade for immigrants, see Ernst, *Immigrant Life,* p. 93. After 1835, when the commercial district was rebuilt after the great fire of that year, rents soared in lower Manhattan.

Sidney Pollard assesses the importance of subcontracting in early industrial capitalist enterprises in England. The large entrepreneur could thereby reduce his supervisory activities and to some degree stabilize his cost structure by paying the subcontractor a fixed price. *Genesis of Modern Management,* pp. 38–39.

18   Degler, "Labor in the Economy and Politics of New York City," p. 111. See also Freedley, *Leading Pursuits,* pp. 126–27, for the difficulties of small manufacturers.

19   Quoted in Sumner, *History of Women,* p. 136.

20   Cf. Virginia Penny on the "tears and sighs of hardworking women." *Employments of Women,* p. 345; Burdett, *The Elliott Family;* "the poor helpless females" mentioned by the National Trades' Union, quoted in Sumner, *History of Women,* p. 141. For the parallel imagery in England, see T. J. Edelstein, "They Sang 'The Song of the Shirt': The Visual Iconography of the Seamstress," *Victorian Studies* 23 (Winter 1980): 183–210.

21   Minute Books, November 15, 1855, SRPW.

22   *Herald,* June 7, 1853. Stott discusses seasonality in the clothing trade and in dressmaking. "Worker in the Metropolis," pp. 147–48. He also notes that women suffered more heavily from unemployment in periods of contraction; at least in the Panic of 1857, when female employment dropped by almost half in comparison to 20 percent for men. Ibid., p. 160. See also Walt Whitman on the sewing women in the *Brooklyn Daily Eagle* (Brooklyn, N.Y.), November 9, 1846.

On the importance of dovetailing employment in a casualized labor market, see Gareth Stedman Jones, *Outcast London* (London, 1971), pp. 39–41. For mentions of both weekly and seasonal unemployment, see Carey, "Report on Female Wages," *Miscellaneous Essays,* p. 267; "Circular of the Shirt Sewers' Association," Shirt Sewers' Cooperative, Broadsides Collection, NYHS; *Daily Tribune,* June 8, 1853; Minutes, November 16, 1854, SRPW; Penny, *Employments of Women,* pp. 114–15.

23   Greeley quoted in Sumner, *History of Women,* p. 136. The German Jews of Chatham Street were the perennial scapegoats of denunciations that depended heavily on anti-Semitic connotations. "A class of beings in human form," angry seamstresses called them after a wage cut in 1831, and two decades later a journalist sympathetic to the seamstresses conjured up the stereotype of the avaricious Jew, the "shopkeeping, pennyturning genius." More prosperous businessmen liked to see themselves as superior in benevolence and moral scruples to the immigrant entrepreneurs and were quite content to see issues of ethnicity obscure those of class. In actuality, their firms—respectable concerns like Brooks Brothers—profited equally from rate cutting, although its practice was less visible. They kept their hands clean because they did not set the piece rates for their outside workers but left it to the contractors, men who were the worst gougers in the trade. *Working Man's Advocate,* September 6, 1831; Foster, *New York in Slices,* p. 13.

24   Carey, "Report on Female Wages," *Miscellaneous Essays,* p. 280. Working-women also suffered from underbidding from farm women in the surrounding

countryside. Sumner, *History of Women*, p. 140; Penny, *Employments of Women*, pp. 112, 345; Freedley, *Leading Pursuits*, p. 127.

25   *Daily Tribune*, June 8, 1853; the workingman's budget is from the *Times*, November 10, 1853.

26   An English traveler in 1819 noted that women who did the skilled work of sewing coats and jackets earned 25–50 percent less than men doing similar work. Stokes Collection Typescript, p. 314. In 1836, journeymen tailors reported they were earning 15 shillings ($1.87) per day with a female helper; until the 1850s, reports state that women's wages at any work remained at or below two shillings per day. *National Trades' Union*, March 12, 1836. See also Feldman, *Fit for Men*, pp. 112–14.

27   Adams, Jr., "Wage Rates in the Early National Period," p. 406; see also *Daily Tribune*, July 9, 1845. On turnouts, see Gilje, "Mobocracy," pp. 175–83. The *Daily Tribune*, July 20, 1850 reported wages for unskilled immigrant men in the city at 9 shillings ($1.12) per day.

Badly off as the outside workers were, there was a seemingly inexhaustible supply of women who could work for less. In 1830, for instance, an employer "sought up emigrants, or went to the almshouse, to have his work done; if he could find no women in his neighborhood willing to undertake it . . . so that he forced them to come to his own terms." *Working Man's Advocate*, September 11, 1830; see also *Herald*, October 21, 1857.

28   Bobo, *Glimpses of New York*, p. 109; see also pp. 107–110. Other references can be found in the *Herald*, June 7, 1853; October 25, 1857; *Daily Tribune*, August 7, 1849, June 8, 1835; *Working Man's Advocate*, April 6, 1844; William W. Sanger, *The History of Prostitution* (New York, 1859), p. 527; *Jonathan's Whittlings of War* (April 22, 1854), pp. 102–103; *The Subterranean*, February 7, 1846.

29   *Daily Times*, February 24, 27, March 1, 1855. A third seamstress sued her employer in court on March 1.

30   "Needle and Garden," p. 170; *Jonathan's Whittlings* (April 22, 1854), p. 102; Bobo, *Glimpses of New York City*, p. 109.

31   *Daily Tribune*, March 7, 1845.

32   Penny, *Employments of Women*, pp. 111, 114, 356. See also Pollard, *Genesis of Modern Management*, pp. 33–34. The inefficiency of putting out is also discussed in Ivy Pinchbeck, *Women Workers and the Industrial Revolution 1750–1850* (1930; New York, 1969), p. 137.

The other drawback of the outside system was the opportunity it gave workers to embezzle goods. Stephen Marglin has argued that embezzlement was widely practiced by English cottage workers in the eighteenth and early nineteenth centuries. He believes that embezzlement was the most serious of the many problems of labor discipline which led capitalists to factory organization: not because factories were initially technologically superior to outwork, but because direct supervision could better control such refractory practices. "What Do Bosses Do? The Origins and Functions of Hierarchy in Capitalist Production," *Review of Radical Political Economics* 6 (Summer 1974): 33–35, 50–51.

There is some evidence of embezzlement among New York workers. One employer told Penny that he had incurred serious losses from unreturned work: "On inquiry at the place where the women said they lived, they would find they had never been there." Another mentioned a blacklist of women who did not return their work, and a third corroborated the existence of a blacklist but claimed that he himself had never had any problems with embezzlement: "If they [the women] should keep them, they would soon be known at the different establishments, and have no place to go for work." Penny, *Employments of Women*, pp. 112, 115, 352. There were arrests of tailors for embezzlement during the tailors' strike of 1850, and one employer raised the issue as a general problem. See *Daily Tribune*, July 26, August 14, 1850. There was an extensive network of illicit trade in New York, comprised of secondhand stores and pawnshops. Evidence that women utilized these networks to sell embezzled sewing is in CGS, People v. Riley, September 10, 1830, and People v. Stebbins et al., December 8, 1834.

33 *Herald*, June 11, 1853; Freedley, *Leading Pursuits*, p. 130.

34 Mayhew elucidated this principle in his investigation of London slop-workers: letters subtitled "Over-work makes under-pay" and "Under-pay makes over-work," in Eileen Yeo and E. P. Thompson, *The Unknown Mayhew* (New York, 1971), pp. 384–88.

35 Penny, *Employments of Women*, pp. 350–51; evidence on the length of the workday is in Carey, "Essays on the Public Charities of Philadelphia," p. 167; "Address of the Shirt Sewers' Cooperative"; Penny, *Employments of Women*, p. 356. See also "Needle and Garden" on the sewing machine.

36 Penny, *Employments of Women*, p. 310.

37 The doggerel beat of Thomas Hood's "Song of the Shirt" captures something of the drudgery of the work itself. The poem is reprinted in "Circular of the Shirt Sewers' Association"; a more accessible reprinting is in *The Penguin Book of Socialist Verse*, ed. Alan Bold (Harmondsworth, Eng., 1970), pp. 66–68.

38 Penny, *Employments of Women*, p. 311.

39 Ibid., p. 356; *Herald*, June 7, 1853; "Circular of the Shirt Sewers' Association."

40 The problem with any sample of outside workers is that the census would have underenumerated the number of outworkers in general and the number of married outworkers in particular. Married women were less likely than single women to declare any paid employment to a census taker: because their work was intermittent, because they deemed wage labor unrespectable for a wife, or because they considered domestic labor their primary employment.

41 Kessler-Harris, *Out to Work*, pp. 27–29.

42 There are allusions to family labor in waged employment throughout New York House of Refuge Papers, HRCH, 1825–60, and the published reports of the Children's Aid Society. For other references and examples see "Needle and Garden," p. 91; *Daily Tribune*, August 28, 1845; *The New-York Cries in Rhyme* (New York, 1832), p. 18; *Herald*, June 11, 1853, October 25, 1857; *Young America* (New York),

October 18, 1845; Penny, *Employments of Women*, p. 155; Mariner's Family Industrial Society, *Twelth Annual Report* (1856), pp. 6–7.

43   Abbott, *Women in Industry*, pp. 221–22. For contemporary references see Penny, *Employments of Women*, pp. 114, 264, 310–11, 312–14, 355; Freedley, *Leading Pursuits*, p. 129; *Daily Tribune*, September 5, 9, 1845; *Working Man's Advocate*, July 27, 1844.

44   Computations are from New York State Census, 1855, Population Schedules, Wd. 4, E.D. 2.

45   Conrad Carl, a New York tailor testifying before a Senate investigatory committee, cited this proverb. Senate Committee on Education and Labor, *Testimony As To the Relations Between Labor and Capital*, 48th Cong., 1885, p. 414.

46   Ivy Pinchbeck makes this point about women in household units of production, although she does not extend it to the development of a system of wage differentials. *Women Workers and the Industrial Revolution*, p. 2.

47   Penny, *Employments of Women*, pp. 113–14, 342–43. The wage differential in these "helping" arrangements was 2:1, reported the *Working Man's Advocate*, July 27, 1844. The women earned about $1.25/week, the men $2.50/week after rent.

48   Penny refers to the learning system throughout *Employments of Women*. See also *Herald*, October 21, 1857. For the Irish garret mistress, see ibid., June 8, 1853.

49   *Daily Tribune*, November 12, 1845. References to the many different kinds of sweaters can be found in the following: *Daily Tribune*, November 15, 1845; *Herald*, October 21, 1857; Penny, *Employments of Women*, pp. 112, 312, 342–43, 356, 452. In *Hunt's Merchant Magazine*, January 1849, is the very interesting piece of information that piece masters in the large establishments of New York made anywhere from $25 to $150 a week, an indication that they were engaged in quite lucrative subcontracting. George C. Foster mentions sweaters and undersweaters in *New York Naked*, pp. 137–38.

50   Depew, *One Hundred Years of American Commerce*, p. 525; Feldman, *Fit for Men*, pp. 106–107. Several inventors had taken out patents on sewing machines in the 1840s, but the stitches unraveled too easily, and the power came from an unwieldy hand crank. In 1846, Elias Howe devised a lockstitch which imitated the hand sewers' sturdy backstitch. Ruth Brandon, *A Capitalist Romance: Singer and the Sewing Machine* (Philadelphia, 1977), pp. 42–89.

51   Senate Committee on Education and Labor, *Relations between Labor and Capital*, pp. 413–14. A machine in the early 1850s was quite expensive ($100–$150) but by 1858 the price had dropped to $50 and there was a substantial secondhand trade. Feldman, *Fit for Men*, pp. 108–109. For another account (from Philadelphia) of how the machine encouraged sweating, see "Needle and Garden," pp. 173–75. Sally Alexander observes that the introduction of the sewing machine had more to do with the available skills and flexibility of the labor market than with the technical requirements of the trade. "Woman's Work in Nineteenth-Century London," p. 97.

52   Thomas Dublin, "Women and Outwork in a Nineteenth-Century New England Town," in *The Countryside in the Age of Capitalist Transformation: Essays in the Social History of Rural America*, ed. Steven Hahn and Jonathan Prude (New York, 1986).

53   Dublin, *Women at Work: The Transformation of Work and Community in Lowell, Massachusetts, 1826–1860* (New York, 1979), pp. 14–22.

54   "Needle and Garden," p. 173.

55   See, for example, *Jonathan's Whittlings* (April 22, 1854), p. 102.

56   Children's Aid Society (CAS), *Seventh Annual Report* (New York, 1860), p. 5.

57   My census sample shows this age distribution among workingwomen in identifiably inside trades.

AGE	NUMBER
10–15	5
16–20	38
21–25	15
26–30	5
31–40	7
41–50	4
50+	6
	N = 80

69 were single, 2 married and 9 widowed.

Source: New York State Manuscript Census, 1855, Fourth Ward, E.D. 2, Seventeenth Ward, E.D. 3.

58   Sumner, *History of Women*, p. 158; *Herald*, June 7, 1853.

59   Ibid.

60   The same writer, for example, refers to the constant rate cutting to which the straw sewers were subjected. Ibid.

   My argument about the significance of inside wage work for women is based on a different premise from Edward Shorter's paean to the effects of wage labor on women in *The Making of the Modern Family* (New York, 1975). But neither do I agree with his critics Joan Scott and Louise Tilly in *Women, Work and Family* that single women's wage work was altogether incorporated into family economies and traditional family values.

61   Penny, *Employments of Women*, pp. 305–307, 321, 344, 348; see also pp. 295–98, 301–303, 312–14, 319–20; *Daily Tribune*, September 17, 1845.

62   In England, factory owners by midcentury had given up employing children in large numbers. Pollard, *Genesis of Modern Management*, p. 185. Pollard also describes similar practices of adult supervision in those English workshops or factories that continued to employ children. On New York, see Penny, *Employments of Women*, pp. 305–307, 319–20, 371.

63   *Daily Tribune*, August 20, 1845; Penny, *Employments of Women*, pp. 295, 364; on the foreman's power over learners see ibid., pp. 292–95, 364; *Daily Tribune*, August 19, 20, 1845.

64   Penny, *Employments of Women*, p. 306; Sanger, *The History of Prostitution*, pp. 533–34. This is consonant with Engels's observations of English factory supervisors at about the same time in *The Condition of the Working-Class in England* (Leipzig, 1845; Moscow, 1973), pp. 186–87.

65   Printers' report on the state of the trade in 1850, reprinted in Commons et al., *Documentary History*, 7:117.

66   See Penny, *Employments of Women*, passim on the sex of supervisors. Mentions of "foreladies" are in the *Herald*, June 7, 1853, October 25, 1857; *Young America*, November 29, 1845. Caroline Dall, reformer and feminist, makes reference to a common belief that women were unfit by nature for the technical skills required in a supervisory role: "an idea has gone abroad, that no slopwork will be fit for sale unless a man inspects it." *"Woman's Right to Labor"; or, Low Wages and Hard Work* (Boston, 1860), pp. 69–71. Here was another ramification of the view of women as "outside" the manufacturing system.

67   Penny, *Employments of Women*, p. 392.

68   Marx, *Capital*, 1:380. For more quotations from employers on female labor, pro and con, see my dissertation, "Women of the Laboring Poor in New York City, 1820–1860" (Ph.D. diss., Yale University, 1979), pp. 104–108.

69   Penny, *Employments of Women*, p. 356.

70   E. P. Thompson, "Time, Work-Discipline and Industrial Capitalism," *Past and Present* 38 (December 1967): 56–97; see also Herbert Gutman's reinterpretation of Thompson's analysis for nineteenth-century America, "Work, Culture and Society in Industrializing America, 1815–1919," in *Work, Culture & Society*, pp. 3–78.

71   *Daily Tribune*, August 20, 1845.

72   Penny, *Employments of Women*, pp. 218–19, 281, 331–34, 392, 438, 458.

73   William Burns, *Life in New York, In Doors and Out of Doors* (New York, 1851), n.p.; Penny, *Employments of Women*, pp. 113, 136, 250, 344. For a mention of a common rule against talking in mixed workrooms, see ibid., pp. 313–14 and *Daily Tribune*, August 20, 1845. There is also counterevidence of women *disliking* to work with men. We need to know more about antebellum working-class women before we know how to weigh this evidence and distinguish between the cases. For example, were married women less likely to take jobs in workrooms where there were men? Penny, *Employments of Women*, pp. 233, 386, 449.

74   CAS, *Seventh Annual Report* (1860), p. 6. "The class frequently labor in company with men or bold women; they are fagged out at the end of the day; they are ignorant and have few resources of an intelligent kind, and with the passion for amusement, or the impulse of vanity, they are often easily led away. There is danger of the same sad state of morals arising among this class, as exists in some of the large English manufacturing towns."

75   Sanger, *History of Prostitution*, pp. 534–35: "The employment of females in various trades in this city, in the pursuit of which they are forced into constant communication with male operatives has a disastrous effect upon their characters." Cf. *Young America*, September 6, 1845: "the want of education and the out-door temptations which belong to the fortunes of so many of them . . . beget habits of levity and idleness," the newspaper charged of the book folders.

76   Engels, *Condition of the Working-Class,* pp. 185–86; the English debate on the morality of female operatives is chronicled in Hewitt, *Wives & Mothers in Victorian Industry,* pp. 48–61.

77   Cf. Sally Alexander on skilled English workers: "Men's desire to confine women to their proper place must be understood—at least in part—as a desire to (legally) control and (morally) order sexuality." "Women, Class and Sexual Differences in the 1830s and 1840s: Some Reflections on the Writing of a Feminist History," *History Workshop* 17 (Spring 1984): 144.

In their objections to inside employment for women, laboring people may have been in part expressing their dislike of the sexual harassment that could go on there. Penny gives one small example of the kind of sexual scrutiny factory girls could encounter: In one building she visited, the stairs were open so that, as women walked up and down, male workers could look up their skirts. See also the case of sixteen-year-old Catherine Runnett, who went to work in a pen manufactory in 1850 and ended up pregnant by the foreman. Penny, *Employments of Women,* pp. 377–78; Runnett v. Bagley, Superior Court, reported in *Daily Tribune,* April 9, 1850.

78   Burn, *Three Years Among the Working-Classes,* p. 85.

CHAPTER 7: WOMEN AND THE LABOR MOVEMENT

1   Richard B. Morris, *Government and Labor in Early America* (1946; New York, 1975), pp. 139–66.

2   Alice Clark, *The Working Life of Women in the Seventeenth Century* (London, 1919), chapter V; (on America) Alice Morse Earle, *Colonial Dames and Good Wives* (Boston and New York, 1895), pp. 55–56.

3   *Evening Post,* July 13, 1819.

4   John R. Commons et al., *History of Labor in the United States,* 2 vols. (New York, 1918–35), 1: 472–83; U.S. Congress, Senate, *History of Women in Trade Unions,* by John B. Andrews and W. D. P. Bliss, pp. 22–49. *Report on Condition of Woman and Child Wage-Earners in the United States,* S. Doc. 645, 61st Cong., 2nd Sess., 1910, vol. 10. (Hereafter cited as Andrews and Bliss, *History of Women in Trade Unions.*)

5   Quoted in ibid., p. 21.

6   The society's membership of 500 women must have included a substantial number of the city's needlewomen. Although the society may have been a successor to an earlier craftswomen's association, its size, as well as its inclusion of all grades of work on the price list, suggests that it also admitted unskilled women. The listing of forty-two women as "tailoresses" in the city directory for 1825 is one sign that there was still a group in the city who identified themselves as established craftswomen. *Longworth's American Almanac . . . and City Directory* (New York, 1825). On the price lists and membership of the society, see *Daily Sentinel* (New York), February 12, July 19, 1831, and *Working Man's Advocate,* July 3, August 6, 1831. I am indebted to Dolores Janiewski for her unpublished essay on the New York sewing women, "Sewing with a Double Thread: The Needlewomen of New York 1825–1870" (M.A. thesis, University of Oregon, 1974).

7   Monroe's speech is printed in the *Daily Sentinel,* March 5, 1831; see also the letters in the *Working Man's Advocate,* June 25, August 6, 1831.

8   Taylor, *Eve and the New Jerusalem,* pp. 1–18 (on Jacobin feminism), 65–68 (on Frances Wright). Claire G. Moses explores analogous feminist developments in France in the 1830s and aptly characterizes Frances Wright as part of a "far-flung" network of feminists within European social movements in this period. "Saint-Simonian Men/Saint-Simonian Women: The Transformation of Feminist Thought in 1830s France," *Journal of Modern History* 54 (June 1982): 240–67. See also Joan Wallach Scott's important essay "Men and women in the Parisian garment trades: discussions of family and work in the 1830s and 1840s," in *The Power of the Past: Essays for Eric Hobsbawm,* ed. Pat Thane, Geoffrey Crossick and Roderick Floud (New York, 1984).

9   An account of Wright's New York sojourn is in Wilentz, *Chants Democratic,* pp. 176–83. The quotation from Wright is in the *Free Enquirer* (New York), March 18, 1829. Owen also crusaded for birth control in the *Free Enquirer,* the iconoclastic paper the two began, although he based his advocacy on neo-Malthusian reasoning rather than on the grounds of women's good.

10   Quoted in Commons et al., *History of Labor,* 1:423.

11   *Daily Sentinel,* February 17, 1831.

12   Ibid., March 5, 1831.

13   The bookbinders' address was printed in the *National Trades' Union,* July 7, 1835; on the Philadelphia Federation, see Andrews and Bliss, *History of Women in Trade Unions,* pp. 39–40. On Lowell, see Dublin, *Women at Work,* pp. 99–103.

14   Katherine E. Kendall and Jeanne Y. Fisher, "Frances Wright on Women's Rights: Eloquence Versus Ethics," *Quarterly Journal of Speech* 60 (February 1974): 58–68; Gerda Lerner, *The Grimké Sisters from South Carolina* (Boston, 1967), p. 189; Smith Rosenberg, *Religion and the Rise of the American City,* p. 120.

       The tailoresses asked Cornelius Blatchly, a Quaker physician and radical essayist, to collect funds for them, and they invited another man to speak to them; otherwise, only women are mentioned in the proceedings.

15   The *Free Enquirer* reprinted a lengthy report on laboring women authored by Matthew Carey (May 6, 1829); beyond that Wright herself did not go. Her New York speeches on women concern education and the common law. The only rhetorical mention of women I have located is an injunction to the "sons and daughters of America," in a speech reprinted in the *Free Enquirer,* April 15, 1829. The observations about women in the audience are in Celia Morris Eckhardt, *Fanny Wright: Rebel in America* (Cambridge, Mass., 1984), p. 223.

16   Wilentz, *Chants Democratic,* pp. 172–216.

17   Ibid., pp. 219–54. The conventions of 1834 and 1835 were held in New York, with delegates from New York and Brooklyn representing 11,500 men in 1834. Commons et al., *Documentary History of American Labor,* 6: 191–92.

18   Ibid., p. 219; *National Trades' Union,* July 11, 1835.

19   Commons et al., *Documentary History of American Labor,* 6:251.

20   Ibid., 6:282–83.

21   Ibid., 6:284. "In the early ages we find that women were usefully, healthily and industriously employed," the men wistfully maintained. Ibid., 6:283.

22   Ibid.

23   Committee on Female Labor (convention of 1836) in ibid., 6:282.

24   See comments on "the prevalence of depravity" at Lowell (convention of 1834), ibid., pp. 217–18; on the moral injuries young workingwomen incurred (convention of 1835), p. 250; and on the damage to the female character involved in wage work in the *National Laborer* (1836), quoted in Sumner, *History of Women in Industry*, p. 29.

25   Quoted in ibid., p. 278. See also the toast by Ely Moore, first president of the New York GTU, to "the female operatives. Noble auxiliaries in the cause of equal rights." Quoted from an 1836 Philadelphia paper in Andrews and Bliss, *History of Women in Trade Unions*, p. 47.

26   Alexander's discussion of the sexual politics of contemporaneous working-class movements in England is illuminating here. "Women, Class and Sexual Differences," pp. 136–40.

27   Commons et al., *Documentary History of American Labor*, 6:284; an analysis of the meaning of the family wage to English workingmen is in Taylor, *Eve and the New Jerusalem*, p. 268.

28   Women themselves, complained the Committee on Female Labor, did not always appreciate the men's kindly intentions: "Females themselves are very blind as to their real interest, and imagine that each effort made to destroy the operation of the system, is destructive to their interest, whereas it is virtually calculated to remove and destroy the very evils they now labor under." Commons et al., *Documentary History of American Labor*, 6:284. On women campaigning against their own employment, see ibid., 6:285. English is quoted in Andrews and Bliss, *History of Women in Trade Unions*, p. 48; see also Laurie, *Working People of Philadelphia*, pp. 70–71, 88, 94–95. A discussion of similar ideological developments in France and England is in Harold Benenson, "Victorian Sexual Ideology and Marx's Theory of the Working Class," *International Labor and Working Class History* 26 (Spring 1984): 5–8.

29   *The Man* (New York), May 27, June 19, 1835; *Evening Post*, July 10, 1835; *National Trades' Union*, August 22, 1835; Andrews and Bliss, *History of Women in Trade Unions*, pp. 32–33, 43–45.

30   Mary H. Blewett, "Work, Gender and the Artisan Tradition in New England Shoemaking, 1780–1860," *Journal of Social History* 17 (Winter 1983): 221–48. Taylor also notes that in England, strong traditions of cooperative organizing between men and women existed in trades that were domestically based. *Eve and the New Jerusalem*, pp. 90–91.

31   I cannot determine whether the strikers were silk spinners, cotton spinners or both. On silk spinning, see Pinchbeck, *Women Workers and the Industrial Revolution*, p. 168; L. P. Brockett, *The Silk Industry in America: A History* (New York, 1876), pp. 35, 115; on cotton spinning, Prude, *The Coming of Industrial Order*, pp. 43, 51–52, 86–87, 116–17; on bookbinding, J. Ramsay MacDonald, ed., *Women in the Printing Trades: A Sociological Study* (London, 1904), p. 7.

32   Sumner chronicles the tailors' hostility to women in *History of Women in Industry*, pp. 120–21. It is worth noting that tailoring, like printing, was a trade where employers invoked the threat of women workers to counter labor militance. See, for example, *Journal of Commerce* (New York), October 12, 1833.

33   On the 1836 venture, see *New York Sun*, March 15, 1836; a full account is in Janiewski, "Sewing with a Double Thread," pp. 50–59. On the 1844 strike, see *Working Man's Advocate*, July 24, 1844; Andrews and Bliss, *History of Women in Trade Unions*, p. 58.

34   " 'The Men Are as Bad as Their Masters': Socialism, Feminism, and Sexual Antagonism in the London Tailoring Trade in the Early 1830s," *Feminist Studies* 5 (Spring 1979), p. 30.

35   Quoted in Wilentz, *Chants Democratic*, p. 253.

36   Alice Kessler-Harris, " 'Where Are the Organized Women Workers?' " *Feminist Studies* 3 (Fall 1975): 92–111; Meredith Tax, *The Rising of the Women* (New York, 1980); Susan Levine, *Labor's True Woman: Carpet Weavers, Industrialization and Labor Reform in the Gilded Age* (Philadelphia, 1984).

37   See, for example, the mentions of women in Evans's *Working Man's Advocate*, August 10, September 14, 1844, June 7, 14, 1845 and in Walsh's *The Subterranean*, September 13, 1845, May 30, November 14, 1846.

38   *Herald*, June 7, 1853; *New York Sun*, March 3, 1845.

39   *National Trades' Union*, July 4, 1835.

40   *Working Man's Advocate*, March 8, 1845; *Herald*, March 4, 1845.

41   *Evening Post*, March 7, 1845.

42   *Daily Sentinel*, March 5, 1831.

43   *New York Express*, March 7, 1845.

44   *Evening Post*, March 7, 1845.

45   Dublin provides an extended discussion of republicanism and labor militance at Lowell in *Women at Work*, pp. 86–131.

46   *New York Express*, March 7, 1845.

47   *Evening Post*, March 7, 1845.

48   *Herald*, June 7, 1853.

49   *Working Man's Advocate*, March 22, 1845, March 8, 1845.

50   *Herald*, March 15, 1845.

51   *New York Express*, March 7, 1845; *The Man*, June 19, 1835; *Evening Post*, March 7, 1845. Similarly, in the New York shirtwaist makers' strike in 1909, employers taunted the girls with sexual slurs and police put them in jail cells with prostitutes. Tax, *Rising of the Women*, pp. 220–21.

52   Wilentz, *Chants Democratic*, pp. 364–86.

53   *Daily Tribune*, September 4, 10, 18, 1850.

54   Ibid., April 9, 1850; Penny, *Employments of Women*, pp. 282–83.

55   Straw sewers had gone on strike again in the late 1840s. *Herald*, June 7, 1853. The 1851 meeting is reported in *Daily Tribune*, February 5, 1851.

56   "Address of Shirt Sewers' Cooperative" and "Circular of the Shirt Sewers' Association," Broadsides Collection, NYHS.

57   Ibid.; Engels, *Condition of the Working-Class*, p. 248.

58   *Daily Tribune,* June 8, 1853.

59   Ibid., December 14, 1850; Andrews and Bliss, *History of Women in Trade Unions,* pp. 61, 89. On the peculiar case of women in the printing industry, see Ava Baron, "Women and the Making of the American Working Class: A Study of the Proletarianization of Printers," *Review of Radical Political Economics* 14 (Fall 1982): 23–42.

60   The Lynn strike of 1860 involved both men and women and was the largest strike in the United States to that date. Women invoked republican rhetoric; most women were involved in the strike as family members. Dawley, *Class and Community,* pp. 81–83, 228. Mary Blewett argues that by the late nineteenth century, *independent* female wage earners were at the forefront of labor militance in the shoe industry. "The Union of Sex and Craft in the Haverhill Shoe Strike of 1895," *Labor History* 20 (Summer 1979): 352–75. Nonetheless, I think that the *persistence* of female republican militance and its *transmission* to successive generations in the shoe industry can be traced to the family culture in which women worked for most of the century.

61   Some excellent feminist scholarship has examined the results of cross-class alliances between middle- and working-class women: Linda Gordon, *Women's Body, Women's Right: A Social History of Birth Control in America* (New York, 1976); Mari Jo Buhle, *Women and American Socialism* (Urbana, Ill., 1981); Tax, *Rising of the Women.*

CHAPTER 8: DOMESTIC SERVICE

1   Catharine E. Beecher and Harriet Beecher Stowe, *The American Woman's Home* (New York, 1869), pp. 320–21.

2   Sedgwick, *Live and Let Live; Or Domestic Service Illustrated* (New York, 1856), p. 71.

3   The ethnic breakdowns of applicants for positions through the employment agency run by the Society for the Encouragement of Faithful Domestic Servants in the late 1820s illustrate the heterogeneity of the class, although the Irish already predominated. The next largest groups were native-born whites and blacks, followed by small numbers of English, Scots-Irish, Germans and French. Society for the Encouragement of Faithful Domestic Servants, *First Annual Report* (1826), p. 3; *Third Annual Report* (1828), pp. 16–17; *Fifth Annual Report* (1830), pp. 7–8. The servant class was also highly diverse in London in this period, recruited from sources as diverse as the impoverished gentry and the rural proletariat, Scots and Irish, blacks and continentals. J. Jean Hecht, *The Domestic Servant Class in Eighteenth Century England* (London, 1956), p. 19.

4   CGS, People v. Linipera, January 8, 1805.

5   See, for example, Minute Books, January 23, 1815, SRPW. The society recognized the impracticability of mothers with more than one child going into service, but the managers had a policy of refusing assistance to women with only one child on the grounds that they would "subject themselves to less distress by going out to service." Ibid., December 12, 1803. The *Evening Post,* October 27, 1815, also

mentions the dilemma of single mothers with many children who were "incapacitated from going into service" in a report on the House of Industry. Matthew Carey maintained that in Philadelphia in the early 1830s, not one in fifty of the hundreds of women desperate for work could go into service because they were needed by their families. *A Plea for the Poor*, p. 8. The relationship of service to workingwomen's life cycles is detailed in Theresa M. McBride, *The Domestic Revolution: The Modernisation of Household Service in England and France 1820–1920* (New York, 1976).

6   The 1855 census reported 23,386 Irish servants in the city, of the total (31,749). Ernst, *Immigrant Life*, p. 215. The preponderance of young Irish women in service is noted throughout the writings of contemporaries, but see especially Penny, *Employments of Women*, pp. 425–26, and Beecher and Stowe, *American Woman's Home*, p. 327. In a statistical study of servants in Buffalo, Laurence Glasco corroborates the basic patterns I have described here. Few native-born women became domestics; the Irish did, but they began to leave service at age 21 to marry, and there were no Irish women so employed after age 26. "The Life Cycles and Household Structure of American Ethnic Groups: Irish, German, and Native-born Whites in Buffalo, New York, 1855," *Journal of Urban History* 1 (May 1975): 339–64.

7   Frances J. Grund, *The Americans In Their Moral, Social and Political Relations*, 2 vols. (London, 1837), 2:6. See also William Cobbett, *A Year's Residence in the United States of America* (London, 1818), p. 340; Carey, *A Plea for the Poor*, p. 9; and Society for the Encouragement of Faithful Domestic Servants, *First Annual Report* (1826), p. 3. The society found "an insuperable pride, which revolts at the very name of servant" which was so strong that when it awarded monetary prizes for longevity in service, some domestics refused the money rather than be named publicly as servants. Ibid., pp. 13–14. For the later period, see Penny, *Employments of Women*, p. 426.

8   On employment patterns for girls, House of Refuge Papers, Case Histories (HRCH), 1825–1860. In 1855, 1,025 blacks were domestic servants. Ernst, *Immigrant Life*, p. 215. For blacks in the retinues of the wealthy, see Ann Sophia Stephens [Jonathan Slick], *High Life in New York* (Philadelphia, 1854), passim. For blacks in brothels, see Sanger, *History of Prostitution*, p. 554. On Germans, see the figures in Ernst, *Immigrant Life*, p. 215.

9   In 1800, a servant's wages were commonly $2/week; in 1835, $1.50/week; from 1845 to 1860, $1/week. Pomerantz, *New York: An American City*, p. 220; Harriet Martineau, *Society in America*, 2 vols. (New York, 1837), 2:249; *The Man*, June 24, 1835; Carey, "Essays on the Public Charities of Philadelphia," p. 193; *Daily Tribune*, November 6, 1845; Penny, *Employments of Women*, p. 426. Like all wage figures from this period, these lack precision and specificity, but they provide a rough comparison to the outside wages that were common for a fully employed needlewoman. In 1830, women sewing low-priced shirts made about 90¢/week; in 1845, moderately priced work yielded about $1.50/week; in 1853, $2.50/week; and in 1859, 83 percent of the women whom Sanger interviewed in his survey of New York prostitution had earned $1–$3/week at their former trades. *Working Man's Advocate*, September 11, 1830, March 8, 1845; *Herald*, June 7, 1853; Sanger, *History of Prostitution*, p. 527.

10   Alan L. Olmstead, *New York City Mutual Savings Banks, 1819–1861* (Chapel Hill, N.C., 1976), p. 51. Saving was a valued part of a domestic's life; Theresa M. McBride notes that it was particularly important in Europe for French girls from the country, who came from a peasantry culturally attuned to accumulation. *The Domestic Revolution*, pp. 82, 97, 119.

11   Charles Lockwood, *Bricks & Brownstones* (New York, 1972), pp. 11–25; Dayton, *Last Days of Knickerbocker Life*, pp. 26–27.

12   A girl committed to the House of Refuge gave this as a reason she had been turned out from one of her positions in service. HRCH, Case #538 (1827).

13   See, for example, Haswell, *Reminiscences of New York*, p. 69.

14   Ibid.

15   Lydia Maria Child, *The American Frugal Housewife* (New York, 1841), pp. 13–18; *The Domestic's Companion* (New York, 1834); Society for the Encouragement of Faithful Domestic Servants, *Third Annual Report* (1828), p. 23.

16   Haswell, *Reminiscences of New York*, p. 70; Martineau, *Society in America*, 2:251.

17   Child, *Letters from New York; Second Series*, pp. 279–80.

18   "Needle and Garden," p. 327.

19   Maria C. Todd Diary, NYHS. My own reading of prosperous women's diaries differs from the view that Patricia Branca develops in "Image and Reality: The Myth of the Idle Victorian Woman," in *Clio's Consciousness Raised*, ed. Mary Hartman and Lois W. Banner (New York, 1974), pp. 179–89. Branca argues that the freedom of Victorian women from domestic work is a myth.

20   Julia Ann Harkness Lay Diary, Manuscript Room, NYPL.

21   Dudden, *Serving Women*, pp. 5, 46.

22   Foster, *New York In Slices*, p. 38.

23   A particularly striking—and sometimes poignant—document in this regard is Julia Lay's journal. A generous and loving woman whose anxieties and concerns dispel any notion that problems of status and class identity are only for the hypocritical and selfish, Lay often wrote of how her acquisitions of furniture and clothes contributed to her very shaky sense of being a lady. The place of the home in developing bourgeois consciousness in Victorian England is discussed in Davidoff, "The Rationalization of Housework," pp. 121–51. For novelists' caricatures of the phenomenon, see Sedgwick, *Clarence*, pp. 43, 52; Hankins, *Women of New York*, pp. 143–49.

24   Quoted in Ryan, *Womanhood in America*, 1st ed., p. 157.

25   *An Authentic Statement of . . . Rose Butler*, p. 6.

26   Lockwood, *Bricks & Brownstones*, pp. 70, 159, 167, 182–83, 186; Blackmar, "Housing and Property Relations," pp. 189–94. There are comments on the bad living conditions of domestics in the *Daily Tribune*, November 6, 1845; Beecher and Stowe, *American Woman's Home*, p. 323; Penny, *Employments of Women*, p. 425; Sedgwick, *Live and Let Live*, pp. 119, 191.

27   Sanger, *History of Prostitution*, p. 527; Augusta H. Worthen, "Servants," *Godey's Lady's Book and Magazine* 68 (1864): 285. See also Dudden, *Serving Women*, pp. 104–154 on the "servant problem" nationwide.

28   Penny, *Employments of Women*, p. 403; *Daily Tribune*, November 6, 1845; also, Foster, *New York In Slices*, p. 39; Beecher and Stowe, *American Woman's Home*, p. 321.

29   *An Authentic Statement . . . of Rose Butler*, p. 10. I have come across other references to arson attempts by servants, one in HRCH, case #2579 (1840); the other, in Elizabeth Bleecker Diary, November 19, 1806, NYPL. The latter is especially fascinating because Mrs. Bleecker seems to treat the attempt—by a black girl —so matter-of-factly. Poisoning seems to have been a form of reprisal associated with black servants. See CGS, People v. Rankin and People v. Margaret and Diana, December 8, 1806 and People v. Sims, July 16, 1835 (a case where a white girl claims she learned about poison from a black woman servant).

30   Leonore Davidoff has argued that a preoccupation with dirt was a new development in the early nineteenth century, and that it was a way that women defined themselves as bourgeois. Up to the mid-eighteenth century, the life styles of the rich and poor were not distinguished by the presence or absence of dirt. Most important, she argues that genteel housewives were as much concerned with ritualistic tidying and polishing as with dirt itself. "The Rationalization of Housework," pp. 127–28. Dudden also stresses the obsession of American ladies with dirt. *Serving Women*, pp. 138–45.

31   *Diary of George Templeton Strong*, 2:2 (entry for January 5, 1850).

32   Alan Gowans, *Images of American Living* (Philadelphia, 1964), pp. 287, 298–300; Celia Jackson Otto, *American Furniture of the Nineteenth Century* (New York, 1965), pp. 119, 122. For mentions of overcrowded Victorian rooms by contemporary New Yorkers, see Thorburn, *Fifty Years' Reminiscences*, p. 208; Stephens, *High Life in New York*, pp. 20–22; Sedgwick, *Live and Let Live*, p. 191, and *Clarence*, pp. 309–310, 319–20. See the Lay Diary for a chronicle of the acquisitions in furniture and ornaments of a modest middle-class family over time.

33   Caroline A. Dunstan Diary, April 7, 1859, NYPL.

34   Lockwood, *Bricks & Brownstones*, p. 178; Sedgwick, *Live and Let Live*, pp. 48–49; John S. Ewing and Nancy Norton, *Broadlooms and Businessmen* (Cambridge, Mass., 1955), p. 13.

35   Groneman, "Working-Class Immigrant Women," p. 258.

36   "It is very common to say, 'There is no use in trying to teach an Irish person.'" Sedgwick, *Live and Let Live*, p. 71.

37   *Three Years Among the Working Classes*, pp. 84, 298.

38   Phila A. Williams Diary, May 13, 1844, Delaplaine Collection, NYHS; Todd Diary, June 2, 1838; Edwin L. Godkin, *Reflections and Comments: 1865–1895* (New York, 1895), p. 64.

39   Leonore Davidoff has analyzed the psychological associations of class, cleanliness and femininity in English Victorian culture in "The Rationalization of Housework" and in her remarkable essay, "Class and Gender in Victorian England: The Diaries of Arthur J. Munby and Hannah Cullwick," *Feminist Studies* 5 (Spring 1979): 86–133.

40   Worthen, "Servants," p. 285. There was a strong tendency among women writers on domestic matters to counsel reform in the class-conscious manner of

dealing with servants so prevalent after 1840, a tendency that produced critical descriptions of mistresses such as this one.

41 Beecher and Stowe, *American Woman's Home,* pp. 325, 323.

42 *Daily Tribune,* September 16, 1846.

43 Dunstan Diary, July 30, August 6, 14, 1857.

44 "The Managers are convinced that the greatest proportion of the Misery, and Poverty which actually exists among the lower classes in this City, arises principally from the two following causes—viz.—Intemperance among the men, and the Love of dress among the Women." Minutes, November 21, 1822, SRPW. See also Society for the Encouragement of Faithful Domestic Servants, *First Annual Report,* p. 12.

45 SPP, *Documents Relative to Savings Banks, Intemperance and Lotteries* (New York, 1819), p. 8.

46 *Daily Tribune,* September 3, 1845; Penny, *Employments of Women,* pp. 325–26.

47 Foster, *New York In Slices,* p. 37.

48 Vere Foster, *Work and Wages; or, The Penny Emigrant's Guide to the United States and Canada* (London, [1855]), p. 9.

49 Dunstan Diary, July 27, 1859.

50 Hecht, *The Domestic Servant Class,* pp. 115–23.

51 Society for the Encouragement of Faithful Domestic Servants, *Third Annual Report* (1828), p. 6. The same tendency in England is described in Pamela Horn, *The Rise and Fall of the Victorian Servant* (New York, 1975), pp. 11–12.

52 Hankins, *Women of New York,* p. 17.

53 Ibid.; *Daily Tribune,* November 6, 1845; see also August 25, 1844. Other descriptions of the finery of poor women can be found in "Needle and Garden," pp. 166–68; [Sedgwick], *The Poor Rich Man,* p. 98. Since prostitutes in New York were recognized by their gorgeous dress, there were erotic associations that underlay gaudy clothing. Caroline Dunstan criticized her servants' dress in her diary, January 5, July 30, 1857. Beecher and Stowe advised a strategy of influence rather than direct interference for mistresses trying to change their domestics' mode of dress. *American Woman's Home,* p. 330.

54 Penny, *Employments of Women,* p. 403.

55 Ibid., pp. 403, 424.

56 Lynn Hollen Lees, *Exiles of Erin: Irish Migrants in Victorian London* (Ithaca, N.Y., 1979), p. 107.

57 Article reprinted in the *Irish American* (New York), July 7, 1855.

58 Penny, *Employments of Women,* p. 403.

59 *Daily Tribune,* November 6, 1845.

60 Minutes, March 27, 1840, Association for the Relief of Respectable, Aged and Indigent Females in New York City.

61 Hecht, *The Domestic Servant Class,* pp. 127–40. Hecht's generalizations for England are confirmed for the United States by one fragmentary piece of evidence, the testimony of the young arsonist Rose Butler about her social life while working in service in 1819 in *An Authentic Statement of . . . Rose Butler.*

62 *Daily Tribune,* September 16, 1846. On the limitations on receiving guests,

see also Penny, *Employments of Women*, p. 424; Burn, *Three Years Among the Working Classes*, p. 84. One of the points Irish women bargained for was time off to wash their own clothes. Foster, *New York In Slices*, p. 2; *Daily Tribune*, November 6, 1845; Penny, *Employments of Women*, p. 149.

63   Ibid., pp. 233, 426; see also p. 424 for the difficulty of getting Sundays off.

64   Bobo, *Glimpses of New-York*, p. 193. See also Sedgwick, *Live and Let Live*, pp. 49–51, 100. There is a vivid description of the Sunday night promenade on Broadway of domestic servants who had just gotten off work in Foster, *New York In Slices*, pp. 99–100.

65   Sanger, *History of Prostitution*, p. 517. The function of intelligence offices in recruiting prostitutes is evident in the HRCH, 1825–60, passim; it is also mentioned by contemporaries: Dall, *"Woman's Right to Labor,"* p. 174; Foster, *New York In Slices*, p. 39; *Irish American*, September 10, 1853.

66   Penny, *Employments of Women*, p. 427.

67   Society for the Encouragement of Faithful Domestic Servants, *Third Annual Report* (1828), p. 23.

68   Beecher and Stowe, *American Woman's Home*, p. 313.

69   Ibid., p. 322.

CHAPTER 9: WOMEN ON THE TOWN

1   Two recent works, Walkowitz, *Prostitution in Victorian Society* and Ruth Rosen, *The Lost Sisterhood in America, 1900–1918* (Baltimore, Md., 1982), set the historical discussion of prostitution on a new footing.

2   *Columbian* (New York), December 30, 1818. Whiteaker also notes the general tolerance for prostitution in the eighteenth and early nineteenth centuries. "Moral Reform and Prostitution," pp. 21–26.

3   J. R. McDowall, *Magdalen Facts* (New York, 1832), p. 7. A Grand Jury investigation of the extent of the problem in 1831 found only 1,388 prostitutes in a ward-by-ward survey taken by the watch. *Working Man's Advocate*, August 20, 1831.

4   National Trades' Union "Report . . . on Female Labor" in Commons et al., *Documentary History*, 6:217, 282; *Working Man's Advocate*, March 8, 1845; Carey, "Essays on the Public Charities of Philadelphia," pp. 154, 161; *Daily Tribune*, June 8, 1853. In the comments of the *Working Man's Advocate* on prostitution and on the Magdalen Society, one can see the similarities of the evangelical analysis to that of supporters of labor. Ibid., September 11, 1830, July 30, 1831.

5   Sanger, *History of Prostitution*, p. 29. Public interest in New York was also prompted by concerns about syphilis. See the comments in the reports from the Penitentiary Hospital contained in Commissioners of the Almshouse, *Annual Reports* (1849–60).

6   Matsell's letter is reprinted in Sanger, *History of Prostitution*, p. 576.

7   Commitments of disorderly house keepers to the First District Prison rose from 17 in 1849 to 90 in 1860. Commissioners of the Almshouse, *Annual Reports*. The magnitude of vagrancy commitments in the 1850s is especially striking compared to the figure of 3,173 commitments for the entire *decade* 1820–30 a Grand Jury gave

for commitments exclusive of assault and battery (which mostly comprised drunkenness and vagrancy). Report quoted in *Working Man's Advocate*, August 20, 1831.

Commitments to the city prisons for vagrancy rose from 3,552 in 1850 to 6,552 in 1860.

YEAR	NUMBER OF MEN	NUMBER OF WOMEN	TOTAL	PERCENTAGE OF WOMEN
1850	1,148	2,204	3,552	62
1851	1,305	2,225	3,530	63
1852	1,797	3,396	5,193	65
1853	2,417	3,824	6,241	61
1855	1,656	3,598	5,254	68
1860	1,816	4,736	6,552	72

Source: Commissioners of the Almshouse, *Annual Reports*. There are no complete figures for 1849, 1854, 1856–59.

Commitments of females aged ten to thirty years old comprised between 49 and 65 percent of the total female commitments in those years in the 1850s when age breakdowns are available (for the First District Prison, the largest in the city).

8   Eighty-eight percent of Sanger's interviewees were fifteen to thirty years old. *History of Prostitution*, p. 452. These women were around marrying age, and there was a demographic undercurrent to their situations: The disproportional sex ratio in New York lessened their chances of marrying.

9   Sanger, *History of Prostitution*, p. 29.

10   Ibid., pp. 549–59.

11   Rosen, *The Lost Sisterhood*, pp. 32–33.

12   Sanger, *History of Prostitution*, pp. 559–73.

13   Citizens' Association, *Report of the Council of Hygiene and Public Health*, p. 26. For descriptions of a similar variety of establishments in London, see Dr. Fernando Henriques, *Modern Sexuality* (London, 1968); Kellow Chesney, *The Victorian Underworld* (New York, 1972), pp. 307–365.

14   The beginnings of the sex trade were already evident in the 1830s, when John McDowall sought to expose the traffic in pornography in the city. Whiteaker, "Moral Reform and the Prostitute," p. 182. George Foster provides a tour of commercial sex establishments in *New York by Gas-Light*. See also Batterberry, *On the Town in New York*, pp. 102, 104 for some of the "lowest" of the city's night spots. Indictments for various kinds of "indecent exhibitions" can be found in CGS, People v. Brennan and People v. Fowler et al., March 22, 1848; People v. Hamilton et al., March 24, 1848 and for obscene reading matter and prints, People v. Ryan, September 28, 1842, People v. Shaw, July 1844, People v. Carns, June 21, 1844, People v. Miller et al., October 16, 1835.

15   Sanger, *History of Prostitution*, p. 492. Sanger estimated that the Panic of 1857 had sent 500–1,000 new prostitutes out on the streets. Ibid., p. 34.

16   Ibid., pp. 524, 528, 529; see also p. 532.

17   Peiss, " 'Charity Girls' and City Pleasures," pp. 74–87.

18   Sanger, *History of Prostitution,* p. 491.

19   Ibid., pp. 473, 475, 539.

20   Ibid., pp. 506–508.

21   The European writers are analyzed in Walkowitz, *Prostitution in Victorian Society,* pp. 36–47.

22   Sanger, *History of Prostitution,* pp. 488–89.

23   Ibid., p. 488.

24   Ibid., p. 524; see also McDowall, *Magdalen Facts,* p. 53.

25   The Irish were overrepresented in Sanger's sample (28 percent of the total population was Irish in 1855); the Germans (16 percent of the population) were underrepresented. Ibid., pp. 460, 536.

26   Ibid.

27   Commissioners of the Almshouse, *Annual Report* (1849), pp. 160–61.

28   HRCH, cases #232 (1827), #191 (1826).

29   Quoted in Robert S. Pickett, *House of Refuge: Origins of Juvenile Reform in New York State, 1815–1857* (Syracuse, N.Y., 1969), p. 3.

30   HRCH, cases #60 (1825), #1559 (1835), #538 (1828). My interpretations of children's lives in this chapter and elsewhere are based on my reading of 455 girls' cases from the House of Refuge—all girls committed each year at five-year intervals 1825–60—and assorted other cases of both boys and girls, totaling about 700 cases.

31   On the Victorian gentleman's erotic fascination with working-class life, see Davidoff, "Class and Gender in Victorian England." The pedophilic propensities of late Victorian men are described in Eric Trudgill, *Madonnas and Magdalens: The Origin and Development of Victorian Sexual Attitudes* (New York, 1976), pp. 90–100 and Ronald Pearsall, *The Worm in the Bud: The World of Victorian Sexuality* (London, 1969), pp. 350–63. Many of Carroll's photographs are in Graham Ovenden and Robert Melville, eds., *Victorian Children* (New York, 1972).

32   Obviously there are problems with using rape records as evidence of sexual expectations and practices; the investigation of a crime is necessarily limited in what it can tell us about legitimated forms of sexuality. Court cases themselves, as I have noted before, present many problems in the authenticity of evidence which was, after all, constructed to persuade a judge and/or jury. Nonetheless, much can be learned. The descriptions of rape, however distorted in the courtroom setting, reveal something of where people, especially women, drew the line between licit and illicit sex. And conflicting evidence in the trials themselves can also be a source of historical understanding, illuminating the different ways in which the (female) victims and the (male) perpetrators perceived and experienced certain sexual acts.

33   In a random sample of 101 rape cases between 1820 and 1860 tried before the Court of General Sessions, 26 involved complainants who were under 16 years of age. Of these, 19 were under 12 years old (the youngest was 4), 5 under 16 and 2 of age unknown.

34   CGS, People v. Hynes, February 17, 1842.

35   People v. Foyce, May 11, 1854, People v. Plonsha, June 14, 1848.

36   People v. O'Connor, August 10, 1849.

37   HRCH, case #712 (1830).

38   McDowall, *Magdalen Facts*, p. 53; Charles Loring Brace, *The Dangerous Classes of New York, and Twenty Years' Work Among Them* (New York, 1872), p. 135.

39   HRCH, case #61 (1825).

40   McDowall, *Magdalen Facts*, p. 53.

41   HRCH, case #1421 (1834), #2480 (1840).

42   Ibid., case #209 (1826).

43   *Diary of George Templeton Strong*, 2:57 (July 7, 1851); see also Robinson, *Hot Corn*, p. 267.

44   [Society for the Reformation of Juvenile Delinquents in the City of New York], *Examination of Subjects Who Are in the House of Refuge* (Albany, N.Y., 1825); HRCH, case #5 (1825).

45   Records of the County Coroner, passim; New York City Inspector, *Annual Report* (1849); Gordon, *Woman's Body, Woman's Right*, pp. 26–71.

46   Ibid., pp. 203–204.

47   HRCH, case #2513 (1840).

48   Sanger, *History of Prostitution*, pp. 488, 500, 502.

49   HRCH, cases #2487 (1840), #3628 (1845), #4882 (1850).

50   HRCH, cases #326 (1827), #737 (1830), #2555 (1840).

51   Ibid., case #2442 (1838).

52   Quoted in Sedgwick, *Poor Rich Man*, p. 168.

53   HRCH, case #576 (1829).

54   Ibid., cases #1613 (1835), #1585 (1835).

55   Sanger, *History of Prostitution*, pp. 494, 496, 536; an early example of the seduced-and-abandoned tale is in Prime, *Life in New York*, pp. 15–30.

56   Ibid., p. 536.

57   HRCH, cases #261 (1827), #1548 (1835).

58   Brace, *Dangerous Classes*, p. 118.

CHAPTER 10: THE USES OF THE STREETS

1   CAS, *Third Annual Report* (1856), pp. 26–27.

2   Smith Rosenberg gives a general account of this shift in *Religion and the Rise of the American City*.

3   "Semi-Annual Report of the Chief of Police," *Documents of the Board of Aldermen*, vol. 17, part 1 (1850), p. 58.

4   Short biographies of Matsell can be found in *Appleton's Cyclopaedia of American Biography; The Palimpsest* 5 (July 1924): 237–48, and Walter Hugins, *Jacksonian Democracy and the Working Class: A Study of the New York Workingmen's Movement 1829–1837* (Stanford, Calif., 1960), p. 103.

5   *The Subterranean*, January 2, 1847; Walsh quoted in James F. Richardson, *The New York Police: Colonial Times to 1901* (New York, 1970), p. 56.

6   "Semi-Annual Report," pp. 58, 62, 59, 63.

7   Buckley, "To the Opera House," pp. 353–66.

8   Emma Brace, ed., *The Life of Charles Loring Brace . . . Edited By His Daughter* (New York, 1894).

9   Beecher, *A Treatise on Domestic Economy* (1841; New York, 1977), p. 14.

10   *Daily Tribune,* July 4, 1850.

11   Bell Diary, entry for April 19, 1851.

12   A striking case of overcrowding is reported in the *Daily Tribune,* June 8, 1853: Eleven women and children were living in a cellar on Avenue C, with "nothing in the world but what they stood up in; and some had even borrowed their rags from their companions." By 1865, overcrowding in New York was greater than in London or any other European city, one investigating committee claimed. Density in the Fourth Ward was an estimated 192,000 persons per square mile, as compared to the recent estimate of 175,816 for East London. Citizens' Association, *Report,* pp. lxxi–lxxii.

13   Statistics on public health come from Duffy, *History of Public Health,* pp. 447, 452–53, 587, 577–79; quote is from Citizens' Association, *Report,* p. 180. On Britain, see E. P. Thompson, *The Making of the English Working Class* (New York, 1966), pp. 326–27.

14   Quoted in Wilentz, *Chants Democratic,* p. 366.

15   Schneider, *History of Public Welfare,* p. 269; Degler, "Labor in the Economy and Politics of New York," pp. 188 and 157–97 passim; *Herald,* October 21, 1857. The quote is in Degler, "Labor in the Economy and Politics of New York," p. 196.

16   Smith Rosenberg, *Religion and the Rise of the American City,* pp. 186–273. To be sure, these reformers had not abandoned the Christian mission of their predecessors. The AICP, the city's largest and most powerful charity at midcentury, was an offshoot of the NYCTS and maintained close intellectual and professional ties with it. Robert Hartley, head of the AICP, was an evangelical convert of the 1830s. The NYCTS itself shifted its aims to more temporal goals during the 1840s. By the late years of that decade the members were presenting information about wages and the cost of living in their annual report along with customary tabulations of the number of souls saved. While the "secular" charities infused the physical surroundings of the poor with moral character, the "religious" charities became interested in the physical character of the immoral life. Charles E. and Carroll S. Rosenberg, "Pietism and the Origins of the American Public Health Movement," *Journal of the History of Medicine* 23 (January 1968): 16–35.

Scientific environmentalism, in secularizing moral concerns, probably popularized reform among a broader clientele—people indifferent or disinclined to organized religion, like Matsell himself, who had grown up in the freethinking milieu of the Owenites and the Workingmen's Party.

17   The conflict between the Methodist ladies and the forward-looking environmentalist Louis Pease over the direction of the Five Points Mission is one example. Pease won. Smith Rosenberg, *Religion and the Rise of the American City.*

18   Griscom, *The Sanitary Condition of the Laboring Population.*

19   New York Assembly, *Report . . . into the Condition of Tenant Houses,* p. 8. See also Citizens' Association, *Report* (1865).

20   New York Assembly, *Report . . . into the Condition of Tenant Houses,* p. 8.

21   Ibid.

22   Ibid., p. 14.

23   Ibid., p. 31. There is more than a hint of racism here, contingent upon a largely immigrant poor: The emphasis on deformed bodily features, and the buried allusions to animals become at moments more explicit. Babies are "weazened" like monkeys and the prevalence of pink-eye among the children invites comparisons to troglodytes, bats and moles.

24   Ibid., p. 12. Poverty, the committee added, was "to be seen in its real aspect at home, and no where else." (Ibid., p. 13.)

25   AICP, *Thirteenth Annual Report* (1856), p. 23; New York Assembly, *Report . . . into the Condition of Tenant Houses*, p. 50. Cf. *Diary of George Templeton Strong*, 2:200: "If the word 'home' can be applied to their wretched abiding-places," he wrote of working-class children (entry for November 30, 1854).

26   AICP, *Fourteenth Annual Report* (1857), p. 21.

27   New York Assembly, *Report . . . into the Condition of Tenant Houses*, p. 32. On the conflation of the problem of poverty with that of public health, see Charles E. Rosenberg, *The Cholera Years* (Chicago, 1962).

28   For the New England situation, see Dublin, *Women and Work*, p. 140 and Prude, *Coming of Industrial Order*, pp. 85–87; on the paucity of apprenticeships, Stott, "Workers in the Metropolis," pp. 116–22; also John Commerford, quoted in Degler, "Labor in the Economy and Politics of New York," p. 157 and CAS, *Seventh Annual Report* (1860), p. 7.

In the visibility of its population of juvenile casual laborers, New York resembled London, where crowds of ragged street children similarly fascinated the respectable. In both cities, children constituted almost one-third of the population. The proportion of children under fifteen years in the total urban population was, in London in 1851, 31.9 percent; in New York in 1850, 31.6 percent. In Paris, in contrast, children under fifteen made up only 19.6 percent of the total population. These figures are computed from Hough, *Statistics of the Population . . . of New York;* Great Britain, Parliament, *Parliamentary Papers*, 1852–53, vol. 88, part 1 (*Population*, vol. 8), p. 1; Louis Chevalier, *Labouring Classes and Dangerous Classes in Paris During the First Half of the Nineteenth Century* (New York, 1973), pp. 224–25, 233 ff.

29   *Diary of George Templeton Strong*, 2:149 (entry for January 14, 1854).

30   Penny, *Employments of Women*, pp. 133–34, 143–44, 150–52, 168, 421, 473, 484; Burns, *Life in New York;* Phillip Wallys, *About New York*, p. 50; CAS, *First Annual Report* (1854), pp. 23–24, *Seventh Annual Report* (1860), p. 16. For the butterfly seller, see Penny, *Employments of Women*, p. 484.

31   The aggressive character of juveniles on the streets and the prevalence of juvenile petty theft is discussed in David R. Johnson, "Crime Patterns in Philadelphia, 1840–70," in *The Peoples of Philadelphia: A History of Ethnic Groups and Lower Class Life, 1790–1940*, ed. Allen F. Davis and Mark H. Haller (Philadelphia, 1973).

The Common Council periodically tried to limit street hawking because of the facility it provided children to steal. *MCC*, 13:393 (December 15, 1823); 17:606 (January 26, 1829); 17:744–45 (March 23, 1829). There were also attempts to constrain scavenging and the trade in scavenged goods. In 1809, a group of citizens petitioned the council to outlaw the secondhand trade in articles from "children, apprentices and others." Ibid., 5:515 (April 17, 1809). By 1817, the council had passed the statute which William Bell was to enforce in 1850, prohibiting the secondhand dealers from trading with minors. *Laws and Ordinances . . . of the City of New-York* (1817), p. 112. In 1823, in consultation with the Society for the Reformation of Juvenile Delinquents, the city's ship carpenters passed a rule forbidding chip-picking in the shipyards, thus abrogating a customary gleaning right of the poor. Pickett, *House of Refuge*, pp. 41–42.

32   HRCH, case #5420 (1852).

33   Wallys, *About New York*, p. 43.

34   HRCH, cases #6032 (1854), #6354 (1855); "Semi-Annual Report," pp. 59–60.

35   See Commissioners of the Almshouse, *Annual Report* (1851), p. 64 for the rising alarm over juvenile crime. Vagrancy figures are also in the *Annual Reports*.

36   Brace, *Dangerous Classes*, p. 135.

37   Foster, *New York in Slices*, p. 20.

38   CAS, *Fifth Annual Report* (1858), p. 38.

39   See the Bell Diary, passim, for examples of the ease with which children sold stolen goods.

40   *Daily Tribune*, June 3, 1850.

41   "Semi-Annual Report," p. 65; CAS, *Second Annual Report* (1855), p. 45; HRCH, case #6032 (1854).

42   Brace, *Dangerous Classes*, p. 91. Cf. CAS, *Second Annual Report* (1855), p. 4: "to *have no home*, but only some lodging-house cellar, or a corner of a garret in which to live; to be cold, and drenched, and hungry all day, pushed, kicked and beaten; to have the child's eager want for affection and love, and to receive only abuse or neglect." Two tales of urban waifs are Maria S. Cummins's immensely popular *The Lamplighter* (1854) and John Treat Irving, *Harry Harson: or, The Benevolent Bachelor* (1844).

43   CAS, *Fifth Annual Report* (1858), pp. 39–40; *Second Annual Report* (1855), p. 45.

44   Ibid., *Sixth Annual Report* (1859), p. 67; *Third Annual Report* (1856), p. 39; *Fifth Annual Report* (1858), pp. 38–39.

45   Groneman Pernicone presents a compelling picture of the ability of immigrant families in the city's most "depraved" neighborhood, the Five Points, to expand and encompass those temporarily or permanently detached from nuclear families in " 'The Bloudy Ould Sixth.' "

46   CAS, *Sixth Annual Report* (1859), pp. 67–68; *Fifth Annual Report* (1858), p. 61.

47   Ibid., *Sixth Annual Report* (1859), p. 58; *Fourth Annual Report* (1857), pp. 43–44; Bell Diary, July 18, 1851.

48   AICP report is from *Fifteenth Annual Report* (1858), p. 38; quote from CAS, *Third Annual Report* (1856), p. 27.

49   Brace, *Dangerous Classes*, p. 47.

50   CAS, *Sixth Annual Report* (1859), p. 9; figures are from Miriam Z. Langsam, *Children West: A History of the Placing-Out System in the New York Children's Aid Society* (Madison, Wis., 1964), p. 64.

51   An important study of the CAS is Bruce Bellingham, " 'Little Wanderers':
A Socio-Historical Study of the Nineteenth Century Origins of Child Fostering
and Adoption Reform" (Ph.D. diss., U. of Pennsylvania, 1984). Bellingham stresses
the semi-independent status of the emigrants, who were largely adolescents, and
also emphasizes the parents' own role in sending children West.

52   Lydia Maria Child, *Letters from New York* (London, 1843), p. 62.

53   Brace, *Dangerous Classes*, p. 234.

54   Lees, *Exiles of Erin*, pp. 35–36. See Bellingham, " 'Little Wanderers,' " pp.
84–204 for a complex and nuanced analysis of parental motives in agreeing to send
children West.

55   CAS, *Third Annual Report* (1856), p. 8.

56   Pickett, *House of Refuge*. This is similar to the shift in criminal law from
corporal punishment to the more "enlightened" environmental techniques of the
penitentiary. See Michael Ignatieff, *A Just Measure of Pain: the Penitentiary in the
Industrial Revolution, 1750–1850* (New York, 1978).

57   CAS, *Second Annual Report* (1855), p. 5. Bender notes that Brace was deeply
influenced by Horace Bushnell, a Connecticut minister important in the dissemina-
tion of liberal theological ideas of influence and women's crucial role in moral
education. *Towards an Urban Vision*, p. 137.

58   CAS, *Fifth Annual Report* (1858), p. 17.

59   Boyer also notes Brace's fascination with street boys. *Urban Masses*, pp. 94ff.
Exemplary passages from Brace's writing are in *Dangerous Classes*, pp. 80–82, 98–99;
"sturdy independence" is from ibid., p. 100.

60   Brace, *Dangerous Classes*, pp. 97–113.

61   CAS, *Ninth Annual Report* (1862), p. 13; *Tenth Annual Report* (1863), p. 23;
Seventh Annual Report (1860), p. 8.

62   Ibid., *Ninth Annual Report* (1862), pp. 17–18; *Eleventh Annual Report* (1864),
p. 28.

63   One historian of social welfare claims the CAS was more influential in the
second half of the nineteenth century than any other child welfare agency. Henry
W. Thurston, *The Dependent Child* (New York, 1930), p. 92.

64   Jamil S. Zainaldin, "The Emergence of a Modern American Family Law:
Child Custody, Adoption, and the Courts, 1796–1851," *Northeastern University Law
Review* 73 (1979): 1038–65; Frederick L. Faust and Paul J. Brantingham, *Juvenile
Justice Philosophy* (St. Paul, Minn., 1975), pp. 52–118; Michael Grossberg, "Law and
the Family in Nineteenth Century America" (Ph.D. diss., Brandeis University,
1979), pp. 257–322.

65   Ex parte Crouse, 4 Whart. 9 (Pa., 1838); Pickett, *House of Refuge*, pp. 75–77.

66   The law is reprinted in the AICP, *Eleventh Annual Report* (1854), pp. 61–62.
On conditions of relief, see *Seventeenth Annual Report* (1860), pp. 31–33.

CONCLUSION

1   Alexander, "Women, Class and Sexual Difference," p. 136.

A Note on Sources

This essay includes those primary sources and secondary materials which I found most helpful. I have not included all the sources on which I depended, since readers who want more detailed information can find it in the notes. Nor have I generally made note of those historical works on women and/or labor published in the last ten or fifteen years, which are readily accessible to the general reader or scholar. In order to help those interested in pursuing further the history of New York, I have listed some manuscript materials which were irrelevant to my purpose but which might help others.

MANUSCRIPT COLLECTIONS

Germinal to this study were the records of female charities on deposit in the Manuscript Room of the New-York Historical Society (NYHS). The papers of the Society for the Relief of Poor Widows with Small Children and the Association for the Asylum for Lying-In Women both contain minute books with the ladies' notes about applicants for aid. Of less value, but still interesting, are the papers of the Asylum for Aged, Indigent and Respectable Females, also at the NYHS.

Diaries of New York women before 1860 are difficult to find; those of laboring women are nonexistent. I located these in the Manuscript Room of the New York Public Library (NYPL): Elizabeth Bleecker Diary, Caroline A. Dunstan Diary, Helen Lansing Grinnell Diary, Julia Harkness Lay Diary. The diaries of Sarah Todd Green, Mary Lorrain Peters, Maria C. Todd and Phila A. Williams are at the NYHS.

General sources on the life of the streets and of the laboring classes are the policeman William H. Bell's diary of his beat at the NYHS and the I. N. Phelps Stokes Collection on New York slums at the NYPL. The Stokes Collection is a massive typed compilation of extracts from nineteenth-century primary sources, cited in full, and thus has the additional virtue of pointing the researcher on to other leads. Finally, the manuscript version of the Philip Hone Diary at the NYHS is indispensable for any student of the social life and politics of the period.

GOVERNMENT REPORTS AND OFFICIAL DOCUMENTS —PUBLISHED AND UNPUBLISHED

Manuscript records of municipal and state officials concerned with the poor are quite helpful in learning about urban class relations. For the very early period,

1789–1820, the Documents of the Common Council, on deposit at the New York Municipal Archives, contain a great deal of information about day-to-day life in the city. I used in particular the papers of the Committee on the Almshouse and Bridewell and the Committee on Charity. The *Minutes of the Common Council,* published in full, are a heterogeneous collection of deliberations, but a complete index helps the researcher locate miscellany that may be useful. The Daily Journals of the New York House of Refuge Papers contain detailed case histories of the poor children incarcerated. They are at the New York State Archives, State Education Department, Albany. The Records of the Foundling Hospital, contained in the Indentures from the New York City Almshouse at the NYHS, are a source of evidence—some of it very moving—about the strategies which poor women used to ensure their babies' survival.

Legal records tell a great deal about gender relations. The Records of Divorce and Separation in the County Clerk's Office, Surrogate Court Building, 31 Chambers Street, New York City, although lengthy and dry, nonetheless offer testimony about the dynamics of marriages. The Coroner's Inquisitions of the New York Supreme Court, on deposit at the Municipal Archives, contain often fascinating details of daily life as well as rare information about abortion and infanticide. Most valuable to me were the Trial Records of the New York Court of General Sessions, also at the Municipal Archives. These contain testimony and documents pertaining to criminal cases tried in the city. The records of rape, homicide and assault-and-battery cases were most relevant to my research, although the court also heard cases of robbery, theft, forgery and kidnapping.

The first census to list women's occupations was the New York State Census of 1855. The population schedules are at the County Clerk's Office. A useful published compilation of census statistics on New York from 1790 to 1860 is Franklin B. Hough, *Statistics of Population of the City and County of New York* (New York, 1865).

REPORTS ON POVERTY

Although this literature is chiefly important for its successive formulations of the "problem" of poverty, some information about social conditions can also be gleaned from it. By the 1840s, municipal officials had caught the British enthusiasm for statistics, and the published reports of the Commissioners of the Almshouse, 1849–60, are packed with statistical information of all kinds on the clients of the municipal welfare system. Other important runs of charity/reform reports are those of the Society for the Encouragement of Faithful Domestic Servants, the Society for the Relief of Poor Widows, the Society for the Prevention of Pauperism, the Association for the Asylum for Lying-In Women, the Association for the Improvement of the Condition of the Poor (all at NYHS), and the New York City Tract Society (available at Union Theological Seminary). Of compelling interest are the evocative and detailed case histories contained in the reports of the Children's Aid Society, also to be found in their entirety at the NYHS. The section on New York in William W. Sanger, *The History of Prostitution* (New York, 1859), commissioned by the city government, provides more raw data on prostitution than I or any other scholar have yet analyzed.

The major treatments of the "tenement class" question are John H. Griscom, *The Sanitary Condition of the Laboring Population of New York* (New York, 1845), "Semi-Annual Report of the Chief of Police," *Documents of the Board of Aldermen*, vol. 17, part 1 (1850); New York Assembly, *Report of the Select Committee into the Condition of Tenant Houses in New-York and Brooklyn*, Doc. 205, 80th sess., 1857; Citizens' Association of New York, *Report of the Council of Hygiene . . . Upon the Sanitary Condition of the City* (New York, 1865).

NEWSPAPERS

Although women are not highly visible in the newspapers of the day, questions of gender can often be read between the lines, and the researcher with a sharp eye can still find in the local news bits of information that bear directly on women. In the early period, the *Independent Mechanic* was the most consistently useful paper. After 1830, news about women and labor begins to appear with some regularity in the *Working Man's Advocate, Daily Tribune, New York Herald, Young America, Daily Sentinel, The Man, The Subterranean, Evening Post*.

CONTEMPORARY ACCOUNTS AND MEMOIRS—PUBLISHED

Memoirs, reminiscences, and accounts of New York society, although often replete with nostalgia, do record otherwise neglected facets of daily life and offer some fascinating observations on gender relations. Among those I used were James Dawson Burn, *Three Years Among the Working-Classes in the United States During the War* (London, 1865), Lydia Maria Child, *Letters from New York* (London, 1843) and *Letters . . . Second Series* (New York, 1845), Abram C. Dayton, *Last Days of Knickerbocker Life in New York* (New York, 1882), Thomas F. De Voe, *The Market Book* (New York, 1862), Reverend Ezra Stiles Ely, *Visits of Mercy* (New York, 1811) and the subsequent *Visits* (London, 1816), Rush C. Hawkins, *Corlears Hook in 1820* (New York, 1904), Grant Thorburn, *Fifty Years' Reminiscences of New-York* (New York, 1845), and especially Charles Loring Brace, *The Dangerous Classes of New York, and Twenty Years' Work Among Them* (New York, 1872).

Published diaries include the *Diary of George Templeton Strong*, ed. Allan Nevins and Milton Halsey Thomas, 2 vols. (New York, 1952)—critical to an understanding of the city—and the more modest but extremely interesting *Diary of Michael Floy, Junior: Bowery Village 1833–1837*, ed. Richard Brooks (New Haven, Conn., 1941).

Some of my most valued findings came from the accounts of labor reformers. Matthew Carey's work is a starting point for anyone interested in antebellum workingwomen. The material on women's wages and working conditions is in *A Plea for the Poor* (Philadelphia, 1831) and scattered throughout *Miscellaneous Essays* (Philadelphia, 1830). Virginia Penny's marvelous *The Employments of Women: A Cyclopaedia of Woman's Work* (Boston, 1863) is a one-woman survey of conditions and wages in every trade in the city where women were known to be employed in 1859.

NOVELS AND JOURNALISM

The lines between novels, journalism and reformers' reports are often blurry: All three forms are structured by similar sorts of plots and narrative concerns—above all the fascination with "life among the lowly." In this vein, the most interesting views of New York are in the books of George C. Foster: *New York In Slices; By an Experienced Carver* (New York, 1849), *New York by Gaslight* (New York, 1850), *New York Naked* (New York, 1850). *The Cries of New-York,* a compilation of street hawkers' songs, is a window into street life. More treatments of the exotica of poverty are in Ned Buntline [E. Z. C. Judson], *The Mysteries and Miseries of New York* (New York, 1848), the journal *Jonathan's Whittlings of War* (New York), William Burns, *Life in New York, In Doors and Out of Doors* (New York, 1851), Solon Robinson, *Hot Corn: Life Scenes in New York Illustrated* (New York, 1854) and the philanthropic *The Old Brewery . . . By Ladies of the Mission* (New York, 1854) and American Female Guardian Society, *Wrecks and Rescues* (New York, 1859).

PUBLISHED TRIALS

The proceedings of sensational trials were often printed up as pamphlets. This literature, especially the murder and rape trials with their keen attention to the comings and goings of the parties involved, are some of the richest sources of evidence about household relations I encountered. Some well-documented ones involving women are *The Hypocrite Unmask'd: Trial and Conviction of John Baker . . . for Seducing Miss Ann Burns* (New York, 1798), *The Only Correct Account of the Life, Trial and Confession of John Banks* (New York, 1806), *Report of the Trial of Henry Bedlow for . . . a Rape of Lanah Sawyer* (New York, 1793), *An Authentic Statement of the Case . . . of Rose Butler* (New York, 1819), *Report of the Trial of Richard D. Croucher . . . for a Rape . . .* (New York, 1800), *Trial for Murder . . . The People vs. George Hart* (New York, 1812), *Report of the Trial of James Johnson, a Black Man, for the Murder of Lewis Robinson, A Black Man* (New York, 1811), *Trial . . . of James Ransom, for the Murder of His Wife* (New York, 1832), James Hardie, *An Impartial Account of the Trial of Mr. Levi Weeks, for the Supposed Murder of Miss Julianna Elmore Sands* (New York, 1800), *Report of the Trial of Levi Weeks* (New York, 1800), *A Brief Narrative of the Trial for the Bloody and Mysterious Murder of the Unfortunate Young Woman, in the Famous Manhattan Well* (New York, 1800). All are deposited at the NYHS.

HISTORIES OF NEW YORK CITY

There is a large body of work on nineteenth-century New York, much of it written in the first half of the twentieth century. For the basic outlines of the economic and political history of the city, I used Robert G. Albion, *The Rise of New York Port, 1815–1860* (New York, 1939), Sidney I. Pomerantz, *New York: An American City 1783–1803* (New York, 1938), James Grant Wilson, ed., *The Memorial History of the City of New York,* 4 vols. (New York, 1893), Jerome Mushkat, *Tammany: The Evolution of a Political Machine 1789–1865* (Syracuse, N.Y., 1971), Edward Pessen, *Riches, Class, and Power Before the Civil War* (Lexington, Mass., 1973). There is a copious literature on New York labor: of greatest use were the sections on New York in John R. Commons et al., *History of Labor in the United States,* 2 vols. (New York, 1918–35) and Carl N. Degler's still-unpublished "Labor in the Economy and Politics of New York, 1850–1860; A Study of the Impact of Early Industrialism" (Ph.D. diss., Columbia University, 1952).

Similarly, the scholarship on New York reform movements and charities is large. A good beginning can be made with Thomas Bender, *Toward an Urban Vision: Ideas and Institutions in Nineteenth-Century America* (Lexington, Ky., 1975), Paul Boyer, *Urban Masses and Moral Order in America, 1820–1920* (Cambridge, Mass., 1978), Raymond Mohl, *Poverty in New York, 1783–1825* (New York, 1971), Robert S. Pickett, *House of Refuge: Origins of Juvenile Reform in New York State, 1815–1857* (Syracuse, N.Y., 1969), David M. Schneider, *The History of Public Welfare in New York State 1609–1866* (Chicago, 1938), Carroll Smith Rosenberg, *Religion and the Rise of the American City: The New York City Mission Movement, 1812–1870* (Ithaca, N.Y., 1971).

Books on New York social life are usually concerned with local color rather than analysis, but they can still be highly informative. Bayrd Still, *Mirror for Gotham: New York As Seen by Contemporaries from Dutch Days to the Present* (New York, 1956) is a compendium of observations from travelers' accounts; also important is Still's *New York City: A Students' Guide to Localized History* (New York, 1965). I. N. Phelps Stokes, *The Iconography of Manhattan Island 1498–1909,* 6 vols. (New York, 1915) takes the reader through New York's history year by year with snippets from contemporary accounts and newspaper reports. The basic social histories include Herbert Asbury, *The Gangs of New York* (New York, 1927), John Duffy, *A History of Public Health in New York City 1625–1866* (New York, 1968), Robert Ernst, *Immigrant Life in New York 1825–1863* (New York, 1949), Alvin F. Harlow, *Old Bowery: The Chronicles of a Famous Street* (New York, 1931), Roy Ottley and William Weatherby, *The Negro in New York* (New York, 1967), Esther Singleton, *Social New York Under the Georges 1714–1776* (New York, 1902), Smith Hart, *The New Yorkers* (New York, 1938), Joel Tyler Headley, *The Great Riots of New York: 1712–1873* (New York, 1873).

WOMEN AND LABOR

The generation of labor and economic historians who wrote in the early twentieth century—most of them associated with John R. Commons—were notably interested in wage-earning women and made the path-breaking forays into primary sources on which women's labor history has since depended. The works which I used most heavily were Edith Abbott, *Women in Industry: A Study in American*

Economic History (New York, 1924), Commons et al., *A Documentary History of American Industrial Society*, 10 vols. (Cleveland, Ohio, 1910–11), Norman J. Ware, *The Industrial Worker 1840–1860* (Boston, 1924), and the two classic volumes in U.S. Congress, Senate, *Report on Condition of Women and Child Wage-Earners in the United States*, S. Doc. 645, 61st Cong., 2nd Sess., 1910: Helen L. Sumner, *History of Women in Industry in the United States*, vol. 9, and John B. Andrews and W. D. P. Bliss, *History of Women in Trade Unions*, vol. 10. Much of this work— especially that of the Commons school—has been amply criticized in our own time for its narrow institutional focus and its almost-exclusive concern with trade union- ism as an index of working-class consciousness. As far as women go, these books —with the exception of Abbott's—tend to adopt an uncritical attitude toward the male-dominated labor movement. They also oscillate between portrayals of women workers as hapless victims or as heroic militants. There is no analytical attempt to connect these two facets of experience. Nevertheless, no historian of working- women today can do without their exhaustive research; these were the scholars who sketched out the outlines of women's movement into industrial wage labor. Finally, a fundamental revision of the woman-and-labor question as the Commons school formulated it was Gerda Lerner's pioneering essay, "The Lady and the Mill-Girl: Changes in the Status of Women in the Age of Jackson," *Mid-Continent American Studies Journal* 10 (1969). Lerner extracted the analysis of workingwomen from an exclusively economic context and refocused the problem on the dynamics of gender relations and class relations between women.

Index

A NOTE ON THE TYPE

The text of this book was set by CRT
in Janson, a film version of a typeface thought
to have been made by the Dutchman Anton Janson,
who was practicing type founder in Leipzig
during the years 1668–1687. However, it has been conclusively
demonstrated that these types are actually the work
of Nicholas Kis (1650–1702), a Hungarian,
who most probably learned his trade from the master
Dutch type founder Dirk Voskens. The type is an example
of the influential and sturdy Dutch types that
prevailed in England up to the time William Caslon
developed his own designs from them.

Composed by
The Haddon Craftsmen, Inc., Scranton, Pennsylvania

Printed and bound by
R. R. Donnelley & Sons, Harrisonburg, Virginia

Designed by
Iris Weinstein